CHARLES BEATTY

Author of

DE LESSEPS OF SUEZ

Ferdinand de Lesseps
A contemporary cartoon

De LESSEPS of SUEZ

the man
and
his times

by CHARLES BEATTY

HARPER & BROTHERS
publishers
new york

DE LESSEPS OF SUEZ

*This book is published in England
under the title of* FERDINAND DE LESSEPS

Library of Congress catalog card number: 56-12440

CONTENTS

ILLUSTRATIONS

The illustrations, grouped in a separate section, will be found following page 128.

AUTHOR'S NOTE

The literature associated with Ferdinand de Lesseps is large. In such a study as this there is space only for strictly relevant material and my bibliography can but indicate some useful sources. With the object of unwrapping a personality from so much paper I have relied largely, but not blindly, upon the Lesseps documents, Bridier, and Edgar-Bonnet. Where opinions differ, as in the case of Ferdinand's father, whether or no he was a secret agent, I adopt the likeliest view. On the death of his elder brother, Theodore, in 1874, Ferdinand became the Comte de Lesseps; but for the sake of clarity I have not changed his style.

Though some of his contemporaries thought his estimate of canal traffic so exaggerated as to constitute evidence of criminal intent, modern returns far surpass his imagination's highest flights. On the 1st of December, 1947, the President of the United States submitted to Congress a programme for the realization of the original Lesseps plan, a sea-level canal at Panama. The cost will be 2,482,000,000 dollars. On the 19th of November, 1954, *The Times* reported that the Suez Canal Company, in their eighth scheme for improvements, would double the existing capacity of the route after excavating 'over eighty million cubic feet, more than four-fifths of the total quantity removed in cutting the original canal'.

We detachments steady throwing,
Down the edges, through the passes,
  Up the mountains steep,
Conquering, holding, daring, venturing,
  Pioneers! O Pioneers!
                    WALT WHITMAN

Chapter 1. ROOTS

Soon after the First Consul decided to attack Egypt instead of England, Mathieu de Lesseps became his Commissary-General at the port of Cadiz, whence the bulk of the expedition was to sail. Although in love at the time, Mathieu was so competent that he even managed to please both the army and the navy. No sooner had the fleet gone – in deepest secrecy lest the move come to the ears of Admiral Nelson, than he rode to Malaga and proposed to the girl. She was Catherine de Grivignée, the daughter of a lawyer from Liège who, as a young man, had settled in Spain and become a prosperous wine merchant. Catherine accepted his suit and they were married in Malaga cathedral on the 21st of May, 1801. It was a smart wedding, attended by a member of the Privy Council of Spain and a crowd of diplomats. The only cloud in the sky was hardly the size of a man's hand – Abercrombie's victory in Egypt. Yet that apparently trivial check to Napoleon's headlong career was, besides a hinge of fate for international affairs, a first cause in the sequence of events which would bring Mathieu's second boy, Ferdinand, as an irresistible force to the apparently immovable isthmus of Suez.

In December the last of the French troops left the country, and soon afterwards Mathieu was summoned from Cadiz to Paris where Napoleon told him: "You have conducted yourself as the most trustworthy and zealous agent of the Government." He was then posted, in a similar capacity, to Alexandria. There he lived so exuberantly that he was even accused of 'keeping a tavern in his house', the implication being that he bribed friendships in the struggle for mastery between the pro-British and pro-French factions. Perhaps he did, but then his official position was only cover for a secret mission one requirement of which was that he should get to know, as intimately as possible, everyone in the country who was likely to become a man of power.

13

In accordance with the Treaty of Amiens the British had also withdrawn their troops from Egypt, and chaos emerged behind them as two great Muslim factions gathered their forces to decide the mastery of the country. Napoleon, who still regarded Egypt as the vital bridge between East and West, was determined that, though he had failed to hold it by force of arms, he might yet succeed in doing so by supporting the winning side and the strongest leader; particularly in the likely event of civil war. Mathieu's task was, 'to seek out a person, bold, intelligent, trustworthy', capable of mastering the remnant of the Mamelukes and creating a strong State; independent of Turkey, hostile to England. The candidate would receive all possible assistance from France, though that, at least for the time being, could not amount to much. Even so the British appointed an agent to work on very similar lines and between them Egypt soon became even more divided by intrigue and ambition. Meanwhile Catherine and Mathieu set up house, and while fulfilling his ordinary commercial duties he began to look about him for the exceptional man who might one day rule Egypt in the name of France. The circumstances which produced him were, many years later, described by Ferdinand:

"One of my father's janissaries brought to him one day Mehemet-Ali-Aga, who at that period could neither read nor write. He had left Kavalla with his little band and sometimes boasted of coming from the same country as Alexander. Thirty years later, when the Consular Corps came to Alexandria to compliment Mehemed-Ali Pacha on the victories of his son Ibrahim in Syria, the Viceroy of Egypt, turning to me, said to my colleague: 'The father of this young man was a great personage when I was a very small one. On the day after he had invited me to dinner I learned that some silver had been stolen from his table, and as I was the only person who could be suspected of the theft I dared not return to the house of the French agent, who was obliged to send for me to reassure me.'"

The young man from Kavalla, a small port on the Macedonian frontier, was an orphan. He had been adopted by the local mayor and brought up to collect taxes. He also acquired a modest business in tobacco, and would no doubt have lived laborious days had he not been drafted with Turkish territorials called up to defend Egypt against the French. He was given the rank of Major, and saw the battle of the Pyramids, from which he was lucky to escape. He was again on the losing side when at Aboukir the French utterly defeated the Muslim army, and on that occasion he was even more fortunate. Driven into the sea, he would have drowned had he not been able to lay hold of the gunwale of a small boat. He was hauled in. The boat was the personal gig of Sir Sydney Smith. So it was the Hero of Acre, so largely responsible for the collapse of Napoleon's eastern dream, who, by saving the life of Mohammed-Ali, eventually confirmed French dominance in Egypt.

After an initial success followed by apparent failure, Mathieu returned to France, looking forward to an interlude of private life in a house which he had taken at Versailles on the corner of the streets *des Réservoirs* and *la Paroisse*. Martin, his father, now retired after being Consul-General at the court of Catherine the Great, lived in the neighbourhood. The forthright old man, who had been twenty when Louis XV came to the throne, looked to the Emperor for the restoration of the glory of France, and his only complaint seems to have been that while both his sons had been made members of the Legion of Honour on its foundation in 1804, he, '*doyen de MM Les Consuls*', had been forgotten. On the 30th Vendémiaire, an 14 (22nd of October, 1805), he wrote from Paris: "The news is victory on victory. They should lead us to the solid peace which the world so much needs. We shall owe it to that most rare genius who brought it to pass." On the 19th of the following month, early in the grey, cold morning, the old man welcomed his second grandson into the world which promised so well for France, and for the Lesseps, her faithful servants. The event is now commemorated by a plaque on the northern wing of the house, if " wing " is not too grand a word in connection with such a modest establishment. Certainly grandfather would quite reasonably have expected that little Ferdinand would become famous, but hardly through the digging of ditches. He and Mathieu must have drunk a toast to him in the family business of diplomacy, congratulating themselves in that the boy, unlike their own generation, ought to have the good fortune to live in times of peace.

In December came Napoleon's noonday. After Austerlitz he crowned himself King of Rome. A wave of patriotic fervour swept France. Let Albion rule the empty ocean! Forget

Trafalgar! Such liquid sovereignty weighed little in comparison
with the solid reality of Bonaparte's dominion over men, cities
and treasure. Yet Austerlitz probably contributed more than any
other event except Waterloo to the ultimate failure of the
Emperor. The Czar took fright, and from being willing to divide
the world with Napoleon, henceforward he became a secret
enemy, awaiting opportunity to curb the ambitious upstart.
Meanwhile there was a great shortage of experienced adminis-
trators for the new French territories, and so Mathieu soon
found his leave cut short. He was appointed Minister to the
newly created Kingdom of Etruria (Tuscany), where he chose
Pisa for his headquarters. So it was in Italy that little Ferdinand
first became aware of his surroundings. Mathieu never saw his
father again, for Martin died within a few days of his golden
wedding, as a consequence of a chill caught while out shooting.
It was a fitting exit cue for a man who, when over seventy, had
begged Talleyrand to find him active service, even in the ranks
'en qualité de simple volontaire' so that he could be with his
Emperor in the field.

At Pisa the de Lesseps kept considerable state. They had a big
house with extensive gardens for the three children to play in –
Theodore, Adèle, and Ferdinand. Beyond the gardens they
looked to the mellow hills, pine trees, and the Arno. Gently the
years passed, and Mathieu's worries were relatively small, such
as fulfilling the following request from Prince Eugène: "The
tobacco they sell us in the Kingdom of Italy is detestable to the
French nose. If you can possibly find in Etruria some good
Virginian or St. Vincent tobacco, in flake or plug, it would be
most kind of you to send me about fifty pounds." This tranquillity must have seemed the more wonderful by contrast with the
dark past and the bright promise of the future. Then in 1809 a
new blow fell. The Kingdom of Etruria was disestablished and
Mathieu appointed Imperial Commissioner to the Ionian Isles,
a post to which he dare not take his family; for until 1797
Corfu, the seat of government, had belonged to Venice, from
whom Russia and Turkey had wrested it. Now, seething within
and threatened from without, the island was no place for a
French family. Still too young to realize what the separation
must have meant to their young mother, the two boys played in
the sun; under supervision which Ferdinand soon came to resent.

He preferred exploring walks, solitary adventure; and even at that early age, began to yearn for deserts, a notion apparently implanted by his first sight of camels: "those fine creatures which I was to meet so often in Africa. In those days wood-merchants used to deliver their goods by loading them on the backs of camels, and we got a great deal of fun out of watching their arrival with their grave and measured gait, bearing on their backs great stacks of timber. The driver used to steer them under the archway with much shouting." Then there were some sad months, caused by a piece of bread-crust which lodged under Ferdinand's eyelid in the course of a tussle with Theodore for possession of a roll. The crumb set up an infection which nearly lost him the sight of that eye and must have been extremely painful. With returning health the spirit of adventure became stronger than before. One day he nearly killed himself when playing alone in the loft, two storeys up. A truss of hay, with Ferdinand on top of it, began to slide towards the door open to the yard. He had no time to get clear and so rode the hay to the ground, where it broke his fall and he walked away unhurt.

There was a gay set round his mother, the attractive grass widow who had such excellent connections and kept such a good table. Her *salon* was the social centre of Tuscany and there were constant visitors, mostly military or diplomatic, from all parts of the new empire. Unknown to most of them, the brief days of glory were already ending, though in St. Petersburg Ferdinand's Uncle Barthélemy was trying to draft a treaty which would prevent the coming clash with Russia. He did succeed, against all expectation, in satisfying the two foreign offices with his definition of respective spheres of influence for the two great countries. It began to seem as though not only would France and Russia compose their differences, but that Russian arms would support France against England. Then, at the last moment, the Czar refused to sign. War became inevitable.

After the retreat from Moscow, the repercussions of that fantastic failure were soon felt down in the Ionian Isles, where among a starving garrison Mathieu stood firm in face of a British squadron. Under threat of bombardment he refused to surrender and when disaffection came into the open he took occasion to write to his military superior: "Accept, *mon*

Général, my assurance that at any hour, any instant, you may count upon me. Whatever happens, it is to you I owe my duty and I desire nothing but to give you proof of it." The note was dated the 10th of May, 1814, when the news of Napoleon's fall had reached Corfu, the only island then remaining in French possession. Still Mathieu and his General refused to surrender, on the ground that they had received no formal orders to that effect. When at last the papers did arrive, over the signature of Louis XVIII, the General went home to imprisonment and Lesseps to dismissal. So for his obstinate endurance Mathieu had to face poverty in idleness. He had spent his fortune in Corfu, latterly even paying the troops by drafts on his Paris bank – which the new Government chose to regard as no responsibility of theirs. Mathieu probably accepted with resignation the turn of fate, realizing that for the new régime to discriminate against him was in a sense a compliment. Louis had to please England. He could not afford to employ friends of the fallen idol.

Catherine brought more bad news when she arrived with the children from Pisa. Her own people had also been ruined by the Emperor's eclipse, so the family's position was now serious; but there was nothing to do except wait, in the hope that before too late some minor appointment would come Mathieu's way. Then the sun emerged from the shadow. Again France rang with ' Vive l'Empereur! '; and in spite of the fierce surge of the wave he sought to ride, Napoleon did not forget his loyal servant, whom he created a Count of the Empire for his services in Corfu, and conferred upon him a highly responsible post:

> "At the Palace of the Tuileries,
> the 6th of April, 1815.
>
> Napoleon, Emperor of the French, has decreed and decrees as follows:
>
> *Article One*
>
> M. le Comte de Lesseps is nominated Prefect of the Department of Cantal.
>
> signed: NAPOLEON
>
> Office of the Ministry of State.   signed: DUC DE BASSANO
> registered the 8th April, 1815.   No. 94."

Aware of the terrible urgency, Mathieu raced down to Aurillac and began by every means in his power to recruit the men whom the Emperor so desperately needed. Yet even as he issued his proclamations he must have realized that many of the best soldiers were dead on the roads from Russia, and with them thousands of irreplaceable horses:

"Brave patriots of Cantal,
  Our country, our liberty is threatened. Hasten to defend it. What French heart will not beat faster for such news. Two battalions of the Guards are leaving for Lyon, and they must be there by the 15th. The slow methods of organization, at which we are working at full pressure, cannot keep pace with our impatience. My compatriots, let us beat the other Departments! Do not let them dispute with us the palm of honour and of patriotism. Come all of you who can take your places in a *grenadier* or *chasseur* battalion. Come to Aurillac to enlist, to get your equipment and papers. I am burning with the desire to tell the Emperor: 'The citizens of Cantal did not need to be drafted. They went of their own free will to where Honour and Country called them.'
                                    Aurillac, the 9th of May, 1815.
                                    The Prefect of Cantal
                                                DE LESSEPS."

In vain the untrained men rallied to the moulting eagles. Mathieu soon had to break the news of Waterloo. And then, under conditions of great difficulty, he went on governing his Department, in which anti-clerical feeling added poison to the bitterness of national disenchantment. He received great credit for preventing bloodshed, and a deputation of twelve chevaliers waited upon Louis XVIII to pray that Mathieu be confirmed in office under the new order. It was in vain. As before, so now, the Anglophile Government dared not employ the man whom the Emperor had called '*le fidèle de la dernière heure*'.

Mathieu had to leave the Prefecture, but he could not take his wife with him because little Ferdinand was ill. The boy had contracted typhoid, and this acute fever was strangely attributed to the fact that he had recently broken an arm during one of his adventures. The boy could not be moved, and so the new Prefect had to leave Catherine in part of the house. She in turn offered to lend him her carriage, only to discover that it had been used to bring back to Aurillac under arrest no less a personage than Marshal Ney, who had been in hiding with a relative of hers. Years later Ferdinand recalled: "I shall never forget the indignation of my mother when she learned to what use my father's carriage had been put. With her Spanish fire she poured the most violent reproaches upon Baron Locard, and she was never able to forgive his part in the proceeding. She would not any longer stay in the Prefecture, and in spite of my weakness, since I could scarcely stand, we started forthwith for Paris."

*　　*　　*

Realizing that he might well pay for his loyalty with his liberty, Uncle Barthélemy had taken refuge in Lisbon and pressed his brother to join him there. But, probably for the sake of the children, Mathieu would not be persuaded, and lived on in Paris in the hope that the storm would blow over and he would be re-employed. The one bright spot in the family's firmament was a grant towards the education of the boys, made by the Emperor during the Hundred Days. Either it had been overlooked by the new authorities or else had charitably been allowed to stand. At all events both Theodore, the elder by three years, and Ferdinand entered the *Lycée Napoleon* – the name of which was soon changed to *Collège Henri IV*. In the same year, 1818, and in the nick of time, Mathieu was offered a consular post. He wrote to Barthélemy on the 16th of September:

"Two hours ago the Minister's nephew, M. de la Roquette, came to tell me that the King signed my appointment this morning, saying to General Dessoles, 'Hello, a Lesseps! My brother had a great regard for that family.' My salary of twenty thousand francs starts to-day. My wife is in a bad way. The children are crying. We all fell on the neck of the good Roquette. It was high time. My watch and all my wife's jewels were in pawn, and there was no money in the house."

Mathieu's appointment took him about as far away as possible in those days, to Philadelphia; so Catherine became again a grass widow, this time with no social round to keep her spirits buoyed. She lived in the Faubourg St. Germain, and her chief consolation was that every Sunday the boys came over from school. They did quite well there, growing with extraordinary rapidity, and, whether or not they learned much, at least they met the right kind of people. For the function of the establishment had not changed with its name. It remained an institution dedicated to the higher grades of State service, for which recruits generally came from such families as the Lesseps, or from the aristocracy.

The son of the Duc d'Orléans was there with Ferdinand, and seems to have been something of a prig. One day he took exception to some boys laughing at him for falling over when a ball hit him. Getting up he picked on Lesseps, made a rush, and Ferdinand knocked him flat. Then papa d'Orléans suddenly appeared and demanded of his son: " What have you been up to? "

" Fighting Lesseps."

" Why? "

" He was laughing at me."

" And because you happen to be a prince you thought he had no right to do so? Lesseps did well to teach you a lesson, and you can tell him so from me."

Less through lack of brains than because of his physical exuberance, Ferdinand was not a distinguished scholar. He had nothing of the moody introspection of the proverbial genius, tormented by interior conflict into the projection of some great work. If he studied enough to pass his exams on the broad curriculum of science and literature, he did no more than that; and his bent, oddly enough in the light of his later reputation, was to the latter. Left to himself there is no doubt but that he would have spent most of his time out of doors, preferably on a horse. On one occasion, probably for a ' dare ', he swam the Seine rather than take the ferry with the other boys:

" With my garters I tied my shoes to the back of my neck, stuffed my shirt into my hat, which I kept on my head, and dropped into the river. With one hand I swam, while with the other I held aloft at the end of a stick my coat, waistcoat and breeches. My endurance was not equal to my initiative. I reached the bank after much effort, but I had swallowed a lot of water and so had my clothes, which were ringing wet. I had to hang them on some nearby trees, and walked about in a state of nature until they had dried."

Fortunately for his independent temperament, organized games were not yet in fashion, and he found his combative outlet in fencing, which he took up seriously and successfully. After four years, the result of his education, both in and out of school, was to fit him for life as it is, rather than as it used to be or as it might be – which is all that books can teach. He was ' *bien taillé pour la lutte* ', an excellent result in view of what lay ahead, though hardly what the origin of the term *lycée* suggests, that

Athenian 'Institute of Higher Studies' where Aristotle taught his grave philosophy among figures dignified as carven draperies. Ferdinand seems to have had no scholastic ambition, but was already inspired by the tradition of his family in foreign service, and this, at first idealized through the eyes of youth, became a life-long point of view. As such it provided a basis for integrity, even intransigence, and was the cause of many clashes with those who would not understand that loyalty to principle above party could make him seem at once Royalist and Republican, Catholic and Anti-Papal, even an impractical dreamer and an unscrupulous opportunist.

His forbears had been for the most part men of martial prowess and civic office, whose reputations, and their sphere of action, spread out from Bayonne until both his father and his uncle, Barthélemy, achieved international influence. Of these the latter was the more famous, and his story provided young Ferdinand with an heroic example of devotion to duty against great odds. For which reason it deserves to be retold in the present context.

Barthélemy was born at Hamburg, where, in January 1766, his father was Consul-General. At ten he could speak three languages besides his own and was an accomplished musician. He was educated at the Jesuit college in Versailles and at seventeen was posted to the consulate at St. Petersburg, where his father was a personal friend of the Czar. His first commendation came when single-handed he dealt with mutiny on the French warship *l'Uranie* at Cronstadt, and, avoiding heavy penalties, got the men to report back for duty. Rewarded by being sent to Paris with despatches, he met there by chance the famous navigator Lapérouse, who took a fancy to him and persuaded both the parents and the authorities to let the young man join a voyage round the world which the explorer was then planning.

By way of Brazil, Cape Horn, Chile, California and the Philippines, the frigates *l'Astrolabe* and *la Boussole* (the compass) in two years reached the Far East, and at length arrived off Petropavlovsk on the northern coast of Kamchatka. There Lapérouse issued orders which at first sight appear callous. Barthélemy was to find his way home, overland. Alone except for such chance companions as might come his way he must cross the most desolate belt of the northern world, beginning at the season

of approaching winter. It can hardly have seemed likely, either
to the Captain or to his young protégé, that they would ever
meet again.[1] Barthélemy described in his journal the parting
with Lapérouse and the captain of the other frigate, on the 29th
of September, 1787 :

" In the evening I had to take leave of our Captain and his worthy
colleague. One may imagine how I suffered when I accompanied
them back to the waiting boats. They embraced me. My tears must
have shown them the depth of my feelings. The officers, all my
friends, who were also ashore, accepted my farewells and expressed
their best wishes for my preservation, giving me what consolation
and help their regard for me suggested. My sense of loss at leaving
them was inexpressible. I had to be parted from them, and found
myself in the arms of Colonel Kasloff Ougrenin, commanding at
Okhotsk and Kamchatka, to whom M. le Comte de Lapérouse had
commended me, more as a son than as an officer to whom he had
entrusted the despatches. Let anyone try to imagine the sense of
frightful emptiness which came to me that moment. Let him think
of himself in my place, left alone upon an almost unknown shore,
four thousand leagues from my homeland."

The drama of this farewell so impressed the Russians who
witnessed it that they named a local promontory Cap Lesseps.
Of the two chief characters it was probably Lapérouse who had
the heavier heart when the frigates set sail next morning. For
young Barthélemy, who evidently had his full share of the
Lesseps charm, soon found firm friends among the Russian
officers, of whom he wrote later that from the very beginning
he did not hesitate to trust them blindly. With four of them,
four N.C.O.s and four men, he left Petropavlovsk at the end of
the first week in October. The average temperature would
already be down to twenty degrees Fahrenheit. It would fall far
lower during the seven months of his thousand-mile stage round
Shelekov Bay and the Sea of Okhotsk to the town of that name,
where he stayed in welcome comfort with the Ougrenins.
Impatient to be on his way with the despatches, he tried too soon
to push inland and was stopped by rivers swollen with the thaw.
Bitterly disappointed, he made his way back to his friends at
Okhotsk. The delay might well have made all the difference
between getting through to Moscow by late autumn or having
to face another winter, perhaps in the central wilds. He started

[1] Nor did they meet again. Both ships were lost.

again early in June, and, striking almost due west, in a month reached Yakutsk on the river Lena. Still on the flood of the thaw, he took four hours to cross that tremendous stream. There-after he travelled by water, a little west of south, until he reached the headwaters in the neighbourhood of Lake Baykal, whence he continued overland to Irkutsk, a hundred miles to the north of Outer Mongolia. His next stage, Tomsk, was some seven hundred miles farther on. After that he had no more to do than keep westward over the Urals. By the time he reached the Volga, a mere five hundred miles from Moscow, it must have seemed to him that he was in suburbia.

Through the toughest parts of the journey, as when alone with a dog-team he was lost in snow, or when living in a hovel where he subsisted on raw fish, he made a symbol of his despatches, keeping them constantly at hand as a defence against despair. Nearing the end of his ordeal, it seemed even more important to deliver them as soon as possible, and he strained every reserve of force to cover the last stages as fast as possible. This impatience nearly cost him his life. He put his head out of the window of the carriage to urge the driver on. A piece of iron tyre, partly detached from the rim of the rear wheel, struck him and seemed to have cracked his skull. Even then his luck held. A doctor was found, who, though drunk, could say that the wound was only superficial. He sluiced the place with vodka and advised the patient to take the same internally. He then proposed a bleeding, but Barthélemy, who had lost a lot of blood already, had still enough presence of mind to refuse this service. Instead he paid the fee and got back into the carriage. He arrived at St. Petersburg during the night of the 22nd of September, 1788, having covered the last four thousand miles in thirty-two travelling days; with eight days lost owing to enforced delays. A month later he was in Paris, where he was fêted as a national hero. Dressed as a Kamchatkan, he was presented to Louis XVI and became quite a favourite at the court. His official reward was promotion to the grade of Consul and re-appointment at Cronstadt. His standing is represented by the terms in which the responsible Minister conveyed the news : " M. de Lesseps cannot be happier at receiving this mark of the King's favour than I am to transmit it." Barthélemy was then twenty-two. The Revolution found him safely out of France, having been transferred to Constantinople as Secretary to the Embassy, a post he owed to his father-in-law, Chevalier Ruffin, whose daughter Rose he had married at Versailles in 1793. After various adventures of exploration, during which he left his family with the Ruffins, he returned to Stamboul in time to be interned when the Sultan took exception to Napoleon's aggression against Egypt, then a province of the Ottoman Empire. With his relatives he spent three years' more or less rigorous imprisonment in the Castle of the Seven Towers. Released at last, they all went home, but there was to be no leave for Barthélemy. Summoned by Talleyrand, he was presented to Napoleon, then First Consul, who promptly sent him back to St. Petersburg where he stayed until war broke out.

In 1812 Barthélemy was designated Civil Governor of Moscow and in that capacity did what he could to mitigate the horrors of the city's rape. After assuring the population that a strong hand would dispense justice and restore order, he proclaimed: "An administration chosen by you shall keep watch over you, your needs and your interests. It shall form your municipality." But he had no opportunity to carry out his promise. Instead he had to watch the Kremlin blown up, and then, beside Marshal Mortier – well named for such a time, took the weary road back to France. They both reached home, and no doubt Barthélemy's experience of arctic survival was invaluable. But he lost his staff and everything he had taken with him to set up his considerable establishment:

"Twenty-two horses, three carriages, my chattels, and all my baggage, which I value at 35,000 francs (say, six million modern francs), and what is even more of an affliction, all my most important papers, the results of thirty years' work. All that exists for me no more. The most extraordinary circumstances, of which history can show no example, have taken from me my chancellor, my young secretary, my valet, and three coachmen, all of whom were in charge of my baggage."

*   *   *

Distance tends to hero-worship, especially from children, and Mathieu's letters from America must have raised his achievement almost to the level of Barthélemy though in a different sphere. Barthélemy was the man of action. Mathieu the man of policy. Ferdinand resolved to follow those parallel footsteps – and in doing so he would hardly have appreciated that neither father nor uncle were in fact anything but exiles, their past achievements of no value or importance to the present Government of France. Also Mathieu was a sick man. As such he was grateful for the gentle life which he was now able to lead, in contrast with what would have been required of him on the Barbary Coast, his special field. And it must have been pleasant, after poverty in the wilderness, to be again a man of influence and substance. On the 13th of September, 1819, he wrote to Catherine: "I am much fêted and honoured, and refused a number of dinners which I did not really want to attend. But evening parties and Tea Parties are always going on, and these I accept because I learn so much. I am working hard at English, and am beginning to be able to keep up conversations 'very confortable'." Catherine was also 'very confortable'. She was soon happily telling Mathieu about a most satisfactory alliance which Adèle had concluded that year, with Edouard Tallien de Cabarrus, the son of a prominent homeopath in a family to which the Lesseps were related. Though his name was Tallien, the son had tacked on de Cabarrus in honour of his mother's connections: "The daughter of the distinguished Spanish financier became the Marquise de Fontenay, later the beautiful and well-known Madame Tallien, and finally the Princesse de Chimay."[1]

In 1822 Mathieu concluded the first commercial treaty between France and the United States, a landmark to which Ferdinand was to refer when he spoke at the inauguration of the Statue of Liberty in 1886. Soon after the treaty was signed, Mathieu was recalled to France, only to be posted again to a place unsuitable for the family, Aleppo in Syria. His health continued to go downhill, and had there been any money left apart from his pay he would have stayed for a time in Paris. But he still could not afford to do so, and was soon writing to his wife: "My heart is breaking because, having had but a brief glimpse of happiness, I do nothing but say good-bye to you. Good-bye my Trina, good-bye my dear, good children. I hold you tight to my heart where I treasure the memories of you." This time, however, he did not go alone but took Theodore with him as student-consul.

[1] Sanci.

Ferdinand had to remain at school, and must have been most resentful of the fact. For was not Syria a land of camels? Once *en route*, Mathieu's spirits soon began to rise and he wrote to Catherine from the frigate *la Médée*:

"Here we are on board. In a few hours our young man will have lost sight of the coast of his homeland. But I am not at all worried on his account. They have told us that we may expect a calm voyage, and it would hardly be possible for a youth to begin his career under happier circumstances. In the way I was received at Marseille, and here in Toulon, he saw how our name is honoured; and it will give him, or rather increase in him, a desire to be worthy of it. I am delighted to be able to tell you that everyone likes him and approves of him. They find him very well set up. He is going to make a journey for which everyone envies him. He starts his journal to-day."

They took six weeks to reach Aleppo. On the way the convoy had to fight off an organized attack by bandits. Hardly had Mathieu settled into the consulate than an earthquake struck the town and brought most of it to ruin. He and Theodore managed to get out of the consulate before the building collapsed. Then the youth insisted upon going back for important papers. He found them, but just as he came out there was a further collapse. He escaped unhurt. Later on, when there was time to consider such minor matters, Mathieu wrote a citation to the Foreign Office which concluded: "It is the Consul of France rather than a father who begs a generous Minister to ask His Majesty for some suitable recognition of a singular act of devotion, and to announce to H.M. that there is a new Lesseps ready to sacrifice himself for the Service." The wreckage in Aleppo covered at least eight thousand dead and for three weeks the stench was such that the remnant of the inhabitants dared not go back there to live. When they did so cholera broke out, the first recorded epidemic in Asia Minor and one which for generations echoed over Europe. Mathieu sent Theodore to Egypt but himself stayed on at the ruined consulate to become the town's commanding officer against the scourge. Though Pasteur was then only a year old, his principle of disinfection was empirically anticipated by Mathieu, who used quantities of lime and its chloride for practical hygiene. The current theory of the cause of most diseases was then little different from that held by the

Greeks well over two thousand years before. This laid down that
the four humours, phlegm, blood, yellow bile and black bile,
were controlled in some way by peculiar qualities of the earth,
air, fire and water in the immediate environment of the patient.
In the case of fevers air was considered to be the principal
culprit, particularly effluvia.

For his devoted service both the French and the foreign Press
gave Mathieu full credit. Though he was awarded the Cross of
the Legion of Honour, his Government gave him not the least
practical award, of which he stood so much in need. In fact the
only item of intrinsic value came from the King of England,
George IV, who with compliments sent a jewelled snuff-box, and
congratulations upon the successful rescue of two British subjects
who happened to be in Aleppo and had been stricken by the
disease.

*   *   *

Ferdinand now left school and briefly studied law, until lack
of money forced him to look for a job. He found it in the army
commissariat, where he was paid two hundred francs a month
and had to work to a routine which he much disliked. Thence
he was delivered through the influence of Uncle Barthélemy,
who took him to his now official post at Lisbon in the same
grade as Theodore was in when he went to Aleppo – *élève-
consul*. Ferdinand was not quite twenty, and though happy at
last to have his foot on the ladder of the family business,
shadows thrown by serious responsibilities ahead tended to damp
his enthusiasm: "How many things must a man know to be a
good consul! For his duties are endless in their variety and of
quite a different character from those of other officials of the
Ministry. They demand a mass of practical knowledge for which
a special education is required. At need consuls should be able
to undertake the duties of judge, arbitrator and peacemaker.
They must be able to do the work of notaries, and sometimes
that of naval commissioners. They are concerned with matters
of public hygiene and are expected to have detailed knowledge
of trade, shipping and local industry." Such was the opinion of
Prince Talleyrand, his father's friend, who in later life gave
Ferdinand some personal advice which he always remembered:
"Diplomacy," he then said, "is not a science of ruse and

duplicity. If straightforwardness is of prime value anywhere it
is in political transactions, for it is that which renders them
solid and durable. People have confused reserve with ruse.
Straightforwardness is incompatible with ruse, but it is not incon-
sistent with reserve, which indeed strengthens the feeling of
confidence."

Such a point of view, unusual for its lack of cynicism in a
cynical old man, had long been a Lesseps tradition. Like his
elders Ferdinand would find that such a simple and ethical rule
could in its application be extremely difficult to handle because
of conflicting loyalties. In his *Recollections* he cited the instructions signed by Louis XVIII in 1814 for the benefit of French
Consuls: "They are political agents, but only in this sense,
that they are recognized by the Sovereign who receives them as
officers of the Government which sends them, and that the principle of their mandate is either specific treaties, or the common
custom of nations, or the general law." The theory is as simple
as it is admirable, but what happens if the three principles of
mandate conflict with one another?

*   *   *

When in 1825 Ferdinand arrived at Lisbon, he was less concerned with the burden of responsibility than with the joys of
a wider freedom and the entrée to high society, which was open
to him as much on account of his cousin, the Comtesse de
Montijo, as because of his own family connections, whose records
under the Empire were by no means a disadvantage in mon-
archist Spain and Portugal. So it was the gaiety of capitals
rather than the solemnity of contracts which took up most of
Ferdinand's attention. For such an ebullient, enthusiastic nature,
his life up to now had been unduly circumscribed. He had been
resentful of routine, school rules and relative poverty; not even
gilded, as in the case of his elders, by the memory of affluence.
For him Napoleon must have been more of a legend than a contemporary figure: in the year of Waterloo Ferdinand was only
ten. Now, with Charles X apparently secure upon the throne, the
future promised fair. There was every reason to look forward to
a rewarding career, if not with the drama of his father's time,
then at least in the hope of some adventure. Nor need adventure,
to this very normal young man, be in terms only of war. He

loved women and he looked up to them, an attitude as rare as it was acceptable.

Though he took his duties seriously enough, he was well content to grasp everything in the way of diversion, of which there was an abundance; but although his social set was young, gay and rich, he also liked to talk seriously of world affairs, or to ride alone through the Spanish countryside, everywhere welcomed as the representative of France. The people seemed to have no bitter memories of the occupation and the aristocracy were Francophile. In the following year the Comtesse de Montijo gave birth to a daughter, Eugénie, destined to be rated the most beautiful woman of her time and to become an Empress. She would also be an indispensable ally for Ferdinand in the course of his long political battle for the Suez Canal. Ferdinand's gilded springtime came to an end in 1828, and by then he was probably bored with the relative sophistication of his life. Camels were calling. His chance to renew acquaintance with them came when his father, after six years at Aleppo, was posted to Tunis; an appointment which was to prove a death sentence. Its only merit lay in the fact that at last Catherine could join him, to re-establish as much of a home as the climate and conditions of the service allowed.

From Ferdinand's first day in North Africa, that brown land of white-clad people and black shadows set a seal upon his heart and mind. The future no longer appeared as a sequence of social occasions punctuated by routine consular duties, and, equally dull, musical evenings when he would be required to take part in quartets at a piano. Though as yet undefined, he was already aware of a serious purpose, and began to read the signs in the stormy political sky. France was again in ferment. The *émigré* Comte d'Artois, who ruled as Charles X, was trying to turn back the calendar to a date before the Revolution. Against him was not only the immemorial surge of the oppressed: a power entirely new was stirring, the Industrial Revolution. For the first time in history communications were quicker than legs. The power of steam drew not only railway trains, it turned the wheels in the factories which, like black scabs, were fast crusting upon the face of Nature. Not less important, it also turned the presses, and distributed provocative news which previous generations had learned, if at all, only when it had grown cold.

Even in the military world there were signs of a French awakening. Perhaps as much to create a diversion from the approaching crisis at home as to put down the Barbary pirates, who still terrorized shipping in the Mediterranean and enslaved their prisoners, Charles sent an expedition to Algiers. It succeeded as much against diplomatic opposition from London as against the enemy in arms. Inevitably England regarded the move as a first step towards a new Empire, for which the pirates had provided no more than a good excuse. Such suspicions seemed to be confirmed when Tunisia and Oran were added to Algeria, together with the virtual control of Egypt through Mathieu's protégé Mohammed-Ali.   Fearing the emergence of another French dictator, this time with Egypt as a power in her own right, British opinion slowly hardened, not in terms of months but over years and decades, into the conviction that France must inevitably make a second attempt to establish a Napoleonic dominion in the Middle East. Ferdinand never seems to have realized how deep was this fear, how general, and how reasonable.

Chapter 2. ROAMING

Ferdinand was now convinced that in Africa lay his life's work, though owing to the exigencies of the service it did not seem that he would be fortunate enough to spend there many years. In fact before his career had properly begun he was fortunate not to be sent home as *persona non grata*; for he helped a criminal to escape the brisk justice of the Bey. The following description of the affair is taken from Alexandre Dumas' *Impressions de Voyage*:

"One day the French consul, M. Mathieu de Lesseps, watched a good-looking young man of twenty or twenty-two arriving at the consulate. He was dressed in the Arab robes which he always wore, though he was born either at Leghorn or Elba. It was Youssouff, the Bey's favourite, one of the officers of Bach Mameluk. As in the Thousand and One Nights, the Princess Kabourah lowered her eyes to her humble slave. But unfortunately between the lovers were set all those obstacles peculiar to the Orient. With the result that the first time the young officer managed to gain entry to the room of the Princess, he was discovered by a slave who reported what he had seen to the Bey, and the Bey made him put it in writing.

"On leaving the Bey's apartments the slave had to pass Youssouff's door, and Youssouff was waiting for him. He grabbed the man as he went by, yanked him into his room and shut the door. There was a sound of clashing blades, cries, then nothing more. Two hours later the Princess Kabourah received a basket of flowers. She lifted the flowers to find a hand, a tongue and an eye. These unusual offerings were accompanied by a note: 'I send you the eye which spied upon you, the tongue which betrayed you, the hand which denounced you.' But Youssouff did not wait for the Princess's answer. As we have already described, he sought refuge in the French Consulate. Mathieu de Lesseps, who knew Youssouff and had a great liking for him, hurried him off to his country house at Marsa on the coast, and told his son Ferdinand de Lesseps, who is to-day (1848) Ambassador at Madrid, to make arrangements for getting the fugitive on board ship."

The incident which nearly ended Ferdinand's career took place as Youssouff was getting into a boat which had been sent from the French brig *Adonis* on the pretext of getting fresh water. Youssouff's agility and the quickness of the men at the oars, saved his liberty and probably his life, while Ferdinand took to his heels and with difficulty made his escape from pursuing soldiers, who fortunately failed to recognize him. Years later the grateful Youssouff became a distinguished officer in the service of France and founded the famous corps of Spahis.

When the time came to draw up a document defining the status of the new French North African possessions, it was Mathieu de Lesseps who drafted it and sent it to Marshal Clauzel by the hand of Ferdinand. No doubt Ferdinand would have been delighted to take it all the way to Paris, but he was not permitted to, and so missed the Revolution of July 1830. After three days' fighting in the streets of the capital, Charles X, whose suspension of the Constitution had been the detonator of the explosion, fled to England; and by so doing must have embarrassed the Lesseps, because the treaty, with its magniloquent preamble, was not signed until after the King's deflation, though the fact was not yet known in Africa. It is dated the 8th of August, 1830, and begins:

" In the name of God the Merciful, the Compassionate, this Treaty which crowns all the endeavours which sought to reconcile with the help of God so many diverse interests, is concluded between The Marvel of Princes of the Nation of the Messiah, the glory of the peoples who adore Jesus, the august scion of Kings, the crown of Monarchs, the shining object of the admiration of Thine armies and Ministers, Charles X, Emperor of France, by the intermediary of his Consul-General . . ."

In the new Assembly the middle classes consolidated their gains at the expense of the socialists and invited a distinguished soldier, the liberal Louis-Philippe, Duc de Chartres, to wear the crown – in a thoroughly bourgeois manner. He accepted, and symbolized the democratic nature of his majesty by ostentatiously carrying an umbrella. Yet he would not go far enough to please the growing power of the Left, nor of the Right wing where Louis-Napoleon was quietly working against him. The change of sovereign made little difference to the Lesseps and it was in the ordinary course of events that Ferdinand was posted from Tunis to Alexandria, with promotion to Vice-Consul, at the beginning of 1832. He was now nearly thirty, and for the

first time would be independent of his father and mother, an
exciting prospect, but overlaid by the knowledge that he would
be unlikely to see his father again. So his enthusiasm for the
career ahead was checked by the pull of filial piety. He must have
felt selfish at leaving his father at such a time, and yet realized
that in the desire to stay at home was concealed a fear of facing
the world alone. However courageous the solitary traveller may
be, he will surely be homesick at the beginning of his journey.
Such stresses change a man's perspective, make the light seem
brighter, the night darker. Trivial events, which previously
would have passed unnoticed, may assume disproportionate
importance; while the intensity of emotion also increases to
produce a more lasting effect in memory than would occur in the
ordinary day.

Such a state Ferdinand de Lesseps must have entered, for on
the passage to Alexandria a passenger died, it was said, of
cholera; and when the ship docked all the rest were immediately
quarantined. Until now Ferdinand's life had been relatively
superficial. The great challengers had not yet barred his path.
In all probability he had given little serious thought to the problems of existence. Now, already resigned to losing his father,
sudden as an unexpected mirror-image he saw his own mortality.
In the long, loaded days which followed, Ferdinand must have
looked the Absolutes in the face. At first in the lazaret there
was nothing else to do, except to anticipate the onset of the
disease while, against all likelihood, hoping that there would
be no more cases. Should others occur, detention would drag on
and on. . . . The cause of cholera was still unknown, and so
there was no specific treatment. The patient's sufferings were
often increased by the practice of withholding water, so that
dehydration was a frequent cause of death. Mortality was anywhere over fifty per cent. The onset was sudden, the symptoms
dramatic and disgusting, giving the affliction an aura of
demoniacal mystery. The period of incubation was short, usually
two or three days, and death might occur within twenty-four
hours. Unable to take his accustomed exercise, cooped up among
strangers any one of whom might by casual contact give him the
disease, Ferdinand took refuge in serious reading. His immediate
superior, M. Mimaut, the Consul-General, brought him books
out of the official library, and among them Ferdinand discovered

Lepère's paper on the *Canal des Deux Mers*, a long memorandum prepared for Napoleon. The survey had been made under considerable difficulties, for not only had the savants to cope with the climate, lack of water, and hostile Bedouin, they were short of the greater part of their apparatus, which had been sunk on the way out. Even so their report remains a classic. It fired Ferdinand's imagination, burning deep. He saw the canal not in terms of politics or commerce, still less as personal gain. His was a spiritual concept, a dedication, an immortality. Remembering his father and looking at those around him, he had need of such a concept, in the same way that through the kindling of faith the soul may become aware of 'salvation' as experience rather than mere belief. Whether the proper description of conversion be theological or psychological, the experience is usually far-reaching. It tends profoundly to influence character. Even if it soon sinks again below the surface of the mind, it is apt to lead to a secret destiny the individual who has experienced it.

When no new cases occurred, medical opinion began to doubt that the fatality had been due to cholera; and a little later it was generally admitted that the cause of death was 'a consequence of indigestion': anti-climax! Ferdinand left the lazaret to take up his duties, which he found far from onerous. No doubt he thought he had left behind him his vision and its dedication. An evocative description of the daily round in Alexandria, which brought Ferdinand many friends who would be valuable in later life, is quoted by Bridier:

"One sits at the hospitable board of the brothers Pastre; one takes coffee, sometimes even hashish, with friends Rouffio and Rolland; one smokes a pipe or hubble-bubble at the home of Dr. Clot Bey; one goes to gossip about *la Patrie* on board ships in the roadstead; one sees dancing-girls and dervishes at Colonel Sèves' place, who has become Soliman Pasha; one plays music and dances in the *salons* of Messrs. Mimaut and de Serisy. Gay cavaliers are by no means lacking. They are recruited from among the young men of the business houses, the personnel of the consulate, from the military staff, and among the many officers and advisers whom Mohammed-Ali, that good friend of France, invites to his country; and pays so generously to command and train his army, to build his frigates, look after his stud, found his schools, and, in a word, regenerate Egypt."

When, as often happened, Ferdinand wished to get away from

society, there was always a thoroughbred Arab horse to be had and the wide desert to challenge him. Already Ferdinand's feeling for the country had deepened far below the level which most foreigners are content to reach. He seriously studied Arabic and steeped himself in the atmosphere of Islam. Nor was he tied to Alexandria. Mimaut took him to Cairo and formally presented him to Mohammed-Ali. Ferdinand handed to the autocrat a personal letter from his father, and the Pasha of Cairo welcomed this second son of his old friend and sponsor as warmly as he had the first: for Theodore, also in the foreign service, had already been there. " It was your father," said the Pasha before his court, " who made me what I am. Remember that you can always count upon me."

*　　*　　*

Time passed easily for Ferdinand, but his father became a chronic invalid. His legs were now grossly swollen. He had insomnia and gastritis. Yet he could not afford to give up, and expected no kindness from the Quai d'Orsay. At last, being unable to walk without support and almost incapable of a legible hand, he wrote an official letter – but not to seek retirement. It was dated the 8th of December, 1832:

"Monsieur le Ministre, a serious illness, which continues to gain ground, requires that I should go to France to consult doctors. Up to now I have done everything possible to avoid making this journey, which in my present financial circumstances and, because of my devotion to the Service, is very painful to me. But the disease continually grows worse and the doctors in this country tell me that they can suggest nothing else but that I should go to France to consult specialists. I would beg Your Excellency to be so good as to obtain for me from His Majesty a leave of absence which I will do my best to make as short as possible. Just now the major commercial matters have been happily concluded. There remain only the ordinary duties which could easily be carried out by the Vice-Consul, or such person as Your Excellency may appoint in my stead for the time being."

Before a reply could be received Mathieu was dead, nor was Ferdinand able to get to Tunis. When he broke the news to Mohammed-Ali that man wept: he who had massacred the Mamelukes, and by sheer callousness caused the deaths of thou-

sands of fellaheen. Soon afterwards it was arranged that Ferdin-
and should quit Alexandria to be Consul Second Class in Cairo.
At last his schooldays were really ended. How wide and pleasant
seemed the land of his adoption, how genial the present invitation to the future! Since Mathieu's day Egypt had vastly
changed. Replacing a crude traditional baronage, the vaunted
principle of Progress was every month more clearly in operation.
Taxes were no longer pocketed by local Beys but were paid direct
to Cairo where they became the basis of a national exchequer.
It was evident from the beginning that taxation alone could not
support the modernization of the country, but cotton was booming and Mohammed-Ali looked to Lancashire for the money to
balance his budget. As for law and order, whereas in Mathieu's
day everyone travelled armed and in convoy, now: "a man
could start from Taurus (in Turkey) cash in hand, and un-
escorted arrive in Senaar, travelling 700 leagues without having
to fear a single incident." Yet the old roots of power remained
behind this façade. Immemorial inhumanities were practised
and the real taskmasters of the people were still the unholy
trinity of fear, want and pain. At first Ferdinand had no occasion
nor desire to quit the brilliant stages which the dictator of his
father's choice had erected in Cairo and Alexandria. Soon he
stood closer to the throne than any other foreigner, and was
the only person permitted to receive at any hour the young
heir, Säid, whose father confessed that he ignored the tutor's
reports and concentrated upon the record of the boy's weight.
The objection to Säid's obesity was hardly aesthetic. It was held
unmilitary and therefore unmanly. The desert Arabs regarded
fat as a feminine attribute. They stuffed their brides with food
and kept them almost motionless to conserve their adiposity.
Lesseps sympathized with the boy and arranged to give him
refuge in the consulate from the rigours of his day, which,
besides as many as fourteen lessons, included running round the
walls of a town or climbing the masts of a ship. Säid used to
arrive tired and famished, for he had been put on a low diet.
Unfortunately for his figure, his favourite dish was macaroni,
and this was generously provided from the consulate kitchen.
Not that Ferdinand merely let the boy laze. He introduced Säid
to the art of fencing and they used to go out riding together.
In later life Ferdinand may well have wondered at the ways of

Providence, which put a king in debt of honour to him for the
sake of some macaroni and some horse exercise.

The Consul's life was a gentlemanly routine which made it
easy for him to forget that when, for instance, Mohammed-Ali
had decided to build a canal from Alexandria to the Nile,
modern methods were conspicuously absent. No survey was
made. No plans were drawn. No transport, accommodation nor
supply arrangements were prepared. Not even tools were provided. But sixty thousand fellaheen at forced labour shifted the
earth with their hands, completed the canal, and left there
fifteen thousand dead. The Egyptian authorities may well have
considered the work cheap, but it must have shocked Lesseps,
and may explain why, in spite of being so devoted to the idea of
the *Canal des Deux Mers*, he never seems to have pressed that
project upon Mohammed-Ali, whose chief engineer, Linant de
Bellefonds, was an old friend who shared the vision. In fact
Linant did the hard work of the surveys from which other
people, including Lesseps, were to profit. It is to Linant more
than to any other individual that the original plan of the Suez
Canal is due.

*   *   *

It was not long before the ambitious Pasha of Cairo, bent upon
independence, found an excuse to employ Egypt's new army
against his overlord the Sultan, and proceeded to wrest Syria
from him. In those days the province stretched northward from
Sinai to Turkey proper. It was inhabited by tough tribes under
sheiks of ancient heritage who were as much opposed to tyranny
from Egypt as from Stamboul. Guerrillas were a continual nuis-
ance, and were dealt with in the modern manner by wholesale
deportations. A minor incident of this kind involved Bethlehem,
from which the entire male population fit to bear arms were
sent to the galleys for life, accompanied by some of their elders.
By this time Mimaut had gone back to France and Ferdinand
found himself acting Consul-General. As such he inspected
prisoners and :

"observed at each of my visits those twelve aged men and the four
hundred young ones who intoned hymns in honour of France. I
asked them what they had done. 'We have been reduced to slavery,'
they said, 'because of our alliance with the chief Abu Gosh.' This

was the chief who commanded the pass where David killed Goliath. Abu Gosh, the descendant of an ancient family dating from 1100, was then resisting with all his might the domination of the Turks over his fellow-countrymen."

Touched by the injustice which enslaved people on suspicion, shocked that it should have been from Bethlehem that these had been uprooted, Lesseps decided to risk an appeal direct to Mohammed-Ali. He did so in spite of the fact that the officer commanding Syria was the Pasha's son Ibrahim, on whose orders the deportations were carried out, and who from a military point of view had reason to consider such measures essential for the pacification of the country. Mohammed-Ali listened to Lesseps, and after some hesitation agreed to release five men each week, at which rate he hoped that Ibrahim would not notice what was happening. This did not satisfy Lesseps, who showed his remarkable flair for the oriental manner by appearing before Mohammed-Ali with his clothes torn to shreds – a disrespectful gesture. An answer to a polite inquiry as to the reason for such a turn-out, Lesseps said boldly that it was really the Pasha's fault because of his niggardly clemency, which had so much increased the importunities of the remaining galley-slaves that on his last official visit they had mobbed him. The gesture succeeded. All the prisoners were set free.

Thirty years later, when Lesseps was deprived of Egyptian labour for the canal and went into Palestine to recruit workers:

"From the first day of my arrival in Jerusalem old men in red robes came to greet me, saying, 'It was thou who didst turn away from us the vengeance of Ibrahim Pasha: be blessed.'"

And when he visited Bethlehem, accompanied by an escort of French cavalry:

"Women burnt incense under the nostrils of my horse and slaughtered lambs in the streets. From windows and roofs they sang our praises and our path was strewn with verdure and flowers. The French officers could not hide their feelings. On arriving at the grotto of the Nativity, an old man came forward and presented to me a child. 'Here,' he said, 'is a son of those whom you saved.'"

When cholera broke out in Alexandria Lesseps was appointed

to head the Public Health Committee. He could have sat quietly behind a big desk taking the credit for other men's work, instead:

"Ardent, indefatigable, sometimes rash, he went to see for himself. Bent over the beds of the dying, he questioned, consoled and aided them. It is to him that we owe the evacuation of the Okelli, a little street called *les Baudets* (the Asses), entirely inhabited by Maltese, among whom the scourge began. From the beginning this Okelli, where the plague made the most fearful ravages, had been sealed off while arrangements were made to evacuate the inhabitants to the lazaret. But the poor wretches were frightened and categorically refused to move. Hardly had M. de Lesseps taken office as President of the *Conseil de Santé* than he went among them, persuading, begging them to go. He did at last convince them. From among the European community a collection was made for clothes and shoes, and that same evening they underwent *spoglio* (purification) and were taken to the lazaret for quarantine; where only three more cases occurred. These unfortunate people, because of the evil which has fallen upon our town, call M. de Lesseps their father and their rescuer. Yesterday he was told that in one ward of the hospital at the lazaret there languished forty-two cases which for several days had been abandoned by the doctors, who no longer dared to enter the room. M. de Lesseps went among them, and did not leave until he had seen them receive all the attention which their condition required. He then appointed a new doctor for the particular care of these patients. The generous courage with which our young consul wrestles face to face with the plague is most worthy of the profound gratitude which all the inhabitants of Alexandria bear him."

The foregoing was written by the Alexandria correspondent of the *Censeur de Lyon*, who would have been even more impressed if he had known under what circumstances Lesseps first saw the inside of the lazaret, when he himself awaited the onset of the disease. The epidemic lasted almost two years, and during all that time Lesseps, freed from routine consular duty, was constantly on the job, travelling as the incidence of the pestilence shifted. At last, in August 1836, new cases ceased to occur and he went home on leave, to receive public acclaim and to be made a Chevalier of the Legion of Honour. He also fell in love.

Agathe Delamalle was the daughter of an old friend of his mother. She had brown hair, blue eyes, and 'her spirit made a great impression on his heart'. Her late father had been Public Prosecutor at Angers (Maine et Loire), and before that he had like Mathieu and Barthélemy, survived the fall of the First Empire. Unlike them, he had sufficiently pleased Louis XVIII to be ennobled by that monarch although previously honoured after the same fashion by Napoleon. He had been a Councillor of State and a Commander of the Legion. At this unfortunate moment poor Mimaut died and Lesseps, instead of getting married, had to go back to Alexandria. Like other members of the family, he seems to have fallen in love quickly, finally and thoroughly. Agathe and he were married as soon as he could again get leave from Egypt, on the 21st December, 1837. The religious ceremony took place at the Church of the Assumption, Paris, where the service was conducted by the Bishop of Morocco, who was also Almoner to Queen Marie-Amélie, wife of Louis-Philippe and daughter of Ferdinand IV, King of the Two Sicilies. The civil ceremony followed at the *mairie* of the *Premier Arrondissement*, where the witnesses were Theodore de Lesseps, then at the Foreign Office, and a gentleman described as 'sometime councillor to the royal court at Paris'. There was also Viscount Delamalle, uncle to the bride. Ferdinand was already moving in the circle proper to his career.

The newly-weds went back to Alexandria, but the following year Ferdinand was appointed Minister Plenipotentiary at the Hague, where a diplomatic tussle was going on because the King of Holland was reluctant to recognize the independence of Belgium. In 1839 he was appointed Consul at Rotterdam, where their first child was born, to die within a month. It was with relief that, on the 15th of June, 1840, he received a new appointment, to Malaga, where his father had been very well liked. Agathe, who was six months pregnant, could not be left behind to travel by easy stages, and as usual her husband was required to hurry. They travelled only on alternate days but even so the strain on Agathe must have been considerable, for the weather was excessively hot and much of the journey had to be by road. The railway ended at Châlon-sur-Saône, but from Lyons they went by horse-drawn barge, perhaps not so restful a progress as it might seem in view of the river's turbulence, to Avignon. The last stage occupied thirteen hours on a particularly rough and dusty road, bringing them to Marseilles where they were welcomed by many friends. Agathe proudly wrote home: "How nice to have a husband who is so much appreciated by everyone."

The voyage was calm, and their new steamer a steady ship, which Agathe particularly appreciated because she was a bad sailor. They put into Malaga on the 7th of July, and she was immediately transported by everything she saw. The consulate was set between mountains and the sea, with a view *ravissante* from the windows. As for the interior of the house: "You cannot imagine how convenient it is. The Chancellery and the reception-rooms occupy the ground floor, while on the first floor are my little *salon*, Ferdinand's study, the bedroom, and a big *cabinet de toilette* . . . I hardly come down except for meals. The rooms are quite small. We shall easily be able to furnish them without too much expense." Ferdinand's pay was twelve thousand francs a year and he had no private means of any kind. It is not surprising that Agathe was soon complaining that the cost of living was 'horribly dear'. But they managed to keep four servants, three of them Spaniards who could speak only their own language, which Agathe did not understand. The fourth was her maid, oddly named Maurice, who promptly fell ill and had to be nursed by her mistress. When she recovered, life blissfully settled down. "Ferdinand is every day more admirable, and every day I love him more. My dear little man is every day more worthy to be cherished. You can be quite happy about him. His feelings about your daughter do not change at all, unless it is that he becomes more and more loving. . . . We are very snug in our little house, and we are always happy together." Their cup overflowed when in September a second child was born, to survive the baptismal name of Charles-Aimé-Marie. But from the professional point of view Malaga was dull, an unimportant post at the best of times. Ferdinand's nature demanded action as his body needed food, and until a local revolution broke out it did not seem that he would be likely to get any. Even then there was no real reason why he should have become involved.

*   *   *

The force of socialist ideas in Spain was a continuing ferment

under successive governments, driven to increasingly harsh
measures by the steady growth of anti-monarchist, anti-clerical
feeling, carried over with bitterness from the time of Napoleon's
occupation. When France had forced the monarchy back in 1823
she did the equivalent of making the King sit on the safety valve
of the political boiler. Thereafter neither Left nor Right could
compromise. Ten years later the situation was in its elements
still unchanged, but pressure had increased and a new factor
added – the Carlist wars, which, by disputing the throne, poised
the country over a pit of civil war. When at last that issue was
decided by the flight of Queen Cristina, it led to the assumption
of dictatorial power by General Espartero, accompanied by
disturbances due largely to the army's divided loyalties. Because
the Queen had been given asylum in France, Lesseps stretched
a point to intervene when General Espinosa, who was loyal to
her, was in danger of losing his life at the hands of the mob.
He arranged for the General to be put aboard the packet-boat
Phénicien, but no sooner had the fugitive left the consulate than
his enemies appeared in force and demanded a search of the
ship. Since only warships were inviolable under such circumstances, they were within their rights. Knowing that he would
have to give way, particularly as he was hardly within the
bounds of protocol in helping a Spanish national against his
own people's new but established government, Lesseps played
for time. He secretly sent a message to the captain of the
Phénicien asking him to transfer Espinosa to a French man-of-
war which happened to be in the harbour; and then went on
talking to the impatient delegation until he judged that the
transhipment ought to have been made. With a show of resignation he accompanied the senior officer on his search, which of
course was without success. Then: "The Captain-General of
the Government forces went ashore with Ferdinand de Lesseps,
who coolly made his way through the crowd which had been
tricked, and whose shouts and threats died away before the
unflinching bearing of the French Consul. So the General
lived to recount the incident in his memoirs, published in
Madrid."[1]

This must have been Ferdinand's first experience of a hostile
crowd. There would soon be others, but in the meantime

[1] Bridier, *Une Famille Française: les De Lesseps*, Paris 1900.

domestic life ran on with tranquil unconcern for Spanish politics.
A northerner, Agathe was delighted with the sunny climate. The
transition from bride to housewife was in her case no enemy of
romance. Their mutual affection continued to increase and every
trial deepened it. This idyll was interrupted by a new posting,
to Barcelona, where the family moved in June 1842, just as a
serious rebellion was about to break out. The detonator exploded
on the 13th of November when a group of thirty wine-smugglers
began a riot because police tried to interfere with their traditional business. The incident gave the military an excuse for
action and at the same time forced the rebels into the open.
They were drawn from many shades of opinion but held in
common an abhorrence of the iron rule of the dictator, who was
treating Catalonia as though it were the conquered province of
an enemy country.

Built on a high terrace, the consulate was within range of two
rival forts, and was also exposed to small-arms fire from the
streets. Agathe piled mattresses against the windows, but even
in her husband's absence she kept the front door open for those
who sought the protection of the Tricolor. Ferdinand had the
entrée to both headquarters, and at considerable risk spent much
of his time shuttling between them. On the 19th Agathe wrote
to her mother:

"I passed a horrible day yesterday. At noon they stopped firing
at the fort. From the top of our terrace we saw the Captain-
General's family going out to embark on the *Méléagre*, but they
were surrounded by boats full of troops and forced to return to
Barcelonette. Ferdinand at once put on his uniform, and, accompanied by a militia officer, set out to complain about this violation
of the flag (he had furnished the refugees with French passports).
They gave him a written order that the embarkation would be
allowed to proceed. Ferdinand left for Barcelonette, which is outside the town, where the steamers moor. From there he had to
go to the Citadel to reassure the Captain-General about the fate
of his family. While he was there the militia started to fire at the
fort and the regular troops replied. Ferdinand was able to get out
by a back way, but coming into the town he had to cross the
place by the Palace under a hail of grape-shot. During those three
hours of his absence I cannot convey to you how I suffered. At
last he came back to me, safe and unhurt. Hardly had he come
in when the fort of the Atarzarnas opened fire with grape-shot on
the Rambla. The shot whistled round us and we took cover on

the garden side of the house. We were between two fires, and both were fiercely burning."

With precarious intervals of calm, this state of affairs went on until Ferdinand was obliged to send his own family on board ship. The regular troops were threatening to reduce the city by bombardment. Agathe next wrote: " The bombardment, which began yesterday, went on without pause until after midnight. To-day the regular troops are in the city. From shipboard we were able to make out that our home has been hit. One shell went through the front door into the Chancellery, where Ferdinand found it. Another destroyed the balcony next to my little sitting-room." Ferdinand went on living ashore, kept the flag flying and his office functioning. Gradually the tension became less acute but the two factions could find no means of compromise, and in the autumn of the following year another bombardment took place – after a series of delays for which Ferdinand's representations were largely responsible. Until the last moment it seemed likely that the threat would not be carried out, but the power against him was too great, and though the citizens were given plenty of warning, the hungry guns were fed.

On this occasion Ferdinand put the whole French colony, some six hundred persons, on board ship, together with as many Spaniards as he could find excuse for, irrespective of their titular allegiance. The rest of the population, having once experienced the effect of artillery fire among their crowded, weak-walled houses, took to the countryside. Through it all Agathe kept up her regular letters to her mother:

" Everybody has gone into the country, sleeping in the open air. The sick from the hospital, the orphans from their home, all have gone. There hardly remain three thousand people in the town, and there are no supplies for the unfortunates out in the country. Someone who came in this morning said she has seen an old man, who was very ill, stretched out on a mattress on the ground during a rainstorm. Nearly all the consuls have gone and the administrative offices are closed. Don't worry, we are well and undisturbed. Pass on our news to my mother-in-law. The upset has prevented me from writing to her because we are busy all day with people coming and going."

Soon afterwards Agathe had to leave. The bombardment took

place, and, and, after a month's fighting, the rebels were finally defeated. A new dictator, Navaez, then sat in the seat of Espartero. Isabella was declared Queen at the age of thirteen, and her mother, Cristina, was invited to return to Spain to look after her. The consulate had not been sacked, and Agathe went back there with her two children, Charles (two) and little Ferdinand, born the previous September. Calmly she set about putting the house to rights. It was Ferdinand's turn to write to her mother:

"Your dear Agathe is a pearl among women. I do assure you I have appreciated her character and good sense under difficult conditions when it was necessary to have all my wits about me, and where I could by no means have been assured of freedom of movement had I a wife like most of those I see. . . . She has borne most heroically the trials which we have had to undergo. I admired her resignation and cheerfulness in circumstances where I have been forced to leave her in order to carry out my duties, which have exposed me to grave dangers. She never said anything, or allowed any expression of emotion which might deter me from what I had to do."

Agathe also sent a private letter: "This revolution has shown how fine he is. Everyone loves and admires him. The authorities trust him. Whenever he appears they say, 'the Consul of France!' and everybody makes room." Nor was his fame only local. From Paris the Foreign Minister, Guizot, wrote a personal note of appreciation and promised a special mark of favour from the King, which turned out to be the Cross of the Legion of Honour. Only England was hostile, though Lesseps had good personal relations with the British Consul during the troubles. From across the Channel it seemed that the re-establishment of the monarchy was another victory for French imperialist policy, and the hero of Barcelona was accused of having played a double game, even of having fomented the uprising which he had done so much to abort. His reputation was saved from a most unexpected quarter, the rebel leader himself, who on principle had at least as much reason for disliking Lesseps as had the English. Ferdinand was, after all, the representative of the country which had forced the monarchy on Spain in the first place.

When the Queen Mother disembarked at Barcelona she called

at the French consulate and told Agathe: "You must be proud to have such a husband, and he must be so happy to have such a charming wife. I know you are soon returning to France, but promise me that you will come back." To Ferdinand she confided: "You will be seeing the King. He is very pleased with you, and told me so several times. We often talked together about you." The Lesseps were to go home on the same ship which had brought the Queen Mother, and before they embarked Ferdinand had to receive a deputation from the French colony: "Pray accept, *Monsieur le Consul*, as a mark of our repect, this gold medal which we have the honour to offer you. It is the result of a unanimous vote. Anxious to understand the significance of the emblems which it portrays, posterity will one day open history at this good page and read: 'At this time Ferdinand de Lesseps, Consul of France at Barcelona, was brave, generous, humane. His conduct was admirable.'"

They were on leave for a year, and when in April 1845 they returned to Barcelona, it was to find a very different atmosphere. The new dictator had learned the lesson at which his predecessor had failed, and the people, with their racial ebullience, were rejoicing in unaccustomed liberty. Soon after the return of Lesseps, Catherine brought the young Queen to Barcelona, attended by Navaez and the President of the Cortes. A great ball was given at which Agathe was the hostess:

"More than six hundred people attended the *fête* at which our gracious sovereign was pleased to take the arm of the French Consul. Diamonds glittered everywhere. Madame de Lesseps received the guests with perfect grace. Her toilette was ravishing, and she wore it with that marvellous air of which only *Parisiennes* have the secret. Let us add that the affection which everyone bears her did not a little to increase the charm of this magnificent soirée, which lasted until dawn."

The ball represented both the pinnacle of Ferdinand's diplomatic career and the peak of his personal happiness. Soon afterwards dark clouds began to lower on his life. The first squall struck when baby Ferdinand fell ill, and in a month was dead. That the town took opportunity at the funeral to show respect for his parents, turning the simple ceremony into a great gather-

ing, would not have weighed against their sorrow, commemorated upon the headstone of the grave: "Pray for those who
weep for you. You shall be the guardian spirit of your brother
Charles, who dearly loves you. Barcelona the 16th of May, 1846,
when with our own hands we reverently enshrouded your mortal
shell. Ferdinand de Lesseps. Agathe Delamalle."

Chapter 3. REVOLUTIONS

With conditions in Barcelona back to normal, Ferdinand had time to continue both outdoor pursuits and his studious interests, chiefly the idea of the *Canal des Deux Mers* and political philosophy, subjects which, though apparently poles apart, had a connecting link in the fantastic figure of Prosper Enfantin, the reigning 'Father' of the Saint-Simonians. This messianic group originated in the mystical communism of Count Saint-Simon, son of the Duke who achieved fame through his intimate records of life at the court of Louis XIV. It is to the Count that the world owes the social theorem which in its original form was phrased: *"à chacun selon sa capacité, à chaque capacité suivant ses œuvres"*; which is not quite equivalent to the usual English version: "to each according to his need, from each according to his skill". This new-model society was to be by no means classless. Otherwise the basis of Saint-Simonism was for its time an advanced socialism, with all the dark, rational principles which seem so right in theory but can only be put into practice by a rule of fear. Enfantin saw himself as the leader of a bloodless world revolution which would abolish most forms of property, particularly by inheritance, and institute a series of castes. The highest of these, nominated by his close associates, the Elect, would to-day be loosely designated Managers. They were to bring about universal peace through the invincible advance of industry. Only the lowest caste would be permitted old-style religion, the effects of which were to be judged entirely by results in terms of efficiency. And yet, parallel with all this, Enfantin claimed to be the founder of a New Christianity, which was anything but scientific. Its sacrament was sex, its first article of faith the belief that in Prosper Enfantin one half of Jesus Christ was incarnate. The other half of Jesus, secretly awaiting the hour of destiny, was in the body of a woman, still unrecognized, who would become his bride and so constitute a new godhead. It seems at least doubtful whether Enfantin him-

49

self originated this idea, but he certainly made use of it. Its probable source was a nocturnal vision by one of the 'apostles'. This enthusiast came into the 'Father's' bedroom at half-past six one morning and announced: "Jesus lives in Enfantin. Thou art one half of the Couple of Revelation." At the time Enfantin was pulling on his socks. He looked up and answered modestly: "*Homo sum* – I am he." Then he admonished the hysterical visionary not to say anything about his incomplete divinity until the Bride should appear.

In spite of such vain imaginings and the cool reception of his claims by level-headed persons, Enfantin not only became the focus of a numerous and wealthy community, but also contrived to be associated with the court and with practical men of the highest standing, not least in the matter of the Suez Canal. The uniform of the sect was a long, belted tunic, giving the impression of a short, fluted skirt worn over tight trousers, so long that they partly covered the feet. The neck of the tunic was extremely low and wide, the gap garnished at the left side by a sash as big as a Scots plaid but made of embroidered silk, which, after going loosely round the neck, cascaded as far as the knees. A vaguely nautical vest, deeply bordered in colour, was visible across the upper part of the chest, and in the case of Enfantin declared, as though it were the name of a ship: LE PÈRE.

Ferdinand had first encountered these exotic creatures when twenty of them, headed by Enfantin, landed at Alexandria in 1833 and called at the consulate where Mimaut handed them over to him; because their professed object in coming to Egypt was to make a survey for the canal which was already his pet subject. They probably did not mention that France would not welcome them, their society having been dissolved over a year before, since when Enfantin had been in prison. The charge on which he had been convicted was the advocacy of free love, but the reality behind the attitude of the authorities was that Saint-Simonism was no more compatible with Catholicism than is Satanism. Indeed the sexual focus of 'New Christianity' suggests a close relationship. Doubtless in an earlier age Enfantin would have burned; the more certainly because of his Luciferian attitude when arraigned. A tall, bearded figure, inclined to fat, he appeared before the court dressed in Hessian boots and a velvet cloak trimmed with ermine. At first he would not speak at all. When he did so, it was not to defend himself but to preach in free verse of which the following is a fair sample:

> " Car si Jésus a été envoyé
> Pour enseigner au monde
> La sagesse du PÈRE
> Moi, je suis envoyé par mon DIEU,
> PÈRE et MÈRE, de touts et de toutes,
> Pour faire désirer au monde
> Sa tendresse de MÈRE."

He explained his silence by saying that he wished to give the court an opportunity to appreciate his beauty and the majesty of his presence. Nevertheless, he entered the prison of Sainte-Pélagie on the 15th of December, 1832, and there he remained while his disciples eagerly awaited the revelation of the Mother, who was supposed to emerge in the following year. Enfantin contrived to keep control of his cult and sent out an inspired order that the Bride be sought in the East, particularly at Constantinople. Some of the ' Woman's Companions ' went there:

" Behold them therefore disembarking in full costume, saluting all women, rich and poor, high and low, according to Enfantin's instructions; and experiencing at the sight of the veiled ladies more than the usual sense of glamour, since it was extremely likely that the ' free woman ' was at that moment in a harem. The Grand Turk prevented possible complications at this point by transporting them to Smyrna. . . . In the meantime the fame of Lady Hester Stanhope had reached the *compagons de la femme*, and they hastened to visit her, a tremulous hope in their hearts, for had she not seen visions of a woman messiah? But this strange prophetess refused to play the part that was all ready for her. The great lady gave them money but would not further their schemes."[1]

So when they arrived in Egypt the Saint-Simonians were not only unwanted in France but also in Turkey, and as he was still technically a vassal of the Sultan, Mohammed-Ali probably needed a good deal of persuasion before he allowed them to stay in Egypt and survey the isthmus; particularly as he had not been informed of their intentions in advance and suspected a French plot, the more easily because he was secretly planning

[1] E. M. Butler, *The Saint Simonian Religion in Germany*, Cambridge 1926.

to invade Syria across the line of the proposed canal. Finding
conditions on the isthmus uncomfortable, Enfantin only spent
a fortnight there before going into Upper Egypt for a holiday.
Out of funds when he returned, he was able to stay on in the
country only through the generosity of friends, of whom Ferdin-
and was sure to have been one. He returned to France at the
end of 1846. As for the Mother, she had by then faded out of
the picture. Even while the Companions were searching Constantinople, Enfantin had a revelation that instead of being
incarnate she would appear only symbolically, as the opposite
pole to his Society in mystic union between West and East, to
be consummated through the making of the canal. The following text represents the vision in all its freshness:

> " C'est à nous de faire,
>   Entre l'antique Egypte et la vieille Judée,
>   Une des deux nouvelles routes d'Europe
>   Vers l'Inde et la Chine,
>   Plus tard nous perçerons aussi l'autre
>   A Panama . . .
>   Suez
>   Est le centre de notre travail,
>   Là nous ferons l'acte
>   Que le monde attend
>   Pour confesser que nous sommes
>   Mâles . . ."

As for Panama, the Comte Saint-Simon had himself suggested
that enterprise as long ago as 1779. Nor was it then a novelty,
having been the subject of various Spanish surveys over the
previous two centuries.

*   *   *

At the other pole of the political world, Ferdinand admired
Jaime Balmès, a philosophical writer and sometime priest whose
ideas tallied closely with what Lesseps had worked out for himself. Balmès was by no means a narrow cleric, and he conveyed
to Ferdinand no specific dogma but rather a faith founded upon
man's incorruptible essence which, because it lives not alone but
as the son of a spiritual father, survives all degradation and
decay. Lesseps had an almost English reticence in matters

theological, and seldom spoke or wrote in terms of religion though he was a Bible student and a practising Roman Catholic. Yet he refused to be confined by a form of words and recognized behind all humanity the same fundamental values which should, but often do not, determine the conduct of individuals and the policies of governments.

With the dawn of 1848, news from Paris became increasingly disquieting. There was much distress and unemployment throughout the country and consequently a rising tide of socialist feeling which the Government seemed incapable of countering, indeed they almost ignored it. "Can you," Tocqueville demanded of the Ministers on the 27th of January, " at this very moment count upon to-morrow? Have you the smallest idea of what a year, a month, or a day may bring forth? " Feeling themselves secure behind a large majority, the Government ignored his warning. Lesseps would not have been so optimistic. Remembering the fate of his father and uncle after the fall of the Emperor, he had reason to fear for his own career, even for his liberty, should another revolution take place. For though the mob fears tradition, it has a long memory, and the Lesseps were friends of kings. No matter that, if anything, Ferdinand's views were left of centre and his record irreproachable. If the red terror should return he was too conspicuous to be passed over.

On the 22nd of February a socialist banquet was banned and the pink Press called for a demonstration by way of protest. It succeeded better than they could have hoped, for the unarmed and quite peaceable crowds put such fear into the King that he promptly dismissed his Ministers. This act so encouraged the Opposition and the mob that next day the streets were barricaded and the city swarmed with determined citizens, who in some quarters flew the red flag and everywhere demanded a republic. The military were promptly called out, amounting to some thirty thousand troops, quite sufficient to control the situation. But their hearts were not in their work. Even the high command hesitated to buy such a throne with blood. Permeating the rank and file the same sentiment gave a sense of unreality to preparations for battle. For the most part the soldiers stood around and fraternized with the crowds. Then they were ordered back to barracks, and clinched the issue by leaving arms and equipment behind them for the rebels to pick up.

Next morning in a hackney cab a stout party left the city under the name of Mr. William Smith, whose destination was London. Yesterday he had been His Most Catholic Majesty Louis-Philippe, King of the French, whose early promise had gone down into such unpopularity that when Alibaud tried to shoot him the would-be assassin told the police: "I admire Jesus Christ. He was a Republican like me, and would probably have been a regicide too." Technically, Louis-Philippe's undignified exit was a formal abdication in favour of a little boy, the son of the Duc d'Orléans, Ferdinand's old schoolfellow. His mother presented the child to the Assembly but their reception was so hostile that she withdrew, and nothing more was heard of the claim while the Provisional Government went about the business of preparing a new Constitution which would echo the former ideals of Liberty, Equality, Fraternity; but in a tolerant and liberal manner, avoiding all excess. The principle of international socialism would be reaffirmed, but there was to be no interference with the affairs of other countries: coexistence rather than world revolution.

In fact the new masters of France were too slow for the mob, which, waving red flags, invaded the Assembly and demanded, among other things, that the ex-King's civil list be applied to the redemption of articles pawned by workers. Lamartine, the effective Chief of State, was an idealist, a poet and a statesman, who had come under the influence of Prosper Enfantin. A fervent orator, he was on this occasion able to save the Tricolor by persuading the people to attach a red rosette to the flagstaff rather than adopt the red flag entire. But in greater matters he failed, perhaps as much because the disintegration of the country had already gone too far for any man to check, as because he lacked the practical force with which to implement his theories. Yet the signs of decay were nowhere apparent. On the contrary all classes were imbued with a pathetic optimism, and seemed to have forgotten the deep chasms which divided them, as between parties, in spite of shared enthusiasm for a new France; again to be the leader of Europe, through whose inspiration the peoples who still groaned under the yoke of monarchy would follow her to liberty. For though she might not interfere, France could prevent counter-revolution abroad by becoming the ally of a new republic against a returning despot. Thus, when

Lamartine addressed Mazzini and his Italian Association as they were about to leave Paris to create the Roman Republic out of the Papal States, he said: " Since France and Italy are all one in our mutual desire for liberal regeneration, tell Italy that she has sons also on this side of the Alps! Tell her that if she should be attacked on her soil or in her soul, we shall offer the sword of France to preserve her from all invasion! "

That was on the 28th of March, the crest of the new socialist wave. On the first of April Ferdinand was startled to receive a peremptory summons to return to Paris, no reason given. He must have travelled in grave apprehension, but a few days later he was writing to Agathe:

"I am in an office next to that of M. Lamartine, who is finishing off some business before receiving me. He has already let me know that at the cabinet meeting this morning I was formally appointed Minister Plenipotentiary at Madrid. So the matter is closed, and I need hardly tell you how happy I am for both of us. I shall know in a few minutes whether they want me to start at once. If necessary I shall say that I am ready to go this evening."

Lesseps probably appreciated the situation better than most of the politicians, who were immersed in their squabbles of the hour. He thought that the monarchy had had its chance and failed. "A republic," he wrote, "is the only possible government for France." Yet he was not anti-royalist, nor was he one of those people who call themselves broadminded because they lack the courage to take sides. He had already learned the melancholy truth that no matter what the label, a man, a party, or a country can be no better than its soul; that neither Right nor Left can of themselves make government good.

"Stability?" Balmès demanded, "in a world converted to the religion of change, what régime can aspire to such a thing? After so many speeches, so many reforms and changes, all questions of government, of public order, have come to rely upon one thing only: force. The improvement of the working-man's lot is certainly an object of the greatest importance; we have to work for it without pause; but those who want to hurry it, those who try to solve the problem in a sense favourable to the working classes and begin by attacking property, directly or indirectly, are the apostles of a tyrannous liberty, an impossible equality. Their crazy plans can have no other result than to cause great social upheavals which

end by crushing the workers themselves. . . . Monarchy can never
be in any country a calculated institution, a mere convention; it
must rest upon feeling and tradition. From the moment when
people begin to analyse monarchy instead of loving it, monarchy
begins to die. . . . Since 1789 France has broken with all her ancient
traditions, and monarchy demands faith, a kind of fealty in
chivalry."

France, he went on, was incapable of such an attitude. After
what she had endured, how could it be expected of her? "Perhaps in certain circumstances the return of the monarchy is not
impossible. What is difficult, if not impossible, is the stability of
the restored monarchy." The quotations are taken from a book
later translated from the Spanish by de Lesseps under the title
of *Judgment on the Revolution of 1848*, which refers not to the
gentle riots of February but to the blood-letting of June, by
which time Ferdinand was far away. He stayed in Paris until
the 28th of April, and left with grim forebodings. Lamartine
feared that the new spirit in France would cause revolution in
Spain, which country was still a rigid dictatorship. "A good
understanding with Spain," he said, "is worth 20,000 men on
the Pyrenean frontier." His implication was that Spain might
strike first in order to prevent the red infection – a 'preventive
war'.

Supported by Marshal Navaez, Isabella was still on the throne,
but the fires of revolt kept on breaking through the crust of
repression. Consequently the new French socialism was regarded
by the Government as a plague which might easily spread over
the whole of the Iberian Peninsula. Under such circumstances
the French Ambassador could hardly expect to be popular until
he had unequivocally demonstrated his own and his country's
opposition to the export of socialism. This Lesseps achieved by
travelling the whole length of the frontier, from the family's
home town, Bayonne, to Perpignan: no easy route. He visited
every customs post and gave strict orders, duly authorized by
Lamartine, against the crossing of the border by propaganda or
propagandists. No gesture could have been better calculated to
impress the Government to which he was accredited.

*   *   *

On arrival in Barcelona, he hired a diligence for twelve

hundred francs, bundled the family in – there was now a new baby Ferdinand as well as Charles, aged seven, and set off for Madrid, a distance of three hundred miles. He got there in three days, and Agathe was soon the mistress of an establishment suitable to her husband's exalted rank. Yet she sighed for Barcelona, where there had been less glitter but she could see more of him. His duties now occupied nearly all his time, and he often had to attended court alone – where he was too well liked to please the Left-wingers in Paris. It was not long before they stirred up trouble, affirming that since he had served the King he ought not to be employed by the Republic. Realizing that his career must ultimately depend upon putting no Government before the country, Lesseps turned a deaf ear, until, at the end of August, he became so exasperated that he wrote to his brother-in-law, Victor Delamalle: "I do what I ought. I act loyally and I want to have my hands free; as I carefully explained to all the members of the Provisional Government in advance. I will not be put in a false position, nor will I tolerate the least mistrust. If they are dissatisfied with me I shall console myself: perhaps they will even honour me with disgrace. But I stay here on the job just the same."

Such an attitude was typical Lesseps, and also typical Ferdinand. His task as he saw it was, with drawn sword, to follow a straight line. The surest way to fall was to step aside to bandy words with narrow-minded men in search of personal power. He had reason for confidence. Lamartine, though of a reddish colour, was his loyal friend vowed to the same service. It was Lamartine who had said: "There is a principle above patriotism itself, the principle of the development of humanity. Put the interests of civilization and liberty above the question of extended frontiers." It was as good a definition of Ferdinand's straight line as he himself could have made, and he exalted it into a working philosophy. a world-line, which may perhaps be condensed into a single unwieldy word: suprapatriotism.

Meanwhile, Agathe had found a wonderful ally for the social battle. That extraordinary woman, the Comtesse de Montijo, was now at her zenith. Besides having great influence in her own right, she was virtually Comptroller of the Household. If her vices were not entirely inconsiderable, her virtues were really remarkable: "Original and bewitching, with Andalusian grace,

English genuineness, French facility; yet always a Spaniard . . .
She was one of those dauntless and glittering women who move
as much by instinct as by stratagem towards the seats of power.
She scattered pleasures about her and made joy an obligation."[1]
Also she was beautiful. She had a mint of lovers and an income
of £20,000 a year. At twenty-two her younger daughter, Eugénie,
was surpassingly lovely. Ferdinand was delighted with her, and
there is no reason to suppose that Agathe had any reason to
disapprove of their cousinly relationship.

The mother of Manuela de Montijo was born de Grivegnée.
Her father was a Scot who had fled the country after the failure
of the Stuart rebellion in 1745. He entered the de Grivegnée
wine business, married the owner's daughter, and in time took
over the firm. Manuela's first husband, Comte de Teba, died,
and she then married Montijo, who also died. Eugénie, who all
her life would be singularly superstitious, began it under por-
tentous circumstances. Manuela was then at No. 12 Calle de
Gracia, Granada, a modest establishment, for the riches came
much later. As her time approached, there were earthquake
tremors, and, rather than be brought to bed in a house which
might collapse upon her, she went out into the garden and laid
little Eugénie at the foot of a tree. In spite of her fairy-like
arrival the child grew to be a terror to her governesses – 'a
young demon'. As an older girl she was still regarded as rather
light-headed, and this reputation persisted in later life, when
her apparent irresponsibility often concealed a serious purpose.
She also acquired a deep-rooted idealism, based largely upon
the ethics she acquired at the Convent of the Sacred Heart in
Paris, an establishment roughly equivalent to Ferdinand's
school in that it catered for the same kind of people. The Convent was even accused of turning out 'female Jesuits' and seeking to 'impregnate fashion with faith'. At all events the curriculum, and the contacts which went with it, could hardly have
been a better social beginning for the fey 'demon' who would
be the last Empress of the French.

The Eugénie of 1848 had few cares that were not in terms of
society, which meant the circle round the Queen and the
Comtesse de Montijo, a gay group, even a naughty one. For
Isabella was no less enthusiastic about life than was Eugénie's

[1] Robert Sencourt, *Life of the Empress Eugénie*, London 1931.

mother. They were the most elegant pair to preside in the royal box at the tragedy of a great nation. . . . According to Lesseps, some three or even four thousand people had recently been imprisoned, deported, or sent to the galleys, without any kind of legal process. The Dictator's reputation, if not his character, was later summed up by an apocryphal story that on his death-bed he declared he had no enemies to forgive – because he had had them all killed. Yet this man of iron, Navaez, did not succeed in taming the young Queen, and on one occasion may have come near to losing his power because he was foolish enough to interfere with her private life. Without consulting her, and without reason given, though everyone appreciated the motive, he banished her friend the Marquis de Bedman; who, after making himself socially conspicuous just across the border, crossed back into Spain and was installed in the palace where it was rumoured that his room was just below the Queen's, with a secret staircase between the two. Navaez feared that Bedman's influence with Isabella might even cause her to dismiss him. Her constitutional powers were sufficient for the purpose, and they were supported by the Church, which he dare not challenge. Navaez rode to the palace and demanded audience. The Queen received him in a small room off the main *salon* where a number of people were soon speculating upon the significance of the Marshal's sudden appearance. Soon they heard his voice raised in anger, protesting that it was impossible to maintain a throne so compromised. The Queen ordered him to withdraw, never again to enter her presence. Navaez stalked out. It seemed that the victor of many battles had been routed by a girl. But as lesser men are apt to do with lesser women, he went straight to her mother. And mother took daughter to task. So the Queen lost her lover and the Dictator kept his job. But, as Edgar-Bonnet dryly comments, that solution to the immediate problem left Navaez ' exposed to similar incidents '.

Behind the froth and frivolity of high society, tragedy was waiting. Before long even Eugénie was touched by it, if only with a finger-tip. Some young officers, among them the brother of an intimate friend, were sentenced to death for mutiny in Valencia. Would Ferdinand intervene? He had really no business to inter-fere in such a domestic matter but he could not deny Eugénie, and at once rode to the palace at Aranjuez, to find that the death-warrants had just been laid before the Queen. Surrounded by her Cabinet and with Navaez at her elbow, she would have had no alternative but to sign had not the Marshal been suddenly called away to see de Lesseps. In his absence the Queen refused to sign, and while she waited, Ferdinand confronted the Dictator with an ultimatum, which, had it not been accepted, would hardly have pleased the new Government in France.

" ' I have come to take leave of you,' he began, ' for you will see that, as the conditions of my mission to Spain were accepted by a sovereign Assembly that I might be able to exercise a salutary influence on your government, if it is learned that Mlle. de Montijo, belonging to one of the highest families in Spain, has unsuccessfully solicited my intervention to procure a pardon which, in my opinion, will strengthen rather than weaken you, there is nothing left for me to do but to retire and take my leave.'
"Navaez listened with amazement while de Lesseps poured out this long sentence. But seeing the determination written on the face before him, he shrugged his shoulders, and held out his hand. With the suspicion of a smile on his grim features he said, ' Very well, Ferdinand, you may be off with these men's heads in your pocket.' De Lesseps did not wait to hear more, but, gratefully pressing the hand offered to him, he hastened back to Madrid. There he learnt that the Queen, at the instance of Navaez, had pardoned the condemned men." (Schonfield.)

Though it must have brought Lesseps and Isabella closer together, the incident does not seem to have made him unpopular with the Dictator; so he stayed on in Madrid, enjoying to the full both the duties and the diversions of his rank and set, but increasingly concerned about affairs in Paris. Two elections had only increased the bitter, inconclusive hostility of rival parties until, by the beginning of June, revolution again became inevitable. This time there was no gentleness. In four days from the twenty-third of the month ten thousand people fell in the streets, among them more army officers than had been lost at any of the great victories of the Emperor. The Archbishop of Paris, who courageously tried to intervene, was killed by a stray bullet. Four generals were among the dead. Behind the open conflict all manner of atrocities took place. Shocked by a single-minded determination to secure peace at home, the people of France proceeded to elect, for four years, a President who should be above Party. They chose Louis-Napoleon, whom the previous

Assembly had tried to exile. He secured five million votes as compared with one and a half million for his runner-up, General Cavaignac, who had been responsible for the appalling victory in June. So, for the first time since 1792, the voice of the people unmistakably spoke; and its desire was not to rule, but to be ruled. The new Chief Executive had every intention of ruling, and one of his first acts was to get rid of Lamartine, put Drouyn de Lhuys into the Foreign Office, and so make the country alter course from port to starboard: "Memories of the Napoleonic legend, dreams of a glorious future, the fear of communism and of clerical propaganda, had deceived the mind of the people, and in consequence the Republic obtained a master."[1] The people had voted for stability, but by concentrating such power in the hands of one man they made a down payment on tyranny – and the instalments would prove ruinous.

In February 1849 the new Foreign Minister wrote to Lesseps: "The President has decided that M. Napoleon-Joseph Bonaparte will go to Madrid as Ambassador. Naturally you will immediately be offered a position similar to that which you are leaving. The two things can be done simultaneously. You will have understood as much without my having to say so. As to your destination, I will let you know that later." So the blow fell. But the new Minister, if curt, was at least civil. With guarded optimism Agathe began to pack, and Ferdinand went to say good-bye to the Queen who told him, "You take with you my esteem and that of all my subjects." Certainly he had earned praise, for while representing the socialists he had risked his own career in order to fulfil Lamartine's overriding demand, good relations between the two countries. And now perhaps his future was in jeopardy again – because he had so well served the Left! Among the French colony in Madrid, however, there were no enemies. As at Barcelona he was presented with a gold medal, and an address which reads in part: "As touching French citizens you have left no unfortunate without help, no injustice without reparation; and it can be said that each day of your administration has been marked by a good deed."

*   *   *

Ferdinand did receive a new appointment when he reached

[1] *Cambridge Modern History.*

Paris, though hardly one the equivalent of Madrid. It was for Berne, and before he could take it up he was caught in a political storm, which broke on the 7th of May. News had just been received that a French Army Corps, sent to overawe the Austrians, the Pope, and the new Roman Republic, had attacked the city of Rome and been beaten back with heavy loss. The President of the Assembly promptly put the blame on the General in the field, Oudinot, but all shades of opinion in the Chamber – where Lesseps was present – were indignant. Uproar continued far into the night. Out of it all the only practical decision to emerge was that an Envoy Extraordinary should forthwith be sent to Italy with instructions to reach a political settlement over the heads of the military, an agreement which must satisfy everyone. Lesseps was chosen for this impossible task. The essence of his formal instructions is contained in the following excerpt from the Foreign Minister's remarks:

"The object which we have in view is to deliver the States of the Church from the anarchy which prevails in them, and to ensure that the re-establishment of a regular power is not in future darkened, not to say imperilled, by reactionary fury. . . . You will therefore concentrate all your efforts upon bringing about such a result with as little delay as possible. . . . Your upright and enlightened judgment will inspire you according to circumstances."

The brief, inglorious history of the expedition began with the sound republican idea that the newly declared Roman Republic, the people's overwhelming choice, should not be allowed to go down under the armies of autocratic Austria, bent on restoring the temporal power of Pius IX. Pius had fled before the republican flood and took refuge at Gaeta under the protection of the King of Naples. The move was precipitated by the public assassination of the Pope's Prime Minister. Mazzini, whose memories of Lamartine's Paris were still vivid, had no reason to suppose that the change of government there would go so far to the Right that the President would be prepared to act, almost before he was settled in office, against both the spirit and the letter of the Constitution which he had solemnly sworn to uphold. Yet French troops had attacked Rome. Why?

When the expeditionary force landed at Civita Vecchia they were unopposed because the Romans still regarded them as

allies. Then Oudinot issued a proclamation and demanded entry
to Rome. Though his words were fair the demand was not. It
was refused. He attacked. He failed. What next? If only Lesseps
could gain time there might yet be a way out of the impasse.
The Pope must make concessions. The Republic must make concessions. And France must save her martial face. Behind all this
lay the President's recognition that in a real sense his power still
lay in the hands of the Pope, because it was the Catholic vote
which had swept him into office. The election had taken place
on a Sunday, which the socialists thought would keep the devout
away from the polls. Instead, whole congregations marched
from the churches to record their votes. Such people could not
be expected to distinguish between the religious and political
issues of the Papacy, nor did the ideals which Lamartine shared
with Mazzini come into the picture. But Louis-Napoleon was
well instructed in these matters. He had himself shared the early
struggle of the Roman patriots. The right thing to do was clearly
to dismiss Oudinot, reaffirm that French troops were only in
Italy for the protection of the legitimate aspirations of the
people, and compromise with the Pope to the extent of bringing
him back to St. Peter's, but not to his temporal throne. Louis-
Napoleon loved power more than he loved principles, but his conscience was troubled.

Without actually saying so, he seems to have tried to convey
as much to Lesseps in an interview just before Ferdinand left
for Rome. After reading the formal instructions from the
Foreign Office, which he properly described as ambiguous –
they amounted to little more than the hope that Lesseps would
offend none yet coerce all three, Pope, Austria, and Rome, into
a compromise, the Prince added:

"That I should do well, if opportunity occurred, to call attention to the fact that in 1831 he had already taken part against the
Temporal Power when he was before Rome in the company of his
elder brother, who died during the insurrection. Upon returning to
see M. Drouyn de Lhuys I was careful not to confide this matter
to him, nor did I make any use of it while in Rome, so as not to
excite public feeling unnecessarily. . . . M. Drouyn de Lhuys'
salon being then full of visitors, as it was his regular reception day,
I took leave of him and was soon travelling in a post-chaise to
Toulon, where telegraphic orders had been sent for a man-of-war
to be got ready for me."

At the same time a telegram went from the Foreign Office to General Oudinot: "Inform the Romans that we do not intend to join with the Neapolitans against them. Follow up the negotiations in the sense indicated by your instructions. Reinforcements are being sent to you. Await their coming. Endeavour to enter Rome with the assent of the inhabitants, or, if you are compelled to attack, do so with the most absolute certainty of success." To a professional soldier smarting under a humiliating reverse, the message meant only one thing. The rest of it was only politicians' stuff, but the one word *reinforcements* told Oudinot everything he needed to know. He was determined that, whatever else happened, France was going into Rome, if only to redeem the honour of her arms. In the middle of the night Lesseps arrived at field headquarters with exactly the opposite point of view, that for the honour of her arms France must not enter Rome except by invitation. At once Oudinot had to send out a stand-still order to units, and although Ferdinand kept his private views to himself, from that moment conflict between the two men became inevitable. At daybreak Lesseps was on his way to Rome.

" At first we had some difficulty in gaining admission, and it was necessary to make a partial circuit of the walls, as several of the gates were barricaded. All along the road were posts upon which were inscribed in large letters the clause of our Constitution which forbids attack upon a foreign nationality. Some of the sentinels upon the ramparts levelled their rifles at us, but my servant, who was sitting beside the driver of our brougham, flourished a white handkerchief, and the rifles were at once lowered. At last I saw a gate open, and a young officer, Colonel Medici, who recognized me, came forward and offered his services, saying that the city would be glad to hear of my arrival. He had me accompanied by a detachment of his men to the Via Condotti, where I alighted at the Hôtel d'Allemagne, thinking it advisable not to go just yet to the French Embassy."

Five days later the situation was so much improved that Garibaldi took all his force, some twelve thousand men, out of the city to attack the Neapolitans. Lesseps was beginning to feel confident that he could get the Roman Government to accept a token entry of French troops, thus saving face for Oudinot and Louis-Napoleon and at the same time avoiding war. But soon resistance stiffened. Fresh news from Paris had caught up with the Minister Plenipotentiary and he was no longer accepted by the Romans at his own valuation. They thought that he must be playing a double game, promising much, with the intention of breaking those promises the moment that French troops were within the city. One day he was mobbed as he drove to the Embassy, and only escaped being manhandled by making a show of pistols, which, he claimed, is always an effective gesture among people accustomed to using knives. Then there was an attempted assassination, which would have succeeded had not a man whose life Ferdinand had saved in Spain informed on the conspirators. Undaunted, he continued to shuttle between French headquarters and the Roman Government. Believing that he was in fact achieving the impossible, he worked day and night. He could not know that even the men closest to Oudinot were determined to win Rome for the Pope, nor that secret instructions from Paris to much the same effect had already arrived. He was: "always on the move or in conference, at high pressure, boiling, feverish, tired, but obstinate." And the day came when it seemed that his task was done. Mazzini and the other two members of the Triumvirate signed an armistice agreement and a Convention regulating all the outstanding differences. War had been averted: face had been saved. Exhausted but elated, Lesseps took the document to Oudinot, who would have none of it. He was now openly determined to fight, but he still had to accept Ferdinand's official status so:

"My firmness, coupled with dropping my hand on the hilt of my sword when the General talked of having me placed under arrest, fortunately had the effect of revoking at the last moment, all along the line of advance posts, the order which had been given for an immediate attack. However, as I was afraid that these orders would not arrive in time to prevent deplorable consequences, I made it known in Rome, whither I at once proceeded, that there was no occasion to feel uneasiness at our movements, which were only intended to enable us to make sure of the positions which foreign armies marching upon Rome might seize."

Next morning the General apologized, but again and again he was driven into direct opposition to Lesseps because of the war-whooping men of Paris and his own childish interpretation of the idea of glory. Meanwhile the Triumvirate and Lesseps hammered away at the technical difficulties which were continually being put up to prevent an understanding. Both sides knew that battle was needless, that the interests of France were not incompatible with the demands of the Roman Republic. Two letters illustrate the situation, the first to the Triumvirs from Lesseps, dated the 26th of May, 1849:

"Gentlemen, I have received with much satisfaction the letter which you did me the honour to address to me yesterday. The explanations which I have already given to the three commissioners of the Roman Constituent Assembly (the Triumvirs), and the communications which I have thought it incumbent upon me to make to the Assembly itself, meet, without exception, all the objections raised in your note; and whenever you see fit to complete the negotiations by sending your commissioners, invested with the necessary authority, it will be very easy, in my opinion, for us to come to a complete understanding and settle the basis of a definite agreement; which must, of course, be one such as will quite satisfy the two contracting parties. . . . There is only one point which could in any way make you feel anxious, and that is the idea that we are intent upon imposing on you by force the obligation to receive us as friends. Friendship and violence do not go together, so that it would be illogical for us to begin by cannonading you as a preliminary to getting you to look upon us as your natural protectors. Such a contradiction in terms does not enter into my intentions, nor into those of my Government, nor of our Army. This was the purport of what General Oudinot said yesterday in my presence to the Roman deputation which came to offer in your name a present of fifty thousand cigars and two hundred pounds of tobacco for our soldiers; and his remarks must have removed any doubt which may have lingered in your minds. . . . It would ill become Frenchmen, noted for their unlimited devotion to their country, to blame other nations for defending their territory against their real enemies, or to compel you to do the very contrary of what they would always do in their own case."

The second letter is from the Triumvirs: Armelli, Mazzini, and Saffi, addressed to M. de Lesseps on the 30th of the month, i.e. four days later. It reads in part:

"It is time, Sir, that this state of things ended. It is time that fraternity ceased to be an idle word with no practical results. It is time that our messengers, our troops, and our arms should be allowed to circulate without hindrance throughout our territory. It is time the Romans no longer had to treat with suspicion the men they have been accustomed to treat as friends. It is time that we should be free to defend ourselves, with all our resources, against the Austrians who are bombarding our city. It is time there should be no mistake anywhere as to the good and loyal intentions of France. It is time that Europe should no longer be able to say that she deprives us of our means of defence, in order presently to force upon us a protection which would preserve for us our territorial integrity without preserving for us what is dearer to us by far, our honour and liberty."

After this, Oudinot refused to co-operate with Lesseps in any way, a discourtesy at least understandable in terms of temperament, because by this time Ferdinand must have been exasperated to the point of hysteria, and might well have called him out. The General sat in his headquarters awaiting with confidence some fresh instructions from Paris which would bypass Lesseps and let the army get on with its war. Lesseps also went on his own way, and was relieved at not having to explain every new development of the negotiations to someone who was on principle opposed to them and desired them to fail. At last he was able to lay upon Oudinot's table a copy of the Convention finally agreed. On behalf of France he signed it then and there, without even asking the General's opinion. Then, having despatched a second copy to the Triumvirs and a third to Paris, he went back to Rome, no doubt congratulating himself upon a *fait accompli*. But no sooner had he arrived in the city than urgent communications were handed to him. One was from Oudinot, refusing to accept the Convention. Another was from the Triumvirs to Oudinot:

"We have this moment received with surprise and regret your despatch of May 31st. The difference of opinion between the General in command and the Minister Plenipotentiary of France was not an event for which we could be prepared; and as this difference of opinion arises with reference to a Convention the spirit of which is in entire harmony with the explicit aspirations which recently emanated from the French Assembly and with the well-grounded sympathies of your nation, it is a very deplorable occurrence, and one which may result in the gravest consequences, the responsibility for which does not rest with us."

Lesseps immediately wrote to the Triumvirs:

"Gentlemen, in reply to yours of this morning, containing General Oudinot's letter and your reply, I have the honour to inform you that I adhere to the arrangement signed yesterday, and that I am starting for Paris in order to get it ratified. The arrangement was concluded by virtue of the instructions which charged me to devote myself 'exclusively to the negotiations and relations which it might be desirable to establish with the Roman authorities and people'."

The last phrase, 'Roman authorities and people' evades the use of the words 'Roman Republic' in accordance with that part of his orders which required him not to give formal recognition to the Triumvirate. Still they were the only people with whom he could have negotiated. . . . That same day, as he was packing up, a telegram arrived, the first official communication to him personally since the mission began. It summarily recalled him to Paris. Unknown to Ferdinand, Oudinot also received his orders then. They were to repudiate the Convention and to attack the city. Such an act would constitute not only bad faith but also a broken truce, for there was a clause in the Convention whereby the armistice remained effective for fifteen days after official notice from either side that ratification had been refused.

In case even Oudinot should shrink from the dirty work ahead, General Vaillant appeared at headquarters, ready to take his place as C. in C. Ironically enough, Vaillant had originally been promised to Lesseps as *his* man should Oudinot prove obstinate! Three days later, the 3rd of June, the siege began. Desperate with the bitter anger of the betrayed, Rome held out until the last day of the month, exacting a high price in blood for the return of the Holy Father to his temporal authority. A fortnight later: "The Catholics saw the close of their cherished crusade: a solemn *Te Deum* was sung in St. Peter's celebrating the victory of France over the Roman Republic, and the unconditional restoration of pontifical authority." (*Cambridge History.*) It subsequently appeared that the Jesuits had helped to finance the invasion; a fact which, had Lesseps known of it, would have made him pause to wonder whether Paris had ever intended his mission to succeed.

By the wording of the telegram of recall he must have realized that something was wrong: "The Government of the Republic has put a stop to your mission. You will be good enough to start on your return journey to France as soon as you have received this despatch." Already worn out, he left Rome at three o'clock in the afternoon and reached Paris at five one morning. Agathe was not at home to welcome him. What could have happened to her? Fear touched him. He routed out a servant. Madame, he was told, had just left for Italy. Madame had received news of Monsieur's illness. . . . Illness? What nonsense! But how like Agathe to go off like that, at a moment's notice, because she thought he might have need of her. They must have passed each other somewhere along the Toulon road. He got wearily into bed. He was never ill: how could such a rumour have started? There must be malice somewhere. Oh, but that would be cleaned up when the major difficulties were dealt with; if there *were* any major difficulties. Misconceptions so easily arise between a special envoy and his Government, particularly when a change of Minister takes place. And Drouyn de Lhuys had been replaced by Odilon Barrot, who was also President of the Council. But that should not make any real difference. Ferdinand had heard Barrot tell the Assembly:

"The Government has decided to despatch a man who enjoys our full confidence, whom we have put to the test in very trying circumstances, and who has always served the cause of liberty and humanity. M. de Lesseps, to give you his name, has been sent. And we have specially instructed him to place himself in immediate communication with the Government and to keep us informed day by day of whatever may happen. We have further impressed upon him that he is to employ his utmost influence so that our intervention may secure genuine and real guarantees for the Roman States."

'Genuine and real guarantees', well, that was just what he had achieved. And he had meticulously kept the Foreign Office informed of every move in the game. There could be nothing to worry about. Everyone who mattered must be in possession of the facts and realize the magnitude of his accomplishment. Certainly he would be congratulated. Perhaps he would even get an official apology for the curtness of his recall in the moment of victory. Poor Lesseps! For nearly twenty years he had been abroad, and, largely because of his own integrity, was the last person to realize that, in the words of the *Cambridge History*: "Whatever chance of success such a mission might have had in Rome, it was condemned in France before it started."

Chapter 4. DEPTHS

Next day Lesseps went straight to the Foreign Office. The new Minister was busy and could not see him. Puzzled, in view of the urgency of his recall, Ferdinand sought out the deputy, Tocqueville, who said that he knew so little about the mission that he was not in a position to comment. Other Ministers could not even be found. Louis-Napoleon did receive him, but hardly mentioned Rome except to say that the Pope was being difficult. As Edgar-Bonnet says: " All the qualified representatives of the Executive were playing at Pontius Pilate." Lesseps was soon to be handed over to his judges, and meanwhile public opinion was being whipped up against him. Someone had already taken the trouble to spread a rumour that he was out of his mind, and had told Agathe as much in the presence of the children. So that was why she had suddenly gone to Rome.

News of the siege arrived, and Lesseps then knew the rôle which was being prepared for him. He was to be a scapegoat, bearing away in the sight of all the people the sins of Louis-Napoleon. He had arranged peace with honour. The Prince-President had chosen war with dishonour. A chasm opened before him. He went back to the flat at No. 9 Rue Richepanse and wrote to Agathe: " It will not be the first time that I have been alone against the world and have won through. Hitherto, attacks have served my own interests because they compelled the examination of my conduct. To-day it will be the same. I well know how to ride out a storm, and that is what one ought to do when one has a clear conscience." Then, by a later post: "I could not be better. I am never so calm as at the very centre of troubles. I am now attacked from every quarter, but one day it will be an honour to have done what I did. I shall tell you everything. And you, who have such heart and such integrity, will see that I have nothing, absolutely nothing, to apologize for about any single one of my actions."

Agathe was soon back in Paris. Together they braced them-

selves to withstand the attack for which the Government paper
National was preparing the public. They had not long to wait.
Barrot, who had told Lesseps: "You must save us. We count
on you," now fulminated in the Assembly that the agreement
with the Triumvirs had annoyed His Holiness and compromised
the honour of French arms. Aghast at the news of the battle
then taking place – a development quite unlooked for by the
vast majority of Deputies, the idea took easy root that somehow
de Lesseps must be to blame. No one could believe in the per-
fidity of the new Prince-President, nor that the commander in
the field had taken upon himself a grave political decision. So the
fault *must* be that of the envoy. Let him stand trial! But how,
since there was no charge to be answered? For the first and last
time in the history of France a Council of State was convened
to act as a kind of Star Chamber Court; but even then there
was so little to go on that no indictment emerged. Technically
the proceedings were only an examination of Ferdinand's
conduct.

Meanwhile the Press demanded: "Is he guilty of abominable
disloyalty or is he a sick man to be cured?" On the 30th of
June, with Rome about to fall, Lesseps for four hours was
publicly examined in the hope that something might be discovered to provide the basis of a charge and make the public
believe he had been guilty of the policy for which the Government, under the Prince-President, was entirely responsible. To
every insinuation Lesseps replied with candour and conviction,
permitting himself no excursions nor seeking to embarrass the
Government in any way; though he must have realized that the
consequences of its aggression would recoil upon France herself, as in fact happened:

"Turned away from its original orientation, which was that of
Lesseps, French policy in Italy achieved neither its immediate
objective nor its ultimate one. It experienced a check, a total check.
The expedition of 1849 was the first fruit of the equivocation which
vitiated the whole foreign policy of the Second Empire. A prey to
vague dreams, the future Napoleon III already began to wish to
reconcile the opposites. Champion of the right of peoples to settle
their own affairs, he destroyed the Roman Republic in order to
establish by force an absolute sovereignty (the Pope's), the principle of which he had never ceased to oppose and yet which could
now only survive by his support. A few years later he would begin

by force of arms that unification of Italy which brought about the
end of the Temporal Power, and meantime could only be sustained
by the presence of his troops. By way of gratitude he gained from
either side nothing but bitterness and even contempt." (Edgar-
Bonnet.)

Failing to gain any better ground, the attack concentrated
upon an attempt to show that Lesseps had exceeded, even dis-
regarded, his instructions. When he proved that he had been
meticulously loyal to them, the court submitted what purported
to be an original document by which he was required "to do
everything in his power to hasten the end of a régime (the
Roman Republic) destined to perish in any case through pressure
of events". Lesseps proved that the phrase had been inserted
later, that it was not in the copy he had been given when he
left for Rome; where at that time General Oudinot was pro-
claiming to the Italians:

"Welcome us as brothers. We shall justify the title. We shall respect
your persons and your goods. We shall co-operate with the existing authorities so that our occupation will not cause you the least
inconvenience. We shall safeguard the military honour of your
troops, associating them with our own for the maintenance of order
and liberty. Romans, my personal devotion is yours if you heed
my voice. If you have confidence in my words, I shall consecrate
myself without reserve to the interests of your beautiful country."

After so much labour, at the risk of assassination and death
by gunshot, the Convention which Lesseps had achieved, against
all expectation and the opposition of General Oudinot, read in
part as follows:

1. The people of the Roman States are assured of the support
of France. They consider the French as an allied army come to
assist in the defence of their territory.
2. In accord with the Roman Government and without interfering in any way with the administration of the country, the
French army will occupy convenient cantonments outside the city,
as much for the defence of the country as for the health of the
troops.
3. The French Republic guarantees the territories occupied by
her troops against all foreign invasion.
4. It is agreed that the present arrangement has to be submitted to the French Republic for ratification.
5. In any case the terms of the present agreement shall not

cease to be effective until fifteen days after an official decision against ratification has been received.

*   *   *

With only one dissentient voice, the Council declared: "for reasons of State" that the conduct of Ferdinand de Lesseps had been blameworthy, but there was still no definite charge and so there could be no specific condemnation. Meanwhile the whole trumped-up trial had failed in its primary purpose, to exculpate the Government from the political consequences of its own bad faith. All shades of opinion were united by the socialists on the basis that the Constitution had been betrayed. The Government's only honest defence would have been the plea that its hand had been forced by the Church of Rome; but that would have admitted to a clerical domination which the country would not have accepted. To admit such a thing would be political suicide. Instead, the Government had to fall back upon the old prescription: force.

"So it is no longer a question of Rome, the Pope, or Lesseps. It is the spectre of bloody insurrection, a new Revolution, which emerges. . . . The rebellion, prepared and awaited, broke out on the 13th of June; but the hesitations of the leaders, the weakness of their troops and the indifference of the people of Paris, permitted the Government of Louis-Napoleon to suppress it without difficulty. The spectre vanished quicker than one would have thought." (Edgar-Bonnet.)

If that ghost had indeed vanished, another was soon to take its place. France still remained more afraid of anarchy than of dictatorship. The reaction against the socialists therefore provided an excuse for disciplinary measures of great severity . . .

"arrests in Paris and in the provinces, prosecutions and a state of siege. Banquets were forbidden, mutual benefit societies dissolved and Republican school-teachers suspended or arbitrarily dismissed. These excessive measures of repression were as ill-judged as the abortive rising of June 13th; besides, they overshot the mark. It became evident that this so-called vindication of order was to culminate in the subjection of the country to the Catholic party." (*Cambridge History.*)

In token of which General Oudinot chose July the Fourteenth

to proclaim the Pope's restoration to his temporal throne; though Pius IX did not occupy that perilous seat until nine months later.

All this and more would have been clear to Lesseps as he considered what ought to be his attitude after his reprimand by the Council of State. He would, for instance, have been aware that Louis-Napoleon had no intention of being dominated by the Pope; so that in future a foreign officer would be in the impossible position of having to please not only the exoteric policy of the Government of the day, but also the esoteric master-policy of the Prince-President, which was likely to be quite different. Lesseps did not wait to find out whether he would be reemployed, but forthwith resigned from the service, at one stroke breaking not only his own career and his financial security, but also the long tradition of his family which had continued their service to the country through a series of past political upheavals in comparison with which the Rome affair was relatively trivial. It must have been a hard decision to reach, but it is difficult to see that with honour he could have come to any other. At forty-three he would have to make a new life for himself, no easy matter though he was young for his age – hardly at all grey, and extremely active. His athletic body had thickened rather than fattened into that of the typical 'pyknik' with 'short legs, thick neck, and relatively large barrel-shaped trunk'. The 'cyclothyme' temperament associated with the type is, as the name suggests, given to alternating moods, in which also Ferdinand was evidently typical rather than exceptional. Though focused by intellect and controlled by will, his tremendous driving-power derived from deep emotion, strong feelings, which, often contrary to common sense, demanded that what ought to be must be. If that trait gave him the strength to attempt the impossible, it was also the probable cause for the suspicion of his sanity at Rome. Already his over-confidence sometimes tended to deceive himself and others. Exaggerated by old age, past achievements and present adulation, it would prove a primary cause of the failure at Panama.

At this time Ferdinand was in a downward cycle. His mood was black. Shocked by the senseless, useless bloodshed at Rome, he must have lost faith in the works of man, and, had he not been blessed with a devoted family, might well have become a bitter cynic. That he did not do so was due largely to his mother-in-law, Madame Delamalle, with the result that, 'active, lovable and gay, exceptional husband and father, so did Ferdinand appear at home during these years which ended the springtime of his life'. In the autumn of 1850 Ferdinand left Paris to take Agathe and Charles, the eldest boy, to Belgium, leaving the other two children behind. Near Liège they stayed at the château of Kinkenpois, belonging to his godfather, who was old enough to have been a Prefect under the First Empire. Ferdinand's mother, Madame Mathieu de Lesseps, whose health at last was failing, was also staying there. The place seems to have bored Agathe, who was accustomed to more social life. " Here," she wrote to her mother, " is the sort of comfort you knew with our grandparents, but no luxury. The interior of the house goes back a century and everything is excessively tidy but out of date. In general it is country life in all its tranquillity with people who like to be quiet. My mother-in-law is better but she does not get much sleep. She is glad to see us."

On leaving Kinkenpois they went all the way to Berne to see what manner of post Ferdinand had missed for the sake of Rome. Agathe was enchanted by the beauty of the setting, and perhaps in her secret heart wished that she were there in the familiar rôle of the distinguished Consul's wife. She had no such love of country life as Ferdinand's, though she was too loyal ever to say so, and did all she could to share his enthusiasms. Even when they had settled down she did not get up at dawn, as he did, ' to plunge into the forest after roe-deer '; but she used to meet him for lunch in some clearing. Apart from shooting, at which he excelled, Ferdinand's passion was still horses, and soon, through the generosity of Madame Delamalle, he would be able to set up a stud. He would also acquire an interesting, full-time occupation. It began to seem as though the loss of his career might yet be the passport to a domestic happiness which otherwise could hardly have been his.

The reason for this change of fortune was that in 1851 Madame Delamalle's mother died, leaving considerable agricultural property in the Berry, that province of central France which centres on Bourges. She appointed Ferdinand her agent, and asked him to find a house for her on the estate. She wanted something out of the ordinary, and he chose an old hunting-lodge which had belonged to Charles VII and by him had been given to his mistress Agnes Sorel, whose claim on history is that she induced him to support Jeanne d'Arc against the English. Agnes is often called *la Dame de Beauté*, but though she was far from ugly, the happy phrase – unfortunately for romance, refers to another property given to her by the King, *Beauté sur Marne*, near Vincennes.

When Ferdinand first saw the hunting-lodge it was in bad repair, but that was a matter of small importance since he intended to modernize and rebuild. Probably he was never happier in his life than when doing so, over the next two years. On the 28th of December, 1852, he could write to Madame Delamalle:

"Dear Mother-in-law, the appearance of the farm, the farmhouse and the château could not be more satisfying. One could not have expected to succeed better with the farm-house. The projecting roof-line makes an excellent effect, and gives the place the look of a pretty little chalet. Agathe is enchanted with it, viewed either from the road or from the yard. Your dwelling is equally excellent. The junction of the old wing with the new has been well done. The pointed tower is well placed. In fact everything seems to have gone splendidly."

There was not a cloud in the blue domestic sky as they celebrated Christmas in Paris before moving into the completed part of the new place— *la Chenaie*, the oak-grove. Because his forebodings about politics had been justified by events, Ferdinand must have found it easy to banish regrets for his lost career. France had become a dictatorship of fear, or an absolute monarchy disguised as a democracy. Every device of tyranny was represented, the informer, the 'approved candidate', the persecution of the Press, secret trial without witnesses or counsel. Savage sentences were passed merely on suspicion. The colour red was banned, and even the cry '*Vive la République!*' was heard no more, by order. The counter-revolution had come full circle when, in that December, such measures gave to the nephew of the first Napoleon a vote of seven and a half millions, against a mere six hundred and forty thousand – to allow him to draw up a new Constitution. Secure in his seat of power, he aspired to be an Emperor in the style of his uncle, and set about unhooding the eagles which had been roosting since Waterloo. But even he

still had to move cautiously. It was not until near the end of
1852 that the man who had lately been content to be called
'Citizen' assumed the purple of Imperial Majesty. On the evening of the second of December: "In a long procession of two
hundred carriages flanked by torch-bearers, the members of the
Senate proceeded in a body to Saint-Cloud, there to hail the
Emperor in due form. The adherents of the older parties had
been silenced; proscription and exile had crushed the 'anar-
chists." (*Cambridge History*.)

Certainly this was not a régime which any Lesseps could
have served with a clear conscience. Ferdinand was well out of
it – except in the social sense which must have been Agathe's
principal interest that Christmas. For Eugénie de Montijo was
to marry the Emperor. Nor was this an arranged marriage but
a love affair of a sort, the origin of which seems to have been
Eugénie's incomparable seat on a horse. Certainly the romance
was pursued largely while out riding, perhaps the only way in
which the couple could secure any real privacy. Even so the
Emperor's intentions remained obscure for so long that Eugénie
had to protest that gossip was making a fool of her. Either he
must propose, or she must go away. He proposed. It is true that
he had hankered after a princess, but the idea had not met with
favour among the royal families of Europe, and when Eugénie
came into his life he was probably grateful to them. She was
twenty-six, in the pride of an extraordinary beauty garnished
by her extraordinary mother. He was forty-four, apparently
secure upon a throne the civil list for which he had just fixed
at 25,000,000 francs a year. And he had an undeniable charm.
Eugénie seems to have had some conscience about her part in
the financial business. She wrote to Ferdinand on the day before
her fiancé announced to the Assembly his intention of marrying
her:

"To Monsieur Ferdinand de Lesseps,
  Rue Richepanse No. 9. Paris.

                                    22nd of January, 1853.
There has never been any question about my demanding from
the Senate a dowry of five millions, nor of less neither; and I give
you my word that I would never do so. I value public opinion too
highly, and know too well the consequences of increased taxation.
I do not wish to take one sou from France, and my only ambition
is to serve as a mediator between the throne and those who suffer.

I give thanks to God for having chosen me for such a great task, while having faith in Him that I may be able to discharge it. Please tell me whenever a hint may be useful, not to me but to France. I am always grateful for the opinions of devoted friends.

Your friend and cousin,

EUGÉNIE.

I am dying to know what effect the speech produced."

The marriage took place on the 30th of January with imperial splendours in the cathedral of Notre-Dame. In spite of the mild weather the building must have been chilly, and it may have been for that reason Eugénie chose velvet – white and uncut, for her wedding-dress, which the *Illustrated London News* described simply as 'perfection', adding: "she bore with great dignity her diadem of diamonds and sapphires, wreathed with orange-blossom". So Agathe found herself related to a reigning Sovereign, with the entrée to a court which promised to be gay. Eugénie for pleasure and Louis-Napoleon for policy both intended to provide France, if not with a revived Versailles, at least with a 'brilliant' social centre. Ferdinand and Agathe would have attended the wedding had not Madame Mathieu de Lesseps died three days before it took place, the first of a series of sorrows. During the Easter term the eldest boy brought back scarlet fever from school – the same which his father had attended and which had now reverted to its original name, *Lycée Napoléon*.

Agathe's devoted nursing saved Charles, but she caught the infection and died of it within a few days. Three weeks later the second little Ferdinand followed her. The other boy, Victor, seemed to be dying, but recovered. So between the first of June and the first of August a disease which in modern times is considered of only minor importance, struck a well-found family with the virulence of cholera. The disease must have been of the fulminating type, now mercifully rare, in which: "the patient is frequently overwhelmed by the infection and may succumb within forty-eight hours from cardiac or vascular collapse."[1] The cause, then quite unsuspected, is a particular strain of haemolytic streptococcus. Incubation may be as little as twenty-four hours and not more than a week. Excepting immunization, there is still no effective treatment, and so poor Agathe did not have a

[1] Albrecht, *Modern Management in Clinical Medicine*.

chance a century ago. The 'pearl among women' who for fifteen
years had filled her husband's heart to the exclusion of all else
– no easy feat – was taken from him just when it seemed certain
that they would be allowed peacefully to grow old together.
Ferdinand, drugged with grief, must have regretted the resistance to infection which he had built up in Egypt. Nothing that
anyone could do or say had power to lighten his darkness, least
of all the flood of polite condolence which flowed over him
because of the 'wonderful spirit and angelic goodness of
Madame de Lesseps'. Among the mass of letters was one from
the Emperor's nephew, the Jérôme who would become known
as Plon-Plon and be the Patron of the Suez Canal:

> "Palais Royal. 15th July, 1853.
> I cannot describe to you how much the news of your frightful
> loss has afflicted me! I understand your sorrow and share it.
> Madame de Lesseps had such qualities as all those who knew her so
> much appreciated. I was with the Empress yesterday when she
> heard the terrible news. She was most dreadfully shaken, and, with
> tears in her eyes, charged me to convey to you how much the death
> of Madame de Lesseps grieves her. More than ever, my dear
> Monsieur de Lesseps, rely upon my affectionate regards. I embrace
> the poor children!
>
> NAPOLÉON BONAPARTE."

*   *   *

Agathe and little Ferdinand were buried in the Paris cemetery
called, after the confessor of Louis XIV, *Père Lachaise*. Unable
to bear the loneliness of the familiar flat, Ferdinand went down
to La Chenaie and left Madame Delamalle to look after the
children who were left, Charles and Victor. She wrote to him
on the 10th of August:

> "Poor, poor, dear son, how I grudge the delay in coming to
> you, to feel with you all the emotions of your poor heart. I always
> divine them, and understand them. Yesterday I was sitting in
> front of her portrait and saw again that dear child through all the
> stages of her life. I loved her very much, and now I think I ought
> to love her more. All the emptiness which she has left in my heart
> shall be filled with what she loved above everything else in the
> world, you and my two little grandchildren. Our Victorinet took
> a great step forward to-day. He is eating better and his walk is
> steadier. If this poor little thing had his charming playmate I am
> sure his cheerfulness would be entirely restored. But who could
> ever replace that child's joy of living, or the goodness of his mother,

our Agathe? Her loss seems to me every day more painful. My thoughts are ever with you. Dear son-in-law, I weep."

Victorinet (Victor) was now his father's second son, and he again fell ill. The sky remained unlighted even by a star when, ten days later, young Charles dreamed while at school that he had seen both his mother and brother and had brought them back from the grave. To this Ferdinand replied:

"My very dear boy, yesterday's letter gave me great pleasure. I miss your company. There was something true about your dream, though I have often been to Père Lachaise and have never brought anyone back. Death does not give up his victims, but one day he will reunite you with those who now seem lost. Waiting for that one needs resignation, courage, confidence in God. I am still able to be happy through you, your conduct, your success. Good-bye, *mon chéri*, I embrace you tenderly,

                                                    F. DE LESSEPS."

He tried to fill the void by becoming preoccupied with practical detail. The rest of the big house was made habitable. The children came to stay. But Madame Delamalle did not care for country life, and with the boys at school in Paris, Ferdinand was much alone: " I pass my days among cattle, pigs and sheep. These last have developed little family sense. Every day I marvel how the farm-girls manage to unite the young with their mothers, which they have no instinct to recognize for them-selves."

That must have been written in the following spring. Even so, outdoor pursuits were not enough to stop him thinking about the past, and it was in these circumstances that he began again to study the question of the canal. They proved almost as potent as those under which inspiration had first come to him in the lazaret at Alexandria. But whereas the canal had then been a dream which one day other men would bring into fulfilment, now for the first time he thought of it as something within reach of his own hand. Into his research went two great mental drives, his love for Agathe and his devotion to the family tradition. The Suez Canal became a surrogate for both of them, at once his love, his ambition, and his devotion to the Lesseps ideal of service to humanity.

                          *   *   *

The historical data upon which he began to work is of notable antiquity. Almost two millenia before Christ, Sesosteris I, Pharaoh, Lord of the Two Lands, connected the Nile with the Red Sea, though the first record implying such a waterway dates from five hundred years later, in the reign of Queen Hatshepsut, 'the first great woman in history of whom we are informed'. This, though an immense undertaking, was not a direct ancestor of the proposed *Canal des Deux Mers* in that, instead of being cut through the isthmus, it ran from the Nile in the neighbourhood of modern Cairo. But the effect was the same. A ship with cargo could travel from one sea to another, making new trades possible, existing ones easier and cheaper. In Hatshepsut's reign, for instance, the myrrh for temple lamps had to pass from hand to hand across the deserts between Punt (Eritrea) and Egypt, a method which could not handle living trees; but the Queen had set her heart upon a line of myrrh-trees along the terrace of her new temple to Amon-Ra, and she had them brought by water:

"The route was perhaps down the Nile and through a canal leading from the eastern Delta through the Wadi Tumilat, and connecting the Nile with the Red Sea. This canal was attributed by the Greeks to Sesosteris and hence may have existed in the Middle Kingdom. In any case the same vessels are shown in the queen's reliefs, both upon the Nile and upon the Red Sea; no shift of cargo is mentioned, and all this suggests the use of such a canal. They arrived at Punt in safety; the Egyptian commander pitched his tent on the shore where he was received with friendliness by Perehu, the chief of Punt, followed by his absurdly corpulent wife and three children. It was so long since any Egyptians had been seen in Punt that the Egyptians represented the Puntites as crying out, 'Why have ye come hither unto this land, which the people (of Egypt) know not? Did ye descend upon the roads of heaven, or did ye sail upon the waters, upon the sea of God's-Land?' The Puntite chief having been won over by gifts, a stirring traffic is soon in progress, the gang-planks are run out, and the loading goes rapidly forward, until the vessels are laden 'very heavily with the marvels of the country of Punt; all goodly fragrant woods of God's-Land, heaps of myrrh resin, of fresh myrrh-trees, with ebony and pure ivory, with green gold of Emu, with cinnamon-wood, with incense, eye-cosmetic, with baboons, monkeys, dogs, with skins of the southern panther, with natives and their children. Never was the like of this brought for any king who has been since the beginning.' After a fair voyage, without mishap, and with no transfer of cargo as far as our sources inform us, the fleet finally moored again at the docks of Thebes."

The foregoing description from Breasted's *History of Egypt* illustrates not only the practability of the route but also its commercial possibilities. For the quantity of material brought back by Hatshepsut's five ships was enormous in comparison with what could have been conveyed overland, including – besides the living trees – no less than 3,300 'small cattle' i.e. sheep and goats, the movement of which would have been quite impossible overland. The canal is shown in a wall-painting of Seti I, about 1380 B.C., but in spite of the obvious advantages it fell into decay, perhaps because of the excessive amount of work required on upkeep; for such a ditch is easily filled in during severe sandstorms, as much as by flooding. It was not heard of again until about 600 B.C. when Necho, that King of Egypt whom Nebuchadnezzar chased out of Palestine, re-excavated most of it, at a cost, according to Heroditus, of a hundred thousand lives. When he occupied Egypt in 521 B.C., Darius the Persian worked on the project, which was still unfinished in the time of Xerxes, some fifty years later. It was probably finished by the Emperor Trajan in the first century A.D.

The reason why Darius failed to finish the job himself is given by Diodorus: "From Pelusium to the Arabian Sea a canal was made. Necho, son of Psammitichus, first began the work; after him Darius the Persian carried it on, but left it unfinished, being told that if he cut through the isthmus, Egypt would be laid under water, as the Red Sea was higher than Egypt." Probably it was not so much inundation that was feared as that the canal, bringing sea-water, would make the Nile undrinkable, a matter of almost equal gravity for a country which had hardly any other source of fresh water. Evidently this had not happened in the past, but the past was forgotten, nor did disaster occur when Trajan succeeded; yet an idea persisted, well into the age of Lesseps, that the enterprise would come to grief because of a difference between the levels of the two seas.

Even Roman engineering skill was not able to maintain the waterway, and, like its forerunners, it merged into the sands. Another five hundred years had to pass before a new attempt was made, after the Arab Conquest. It is said that in A.D. 788 Harun Al-Raschid, Caliph of Baghdad, conceived the idea of an alternative route directly between the seas. If such be the case, then although no practical work was undertaken, it is to

the Commander of the Faithful in the epoch of the Thousand
and One Nights that the origin of the modern Suez Canal should
be credited. Meanwhile the indirect route remained in use for
a century or so, and was then deliberately destroyed in order
to starve the inhabitants of Medina, who have always been
dependent upon waterborne supplies. The advantages of the
canal, as recognized by so many generations, remained a spur
to further endeavour and at the end of the fifteenth century a
plan was put forward by the Republic of Venice whose suprem-
acy was threatened by the discovery of the Cape route to the
East. Even Venice could not afford to put so great a work in
hand and so it remained on paper. Then in *Tamburlaine* (1587)
Christopher Marlowe echoed the poetic idea which was to be
taken up by the Saint-Simonians:

> "Whereas the Terrene and the Red Sea meet
> Being distant less than a full hundred leagues,
> I mean to cut a channel to them both
> That men might quickly sail to India."

But no one else aspired to it until, at the instigation of the
philosopher Leibniz, Louis XIV seriously considered the conquest of Egypt for the purpose of making the canal; and doubtless Napoleon I would have made the attempt had he been able
to keep his footing in the country.

The next practical step was taken by Prosper Enfantin in
1847 when he formed a Survey Committee, composed of
engineers of international reputation, most of whom had no
connection with Saint-Simonism, though they held their meetings at Enfantin's house in Paris. At this time he and his
'apostles' had some influence with Louis-Philippe and consequently the fall of that monarch dealt a hard blow to the faithful, who were never again of significance as an organized body.
But thanks to the engineers, France and Egypt both gave their
blessing to the work and a Company was duly registered, with a
capital of 150,000 francs, so constituting a definite beginning for
the modern enterprise; which Lesseps was able to take over
only because the Survey Company did not, as it should have
done, develop into a Construction Company. Clouds of vapour,
without glory, still trailed behind the Saint-Simonians. Linant
de Bellefonds, Egypt's foremost engineer, broke with them,

refunding five thousand francs which they had paid him. He turned his considerable energies away from the canal to the barrage which Mohammed-Ali urgently needed in order to prevent the repetition of a Nile flood which had recently caused great damage in the Delta. Robert Stephenson, son of the great George, and the only Englishman on the Survey Committee, went back to London and pronounced against the canal. His opinion had tremendous weight, partly because it was what Westminster wanted to believe, and partly because British industry could look forward to little business in the building of a canal but a great deal of business in the construction of the Cairo-Suez railway. Stephenson eventually completed the Alexandria-Cairo run at a cost of well over a million pounds (£11,000 per mile). He personally received £55,000 – no small inducement in favour of rail against water!

Other Englishmen had already given the matter of communication through, or over, the isthmus their considerable attention; so that though the basis of all the early plans was the survey of Linant de Bellefonds, by her own initiative England was as well informed as France by the time that Lesseps entered the field. A dramatic beginning was made during the French Revolution when the British Consul, George Baldwin, climbed the Great Pyramid and poured out three libations upon the top of it. They consisted of water from the Thames, the Ganges and the Nile, thereby invoking the union of the three rivers. In 1837 a curious pamphlet had appeared in London. Largely in defence of Mohammed-Ali, it was by 'T. Waghorn, General Agent for Steam Intercourse *via* the Red Sea, between England, India, Ceylon, China, etc.' It was dedicated to Parliament. 'Steam Intercourse' was a label for the Overland Route for which Waghorn had laboured twenty years. Originally he had been a Lieutenant R.N. employed by John Company in Calcutta. Passionately convinced of the superiority of the Overland Route, he spent years shuttling between London and Bombay with copies of letters sent round the Cape, until: "On October 1st, 1845, the mail left Bombay, reached Suez on the 19th, Alexandria on the 20th, was taken *via* Trieste, Bavaria, the Rhine and Belgium, and was delivered at the London Post Office, on the morning of the 31st." Passengers had a painful if picturesque transit from Suez to Cairo, whence they took train to Alexandria.

They jolted along the desert tracks in six-seater wagonettes which took thirty hours at best, an average of four miles an hour, under trying conditions aggravated by lack of palatable water. Even coal for the ships in the Red Sea followed the same route, on camel-back, a titanic undertaking in any terms, whether of cost, labour or sheer hardship to man and beast.

Even so the Overland Route handled upwards of ten thousand passengers every year; but Waghorn in his lifetime got little credit for the self-sacrifice he had displayed. He died in harness, 'deceived, exhausted, ruined' (Edgar-Bonnet). Years later Lesseps unveiled a monument to him and said: "He opened the route. We followed . . . When English seamen pass this memorial erected by the French, they will remember the close alliance which ought always to exist between two nations put at the head of the world's civilization, not to ravage, but to enlighten and pacify it."

There was no such alliance in 1853. England and France stood over Egypt like dogs over a bone, and in spite of French ascendancy within the country, the strategic dominance of England remained as unquestionable as it had been when in 1840 Lord Palmerston wrote to his Ambassador:

"Tell M. Thiers (French Ambassador in Cairo) that if France throws down the gauntlet we shall not refuse to pick it up; and that if she begins a war, she will certainly lose her ships, colonies and commerce before she sees the end of it; that her army in Algeria will cease to give her anxiety, and that Mehemet Ali will just be chucked into the Nile. It would certainly be a good thing if he could be got rid of altogether, yet that is improbable for he will give in long before matters come to such a point. We do not want to oust him from Egypt if he is content to spend the rest of his days there as a faithful servant."

Palmerston's confidence in his judgment that Mohammed-Ali's power would crumble at the test, was justified in the following year when the old tyrant, having had to evacuate Syria in face of Anglo-Turkish combined operations, made his submission to the Sultan whom he had defied. The following letter to the Grand Vizier, Mohammed-Ali's particular and personal enemy, was written in January:

"When Your Highness shall, please God, have taken note of

my prompt submission, you will lay it at the feet of my august and powerful Sovereign, of whom I am so proud to be the faithful servant; and you will employ your good offices in order to cause a man advanced in age and faithful, who has grown old in service, to experience without ceasing the effects of his master's clemency."

"On receipt of this, Palmerston obtained the consent of the Powers to a joint request, asking the Porte to bestow the inheritance of Egypt on the Pasha. This memorandum of January 30th was followed by the firmans (decrees by the Sultan) of February 13th and June 1st, 1841; and Mohammed-Ali was left in peaceful possession of the province which he had won by the massacre of the Mamelukes thirty years previously." This origin of the Egyptian dynasty with which Lesseps would have to deal is of continuing significance. In 1850, at the age of eighty, Mohammed-Ali died. Though he had more than eighty-four children only four survived him, and none of these was as old as his grandson Abbas, who accordingly inherited. Abbas Pasha, Viceroy of·Egypt, was an ascetic reactionary who did all he could to undo the modernization of the country which his grandfather had so enthusiastically begun. He even shut the hospitals and dismissed the teachers from the new schools – though some of them existed only on paper and others had no pupils because of the mistrust of the people in general. If all that a boy can look forward to is a slave's life, tied in fact, if not in name, to the land, the tax-gatherer and the corvée of forced labour, education has little point. And girls were not supposed to go beyond their homes until they married, or otherwise transferred to a similarly restricted environment. Abbas is credited with defining his own motive in these terms: "My grandfather thought himself an autocrat. He was one to his subjects and to his children; but to the Consuls of Europe he was no more than a shoe. If I too must submit to someone, let me be the servant of the Caliph, and not of the Christian whom I hate." The best of his reputation was that of 'a Turkish gentleman of the old school'. He was a recluse, rarely leaving his guarded apartments, and as such attracted rumour; but it is likely that the stories of his cruel depravity, such as sewing up women in sacks full of rats, were, if not entirely imaginary, then grossly exaggerated. The large European community in Egypt, which had hitherto enjoyed great privilege and influence, did not take kindly to being shut out of the court, even when it had lost the glitter which Mohammed-Ali had bestowed upon it.

In particular Abbas blamed France for the misfortunes of Egypt. France had produced Napoleon, and if the same country had also set up Mohammed-Ali, it was only to make him a puppet and then force him to break with tradition, at the risk of bankrupting his kingdom in order to modernize it. Abbas had no use whatever for modernization, and he was glad enough to turn away from France towards England because the latter was trying to preserve the *status quo* in the Near East. None of this daunted Lesseps. As early as July 1852, before Agathe died, he had drawn up a long memorandum on the subject of the canal, and had it translated into Arabic for transmission to the Viceroy through an old friend; who wrote back to say that it would be a waste of time to pass it on. Lesseps then tried at Constantinople, but the Sultan ruled that it was none of his business, being, under the Palmerston plan, a matter entirely under the control of the Viceroy.

So these efforts failed as completely as had Linant's bid for the support of Lord Auckland, Governor-General of India. It seemed as though the canal must still remain a dream, and one likely to outlast the lifetime of Ferdinand de Lesseps. If he still kept up his interest in the project, it must have been because of a psychological need; for there was nothing practical that he could do about it any more. As though some mountain-moving engine were harnessed to a plough, he found satisfaction in land and buildings, crops and stock.

Chapter 5. HEIGHTS

To Monsieur S. W. Ruyssenãers,   La Chenaie,
    Consul-General of the Low Countries   15th September, 1854.
      in Egypt.

" . . . I was busy among masons and carpenters, putting an extra
storey on Agnes Sorel's old manor-house, when the postman
appeared in the courtyard with the Paris mail. The workmen passed
my letters and papers from hand to hand. Imagine my astonishment when I read of the death of Abbas-Pasha and the accession
to power of that friend of our youth, the intelligent and warm-
hearted Mohammed-Säid! I hurried down, and at once wrote to
the new Viceroy to congratulate him. I reminded him that I now
have leisure from politics, and that, if he will let me know when
he returns from Constantinople, where he will have to go for his
investiture, I would use it to pay my respects to him. He answered
without delay, and appointed the beginning of November for our
meeting in Alexandria. I want you to be one of the first to know
that I shall punctually be there. What good fortune to find ourselves together again on our old ground in Egypt! Before I arrive,
not a word to anyone about the project of cutting the Isthmus."

So two slaves with a grudge, who had dared to murder
Abbas in his safely secluded apartments, gave the cue for a
land-agent, a widower with a broken career behind him and no
future but in terms of the farmyard, to step on that stage where
statesmen play always the same old tragedy *Balance of Power*.
It was just because the canal would upset the precarious balance,
of which Turkey was the beam, that Lesseps from the beginning
seemed to be taking a villain's part; and not only to most of the
audience, but also to many of the actors. Of this he was ignorant,
and, had he known, it would have made no difference to his
conduct. After such a total eclipse all that mattered was that
the sun was again shining. And had he any doubts about the
omens, they would have been dispelled by his reception at
Alexandria. From the moment he was met by one of the Viceregal carriages it was clear that he was the favourite of the hour.
A palace, lately the residence of a princess, who had laid there

an heir for Säid, was placed at his disposal. The huge rooms were
heavy with silks, ebony, marble, gold. The wash-basin and ewer
were of solid silver. In addition to a corps of household servants
there was a squad of coffee-makers and a *chibouki-bashi*, 'escorted
by four acolytes with their insignia, consisting of a dozen long
pipes with big amber bowls encrusted with diamonds'.

The next day the Viceroy received his old friend at the Gab-
bari Palace, and, with his usual tact, Ferdinand took care to
make his appearance and manner as acceptable as possible. For
though in Paris they had been friends on equal terms, the last
time this now almost absolute monarch had seen Ferdinand in
Egypt was during those macaroni days, of which a proud Prince
might not wish to be reminded. So Lesseps put on his old uniform – knee-breeches, gold-laced claw-hammer coat, cocked hat;
with epaulettes, decorations and a *grand cordon* to show the
most formal deference to this enormous man who held his dream
of twenty years in one fat hand. For Säid was now huge, and
he would reach twenty stone:

"One of those hearty colossi, good livers, big jokers, great eaters,
and magnificent drinkers. His hand was of a size to box the ears
of elephants; his face wide, of high colour, and with a full beard,
showed geniality, sincerity, courage, and cynicism. . . . He jovially
decapitated misbehaving sheiks and made a jolly bonfire of eighty
million piastres of village tax arrears. He entertained visiting
Sovereigns with funny French stories, and made his pashas, with
lighted candles in their hands, wade with him through loose gunpowder to test their nerves. . . . He covered his parade-ground
with iron plates to keep the dust off his Paris clothes. Life with Säid
was never dull. 'Give him two hundred!' he would shout, without
explaining whether he meant *kurbash*, the whip, or *baksheesh*,
cash. He was popular as a gross joke, and some of his reforms, such
as the abolition of slavery (1856), of corporal punishment (1863),
and of conscription, were much appreciated jests."[1]

He was a man after Ferdinand's own heart, and though in
the Frenchman there was nothing of vulgarity, he was full of
gusto and could go, with a real understanding of the oriental
viewpoint, a long way towards sharing the Prince's enthusiasms.
So from the beginning of their renewed friendship the two men
understood one another in a way which Säid could hardly match

[1] D. A. Cameron, *Egypt in the Nineteenth Century*, London 1898.

with any other European. It has been suggested that greedy Lesseps was sly and calculating with his magnificent patron; but craft was not in his nature, nor in his tradition, nor in his record. Also it would have defeated its own object, and had he tried it, Lesseps would have failed; for the Viceroy was surrounded by masters of expediency and double-dealing. Also Säid knew Ferdinand as well as Ferdinand knew Säid.

Eager to play with his new toys and particularly fond of soldiers, the new Viceroy went on manœuvres before going to Cairo for the formal inauguration of his reign; and he invited Lesseps to accompany him on a ten-day excursion into the Western Desert. So instead of having to seek audience of a Prince fumbling with the reins of power, Ferdinand would be able to lead up to the matter of the canal under far more favourable circumstances. By the 15th of November he felt that the royal iron was hot enough to strike:

" At five o'clock in the morning I was outside my tent. I was wearing a red dressing-gown, and must have looked like a sheik of Mecca as I washed up to the elbow. Anyone might have taken me for a true believer. In the time of the Inquisition I would have been burned alive; for you know that among the crimes which called for torture and the *auto-da-fé* in the first rank was washing the arms up to the elbows.

" The camp was beginning to stir and an increased clarity announced the coming of the sun. I put on some clothes warmer than my dressing-gown and went up to my observation post. A few rays of light began to define the horizon. To my right the east was already bright, to my left the west remained sombre and dull. Suddenly from that side I saw a rainbow of the most brilliant colours with its two ends plunged from west to east. I admit that I felt my heart beat and had to check my imagination, which would have interpreted as the success of my project to-day, the practical union of Occident and Orient, that sign of which Scripture speaks: ' And God said, this is the token of the covenant which I make with you and every living creature that is with you, for perpetual generations. I do set my bow in the cloud, and it shall be for a token of a covenant between me and the earth.' The Viceroy helped me to emerge from my preoccupation. He was coming towards me. We wished each other good-day with a firm handclasp *à la Française*. He told me that he intended to make that morning a part of the expedition we have been talking about the night before, so as to see from the high ground all the details of the camp. We mounted our horses, preceded by two lancers and followed by the Staff."

When the cavalcade reached the highest point, the Viceroy
sent an A.D.C. for his caravan: "a kind of omnibus, drawn by
six mules and furnished as a bedroom". It arrived at a gallop,
so the hill could not have been particularly steep. The two men
sat down in the shade of the vehicle and the Viceroy amused
himself by having a stone wall built round them by the light
infantry of the escort, who collected stones from the surrounding desert. They left an embrasure for a gun with which to salute
the rest of the troops—there were ten thousand of them in all, as
they marched past. Lesseps gained considerable prestige by putting his horse Anizé, named after the tribe by whom he was
bred, at the wall and clearing it in each direction, a particularly
popular move because the stallion had been the gift of the Viceroy; who now went off to his siesta in the caravan. Lesseps rode
back to the camp and lunched with the Prime Minister,
who had been in his confidence in the matter of the canal,
and now agreed that Säid was in the mood for a direct
approach.

"Guided by the happy omen of the rainbow, I hoped that the
day would not go down without a decision on the subject of piercing
the Isthmus of Suez. At five o'clock in the evening I mounted,
and rode to the Viceroy's enclosure, where I again jumped the wall.
The Viceroy was cheerful and smiling. He took my hand, and,
keeping it for a moment in his own, led me to sit down beside him
on the divan. We were alone. The tent-fly allowed us to see the
splendid setting of the sun whose dawn had so much moved me.
At that moment, when I was about to ask the question which
would make so much difference to my future, I felt calm and
confident. My studies and meditations on the *Canal des Deux
Mers* were clear before me, and the realization of the plan seemed
so feasible that I did not doubt that I would be able to communicate my conviction to the Prince. I put forward the project without
entering into details, relying on the principal facts and arguments
from my memorandum, which I could have recited from one end
to the other. Mohammed-Säid listened with interest to my exposition. I begged him, if he had any doubts, to tell me them; and he
did offer several intelligent objections to which I replied in a manner
calculated to satisfy him. Then at last he said to me, 'I am persuaded. I accept your plan. For the rest of the journey we will
concern ourselves with means for its execution.'"

The above quotation, and the others in this chapter, are from
Ferdinand's *Lettres, Journal et Documents* (1865), in which the

words of Säid's decision are italicized, presumably because they
represent the source of a Nile of words, which immediately
began to flow as Säid summoned his Staff to hear the news:

"They sat on mats in front of us, and he described to them the
conversation which he had just had with me. . . . These improvised
councillors, more accustomed to judge an equitation exercise than
an immense undertaking of which they could hardly be expected
to realize the implications, opened their eyes wide, and, turning
to me, gave me to understand that a friend of their master, whom
they had just seen jump over the stone wall, could hardly give
anything but good advice. From time to time they raised their
hands to their foreheads in token of agreement with the measure
about which the Viceroy had been telling them. The dinner-table
was brought in, and, as though to show that we were all of one
opinion, we dipped our spoons in the same tureen, which contained
an excellent *potage*. And that is a faithful account of the most
important negotiation which I ever have done, or will ever
do."

At eight o'clock Lesseps left the enclosure to go back to his
own tent, but first he called on the Prime Minister to tell him the
good news and thank him for his part in preparing the ground.
Understandably, Ferdinand found that he could not get to sleep,
and so sat up to write a *précis* of the original memorandum.
Leaving out the historical introduction, these are the main
points of it:

1. The canal will tend to preserve the Ottoman Empire because
it will force the Powers to sustain Turkey as the guarantor of its
neutrality; the Powers being too jealous of one another to allow
one of their own number to play that rôle.

2. Lepère wanted ten thousand workmen, four years and thirty
or forty million francs for the indirect canal *via* the Nile. Paulin
Talabot, Stephenson and Negrelli, working with a Survey Company
(Enfantin's), adopted the indirect route from Alexandria to Suez
via the Nile at an estimated cost of 130 millions for the canal and
20 millions for the port and harbour of Suez. Linant Bey, for thirty
years inspector of the Egyptian canals, who had made a life study
of the question, proposed to cut a direct line with a port in Lake
Timsah. Gallice Bey, who planned and built the fortifications of
Alexandria, made a similar proposal to Mohammed-Ali. Moguel
Bey, chief engineer for the Nile Barrage, was of the same opinion.
Count Walewski undertook to support the plan and present it to
the Powers in 1840, but political events prevented him from doing
so.

3. A detailed survey will determine which is the most convenient route. It is only a matter of choosing the best.

4. Though difficult, there is nothing about the work itself to deter modern technical methods. Success is no longer in doubt, it is only a matter for money and *esprit d'entreprise*.

5. If expenses are kept in proportion to probable earnings the business will be solvent.

6. Though construction costs are likely to be very high, they will not be out of proportion in view of the usefulness of the project and the profits from halving the distance to the Indies from both Europe and America.

7. Confronted with such figures (those of the relative distances) comment is unnecessary. They will show every nation in Europe, and the United States of America, that they are equally concerned with the opening of the Suez Canal and its rigorous, inviolable neutrality.

8. Mohammed-Säid has already recognized that there is no other work of such grandeur, such a title to glory, such a passport to riches. The name of the Prince who opens the great Canal will be blessed century after century to the most remote posterity.

9. The pilgrimage to Mecca will be facilitated for all time.

10. A great impetus will be given to long distance navigation, and emigration from Europe to the vast countries of the East.

11. By the Cape route the annual passage of shipping amounts to some 6 million tons. If only one half of this went through the Red Sea, commerce would save 150 million francs a year. It is obvious that the Suez Canal will cause a considerable augmentation of tonnage, but on the basis of only 3 million tons, 30 million francs (£1,200,000) would be earned annually for a due of 10 francs per ton.

12. The Suez Canal will be easier to make than that of Panama, which is already in preparation. It will be more useful and less expensive.

13. The Suez Canal project is sure of the support of all enlightened persons in all countries, because it is of such importance for the future of the world, and therefore will be free from all serious opposition.

* * *

These statements are lucid and reasonable. They convinced the Viceroy. But in some respects, notably time and money, they proved to be misleading, as much to their author as to anyone else; for they were the work of a visionary. As fiction has its own truth, so vision has its own reality, to which, in supreme examples, the facts of earth give way. But Ferdinand de Lesseps,

though perfectly sincere, was by no means a sage. Fascinated by
the light, he dared not look into the shadows. The future was
to be the fulfilment of the vision, to which all facts must conform. Had he been better able to distinguish between the general
and the particular, or personal, he might have been happier, his
friends more numerous, his enemies fewer: but he would not
have built the canal. He selected data with the conviction that
success would be achieved in proportion as he believed in it,
and communicated that belief to others. So he tended sometimes
to be misled, and to mislead his friends. A greater man, even at
this stage, would have had the courage to warn the Viceroy of
the risks ahead, taking the chance that he might abandon the
project. Lesseps dared not do so, and so committed, if negatively,
his first small deception. Yet, as the alchemist gave all to his
Magnum Opus, holding nothing back; and as others have found
in more prosaic circumstances that the key to success is sacrifice,
so Lesseps was unselfishly devoted to his dream. It is not the
record of his faults which matters now, they were fewer than
most people's, but that practical projection of a vision which
is genius.

When allowance has been made for the fact that the data
from which Ferdinand drew his conclusions had been provided
by independent experts, the aura of wishful-thinking still sur-
rounds his *précis*. For instance the phrase 'success is no longer
in doubt' was true in terms of self-confidence alone. Many
responsible people still held the technical difficulties to be insur-
mountable, and the political obstacles were likely to be no less
formidable. Though France and England were temporary allies
against Russia on behalf of Turkey, their long hostility was
good reason for expecting that England would hardly stop short
even of war to prevent the further growth of French influence
in the Middle East. By the same token, the chance of the Powers
handing over to Turkey the protection of the world's most
coveted waterway was remote. After generations of intrigue,
conflict, and the worship of the Balance of Power, they could
hardly for long agree about anything. Each would tend to
oppose a scheme which tended to disturb the Balance, unless
exclusively in its own favour.

In terms of commerce Lesseps was equally optimistic. Whatever the type of craft which he envisaged, the reality was still

sail with an occasional paddle-wheeler, sail assisted. Steam could not be used on long voyages because the machinery was so inefficient that coal usurped cargo-space and made the payload too small. It was not until the seventies, when the compound engine came into use, that the difficulty was overcome by using exhaust steam to drive a second, third, or even fourth piston. And sail was better adapted to the longer route than to the narrows of the Red Sea, which, with contrary winds, was terribly slow and arduous. Nor was the Mediterranean without its dis-advantages. Sailing ships would be at the mercy of corsairs in times of peace, and of enemy steamers in war. As for the financial side, the implication as to capital cost proved disastrously low, partly because, in spite of Ferdinand's claim to the contrary, available techniques were not adequate to the task. The original estimated capital was 200,000,000 francs.

The capital position would be reflected in the profits, where the chief source of error proved to be traffic receipts. The required three million tons did not pass through the canal until twenty-one years after it was opened. And yet in the long run the earnings of the enterprise have been far greater than even Lesseps dreamed. In principle he was as right as he could have been had he seen the future in a crystal; but he was grossly inaccurate when judged by the standards of common sense applied to the data available in 1854. On the other hand, who could have made an accurate estimate in face of so many unknown or at least incalculable factors? And Ferdinand was not an engineer, nor any kind of scientist. He was not a financier, nor had he experience of handling large sums. He had been a consul but never a statesman. In comparison with the wide issues raised by the canal even his ambassadorial duties had been relatively parochial. Above all he was not a plodder, but had the intuitive, emotional temperament which is concerned with principles and qualities rather than with the counting of quantities. The tendency of such men is not to work out the answer to a problem but to guess what the answer ought to be. Then, if they must calculate, they do so only in order to justify their original inspiration. Right or wrong, they usually burn like meteors through the sky of their generation, but seldom leave behind a trace upon the earth. It is a measure of Lesseps that he had the practical ability and immense determined patience to condense his vision, in reality which must remain long after his denigrators have been forgotten.

*   *   *

It was now plain to the Egyptians that Lesseps was no mere social lion but a man with considerable influence in the country, and so the deference with which he was treated – and the state in which he was kept – were further increased. He rode at the right hand of the Viceroy, taking precedence over both the Prime Minister and the Commander-in-Chief. Such marks of favour implied that Säid believed his guest to be much more than a private individual with a commercial proposition. Had not his father represented the first Napoleon? What more natural than that France should require the son to continue that policy towards an independent Egypt barring England's route to the east? Säid was no fool. His munificence to Ferdinand was also a compliment to France and a tacit acceptance of his rôle as her protégé after the precedent of Mohammed-Ali. If Ferdinand failed to realize that he was still considered to be a secret agent, it must be remembered that he had an extraordinary innocence where people's motives were concerned. This, with a certain personal vanity, inevitably reinforced by his Arabian Nights treatment, explains why he was so shocked and bewildered when he discovered that among the diplomats his motives were regarded with suspicion and his project rated as cover for a devious French imperialism.

No doubt the Egyptian intelligence service soon found out that he was in fact only what he claimed to be, that he had no official standing whatsoever. By then it would be too late for the Viceroy to draw back, and London could not be blamed for continued suspicion. If Ferdinand de Lesseps were not a political agent why had he put on full-dress diplomatic uniform when he first arrived? What alternative explanation was there for his sudden emergence, from a retirement clouded by the Rome affair, to stand as it were behind the Egyptian throne? Why did Säid continue to treat him almost as royalty? On one occasion, for instance, he and the Viceroy were cantering side by side in the desert when the great diamond *chelengk* fell from the Prince's headdress. Lesseps reined in to retrieve the jewel

but Säid would not let him perform such a humble gesture and
the diamonds were left lying in the sand. That evening Säid did
not feel well. He had a cold coming on and retired to his caravan,
asking Lesseps to preside at dinner, a meal of eight courses prepared by twenty-five cooks. The cooks used wood-burning stoves
and Ferdinand was impressed with the waste of the expensive
fuel, which had to be brought from the Delta.

When Säid reviewed his army, Lesseps was beside him:

"The troops defiled beneath us between two knolls, the soldiers
cheering and waving their rifles as they passed the Viceroy. The
sun made their arms flash and a squadron of cavalry, with breast-
plates and the ancient Saracen helmets, were particularly conspicuous. The brown faces of the Arabs were striking under their
helmets. The review over, we went to take the head of the column,
preceded by a dozen Bedouin horsemen serving as scouts and
guides. Renewed cheering saluted the Viceroy and blended with
the military music. These parts had seen no army on the march
since General Bonaparte's expedition. Our brave soldiers of the
Republic had to undergo plenty of hardship and privation where,
forty years later, we were making a *promenade militaire* in all
possible comfort."

The royal entourage had furnished tents and not only water but
ice. In their armour under the sun the cavalry can hardly have
been so comfortable, and the gunners had cause to complain
when Säid sent them through an area of soft sand because someone had asserted that it could not be crossed. On the 20th of
November they reached the Nile near Neguileh, by which time
the Viceroy seems to have recovered from his cold. He installed
himself in the royal yacht *Mahroussa*, for which Mohammed-
Ali had paid an English builder two and a half million francs.
Showing Lesseps round, Säid exclaimed: "You know I am not
responsible for this folly, but I benefit from it." Even Ferdinand,
who by now was not easily impressed, found it 'dazzling'. He
recorded:

"Nothing can give an idea of the luxury of the appointments,
the pictures and the furnishing of this vessel. The doors are of
oak and lemon-wood, their locks and hinges of solid silver. There
are panels representing rivers and animals, painted by the most
distinguished artists, staircases with bannisters and rails of silver,
divans covered with cloth-of-gold. There is a saloon forty feet long,

a dining-room, a boudoir, offices, and bedroom, furnished like the most magnificent palace."

Even so there was not enough room for Lesseps to be able to live aboard. He had to put up with Säid's second-best yacht, *el Ferusi*, the Turquoise. Her saloon was relatively modest and the divans were covered only with gold brocade; but she was superior to the several other craft which accommodated the rest of the entourage. Ferdinand did not even have the ship to himself but had to share with a Pasha and a Bey, who had rooms of their own; even so his position was now so secure that on the following day he not only gave the Viceroy his *précis*, but also a draft of a firman which he proposed for the authorization of the work. Säid read through the *précis*, suggested some minor amendments which were readily adopted, and gave his consent in principle to the terms of the firman.

When the flotilla reached Cairo, Lesseps was told to await the arrival of a carriage which would take him to his new abode, the Palace of Foreigners. Preceded by two running footmen bearing silver-mounted staves, drawn by four matched white horses, a royal *berline* arrived. The negro coachman, in splendid livery, drove at a fast trot, or even a canter through the crowded streets. Pedestrians who did not flatten themselves against the walls in time were treated to curses and blows by the running footmen. Lesseps took the first opportunity to remonstrate with his servants, but he found out later that the people took a certain pleasure in such scenes. They were wont to exclaim admiringly, "There goes some great personage. *Machallah!* Glory to God." And he comments: "Such is the Orient, and so it has been since biblical times. Do we not read how, after Joshua had massacred all the inhabitants of Jericho, even the women, the children and the asses – 'And so was made manifest the power of God'?" His eyes were wide open. He saw and understood cruelty as an historical trait, which must be accepted only in so far as it could not be changed. And he did change it whenever he could. Within the limitations imposed by custom he tried to show that even slaves are people, and his vision of the canal included increased well-being for those who worked on it. Even so, he was later accused of callousness over labour conditions.

At the palace he was welcomed like a king: "The *nazir*

(major-domo), a dignified old gentleman with a grey beard, who looked like a portrait of François I, ran to the door as I began to alight, and assisted me indoors, followed by the household staff." Before being left to himself he was informed that he had the use of twenty horses, ten for harness and ten for the saddle, a gilded state coach, the *berline* in which he had arrived, a barouche, and a *mylord* (phaeton). Dinner would be for twelve *couverts*. The journal does not mention whether the other eleven places were for his own guests or for other foreigners living in the palace. Next morning he went to see the British Consul-General Sir Frederick Bruce, with whom he had a long conversation and came away with the conviction that though no official attitude could be discerned, it was clearly Bruce's personal conviction that England – following the Sultan's opinion – must regard the decision to make the canal as one entirely within the jurisdiction of Egypt. The question was therefore commercial rather than political, a matter of how to find the necessary capital. Lesseps left a copy of his *précis* and, with no misgivings, went to report to the Viceroy.

The day following, being the 25th of November, Lesseps was summoned to the Citadel at nine o'clock in the morning. He found Säid sitting on the throne of Mohammed-Ali: " who had often received me, and where he had told me one day the tragedy of the massacre of the Mamelukes." The whole of the diplomatic set and the court were present to offer congratulations and good wishes. It all seemed very dull and ordinary until:

" Scarcely had the consuls in uniform taken their places and paid their respects, than the Viceroy, to my great surprise, had the happy inspiration of announcing publicly his decision to open up the Isthmus of Suez by a sea-water canal. He added that he had chosen me to float a Company on capital to be drawn from all the Powers, to which he would concede the right to carry out and develop the enterprise. Turning to me he added, ' Is it not so – we are going to do that?' So I commented briefly on the Prince's statement, crediting him with the idea of the project and being very careful not to ruffle the susceptibilities of the foreigners. The consul-general of England seemed rather embarrassed. The consul-general of the United States, to whom the Viceroy had said: ' Well, Monsieur de Leon, we are going to queen the pawn against you over the Isthmus of Panama, and we shall finish before you,' had on the contrary, taken the news well. He replied in a way which made me conclude that his opinion was favourable."

So in dramatic circumstances which must have gratified both
Lesseps and the Viceroy, the news broke in every country that
the moderns would overpass the ancients and cut the great canal
from sea to sea. There was a flurry of activity, political, financial, and impurely personal. Everyone who might conceivably
have something to gain, or lose, by the enterprise, began to
clamour; and it soon became evident that the Viceroy's precipi-
tate declaration, made before any of the Powers, including
Turkey, had been consulted, was an error. Yet had he waited for
the Sultan's approval, it might have been long delayed; and
had he deferred until all the Powers were in agreement, he might
have had to wait for ever.

Chapter 6.   DESERTS

Not the least remarkable quality of Ferdinand de Lesseps was his ability to get things quickly done. Once a decision had been taken he put his whole force into its application, and, as though he were a shunting locomotive, men soon found themselves being marshalled like trucks to the train of his intention. In a word, the power of Lesseps was momentum, and nowhere was it more difficult to get things moving than in Egypt. There was every reason to suppose that even after the Viceroy had made public his approval of the project, time and time again would be required before anything practical could be done about it. Yet only five days after the announcement, Säid Pasha signed the firman, not as a mere confirmation of his approval but as a legally binding document with twelve clauses. Between them they defined all the more important issues involved, and they still provide the historical basis upon which the Canal Company operates. The original firman also defines the fundamental issues of the Canal Zone. The document is given in full by *Bertrand et Ferrier*, from which text the following points are taken:

1.   "Our friend M. Ferdinand de Lesseps" is given exclusive authority to float and direct an international Company.
2.   The Director of the Company shall always be appointed by the Egyptian Government.
3.   The Concession, and all rights enjoyed by the Company, shall be for ninety-nine years from the date of the opening of the canal.
4.   The cost of works shall be borne entirely by the Company.
5.   The necessary land and materials shall be furnished by the Government without charge. (No mention of labour: materials undefined.)
6.   If, as the result of making a fresh-water canal, land which is now desert becomes fertile, the Company shall enjoy it free of tax, for the first ten years out of the ninety-nine of the Concession. After that the Company shall pay the rate applicable to land in an equivalent state of cultivation.
10.   On the expiry of the Concession the Egyptian Government shall resume all rights, subject to an amicable arrangement, or

arbitration, as to the indemnity payable to the Company for its installations and equipment.

11. The Statutes of the Company shall be approved by us (in this case the Viceroy, otherwise the Egyptian Government), and all changes must receive our previous sanction. The list of Founders shall be approved by us.

Over the Viceregal seal at the bottom of the document there appeared the following codicil:

"To my devoted friend of high birth and exalted rank, Monsieur Ferdinand de Lesseps. The Concession granted to the Company requires ratification by His Sublime Majesty the Sultan. I send you this copy for your personal use. As to the actual work of construction, it should not be begun until the authorization of the Sublime Porte has been received.

The 3rd Ramadan, 1271."

This post-scriptum caused Lesseps no immediate anxiety. He was already making up a party for personal reconnaissance, taking with him the two men who knew more about the canals of Egypt than anyone else in the world – Linant and Moguel, both loaned by the Viceroy. The approval of the Sultan, thought Lesseps, was only a matter of form. Asking for it was a mere act of deference, and by the time the plans were drawn in detail the way would be clear. So confident was Ferdinand that, presumably through his influence with Eugénie, it was at once arranged to confer upon Säid the *grand cordon* of the Legion of Honour. Although technically the award of the Legion itself, the gesture was naturally interpreted as confirming Ferdinand's quasi-official status. The ceremony took place on the 22nd of December and began with a procession, led by all the members of the Legion who could be mustered at short notice. They were taken to the Citadel in state coaches, preceded by a squadron of lancers. Ferdinand's own coach was first in line: "The people ranged themselves respectfully along the route, and from the base of the Citadel to the forecourt the way was lined with infantry . . . The Viceroy, surrounded by his high officials, came to the door and received from Monsieur Sabatier, the French Consul-General, a letter from the Emperor."

After the usual flowery preamble this letter promised to the Viceroy, in his support of the canal project, not only the good

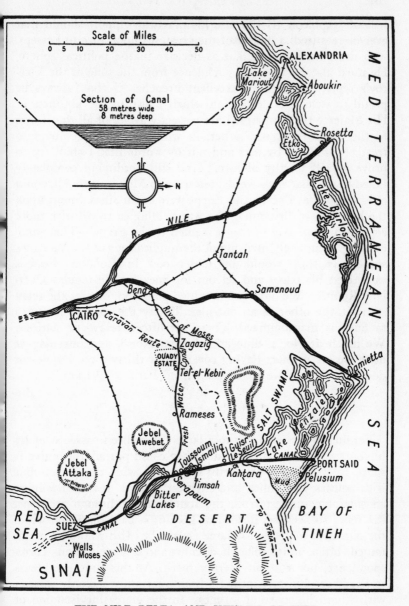

THE NILE DELTA AND ISTHMUS OF SUEZ

A sketch map based on Bertrand et Ferrier, 1887. The great network of
canals and Nile channels not shown.

will of Napoleon III but also his practical support should that
ever be required; a matter of the greatest importance to Lesseps,
who must have regarded it as decisive in the political sphere.
He must also have gained confidence from the tone of the Viceroy's reply, delivered in excellent French: "I shall always be
proud to wear this decoration which I owe to the kindness of
His Majesty the Emperor. I am perfectly aware of all that I owe
to the memory of my father, in whose footsteps I intend to
tread. It shall be by acts and not by words that I shall try to
prove myself worthy of him." And still Ferdinand completely
failed to see that such words, referring to Mohammed-Ali, could
only mean that France and Egypt were again allies, intent upon
the hobbling of Britannia, who was striding eastward with more
arrogance than ever – or so it seemed to the French. That same
evening, completely unaware of the implications of the Viceroy's
speech as they would be understood in London, Lesseps
assembled his party and set out for Suez by the regular Overland Route: "We have two mounted post-boys, one for the relay
stations, the other as an outrider. To-day the road from Cairo
to Suez is macadamized. There are fifteen relays or stations.
We lunch at No. 4, dine and sleep at No. 8, and next day at
noon we are at Suez having covered our thirty-three leagues of
desert as though we were going from Paris to Orleans."

*　　*　　*

Ferdinand's journal has to a large extent been passed over by
his biographers, usually because they could not afford to give it
space in works not primarily concerned with the person but
with politics, economics, and engineering data. It is, however, of
considerable interest from the standpoint of human relations,
the more so because, instead of keeping a bald diary, he wrote
the narrative to please Madame Delamalle, with whom he maintained, often under difficult circumstances, a continuous correspondence, not without literary merit. At this time she seems
to have been his only intimate friend, certainly the only woman
with whom he spoke of business. In the increasing isolation of
power and responsibility he needed her as his one safe confidante
in a world of double talk and double dealing. Not that the letters
are concerned with business, rather they form a balanced narra-

tive, not crowded with detail but giving enough to keep her up to date with the growth of the great project. Often he tried to invoke for her the atmosphere of Egypt, as in the following piece written at Suez on Christmas Day 1854:

"The rising sun is lighting up my room. I open my window and remain for a few moments in contemplation. In front of me the rising waters of the Red Sea are coming to bathe the walls of the India Hotel. To the right are the Attaka Hills. To the left, in the distance, is the beginning of the chain which ends in the peak of Sinai. This part of the coast has a roseate tint which is reflected in the water; and that, I suppose, is what gave the gulf the name of the Red Sea. People are beginning to move about on the quay. Small boats, the oars mere poles with discs at the ends, are going alongside vessels which have recently arrived or are about to leave for Jidda. With no decks, raised poop and sharp prow, they resemble Chinese junks. The dress, of both natives and strangers, as with the furnishings of the houses, gives one an advance taste of Arabia, India, and China. I notice that the locals are slower in their movements than anywhere else in Egypt. Suez itself is a mere point surrounded by deserts, and its population, of three or four thousand," (to-day about 110,000), "is wretched. The only water available is brackish. Our canal will give them both the water and the incentive which they need.

"I go up to the flat roof of the hotel, from where one can take in all the features of the surrounding country. I do want to see everything for myself and not to overlook a single detail, so that once having understood, I shall be able to explain to others who are not engineers. Linant and Moguel have asked me always to tell them my observations and opinions. People told me that they might not get on together, and the Viceroy himself suggested that I take only Linant. But in such a matter as this I would rather have the benefit of two opinions even if they are different. Linant knows the geography of the entire country. He made the map, and he has also studied the geology on the spot. The whole of the canal-system of Egypt is familiar to him. As for Moguel, he is the man who made the great water-works. If no one could be better than Linant for engineering a canal through the ground, Moguel's opinion is pre-eminent as to the question, still not determined, of the two entrances, one from the Red Sea and the other from the Mediterranean.

"My friends have still not appeared in the corridors of the hotel. I am going to wake them up and propose for to-day an excursion into the desert as far as the ancient canal of the Kings. . . . We started after breakfast, some on horses, others in a vehicle, and escorted by fifteen mounted bashi-bazouks. We came to a place where the two banks of the old canal are still clearly visible. We

measured the bed, which has a width of seventy elbows of Heroditus (about seventy-three feet). On the way back we took our siesta
in one of the tents provided for our journey. Linant's man, the
negro Abdallah, served excellent coffee. My famous Ibrahim has
disappeared into obscurity. No doubt to cut more of a dash, he
had bought himself a beautiful gilt sword, an officer's cane, patent-
leather shoes, and a startling cummerbund, etc. But where did he
get the ignoble metal with which to purchase such beautiful things?
From the pockets of my clothes and in the rooms of the Palace
of Foreigners. When the facts had been thoroughly proved, my
Ibrahim was thrown out neck and crop, but without scandal, to
go hang himself elsewhere."

Not all the party's excursions were surveys, nor was Lesseps
taken up with technical issues to the exclusion of his wider interests. He had always been a student of the Old Testament, and
took a lively interest in comparing the terrain he saw with what
it must have been like at the time of the Exodus. Twice he tried
to cross the Gulf to visit the Wells of Moses, but on the first
occasion a storm blew up and made it unwise to try to land, and
on the second the engine of their small steamer broke down.
After repeatedly drawing the fire and hammering away at a
broken pipe, rekindling, and getting pressure again only to have
another burst, the party had to sleep aboard. Next day they
managed to struggle back to Suez. Fortunately there were no
women aboard on that occasion, as there had been on the first.
Then the journey had been undertaken at the invitation of the
owner of the principal well, who arranged a luncheon there with
whole roast sheep as the *plat du jour*. His wife and his sister-in-
law, 'dressed in the most elaborate oriental costume, with their
eyelids, eyes and hands painted', must have been very uncomfortable during the storm; but at least they did not have to spend
the night in the cold cramped quarters of a boat with no
cabin.

The weather was often bad during the three weeks the party
were in the desert, and they were as much troubled by the
intense cold as by the incessant wind. Lesseps in his journal
looked back to the time when this land of Goschen (Gessen)
was fertile pasture, grazed by the herds of the Hyksos, those
'Shepherd Kings' who twice humbled Pharaoh, and of their
Hebrew congeners; from among whom arose Joseph the son of
Jacob, unwitting father of the captivity. Lesseps quoted Genesis

XLVI, 33, 34: 'And it shall come to pass when Pharaoh shall call you and shall say, What is your occupation? That ye shall say, Thy servants have been keepers of the cattle even until now, both we and our fathers: that ye may dwell in the land of Goschen; for every shepherd is an abomination unto the Egyptians." Deep in the solitude of rock and sand, shivering in his tent, de Lesseps wrote:

"The implications I draw from these passages in the Bible suggest that the land of Goschen, which will be traversed by our fresh-water canal, ought to become at least as fertile as it was in antiquity; and that the climate will be healthy for farmers. Even to-day, as in the time of Moses, the tribes of Arabs which sometimes camp here are generally free from epidemics, in spite of their contacts with the population of lower Egypt."

This vision of a renascent land of Goschen was a potent factor in his imagination. He saw it as something almost as important as the canal itself, a spiritual symbol which would confer material benefits upon humanity. In later years he was, on this issue as on so many others, accused of cunning and greed; yet it would be absurd to suggest that consciously there was even a trace of either at work in such an idealist. To have lowered the level of his endeavour to that of mere business would have taken from him the saving grace which had survived the death of Agathe – his capacity for devotion.

*　　　*　　　*

On the 30th of December the main reconnaissance began by following the route of the proposed canal northwards; though, owing to quicksands, it was often impossible to get closer to it than a mile or two. So the party bore westward, keeping to the higher ground except when engaged in taking levels, and so entered the almost featureless solitude through which the Exodus passed:

"'Speak unto the children of Israel that they turn back and encamp before Pi-hahiroth, between Migdol and the sea, before Baal-zephon: over against it shall ye encamp by the sea.' This place is in fact between the ancient lagoons of the Red Sea, the level of which is below that of the sea. So they will become lagoons again when the canal is opened. The Israelites, aided by the storm described in the Bible, must have passed the evening, at low tide, in the depression between Lake Timsah and the Bitter Lakes. They would be among long sand dunes which by moonlight give the effect of limewashed walls. In the morning, the wind having fallen, the Egyptian troops in pursuit of the Hebrews were overwhelmed by the tide and the quicksands in the valley."

He is equally critical of other miracles. The Wells of Moses, which earned their name because Moses made them sweet, he equated with a story of Linant's that the Arabs of Sinai treat brackish water by throwing into it a shrub called *arak*, being a variety of berberis, which reduces the bitterness. Manna he identified as the condensation of a plant-leaf exudate, fallen to the ground. The pillars of fire and of smoke were probably poetic symbols for Arab pathfinders, who carried torches made to give out smoke by day and fire by night, so that the position of a caravan is always indicated. Their own establishment consisted of thirty-three camels and dromedaries, in charge of fifteen Bedouin who slept among them. Poor Moguel could not endure the motion of a dromedary, so for his benefit there were two asses and a groom. The camels were not used for riding but as pack-animals. The best of dromedaries were those which got up quickest when being mounted:

"One needs plenty of alacrity for this business, because the moment the right leg is passed over them they jerk to their feet. So one has to lean well forward, then quickly backward as the animal stretches his hind legs. . . . I was comfortable on mine at once because I have for some time been in training, and can endure both the long-striding gait and the bumping trot. Between those extremes there is quite a comfortable pace."

Close to the camel-lines was the 'farm-yard', consisting of a quantity of chickens, turkeys and pigeons. The birds – except presumably the pigeons, were allowed to roam during the day if the camp remained in the same place; and Lesseps was impressed by the fact that they never strayed. It was as though the desert impressed them also with the completeness of its historic desolation. There must have been several personal servants, though Lesseps did not mention how many, not only to do the camp chores but also to stand guard over the water, which was placed between the two principal tents. There were twenty kegs of it, which, having come all the way from the Nile, could hardly have remained palatable. The tents, only three in all, were divided as between Lesseps and Linant (No. 1), Moguel and Aivas, who was Linant's Egyptian secretary and assistant, (No. 2); and the servants in No. 3. All were bell-tents twenty feet in diameter, but there was also a 'long' tent used as a cookhouse; for there seems to have been general agreement that just because they happened to be living in a desert, condemned to drink bad water, there was no reason why they should not eat well. The attention to this important detail seems to have been common in Egypt at that time, not only to the Turks but also among the English; for Lesseps records the following dinner with Mr. West, Consul at Suez: "Mutton from Calcutta, potatoes from Bombay, *petits pois* from England, Egyptian chickens. We drank Ganges water, French wines, Moka coffee, and China tea."

The interior of No. 1 tent was Spartan. On either side of the pole were two mattresses, each covered with a carpet to form a *divan du jour*, and within reach of rifles clamped to the pole. Close by were packed saddle-bags, two for each person. Behind the tent-pole and level with the heads of the beds was a stake with a board across the top to support an oil lantern, and hooks at each side for watches. The pillows consisted of saddles covered with Senaar sheepskin dyed red. The only furniture was a trestle table. By New Year's Day 1855 Lesseps was convinced that there was no topographical obstacle to his plans; indeed he found the terrain easier than he had expected because of evidence that the depression where the Bitter Lakes now are was substantially lower than the level of the Red Sea, and in the time of Moses must have formed an extension of it. On the third of the month of January they visited Rameses, where Linant sketched the statue of Sesosteris and his two sons. Lesseps picked up bricks such as the Israelites made – he says nothing of straw, which in any case was employed according to the type of clay rather than to make the work lighter. On the fourth they made the circuit of Lake Timsah: "It is a magnificent natural port, six times bigger than Marseilles; and it will be even more useful because it will be easily connected with the cultivated lands of Goshen, and with the interior of Egypt by a canal joining it to the Nile." Next day a storm brought heavy rain which wrecked the tents. Though Linant managed to get out of No. 1 in time, Lesseps was trapped within. While all hands battled with the guy-ropes, he 'acted as a flying buttress' to the tent-pole – 'What a ridiculous situation for the future Director of the *Canal des Deux Mers*! ' On the seventh the weather, though still cold, abated and they moved north of Lake Timsah to survey the site of what is now Ismailia; then northward again, they glimpsed the waters of Lake Menzaleh: "Formed partly by the Nile and partly by the Mediterranean, the shores offer plenty of opportunity for communication between Pelusium and Damietta." On the ninth the party again changed direction, this time towards Tineh and Pelusium, which Lesseps says mean the same thing – mud. Of the ancient city of Pelusium nothing remained: "So we saluted the Mediterranean, promised her a visit from the Gulf of Arabia, and took our leave. We have finished the first part of our reconnaissance and the result is that our project is feasible. Soon, I hope, the report of the two engineers will prove it."

So the party turned back towards Cairo, in cold so bitter that in order to keep warm they had to walk beside their beasts. What must have been a miserable day was provided with some comic relief through the panic of the asses' groom. Convinced that any Bedouin was likely to murder him, he created a scene when he came upon a group of them with rifles over their shoulders, insisting that they must be bandits. The party reached El Guisr by five o'clock and pitched the tents on some of the highest ground in the Isthmus. Next morning they set off again, and after five days' arduous travel reached Cairo, where Lesseps immediately sat down to write his detailed instructions to the engineers. This concise and entirely fair document formed the basis of their report, in the preparation of which they had complete freedom of action. Each of them, high ranking in the Viceroy's service, had the strongest personal reasons for not allowing wishful-thinking to cloud his appreciation of the situation. It is particularly significant therefore that in the matter of costs they agreed closely with the figure given by Lesseps to Säid, a capital of two or three hundred million francs. The facts upon which this estimate was based were all set out in full, and every conceivable factor was considered upon independent data as well as against the record of previous surveys; so in this important respect Linant and Moguel gave expert confirmation of the estimate in the famous *précis*, which otherwise might seem unduly hopeful.

*　　　*　　　*

Lesseps now found that he had left behind the cold and storms of the geographical desert only to run into a howling wilderness of words. The premature announcement of the Viceroy's intention to cut the canal had taken the world's attention even from the infamous Black Winter in the Crimea, where French and English were freezing side by side. As news the effect would to-day be equivalent to the abrupt announcement of a decision to build the Channel Tunnel; though the canal was far more controversial. Instead of concerning only two countries, it focused the jealousies and morbid memories of all Europe. As Renan would say when it was in being: "Cut, the isthmus becomes a strait, a battlefield. A single Bosphorus had hitherto sufficed for the troubles of the world; you have created a second and much more important one. In case of naval war it would be of supreme interest, and a point for the occupation of which the whole world would struggle to be first. You have marked out the field for great battles in the future."

Lesseps must have been reminded of his return from Rome. Again where there had been warmth there was coolness, and where there had been trust there was suspicion, even hostility. This he might have expected; instead he seems to have been surprised that England, in particular, did not at once share his vision. He remained unable to appreciate that in London the realities of the hour, and of history, dictated conclusions quite different from his own. After centuries of Turkish alliance, the first Napoleon reversed French foreign policy by his Egyptian adventure. Though as a feat of arms it failed, as a cultural conquest it unquestionably succeeded; and upon that culture Mohammed-Ali fed until he considered himself strong enough to challenge not only the Sultan but the Sultan's ally, England. Even without the canal, the possibility that Egypt might become a Power in her own right, but under French influence, had been enough to make Lord Palmerston curtail Mohammed-Ali's ambition. Since then not only had Syria been restored to the Sultan but, in a sense, Egypt also. After 1841 Cairo had no valid independence, notwithstanding the dynastic rule which England herself had instituted.

In 1855 the memory of the first Napoleon and of Mohammed-Ali was ominous. Both France and Egypt harked to the future for echoes from the past. That the new Emperor of the French was about to pay a state visit to Queen Victoria did not lessen the implications of his name, to which he owed much of his personal power. For that very reason, sooner or later, he would be compelled to unhood the eagles. That is what his people expected of him, and might even demand. As for Egypt, that Säid was gross and genial did not alter the implications of another of his personal characteristics, greed. The canal would set a tactical barrier between him and his overlord in Stamboul. It would geographically separate Egypt from Turkey. And in order to control the traffic, a life-line upon which grand strategy would soon depend, there was required only a very moderate disposition of troops, a task well within the capacity of Säid's small army. Who held Suez, let alone Port Said, became by that fact an arbiter of power in time of peace. In war only the most costly large-scale operation would succeed in controlling the canal and its traffic against Egyptian wishes.

In terms of *realpolitik* the dream of Lesseps seemed no more practical than had been the vapourings of the Saint-Simonians. Even the commercial benefits – which the canal would be likely to confer chiefly upon English shipping on the India run – were, among statesmen, of no account. Business was restricted to its own sphere. When the Foreign Office spoke, merchants were expected to be silent. Sir Frederick Bruce privately set down the essence of the official view:

"For both commercial and military purposes we are nearer to India than any European nation except Spain and Portugal, which are nothing. When the canal is open, all the coasts of the Mediterranean and the Black Sea will be nearer India than we are. The first proposer of the canal was Bonaparte, for the purpose of injuring England. At present India is unattackable. It will no longer be so when Bombay is only 4,600 miles from Marseilles; and although we shall be able to send troops through the canal, our present position of perfect safety is far better than the amplest means of defence."

At this time imperial Turkey was, as regards Egypt, little

more than a façade, a stage where diplomats acted at court
according to the rules, and then from behind the scenes, themselves largely governed the Ottoman Empire's foreign relations.
The Sultan, operatic, colourful, atavistic, and in a sense magnificent, was in that particular context only a puppet controlled by
foreign Ambassadors. And each of them knew that the alliance
of to-day is apt to change to-morrow. This was true even of the
Anglo-French entente, founded upon the Crimean battlefields;
for in the following year, 1856, France supported the ex-enemy
over a frontier dispute. What the diplomats did share was a
common belief, almost a faith, in the principle of the Balance
of Power which, it seemed, Lesseps was attacking. He wanted to
alter the geography of power. Who could tell what the effect
would be? Did it matter that in the long run humanity might
be happier and more friendly? International officers, a close-
knit community in spite of chameleon policy at home, would
gladly have ignored this Frenchman's aspiration. And they
would surely have done so had it not been for the threat to the
Balance. Dream or no dream, such a person could not be ignored,
particularly if there were a secret plan behind him; and few
responsible people could imagine anyone putting forward so
vast an enterprise without some ulterior motive.

To his surprise and fury Lesseps found himself attacked not
only by his enemies but also abandoned by erstwhile friends,
whose bold offers of support shrank into hazy affirmations of
continued goodwill. First of these was Napoleon himself, who
back-pedalled with remarkable facility considering that Säid
had just acquired the *grand cordon* for the sake of the canal.
Even Eugénie could not get her husband to do more than opine
that the affair would work out in the end. With a visit to
England in prospect he could not afford to jeopardize the
entente. At the Porte there was a new subject for discussion over
the interminable cups of coffee; but no one, least of all the Grand
Vizier, thought of taking any action over the Viceroy's request
for the Sultan's ratification of the firman of Concession. "They
are waiting," Ferdinand wrote, "for their orders from London
and Paris."

In addition to official circles, Ferdinand was assailed by the
remnant of the Saint-Simonians, who affected to believe that he
would hand over his concession to their moribund Survey Com-

pany, on the ground that it was Prosper Enfantin who first put the idea of the canal into Ferdinand's head. When he pointed out that there could be no property whatever in the notion of the canal, about which so many people had for centuries been concerned, they accused him of bad faith. "Treachery!" exclaimed Enfantin, and set out by stealth to persuade the Emperor that if Lesseps would not surrender the concession then France should proceed – presumably without even the Viceroy's authority – with the original Saint-Simonian plan for an indirect canal *via* the Nile. Napoleon did not listen to Enfantin. The subject as far as he was concerned was in abeyance. Enfantin and his friends, some of whom were level-headed characters, went back to the idea of forcing Lesseps to give them a share. Soon they were threatening: "If we are to play the Rooks, we shall act without you, the concessionaire. And then we shall see how you will be able to refuse the conditions which we offer." The reference is to a bargain to be struck when Ferdinand, faced with the need for capital, would have to appeal for French credits. Enfantin was working to gain control, through the big bankers, of the machinery of credit in so far as it applied to such an enterprise. Then Lesseps would either have to accept the money on Enfantin's terms, or give up. Such was the theory, but Ferdinand was convinced that it would have no practical success, and after he had received an ultimatum to the effect that dreadful things would happen to him if he did not capitulate within fifteen days, he refused to have anything more to do with the Saint-Simonian faction and no longer acknowledged their letters. On the 22nd of January he wrote to Madame Delamalle:

"I am going to accomplish something without expediency, without personal gain. That, thank God, is what has up to now kept my sight clear and my course away from the rocks. I shall be resolute in it, and since no one can make me deviate, I am confident I shall be able to pilot my ship into the port we may well call *Saïd*; for the name of the Viceroy also means 'happy' in Arabic. The one thing that is happy about my goal, is that my actions are not accountable to, nor can they be disowned by, any government. The scalded cat fears cold water."

All of which, though true, left him upon a lonely road. He was without official encouragement even from his own country.

He had neither rank nor office; in the absence of which all the best doors remained closed. His record was suspect. There had been rumours that he was not quite right in the head, and to many people it must have seemed that he was obsessed with the idea of the canal. Either that, or he must have some dark purpose. Outside the close circle of his few intimate friends, it could hardly occur to anyone that Ferdinand de Lesseps wanted to dig his ditch not for power nor money, nor even out of patriotism, but for love; a motive so unusual as to be unbelievable.

Chapter 7. OPPOSITION

"Alexandria, 27th of January, 1855.
The Viceroy is sending me to Constantinople where he thinks my presence has become necessary. Furnished with the most potent letters of introduction I sail to-day on the packet-boat *Pharamond*. Should there be any difficulties about the practical organization of our Company, it is well to know that Mohammed-Säid is ready to make a start with his own resources, those of his country, and of my own friends. As I left him he said, 'When we have made the fresh-water canal from the Nile and let the Red Sea into the Bitter Lakes – which is certainly within our means; then we can afford to wait for them (the capitalists) to come to us.' I can only repeat what I have already written, that there is nothing definite to be done in Europe until my return."

In fact nothing further could be done until the Sultan ratified the Act of Concession, which was the object of Ferdinand's journey. He arrived on the 18th of February and was so well received that any mild misgivings he might have had over the delay were soon dispersed. The Grand Vizier was accommodating and personally sympathetic. The Sultan graciously received him. The British Ambassador went out of his way to be civil, and the rest of the diplomatic circle followed his lead. All of which Lesseps took as a compliment to the canal when in fact the motive was largely respect for a personage of consequence. For in spite of his lost career Ferdinand de Lesseps was still a man to be reckoned with. He sat at the right hand of the new Viceroy. His cousin was Empress of the French. He had friends in every capital, and his brother Theodore, Comte de Lesseps, was high up in the French Foreign Office. Also he had distinguished ancestors, not unconnected with Turkey: a matter of importance in Stamboul.

When, in spite of all this friendliness, the required document still failed to appear, Lesseps for the first time began to think there must be a more serious reason for the delay than the chronic lethargy of the Porte, backed by a desire to put the

Viceroy in his place. But he was still confident of the outcome, if only because there had been no real need for Säid to refer the matter to the Porte in the first instance. He had done so, as Edgar-Bonnet says, 'as an act of respect towards his suzerain rather than a specific request'. The precedent was clear. The Act by which Mohammed-Ali's dynasty was established had no provision to allow the Porte to interfere in the internal affairs of Egypt; and accordingly the late Abbas Pasha, that most punctilious Turk, had not thought it necessary to refer his railway project to the Sultan, though Austria and France promptly protested that he should have done so. They had been overruled by the British Ambassador, Lord Stratford de Redcliffe, who was now doing his utmost to prevent Säid from acting independently in what amounted to a parallel case. For if the railway was an 'internal' matter, so surely must the canal be also, since both traversed only Egyptian territory. Lesseps had heard that Stratford was personally opposed to the canal, but also that no instructions in the matter had been received from London. It was therefore with his usual ebullience that he accepted Stratford's invitation to dinner, and after the meal he turned on the impressive power of his enthusiasm. The two men seemed to have formed a definite respect, if not a liking, for one another, and Stratford did not conceal his private appreciation of what the canal might accomplish; but he terminated the interview by saying: "Your explanations are all very fine. If you succeed the affair will doubtless bring you much honour. But for a hundred years it will not be practicable. The moment is inopportune." To which Lesseps replied: "If it is inopportune for you who do not want it, it is opportune for me who do want it. Why postpone it for a hundred years? Since I have complete faith in the outcome I am in a hurry to make a start. And you: you ought to be in even more of a hurry."

The thrust was shrewd. Neither of them was any longer young, and if Lesseps could not expect to live to see his dream's fulfilment, then Stratford was even less likely to be present at the inauguration. To almost anyone but Lesseps the hint would have been sufficient, but his skin was already thickening. He was no sooner back where he was staying than he wrote a long note proposing himself for the following afternoon, to complete

Lord Stratford's conversion. In reply he received a neat but kindly snub:

"I am writing to you early not only to acknowledge receipt of the papers which accompanied your note, but also to ask you to put off until some other day the visit which you propose. Business which I cannot postpone prevents me from accepting your offer for to-day. You are right in thinking that I wish to study the subject. My desire is not less than it would be in relation to any other great enterprise touching the interests of more than one State, and which, though attractive enough in theory, evokes divided opinions on the practical level. Sir, you have too much insight and experience to take it ill that I stand where I do. The various matters which you have dealt with so tactfully and in a manner complimentary to myself, nevertheless belong to the sphere of high politics. In a position such as mine, personal independence has its limits and should withdraw before the exigencies of duty."

Even then Lesseps would not give up. Though he did not again try to see Stratford privately, he sent him a full report on the canal and covered it with a letter setting forth his own answers to what he conceived were Stratford's real objections. They were wide of the mark. Realizing at last that Stratford was the real source of delay over the ratification of the firman, he then betook himself to the Grand Vizier, Reschid Pasha; no doubt to represent that the British attitude was an affront to the Sultan. But Reschid was a realist, one of the few men upon whom Lesseps could make no impression. An aristocrat, he had been educated in England and France without coming under the spell of Progress; and he cared far less for the squabbles of the West than he did for peace at home. It was enough for him that the canal might stir up trouble, and he had no desire to see Säid grow strong; but he nevertheless allowed Lesseps to believe that he would do everything necessary to get the required ratification. So confident was Ferdinand that he even arranged for his departure on the date when the documents would be ready. The day came, but instead of the Sultan's unqualified approval, the official envelope contained only a request for more details, that perennial standby for procrastinating bureaucracy. Now thoroughly roused, Ferdinand cancelled his passage and again tackled the Vizier, with the same result as before. The matter, said Reschid, was in hand. He would see it through. Monsieur de Lesseps would, however, appreciate that official channels dis-

like haste. Perhaps it would hardly be worth his while to continue to stay in Constantinople when no doubt his valued
presence was urgently required by the Viceroy. So Ferdinand
departed with no more progress made than is represented by
the following letter to the Viceroy from the Vizier:

"Your very humble servant has the honour to inform you in
the matter following . . . Monsieur Ferdinand de Lesseps is about
to return to Your Highness, who, having deigned to introduce
him, may be assured that he merits every consideration and
respect. He came here with regard to the matter of the canal, a
most praiseworthy enterprise. I have had the good fortune to see
him on several occasions during his stay in Constantinople and
have discussed with him at length a number of subjects. He has
also had the honour of being presented to His Highness the Sultan,
and to be the recipient of the highest favours from him. In conformity with the Imperial Directive on the interesting subject of
the canal, the matter is at this moment receiving the attention of
the Council of Ministers. Monsieur de Lesseps, unable to await the
outcome of these deliberations, has arranged for his departure. I
hope shortly to communicate to Your Highness the result in detail.
L. S. MOUSTAFA-RESCHID."

*   *   *

The real situation, of which Lesseps still remained almost completely ignorant, was as follows. The Vizier had been playing
with him and so had Stratford. As early as January they had
discussed the implications of the canal in secret and agreed to
oppose it. There may have been no need for Stratford to use
persuasion, still less a threat of force, for recent history read
the same way both to the Turk and to the Englishman. They
shared two great anxieties, the power of Russia and the potential
power of Egypt, either of which could bring down the remnant
of the Ottoman Empire. As far back as 1838 Lord Palmerston,
then Foreign Secretary, had written:

"The Cabinet agreed that it would not do to let Mehemet-Ali
declare his independence, and separate Egypt and Syria from the
Turkish empire. That would result in a conflict between him and
the Sultan, the Turks would be defeated, the Russians would fly
to their aid, and a Russian garrison occupy Constantinople and the
Dardanelles, which, once in their possession, they would never quit.
We are prepared to give naval aid to the Sultan against Mehemet,

and intend to order our fleet to Alexandria, so as to give Mehemet an outward and visible sign of our inward resolve. We should like the French to go there at the same time. I write this on the supposition that France is honest, and can be trusted. It must not be forgotten that one great danger to Europe is the possibility of a combination between France and Russia which, though prevented at present by the personal feelings of the Czar, may not always be as impossible as it is now."

Had the Czar only listened to his own Foreign Office, particularly in the days of Barthélemy de Lesseps, Palmerston's nightmare might well have become a reality. Instead came the Retreat from Moscow, and thence an accountable fear of Russia in France, which grew steadily until the outbreak of the Crimean War. In his book *Histoire de la Turquie* (1855) Lamartine wrote:

" No, Europe is not reduced to the extremity of having to resign herself to the omnipotence of Russia as though to the rod of destiny. In breaking out, the North has misread the times. Turkey is not dead, and the Occident, far-sighted and resolute, will defend in the Orient those racial and territorial integrities which, if they be lost to any one people, may soon be lost to us. The tocsin of peril for Europe rings in St. Petersburg. Extending from Poland to Persia and China, Russia already weighs too heavily upon the world. If one adds the weight of the hundred thousand square leagues of the Ottoman Empire in Asia and Europe, the balance of power is tipped; and the Russian scale will carry for all time the political and geographic hegemony of peoples. One looks to a Czar already recruiting his army from among 65 million men whose sole duty, as in the times of Atilla, is to die well in the service of the master. One adds to this power the potential of 40 million Ottoman subjects, and of 25 million Persians who already tremble before the advance-posts of Russia; 130 millions of men in the hand of a tyrant, to oppress 120 millions of others. What will happen to the Black Sea, the Danube, the Adriatic, the Mediterranean? What will happen to the French empire? Continental France can no longer move within her own frontiers without coming up against Germany, the advance-guards of Russia; or without touching Russia, the reserve of Germany. This is not the fortuitous and temporary coalition of 1815, it is an alliance in perpetuity. A single power, Russia, will dispose all things. Every evening she will be giving Europe her orders."

Not only had a new Napoleon risen to supreme power, there might also be a new Mohammed-Ali whose aspirations would be the more easily achieved through the construction of the Suez

Canal. It would physically divide him from the Sultan. It would earn the money needed for his war machine. It would provide a direct incentive to that militant Egyptian independence most likely to call down the Russians. So Lesseps had been wasting his time when he sought to convince Stratford of the canal's advantages. Had they been even greater than Lesseps himself believed, and had Stratford been completely persuaded that the scheme was eminently practical, he must still have opposed it because of strategic realities. To deal with those, Lesseps would have had to discuss not the isthmus but India, not peace but war. For the inevitable focus of the British appreciation was that the canal could easily become an unwelcome *casus belli*. From such a premise, definite if undeclared, it was inevitable that English statesmen should argue as passionately, and as unreasonably, against the project as did de Lesseps on its behalf. Each side sincerely believed that its own attitude alone was right and reasonable. But Lesseps at least looked to the future in terms of creative activity. The statesmen looked to the past, dreading destruction. Shut in by the blinkers of their preconceptions, neither could see the other's point of view; in default of which he was debited with the worst of motives. Edgar-Bonnet cites a *Times* article of the period which admirably makes this point. Unfortunately he does not give the date so the text is re-translated from his French : " It is one of the sorrows and infirmities of the human spirit that nothing good nor great is accomplished on earth without coming up against the gloomy, the jealous, the alarmist and the pessimist, which by their narrow and vociferous negations pin down the world, immobile."

On the 5th February Säid received Lesseps on one of his yachts near the Nile Barrage, where he was handed the Vizier's letter. The Viceroy was delighted to see his friend and does not seem to have been unduly surprised or disappointed that more had not been accomplished at Constantinople. But he complained that he was being pestered, particularly by the British Minister, who was making his life a burden with threats of what might happen. This was in spite of the fact that officially both France and England had decided not to intervene, preferring to rely, for the time being, upon the infinite capacity for delay inherent in the traditional procedures of the Porte. There were, however, many ways of getting unofficial voices to reach the Viceregal

ear, which received a hint that England might support the
scheme if Suez were ceded to her, or, alternatively, that if it
were not dropped the fleet would bombard Alexandria. No
wonder that Säid was glad to see Lesseps, the one person who
might be able to sort the more outrageous fictions from those
which contained a few grains of facts. Between them they must
have concluded that Napoleon would have pressed the matter
at the Porte had he not been afraid, for the time being, of offending his ally England; and that England would officially have
opposed Napoleon, even at the risk of the entente's failure, had
it not been necessary to preserve a common front for the sake
of the Crimean War. As for the Sultan, he would have to ratify
the firman sometime, if only to show that he was not to be
ordered about, especially upon such a domestic issue. But when?
No guess was good enough, and meanwhile, because of the terms
of Säid's own Concession, nothing could be done. It seemed as
though Lord Stratford de Redcliffe had not been so far wrong
when he mentioned a hundred years.

To culminate these troubles news came from France of an
independent move to put forward, with adequate financial backing, the old Saint-Simonian plan for an indirect canal. It was
not so much the plan which was a threat – Säid said that he
would never consent to have Lower Egypt cut in half, quite
apart from the technical difficulties of the route; but how would
the Lesseps Company get backing if there were an effective
rival in the field? Even Säid, convinced *canaliste* that he was,
could not be expected to hand over large sums if the work might
be brought to nothing for lack of the indispensable foreign
capital. Then there was Madame Delamalle, warning Ferdinand
that he really ought to come back to Paris because there was so
much gossip behind his back, so many intrigues. Nor was hers
a feminine resentment that her protégé was not getting his due.
The Count was keeping in close touch with Eugénie, and was
equally disturbed by the Emperor's apparent weakness and
vacillation. If Ferdinand did not soon take the matter in hand,
his name and his dream would collapse as those of the Saint-
Simonians had collapsed, under a muddy flood of words.

Already what little standing he still had with the Quai d'Orsay
had been weakened through a request by the British Ambassador to be informed of the relationship between Lesseps and the

Government. The reply was that Lesseps had no connection whatever with the Government, and that he was acting entirely as a private person; a true bill, but something less than he might have hoped in view of Säid's *grand cordon*. And, as might have been expected, England did not believe it. The Foreign Secretary, writing to Lord Stratford de Redcliffe, summed up: "All that the Pasha and M. de Lesseps want is to dig a ditch wide, deep and easily defended, across the route which links Syria and Egypt . . . And they will do it at the expense of the dupes whom they will persuade to invest their money in the speculation; which the Pasha and Lesseps will liquidate after they have achieved their political object."

Soon Säid received a blow from another direction. Reschid had an influential friend called Kiamal, whose sister was married to Säid. Kiamal now took advantage of the relationship to pass on the real views of Reschid, which he had not dared to express to Lesseps: "I am pained to notice how Your Highness is throwing himself into the arms of France, whose government has not more stability than her agents. France can do nothing, either for you or against you. But England can do you much harm, and her agents are always supported . . . The Sultan is much annoyed. The only way to calm him is not to mention the Suez Canal."

It was a small but welcome compensation to Lesseps when Reschid over-reached himself to the extent of offending against diplomatic protocol in his effort to put pressure on the Viceroy. His letters evidently found their way to Paris, whence an official protest was launched and Reschid had to resign. So perhaps he was not quite so subtle as his reputation suggested. This little victory did much to cheer Säid, who had been badly shaken. It was one thing to announce his gracious royal patronage, it was another to have to defend its object against attacks which continually reminded him that his throne was in the gift of the Powers. His temper began to suffer, a foretaste of the oriental pique which later on he would indulge more violently. He must seriously have considered revoking the Concession, an act which at one stroke would have brought him not only peace and quiet, but an increased popularity with the two capitals which could do most to make his reign easy, London and Stamboul. But Säid's sense of loyalty was tempered better than his body, and though by a show of cleverness he might have excused such an act, on the ground that since the Sultan evidently did not intend to ratify it was his own duty to withdraw his patronage, he would not let down his friend. That Säid Pasha kept faith with Ferdinand de Lesseps when all the world seemed to have turned against them is a welcome gleam of sunlight upon a sombre landscape shadowed by intrigue and base motive. Had the Viceroy done what any cynical diplomat would have approved, and used his royal prerogative to drop the man whom he had raised up, the canal would have been doomed.

*   *   *

Upon the political level the order of battle was now tolerably clear, with Säid and Lesseps on the defensive against the English attack, hoping for some circumstance which would bring them help from France. Such a stage had not yet been reached either on the financial or on the technical level, all practical development being held up for want of the Sultan's approval. But while Lesseps was busy among the diplomats, Linant and Moguel had been working on their report. It was transmitted to the Viceroy on the 30th of April (1855) and in an unmistakable manner confirmed, with all supporting details, both the route and the specifications of the canal. It also confirmed the original estimate of three million tons annual traffic, and that a proper due would be at the rate of ten francs a ton: "Is this figure exaggerated? Will it be easily payable by shipping? The authors of the preliminary scheme can show that the economy resulting from the shortening of the route is of the order of sixteen francs per thousand ton-leagues. In such circumstances the tariff is legitimate and moderate."

In his covering letter Lesseps made it clear that though he had every confidence in the two Egyptian experts, he regarded it as essential that their report be submitted to the best European brains. The committee should assemble in Egypt, repeat the reconnaissance, and amend the plans according to their own opinions; thus providing as nearly an unassailable basis for the floatation of the Company as could be contrived – and confounding those who opposed the enterprise with the contention that it was technically impossible. The idea of a further reconnaissance

pleased Säid. It would save his face by giving him something
to do while the Sultan was deliberating. It would check all that
Lesseps and his own engineers had been telling him, and it
would provide a better international platform than the narrow
one on which he had so far been working. He began to take
courage again, and soon sent Lesseps off to Paris with two objects
– to discover the real attitude of the Emperor, and to resolve the
financial difficulties. If he succeeded in the first, the result was
not particularly encouraging. As to the second, he sidestepped
the issue by transferring his activities to London; but not before
he had succeeded in getting Napoleon to change his Ambassador at Constantinople, appointing a personal friend, loyal to
both Lesseps and his canal. On the 5th of June Lesseps wrote to
the Emperor:

"Since the two governments" (French and English) "have in a
sense undertaken not to act officially in Constantinople on the subject of the Isthmus of Suez, and to let the matter resolve itself as
between the Sultan and the Viceroy, it is essential to maintain this
situation for the time being. That is to say, without being more
precise, that the French Ambassador should refrain from pressing
officially in favour of ratification, and that the English Ambassador
should abstain from asking for any engagement against ratification.
If this understanding were broken by Lord Stratford, then Monsieur
Thouvenal would be free to act."

Lesseps probably thought that Stratford would not long
remain inactive, in which case the situation would soon turn to
his advantage as Thouvenal invoked the Imperial authority.
That assessment was shrewder than he knew, for at the time
Turkey was expecting that Napoleon would make a state visit
to the Sultan; and if it took place even Stratford was of the
opinion that as between the two heads of State, the matter might
well be settled in a spirit of oriental courtesy to a guest; necessarily in favour of Lesseps. The Emperor did in fact pass on to
Thouvenal the note which Lesseps had written and added
instructions that the Ambassador would do well to conform to
the policy it suggested. He then invited Lesseps to a *soirée* at the
Tuileries, where presumably it was not proper to talk business,
at least not serious business. Certainly the Emperor seems to
have avoided the question which Lesseps must have been so
eager to ask: in what circumstances would he act in accordance

with the promise given to Säid in the citation which accompanied the *grand cordon*? Instead the Emperor returned to a proposal which he had first made soon after Ferdinand's arrival, that he should carry out a publicity campaign in England. Then, having succeeded in gaining British sympathy and encouragement, it might be safe for France to take a stronger line. In the first instance, Napoleon suggested that Lesseps should address himself to the editors of *The Times* through the good offices of their Paris correspondent, Mr. O'Meagher, who had known him both in Barcelona and in Madrid.

O'Meagher furnished Lesseps with a lengthy appreciation of the situation with regard to the canal, so that the London office should be properly briefed. This document claimed that Lesseps had, up to now, refused to accept financial backing elsewhere in the hope that England would take up an appropriate share in the project, which was calculated to benefit her more than any other nation. O'Meagher added that on commercial grounds there was no serious opposition in England, and that the usefulness of the canal had been demonstrated by ' Sir James Wetch, Royal Engineers, and our celebrated author Charles Dickens'. Contrary to the ominous historical echoes which Stratford and Palmerston expected to hear, 'the opening of the Isthmus of Suez would increase the power of England both militarily and commercially '.

As to the financial side of the matter, Lesseps, as usual, went straight to the top. On the 14th of June he wrote to Ruyssenaers, now Ferdinand's official representative in Egypt as well as being the Dutch Consul-General:

"I send you a note written by Baron James de Rothschild, to whom I was able to render some service while I was Ambassador at Madrid. We have had the conference which he proposed. He asked me what my intentions were as to the financial organization, and I told him frankly that I did not wish to be committed to anyone. The matter still needed working out and uncertainties banished from the public mind. But the moment that circumstances permitted, he would be one of the first people whose assistance I should seek. Baron Rothschild was in complete agreement, said that I had adopted a very good method, and offered me all his services. When I told him that I was going to London he gave me a letter of which I send you a copy because it seems to me, coming from the prince of finance, one of the best symptoms."

To most people the note would not have been particularly encouraging. It was in the usual form of an introduction, commending Monsieur de Lesseps and asking the London House to consider his 'interesting information, of which, as do I, you understand the importance'. Nor was Rothschild the only string to the Lesseps bow: "Lord Ashburton, brother to the great banking house of Baring, London, has written to his family and friends in a manner most favourable to the Suez Canal; and I shall find a warm welcome among them." Financiers were naturally eager to see what could be done with such a great operation as the canal portended. What a splendid speculation it would be! And perhaps, later on, there might be a chance to gain indirect control of the Company. But Lesseps, much though he wanted to do so, was still not in a position to deal with practical matters. He had to wait upon a thaw in the political icefield which now held the whole enterprise in its grip. Not that he had the least intention of merely waiting. A passive attitude was one of which he was constitutionally incapable.

He arrived in London on the 24th of June, 1855, and though this was his first visit to England, the language appears to have presented no great difficulty. With characteristic drive, within four days he had arranged to be received by the Foreign Secretary, Lord Clarendon. In spite of the usual civilities, it was soon evident that he was fast upon the rocks, for Clarendon, while promising to re-examine the whole question in the light of what he had just been told, made it clear that the policy which the Government were bound to follow was necessarily hostile to the canal as a matter of principle. Undaunted, de Lesseps then decided to beard that old lion, Lord Palmerston, in his den. At first glance he had little chance of even getting inside No. 10 Downing Street, for protocol had already been satisfied by his interview at the Foreign Office. But, as usual, he soon found an appropriate social introduction, this time through Lady Tankerville, a friend of Lady Palmerston. The result was a private interview with the Prime Minister in his study, an encounter which must have been charged with feeling. The two men, so unlike and yet having in common a singular strength of character, conducted a polite, even genial conversation in general terms. The Prime Minister could not very well tell his visitor that he believed the canal to be a mere pretext for secret diplomacy in the Middle East, but very fairly, he did show Lesseps the firmness of his resolve.

"'I do not hesitate,' he said, 'to tell you my apprehensions. They consist first in the fear that the commercial and maritime relations of Great Britain may be upset by a new route, which, by accepting the shipping of all countries will cause us to lose the advantage which we already possess. I would also admit that I cannot be confident in the future of France, a future which any statesman must consider in the light of the most unfortunate eventualities which might occur, even though our confidence in the Emperor's loyalty and sincerity is complete. But after him circumstances may change.'"

He might well have added that they were already changing. In spite of success in the Crimea the entente was strained and a change of policy was no longer a matter as between Lord Palmerston and his French opposite number – or even as between the Queen and the Emperor. In both countries the rulers were still, in the last analysis, the servants of their peoples. Though Napoleon had been behaving as a dictator, the roots of his power remained firm in the soil of France. He knew only too well what was demanded of him as the price of his elevation: glory abroad, the rebirth of a hero myth and the satisfaction of the national vanity. This alone was enough to alter England's attitude from one of moral support against Russian imperialism to an understandable distrust of the Gallic equivalent. In the social set in which Ferdinand moved it was common gossip that Paris society was increasingly Anglophobe: "In December 1855, even before hostilities ceased, Napoleon was already dreaming of a great conflict of nationalities." First in the minds of educated people, and then through the lower strata, mutual distrust gained ground between the two great nations. The English expected the French to seek revenge for the fall of the First Empire. The French sought to redress the sense of inferiority which the 'luck' of Waterloo had injected into the heirs of the *Grande Armée*. No doubt intellectually the majority of aristocrats, soldiers, diplomats and business men desired the strengthening of the alliance. Every reasonable man must have thought along those lines. But where pride and the loyalties of the heart are concerned there is little room for reason. If in Europe the two nations found room to walk abreast, or even arm-in-arm,

Viscount Ferdinand de Lesseps
"He suppressed an isthmus."
From *Vanity Fair*, November 27, 1869

Ferdinand de Lesseps
From a portrait in the
Musée de Châteauroux

Napoleon III
Photo by Nadar

Empress Eugénie of France
Lithograph

Lord Palmerston
Likeness from last photograph from life

Ismail Pasha, Viceroy of Egypt

Culver Service

Mohammed Säid,
Viceroy of Egypt

By courtesy of the Suez Canal Company

The Suez Canal, from the Red Sea approach

An early drawing

Culver Service

The Suez Canal
View from the Plateau of El Guisr

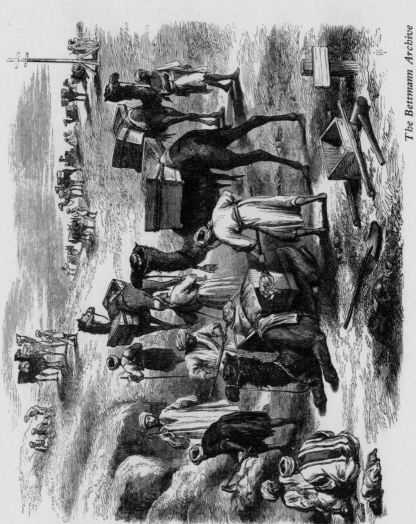

The Isthmus of Suez Maritime Canal: workmen loading dromedaries

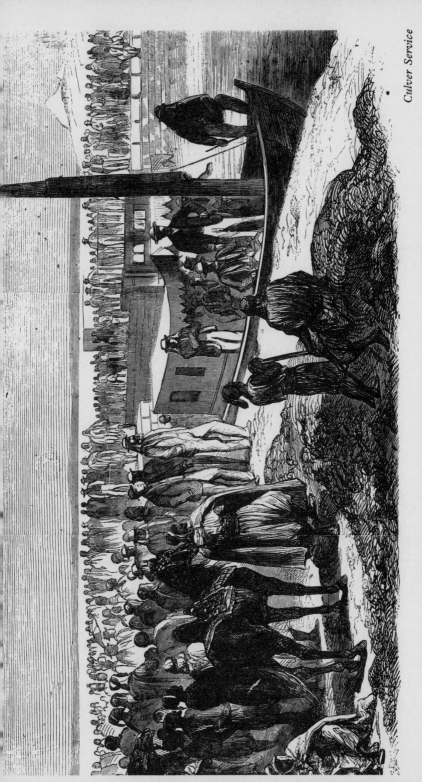

The first boat passing through the Suez Canal, on August 15, 1865

Ceremonies marking the opening of the Suez Canal at Port Said, November 17, 1869, in the presence of the Khedive, the Empress of the French, the Emperor of Austria

French and British officials being invited to a festival at Ismailia to celebrate the opening of the Suez Canal
From the *Illustrated London News*

Brown Brothers

Shipping on the Suez Canal enroute to the Mediterranean

Ferdinand and Hélène de Lesseps and their children

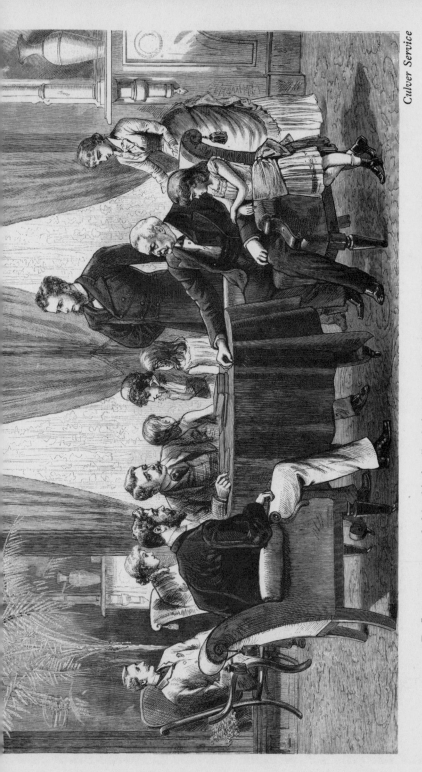

De Lesseps surrounded by his family, being interviewed in the Windsor Hotel, New York

From *Frank Leslie's Illustrated Newspaper*, March 20, 1880

Gulliver Lesseps among the Lilliputians
"The little people trying to tie down the strong man."
From *Frank Leslie's Illustrated Newspaper*, February 21, 1880

Digging the Panama Canal under the French

Panama under the French

Office of the Company, Panama, July 4, 1885

"Is M. de Lesseps a Canal Digger or a Grave Digger?"

that was no reason why England abroad should yield her pride of place, nor France neither. That for one the dominant position happened to be in Turkey, and for the other in Egypt, made for a basic attitude of wary suspicion which no amount of rationalization could modify. It could be changed only by the birth of a new fact. Both sides dreaded change, and so were fundamentally opposed to the canal, not so much for what it might become as because it was already an unavoidable issue.

As though to mollify any hurt feelings, Lady Palmerston asked Ferdinand to be her guest on the following evening at dinner. The French Ambassador was also invited and Ferdinand may well have thought that between the two of them at least some slight concession might be won. Palmerston must have been equally confident, and with more reason, that Lesseps was about to receive his *coup de grâce*. For he knew that the Ambassador, Comte de Persigny, sometime non-commissioned officer and, according to Edgar-Bonnet, a place-seeking snob, had become more English than the English. He would have been even more assured that there would be no more trouble over the canal had he realized that Persigny had a grudge against Lesseps and was working secretly against him, persuading the Emperor that to proceed with the scheme was perilous out of all proportion to any good that might emerge from it. He succeeded so well that Napoleon eventually agreed not only to go back on his word to Lesseps and his written undertaking to Säid, but even to authorize a joint Anglo-French *démarche* at Constantinople with the object not merely to postpone the canal but to prohibit it. The only qualification was that it must on no account seem as though the French change of attitude had been inspired from London.

So, though he did not feel it at the time, Lesseps was stabbed in the back by his own Ambassador. In all probability the world would have heard nothing more of him or his canal had he suspected such treachery. But he still thought that his only enemy was the traditional British attitude of extreme caution. He did not believe that England, nor even Palmerston, was actively hostile, merely 'fifty years out of date'. And he continued to think that as soon as the time was ripe the Emperor would come forward, take the canal under his august protection and make the enterprise a triumph for the entente, a common bond to strengthen, far into the future, the alliance between the two countries. But he was not so ingenuous as to suppose that Napoleon would act until some improvement had been effected in the existing situation, and, the political level being still frozen, Lesseps therefore decided to appeal direct to English public opinion. If he could only work up enough warmth among commercial interests, they in turn might thaw out the politicians, and then the Emperor would honour his undertaking. Far from indulging in despair, Ferdinand's agile mind was already leaping from branch to branch of the tree which he now proposed to climb until he stood at the top of an influential organization which even Lord Palmerston would neither be able to ignore nor to dismiss.

And if de Lesseps were able to change the British attitude quickly enough, then it would not matter that Persigny's plan had already been approved by the Emperor. Napoleon would much prefer to support Lesseps if possible; but the vital factor was now the sympathy, even the enthusiasm, of the British business man; which at first sight seemed unlikely to be in evidence. Everyone interested in the eastern trade realized that under certain circumstances the canal might be a great boon, but those circumstances were not yet in sight. New ships would be needed, better engines, and a host of navigational and economic problems would have to be solved before the new route could pay a dividend.

Such technical considerations, together with the complexity of the canal issue, were too much for Ferdinand's superficial command of English; and the fact that most of his speeches of exposition were made for him by his agent, Mr. Lange, no doubt contributed to a cumulative misunderstanding. He failed to appreciate adequately the British standpoint, and his audiences were similarly in the dark about his personal attitude on specific points. Even so he was a great success, both as an individual, and as the originator of one of the biggest propositions ever put forward to private enterprise.

Chapter 8. ORDER OF BATTLE

On his new tack de Lesseps found the wind of fortune fair. His circle soon included almost everyone of importance in eastern trade, together with a number of Members of Parliament and City personages. He was everywhere accepted socially, and his extraordinary capacity for inspiring confidence was soon turning indifference into friendly interest. No doubt some part of this change was due to a revival of mutual goodwill between France and England at the conclusion of the Crimean War, but it was from the personality of Lesseps that the indispensable momentum came. Everyone was talking about him, and the papers were full of his canal. Besides becoming a regular diner-out, Lesseps produced a series of pamphlets, notably: *The Question of the Isthmus of Suez submitted to English Public Opinion – 'aperire terram gentibus'* (London: July 1855). It contains the following paragraph upon the object of his effort and its scale:

"We consult with the India Company, the business houses of Australia, Singapore, Madras, Calcutta, Bombay; City interests, the ship-owners of London and Liverpool, iron-owners, the makers of machinery, the Peninsular and Oriental Steam Navigation Company, the Directors of banks and the great industrial concerns, the Chambers of Commerce, the coal-owners (who in 1853 exported 4,309,255 tons of coal to the value of £2,127,156, and who will, by the opening of the Isthmus of Suez, considerably augment this immense quantity). I am concerned with their interests. I await their judgment."

As to the last two sentences, the Prime Minister might have said the same. Grand strategy apart, in time of peace he had at least this in common with the wage-earner, that he too was ultimately a servant, albeit the major domo, of the employers. They were the people who paid the fivepenny income tax and whose aggregate business was the wealth of the country. So warm was the welcome to the Lesseps vision of an increased export trade, already the life-blood of the Empire, that on the ninth of the month he could write to Ruyssenaers: "With the exception of Lord Palmerston, English opposition is a phantom which evaporates as one goes forward." Sustained by a flattering clamour, either ignorant of or ignoring the silent forces gathering against him, he pressed on with the selection of a technical Commission, to meet on the Isthmus in the following November. As their duties would have nothing to do with construction, the Porte could hardly object; and meanwhile every week brought an increase of acclaim. In France this development caused the Persigny plan to be dropped, and the Sultan, 'sick man of Europe', was left as before, without direct pressure from either of his jealous nurses.

In August, when the people of his set were no longer to be found, except perhaps on a grouse moor or at a country garden-party, Lesseps withdrew to *La Chenaie* and there began the immense task of organization, not only for the forthcoming scientific Commission, but for the Company itself – constitution, membership of the Board, objects, intentions, plans, methods, finances. From the very beginning he had been determined 'to keep the reins in my own hands'. Indeed he had no alternative – an argument he had used against Prosper Enfantin; for it was to him personally that the Viceroy had given the original firman. Without him there could be no Company, and no canal. He made good progress with the paper work, and on the 13th of September reported to Theodore:

"I continue to receive gratifying letters and interesting documents. Tell our excellent Minister (Count Walewski) that the interest of the Empress in the canal remains and will continue. The reserve imposed by political considerations has not changed the feelings which she expressed when he took office, advising him to be zealous for the success of our enterprise. All the Ambassadors replied favourably to my choice of the leading engineers in their respective countries, who have been asked to join the international scientific commission. I have received propositions from capitalists and middle-men who want to take work on contract, to advance money and accept shares in payment – of course with a good commission. The moment has not yet come to begin such discussions. Without refusing, without putting anyone off, I leave the matter as it stands. I also have numerous private requests for shares, which I acknowledge with thanks but limit myself to writing down the applications. . . .

"In Egypt everything moves as though the Company were already functioning, quietly but surely; and the preparatory work is going forward towards the day when we arrive with the senior commission of European engineers. There is now on the Isthmus, along the projected route of the canal, a group of Egyptian engineers supported by half a batallion of sappers. They are taking a series of levels along the line, and there is another group making soundings at close intervals, so that we shall know in advance the kind of ground we shall have to deal with. The transport, tentage, and provisions for them all require 128 camels. . . . I am busy at work which needs a lot of care, drafting the Articles for the future Company. I have for reference the statutes of all the well-known Companies. My dear brother, I really ought to thank you for all you have done since the beginning of the scheme. You and Madame Delamalle have greatly contributed to the success which, sooner or later, is inevitable."

A few days later he wrote a long letter to Ruyssenaers, full of enthusiasm. His correspondence, always considerable, must at this time have been enormous as he continued to work upon public opinion:

"French, English, Italian, Spanish, German and American papers continue to keep their readers informed about the cutting of the Isthmus of Suez and to speak favourably of our enterprise. My French publication produced an excellent effect. The preliminary report of His Highness' engineers (Linant and Moguel) has been appreciated as it deserves. . . . Some English papers have made criticisms which I feel ought to be answered and I have asked Mr. James Wilson, M.P., founder of *The Economist*, the most important weekly review in England for industrial and economic matters, to do so. . . . You and the Viceroy, don't you worry about my suggestion that the choice of the chief of the enterprise ought to be submitted to the interested parties at some future time. That is how it is done in all big industrial concerns with shares. But to conform to the intentions of His Highness our statutes will lay it down that the first board of directors and its president shall be chosen by the Viceroy. They will stay in office throughout the duration of the work of construction and for so many years after the canal is open to navigation."

On the 25th of October *The Times* published a highly critical article which, far from doing Lesseps any harm, provided a well-timed stimulus for the next phase of his campaign. This consisted in publicity for the technical Commission, the membership of which had only just been completed. The attack was nothing new. It contended that the canal was not possible, or if it was, then it would be futile because shipping would still prefer the Cape route. On the 30th Lesseps wrote a long rejoinder in which he had no difficulty in turning the attack to his advantage by pointing out that no construction would be put in hand unless the best brains of the scientific world were agreed that it must succeed. As for the Cape route, if the long haul were really preferable, why did an increasing proportion of traffic pass overland, in spite of the expensive difficulties of the Egyptian transit? He then gave a list of the members of the Commission, all of whom were of the highest reputation. There were three from England: Rendel, MacClean and Commander Hewet, R.N., 'who has spent twenty-seven years in the study of the hydrography of the Red Sea and the Indian Ocean'. Italy supplied two, Prussia one, Holland two, Spain one, and France two – the Inspector-General *Ponts et Chaussées* and the navy's senior hydrographer.

"'Surely,' exclaimed de Lesseps, 'a Commission of such standing should reassure all misgivings and counter all distrust, uneasiness and timidity! Your correspondent cannot imagine that so many distinguished persons, charged with such an important task, and who occupy in their own countries the highest and most respected positions, are going to lend their names, in the presence of all Europe, to irresponsible illusions; or be so little concerned for their own honour and the pockets of the shareholders that they should treat their responsibilities lightly? To decry is the habit and the sole strength of base natures. To press on, in company with all men of goodwill, is the mark of the high-minded and creative persons. I owe, Sir, this public testimonial to your admirable paper, the first, by initiative and encouragement, to support an enterprise which will be one of the landmarks of our century and a memorial to the eternal glory of the Prince who conceived it and intends to carry it out. To-day all Europe desires the success of the work. It will witness to the impartiality and understanding which you lent to it; and I know that there will be your best reward.'"

*   *   *

Since Persigny's plot failed there had been virtually no diplomatic activity for six months; and the Sultan, for once permitted to make up his own mind, now did so in a sense unfavourable to Lesseps. Unlike other interested parties, he cared nothing for the commercial implications and was not susceptible to democratic pressure. He had no need to wait for the report of the technical Commission, nor did he see the project as a great adventure. He had no respect for machinery and no liking for what the West called progress. Such views, however, were not for publication until the Powers had reached a final impasse, and so the secret of the Sultan's veto did not go beyond his Inner Council. Lesseps remained in ignorance that another court card had been played against him, one which could not be trumped by anything in this three-suit pack, the diamonds, spades and clubs of international business, where there are no hearts.

He felt fairly safe. It would be an obvious tactical error for any opponent to attack before the Commission reported. Their criticism would provide the enemy with ammunition; their commendation would be the best defence, particularly against the charge that the task was impossible. That bludgeon would have to be exchanged for a rapier, or even poison of the kind which had proved so effective in the Rome affair. But the time was not ripe. Friends and enemies alike were still excited by the grandeur of the project, as though it were an idol of the Religion of Progress, symbol of the thrusting technical competence of which the temple was the Crystal Palace – which three years before had housed the Great Exhibition. In fine, popular opinion saw the canal less as a specific work of engineering than as an almost Saint-Simonian portent, omen of peace and plenty.

Fortunately for Lesseps, Säid also saw it in that light. In spite of his shortcomings he was a sincere follower of progress, and sought to make Egypt a prosperous country within the network of industrial states which he had been brought up to believe would beneficently rule the world. With more luck and better judgment he might have been an Egyptian Ataturk. If he was extravagant in public works he had a precedent in the railway mania of the forties. Relatively, the Viceroy's enthusiasm for investment was less speculative, more understandable and rather pathetic. For, at least at the beginning of his reign, it was his belief that if only he undid the reactionary work of Abbas and forced Egypt to catch up with France, then France would in turn bless Egypt, and all the costs would be repaid with interest. It was his desire to do well which first brought him into public debt, and at the end it was not so much he as his creditors who robbed the country of the harvest for which, in the canal as in other matters of modernization, he was now lavishly sowing. His next meeting with Lesseps was on the 19th of November, 1855, another crucial day with a good omen, Ferdinand's fiftieth birthday:

"On the Damietta branch of the Nile.
Yesterday at three o'clock I left Alexandria by rail, and at seven I was at Kaferlais, where a steamer was waiting to take me to the Barrage. This morning the Viceroy passed by with his flotilla of steamers. He stopped, sent a boat, and when I was aboard, threw himself into my arms and embraced me very cordially. He was visibly moved. His first words were the most friendly possible. I had luncheon with him and we talked for four hours. All our plans for future operations have been concerted just as I wished. He wants all the members of the Commission and my companions to be his guests. He will give them the best welcome and splendid hospitality."

The companions of Lesseps were his eldest boy, Charles, then fifteen, and two neighbours from La Chenaie called Lafosse. The Viceroy received the Commission on the 23rd, and promptly sent the whole party up river to enjoy a short break before beginning their labours on the Isthmus. On the 7th of December Madame Lafosse wrote to Madame Delamalle:

"Up to now it has been enchantment upon enchantment. This Assuan where we now are is enough to dazzle European eyes. There is nothing like its boiling cataracts, the rolling black waves, huge and superb. The women are the most lovely Florentine bronze colour and the children are delightful. In fact everything is most agreeable and attractive; but the heat is really tropical, which makes me think of the Nubians, who wear practically nothing, as being well off. There is usually something to replace the fig-leaf after they are eleven or twelve, and under twelve the boys gird their loins with a little palm-frond cord. Remembering my age I can view all this without shuddering with horror; and I can even assure you that they are usually well set up and quite a pleasure to look at. The bronze colour of the skin stops one thinking about it being indecent. How lucky we are to be making such a journey in so much comfort! Luncheons and dinners are sumptuous. Everyone has five glasses and there are five kinds of wine to fill them. Champagne flows as though it filled the Nile. The Commission is always good-humoured. They sing, they laugh, and they are full of enthusiasm for the Suez Canal. I don't suppose there will be the slightest bit of opposition. You need not have the least anxiety. All that your dear Ferdinand has put into it in the way of energy, talent and skill, will be returned in good success which will cover him with glory. You know, you will have to be proud of your son-in-law when that happens. An Englishwoman, the wife of one of the Commissioners, was telling me yesterday that she is in heaven because one eats so well. And, 'Ah,' said she, 'isn't Monsieur de Lesseps handsome? And his son – what a good-looking young man!'"

Even the older members of the Commission waxed poetical over the beauties of the scenery, the magnificence of the Pharaoic monuments, the sense of time and destiny; yet not all their impressions were so solemn: "Those lovely days! Those days of fish, cactus, girls of eighteen and the cries of the camels." All too soon the magnificent free holiday was over and the boats returned to Cairo, where Lesseps stayed with Ruyssenaers for two days while he completed the complicated arrangements for the desert journey to Suez – which was also to be made not by the Commission only but by the whole party. On Christmas Day, Madame Lafosse again wrote to Madame Delamalle:

"Dear and good friend, nothing new. We love you always, Monsieur Lafosse and I. Our last word, written in the shadow of our camels, was for you. Since then we have been separated, and we have left your excellent son-in-law at Suez, surrounded by *savants*. That dear 'son of the sun' as they call him – he no longer warms us with his sacred fire, but his beneficent light is still with us even here, and when we utter his name it is everywhere, 'Open Sesame'. You know that we left Cairo in a caravan. I was in a palanquin, *chère amie*, neither more nor less than a Sultana. Always *The Thousand and One Nights*. You cannot imagine the fairy-tale look of our caravan, 170 camels and 30 dromedaries, splendidly furnished with oriental carpets, some of them fringed with gold, and Angora goat-skins dyed cerise. The men with their white *burnous* and their heads covered Indian-fashion with strips of gauze wound round and round; and the Bedouin escort with their red cloaks and damascened arms, are really splendid. I can still see myself, surrounded by all that, dining in the middle of the desert upon roast gazelle. Here they hunt gazelle as we do hares at La Chenaie. It is delicious, much better than roe-deer.

"The desert seems awe-inspiring and vast, but less sad than I expected. And, just so that we lacked for nothing, there were the most remarkable mirages, with water, woods, and lovely *châteaux* surrounded by trees! It is not imagination. Everyone saw the same. What is so odd is that one sees exactly as though the scene were reflected in a lake. And it certainly isn't hunger and thirst which makes one see mirages. The Commission does not at all suffer in that way. Even in the desert they still serve Champagne. In spite of the prohibition in the Koran, the escort of the Viceroy's guards take it in their gourds, made from a kind of wrinkled coconut. One of these Arabs, a Pasha if you please, whose tongue had probably been loosened by the Champagne, told us that he had had 280 children. Since he was the governor of a province his companions thought it quite likely. One imagines that such men must lead very busy lives."

* * *

Before the Commission began its serious work, which would take the members all the way to Pelusium, de Lesseps addressed them on behalf of the Viceroy. He made it forcibly clear that they were required to act entirely as their knowledge and conscience might dictate. They were to avail themselves of all the data which had been collected on the subject but under no circumstances were they to be bound by it. They were at liberty to reject the whole scheme as put forward by Linant and Moguel, or any part of it; and they were to take into consideration any alternative which might seem practicable. In a week or so the Commission returned to Cairo and gave their preliminary findings in unequivocal terms. The indirect route *via* the Nile they found extremely difficult if not impossible. The direct route, as envisaged by de Lesseps, they entirely approved, even to the costing; with the relatively minor amendment that the Mediterranean port should not be near Pelusium but twenty-eight kilometres farther west – the present Port Säid. "The work," they concluded, "is easy and success is certain. The results in terms of world commerce will be immense."

Lesseps walked on air. Though before putting their names forward, presumably he must have been fairly sure of the general views of the delegates, it was wonderful to have this unanimous expert opinion. After all, he was not an engineer, and though Linant and Moguel were well up in their particular field, they were necessarily somewhat out of touch with mechanical developments and scientific matters generally. Happily he wrote to Madame Delamalle assuring her that after this triumph it could not be long before the first blow of the pick would inaugurate the actual work of construction. He felt that nothing could now stop him. He believed that Science was invincible and that he had been given its sword. On the 17th of February he left Egypt for Paris with the intention of introducing into the Peace Treaty, then being drawn, a clause by which the Powers would guarantee the perpetual neutrality of the canal. This, he thought, would finally scotch any opposition on the part of the Porte, or even Palmerston. It might have done; but the conference had more pressing business to consider, and in spite of his influence Lesseps was unable to even gain formal consideration of his proposal.

This setback does not seem to have worried him in the least. Blithely he went on to London, where he again secured a private interview with the Prime Minister, no doubt with the intention of presenting him with what was virtually an ultimatum, that with or without England, the canal would soon be begun. He walked into a brick wall. Not only was Lord Palmerston completely unimpressed by the Commission's evidence, he told Lesseps that Lord Stratford de Redcliffe would now be instructed to press the Sultan to use his veto. On the 7th of April Lesseps wrote of the interview:

"I found Lord Palmerston just where he was in 1840, full of mistrust and prejudices with regard to France and Egypt. He was very polite and in some ways extremely frank. . . . But he spoke to me with regard to the Suez Canal in the most contradictory, incoherent, and, I will even add, the most senseless fashion imaginable. He is firmly convinced that France has long pursued the most Machiavellian policy in Egypt against England, and that the fortifications of Alexandria were paid for by Louis-Philippe or his Government. He sees in the Suez Canal the consequences of this policy. Upon the other hand he insists that the execution of the canal is materially impossible, and that he knows more about it than all the engineers in Europe, whose opinions will not alter his. Then, regardless of the fact that he had just proved the scheme to be impracticable, he indulged in a long tirade upon the drawbacks which would result for Turkey, and for Egypt herself, from the Viceroy's Concession and the realization of the enterprise. Finally, without any sort of reticence, he declared he would continue to be my adversary. I could not help asking myself whether I was in the presence of a statesman or a maniac."

Palmerston may well have asked himself the same question. Particularly when confronted with opposition not amenable to argument, Lesseps was apt to lose all subtlety and seek to break through to his objective by sheer oratory and emotional intensity. In this way he often succeeded in projecting to his audience his own conviction, not so much because of what he said as by the way he said it. Veteran of so many debates, Lord Palmerston was the last man likely to be impressed by such a manner. Indeed, it would have made a very bad impression, suggesting that there was nothing solid behind the airy words; and if that were so, then Lesseps must be either a knave or a fool. So Palmerston was more than ever convinced that the whole fantastic scheme was cover for a strategic plot, to which Lesseps might or might not be privy. In either case his promotion of the Company appeared to be a palpable fraud. Whether construction was in fact feasible, or what the commercial results would be, were quite secondary considerations. Suez, even Egypt, was small beer in comparison with the overriding realities which it seemed that Lesseps obstinately would not recognize.

In fact he could not. His fanatical one-track mind made him see the canal out of proportion, as an altar of dedication if not of sacrifice. A cooler head would have realized that in trying to batter down the Prime Minister's prejudice he was only destroying his own case. A wider vision would have seen the Englishman's attitude clearly and understood from its very inconsistencies the entirely natural assumption from which they all sprang. For how could Palmerston have told this Frenchman that in spite of the public rejoicing on both sides of the Channel, over the peace treaty which had been signed in Paris on the 6th of March, Napoleon was already showing symptoms of the same ambitions which had led his great namesake into Egypt in the first place? Palmerston had come to distrust Napoleon, and he was by no means alone in his suspicions. At the Horse Guards officers were planning a ring of forts round the island against the day when the Emperor's juggling with the principle of self-determination should provoke an invasion attempt. Nor were they without justification for their anxieties. The strategists of the 1850's regarded the marine propeller much as their successors of the 1940's regarded the airscrew. Both were potential weapons which yet might break Britannia's shield, although to Bonaparte it had proved impregnable.

With his diplomatic background and training Lesseps should have taken such factors into consideration, but he appears to have ignored them, and so gave the old man – he was seventy-two and feeling older, an impression of dangerous irresponsibility; not only because of the canal but also because of his friends in high places. Doubtless Palmerston would have preferred not to have received him at all, but dared not risk appearing uncivil. As usual at the end of a war, the country was ready for a change of government, and he needed every supporter he could find. He quite expected that he might soon be out of office, and even if he were returned the Queen was quite capable of refusing to accept him as her Minister. She had already dismissed him once, six years earlier. She disliked his independence, his high-handed actions and his unalterable opinions, which were so often justified by events. Napoleon and his Empress would soon be at Osborne as her guests. It would never do to have Eugénie complaining that Ferdinand de Lesseps had been badly treated.

Both the Queen and her Consort had received Lesseps and formed a good impression of him. Albert had been particularly encouraging, as was natural for a man with his interests, the promoter of the Great Exhibition. He evidently regarded Lesseps as another apostle of progress and accorded him a long private interview at which he frankly supported the canal. Nor did he speak only for himself: "He told me that the Duke of Brabant was interested in the enterprise and had already commended it to him. I was received in the kindest way by the Duke of Cambridge, who expressed to me very freely and without the slightest reserve, his sympathies with the project." The state visit took place in the following August, when the canal was evidently a favourite topic. Since Napoleon's only reason for holding back was his fear of England, he would hardly have concealed his real feelings from Victoria, who must also have been impressed by Eugénie's emotional and idealistic views. Victoria already regarded her with admiration, reputedly because at first meeting the Empress had made the most beautiful curtsey imaginable. Since Albert was already converted, it may be assumed that when the Prime Minister and the French Ambassador were summoned to discuss the matter, Royalty was solidly in favour of Lesseps. Resolute as ever, Lord Palmerston

refused to change his tune, though he did have to agree with
the French Ambassador to remain neutral at Constantinople, an
engagement never confirmed.

*   *   *

Lesseps could now do no more in England where in business
circles the idea of the canal was now going ahead under its own
steam. He therefore returned to Egypt as a fool to his paradise.
For not only had he grossly underestimated the Prime Minister,
he was still ignorant of the intentions of both the Emperor and
the Sultan, and he was full of confidence in Säid who now
would have preferred never to have heard of the canal. Like
most people whose good intent is founded upon proud selfish-
ness, Säid soon tired of his toys. Unquestionably he had been
sincere in his original patronage of Lesseps, but at the time when
he gave the all-important Concession he had no experience of
power politics and could hardly have expected that there would
be any more unpleasing sequel than perhaps the boredom of
overmuch praise. Everything now seemed to have gone wrong.
Because of his altruistic impulse to perform a great public service nothing but trouble had come to him. On all sides there
were anonymous voices, whispering, wheedling and threatening.
Whoever wished to reach the Viceroy's ear would approach some
official, give a present, state an opinion; and in due course that
view would be current at court. Usually these voices emanated
from some consulate which could not officially say anything on
the subject. Even the French Consul-General was an undercover
enemy who held that the possible benefits of the canal were not
worth the risk of further offence to England. The English were,
of course, represented by Palmerston's mouthpiece; and, while
the Sultan's Inner Council were still supposed to be examining
the question, their agents poured more poison into the royal
stew which already contained so many noxious ingredients.
Like green corn the Viceroy's officers bowed to this new wind.
They regarded their master as expendable, and were anxious
to stay in office if the Powers should decide to replace him by
some more amenable puppet. "Poor Säid," they were saying in
effect, "he tried to please everybody, and now even the French
are against him."

" Almost the whole entourage of Mohammed-Säid bore towards the Suez Canal a hostility which did little to encourage him. The princes nearest to the throne did not conceal their antipathy. As for the Turkish officials, who, as in his father's time, occupied all the highest positions in the Egyptian administration, they were nearly all hostile; including the most prominent among them, Nubar Bey, who would play an important part in the history of the canal. Nor was that all. To declared enemies were added false friends; among them the French colony in Egypt, who were neither the least active nor the least dangerous. They had begun by being favourably disposed, but when the tenacity of Lesseps made it seem likely that in spite of everything the canal would not prove a chimera after all, then the French besetting sin, jealousy, began to play the dominant rôle. A whole clique of intriguers surrounded Mohammed-Säid. The opportunists, come from all the corners of the earth to prey upon Egypt, had very long teeth. Literature has crystallized their types, such as Bravay, the 'fixer' of Balzac, a person of mediocre character and the most obscure origins. It was after visiting Egypt that Alphonse Daudet created 'Nabob', Edmond About, and made him tell tall stories such as were then current among speculators: 'The Isthmus is a witch, seducing the capital of imbeciles; but we of Alexandria, we have things just as we want them. There are fifty or sixty amateurs down there who have nothing to do but to lunch by day and dine by night and drink Champagne. When they are down to their last farthing, M. de Lesseps gets hold of his gold mattock and *crac*! 100 million falls into their laps from heaven.'" (Edgar-Bonnet.)

The hard core of this Alexandrian opposition seems to have been due to the reasonable fear that when the new ports came into operation they would ruin the old town's trade. On the other hand there was suspicion that, for the Emperor to have deserted him, Lesseps must have done something wrong. And it certainly did seem as though Napoleon had turned his back:

" All through the years of uncertainty Mohammed-Säid put his trust in a definite word, a firm act, on the part of Napoleon III. With impatience he used to await each batch of news from France. Hardly had the mail-boat entered harbour than he would be demanding information from Ruyssenaers. Always he began in high hope, but instead of the Emperor's encouragement would come some new pronouncement by Palmerston, or a venomous article in *The Times.*"

The climax came when, unable to stand the pressure any more, Säid ordered Linant and Moguel to stop their preparatory work. "Your canal is a lost cause," he said. Fortunately Lesseps himself arrived soon afterwards and was as well received as ever. "You put me right with humanity again," the Viceroy told him. It did not take long for Ferdinand to restore confidence. At least for Säid, his faith was still highly infectious. Both in the ground and on paper the work restarted, if indeed it had ever completely ceased. In particular an employment policy was formulated, applying Ferdinand's idealism to counter the dreadful record of Turkish inhumanity. The original document setting out the general requirements and conditions was drafted by Lesseps and submitted to the Viceroy on the 20th of July, 1856. It is a model of straightforward language, laying down the basic simplicities for an extremely complex operation; and yet it proved to be the edge of a battle-axe which would split Egypt, fell Säid's successor, and with victory in sight, cause the labour force to melt away. The principal clauses are essentially these:

1. The Act of Concession contains an explicit assurance that the *Compagnie Universelle* will have placed at its disposal all the labour required. (The Act quoted is the formal one which confirmed the Viceroy's personal authorization.)

2. Workers will be paid a third more than they would normally receive in Egypt.

3. In addition to their pay, workers are entitled to food, accommodation, medical and other welfare services. "We believe this to be the first time that such services have been introduced, even in Europe."

4. Piece-work will not be required to exceed the norms laid down in Egypt by the Ministry of Works.

There is no mention of how the labour was to be supplied, but it was assumed to be through the call-up, that *corvée* which in Egypt, as formerly in France, was so much a national institution that hardly anyone could imagine how the country could be carried on without it. Though the system had lent itself to abuse, notably by Mohammed-Ali, there was inherent in it no more slavery than there is in modern conscription. Egyptian law recognized a profound difference between the *corvée* as the old villain-labour (predial slavery) or, in modern terms, the call-up; and *travaux forcés* or hard-labour, a judicial penalty as opposed to a social obligation. A large proportion of the population were in any case slaves, though in the Islamic rather than the western sense. They had to do what they were told, but they had rights under the law and in the Koran, which contains the injunction, " see that ye feed them as ye feed yourselves, and clothe them as ye clothe yourselves ".

In addition to a sincere humanitarian impulse, Lesseps had a strong practical reason for devising the best possible working conditions. They would attract widespread and most favourable publicity, not only for himself but for the Viceroy, whose reputation in England was under a cloud. Yet it was on this particular issue that the enemy was to come closest to breaking both Lesseps and his canal, not because working conditions were so bad as because the word *corvée* was equated with slavery, against which a passionate campaign was in progress. In Arabic there is no real equivalent term for slavery in the western sense. The nearest meaning is something like the state of being a chattel, like an Englishman's wife in the age of William Cobbett who declared, "Talk of serfs! Did feudal times see any of them so debased, so absolutely slaves, as the poor creatures who, in the 'enlightened' north, are compelled to work fourteen hours a day, in a heat of eighty-four degrees, and who are liable to punishment for looking out of a window of the factory? " Cobbett had been dead for twenty years, but conditions in the 'enlightened north' were still appalling; and to a large extent their alleviation would depend upon the Suez Canal which would reduce the price of manufactured cloth to the purchaser in India.

In spite of the new lease of faith which Lesseps had conferred upon the Viceroy, Säid became increasingly a prey to worry. He lost his hearty appetite and his sense of humour. His one desire was to 'hide behind a tree', and Ferdinand must have realized that such an attitude would involve a progressive risk to the canal. Indeed it began to seem as though the only factor which still prevented Säid from taking the obvious step of withdrawing the Concession was his sense of pride, of 'face'. It is a tribute to both men that he did not simply dismiss Lesseps, nor even make of him a scapegoat, to bear into the wilderness the whole responsibility of the failure of the Viceroy's glorious project. Instead it was decided that the best thing to do would be for both men to disappear for a time – out of reach of those with 'the long teeth'. Lesseps suggested a progress through the

Sudan to Equatoria, the former sunk in chaos and oppression, the latter still largely unexplored. From neither province had there yet emerged anything to Egypt's credit, least of all money or money's worth. Lesseps wrote in his journal:

"He was getting thin, poor fellow. I said to him, ' There's only one thing to do. We could study the canal. It is in the desert, outside Egypt proper; but there would be people even out there, and others would be sent to persecute you. . . . Let us act otherwise. There is in the Sudan a population which has been oppressed by your family. Your own brother was killed there, near Khartoum. . . . Mohammed-Ali sent one of his sons to collect the tribute which had been levied by his son-in-law. This consisted of 1,000 loads of straw, 1,000 loads of wood, 1,000 young males and 1,000 young females; all of which were duly brought to the camp. While the staff were at supper, local chiefs set fire to the perimeter.' It was in this context that the Viceroy agreed to come with me, alone except for a few soldiers."

It must have been hard for Lesseps to leave civilization behind. All over Europe and in America the pot of his publicity was coming to the boil. He could hardly afford to be out of touch with Paris and London where his future hung upon such a delicate balance. Three months would be required for the expedition, which would not escape the usual risks inseparable from a long trek among embittered people. On the other hand there was for the time being nothing which he could accomplish in Europe. And the situation might well change for the better while he was away. Palmerston might fall and a new House of Commons prove more progressive than the old one. In that case Napoleon might well overcome his unworthy hesitations, honour his promise to Säid and at the same time please not only Eugénie but also Albert, and therefore Queen Victoria. But a more personal consideration may have been the most important of all. At the beginning of Säid's reign it had been close contact with the Viceroy on his military progress which had cemented their old friendship upon a new basis; so now a fresh opportunity presented itself at a hardly less crucial time. Of the two personalities, that of Lesseps was by far the stronger, and he had the immense advantage of knowing what he wanted while Säid was full of a mere generalized intent to do well. But the Viceroy had no longer any private life, and it may be presumed that, if there were any agreement at all among Turks, Egyptians, and the foreigners who lived among them, it was to the effect that Lesseps was a dangerous power to have behind the throne.

Ferdinand himself must have been aware of this feeling, and though the canal filled his cup of ambition to the brim so that he had no thirst for any power of State, he must also have realized that the issue had narrowed to a simple choice. Either he was to be Säid's favourite, with all the consequences, or he had no place near him, not even for the sake of the canal. If after this long journey he could return to Egypt in the knowledge that Säid would never again withhold his personal loyalty, beyond mere patronage, then even the loss of influence in Europe would have been worth while. In all probability Lesseps now decided that, once quite sure that Säid would stand by him under even the most adverse circumstances, he would press on with the canal in defiance of the rest of the world. Therefore he suffered far more than physical injury, which was considerable, when an accident intervened to prevent just that intimate companionship upon which his heart was set:

"On the 26th of November my steamboat was still alongside the quay of Boulac when, towards midnight, I was in my cabin, which opened to the bridge. My mosquito net caught fire and in a few seconds the whole room flared up. After the first shock of the burns I felt the pain ease and thought it due to asphyxia from the smoke. I made a great effort and got to the door, which yielded. I burst on to the bridge, ordered the captain to cast off and get under way. Part of my body was raw. There were several second-degree burns on my legs. I had to be carried to a bed, and there, after covering my skin with cotton, the painful places were continuously irrigated with Nile water. Thanks to the care and the society of my travelling companions, Doctor Abbate, Motet Bey, and Vernoni, I did not even have fever. However, when the Viceroy came to visit me it was not possible for me to rise. I told him that my accident must be a good omen for the rest of the journey in that we had thus paid in advance our debt to bad luck."

* * *

When by the 18th of December the burns were still unhealed, the Viceroy left Lesseps behind. The cataracts prevented further progress by river and a long ride across the desert was clearly out of the question for an invalid. A week later, the lesions still

open, Lesseps would wait no longer. He could not walk, but he
had himself hoisted on to a camel, and for six days followed
the route marked by the skeletons of animals abandoned by the
Viceroy's caravan. He reached Abu Hammad on the evening of
New Year's Day 1857, after a ride of thirty leagues, and was in
time to offer to the Viceroy the conventional congratulations.
He was also able to help him through a mood of black despair.
From Abu Hammad the party took to the Nile again aboard
steamers based on Khartoum, and Säid was so much recovered
from his melancholy that at Shendy, where a hundred and fifty
thousand inhabitants had assembled, he created an excellent
impression. This was within the area where his brother had met
such a terrible end, and therefore the same country which had
suffered most from the vengeance which followed. The people
must have come into the town with a minimum of confidence,
but Säid, with two theatrical gestures, won them over. He had
a slave-owner chained in public for cruelty to a female domestic,
and he caused all the cannon from the fort to be thrown into
the river. Lesseps remonstrated at this, but was told that not
one of them was capable of firing a shot. Then Säid

"declared that he would send back into Egypt all the Turkish
officials, and would institute self-government through municipal
councils, which, since the beginning of the world, have been the
chief element in all organized societies. I was told to stay behind
for a few days in Shendy so as to superintend, with His Highness'
Ministers, the creation of the councils, which were composed of
heads of families appointed by election."

So it was Säid who first recognized the necessity for self-
government in the Sudan, and de Lesseps who took the first
practical step towards it. He must have believed that the cure
had worked upon his friend, that the melancholy mood was
permanently defeated. But on the very first night that they were
together again, in Khartoum, there occurred a much more
serious outburst than any which had preceded it:

"Scarcely were we settled at the dinner-table than I saw his
expression harden. He again deplored the impossibility of finding
a way to undo the evil which his people had wrought, and said
that nothing remained but to evacuate the country. . . . I reminded
him that he had the means to repair the damage and do good;

that with his absolute power he had only to will it and it would
happen. For a few moments he remained silent. I saw the blood
darken his face. Abruptly he got up, unfastened his sword-belt,
detached the sabre and threw it against the wall. His fury was
unbounded. He told me to go to my room. He declared that he
would spend the night in his hall of audience. None of the
ministers nor his intimates dared go near him. With them I went
into the apartments richly decorated and furnished for the Viceroy.
All night long we were on tenterhooks. From time to time we sent
a messenger who reported that his fury was unabated, and that the
Prince was striding up and down in an agitated manner. At three
in the morning he called for a bath, and at first light summoned
me.

" 'Lesseps,' he said, ' you once said that you wanted to explore
the White Nile. I have had boats made ready for you and your
party. They are to leave when you wish.'

" 'You were *souffrant* last night?' I asked him. He answered,
'It was not on your account. It was against myself. I saw the
evil but not the remedy for it. I was irritated at not having had
your practical idea about giving the country a code of law and
trying to organize it. When you come back you will find you can
be quite happy about me. . . .'"

So Lesseps, after being cheated by the accident of that
intimacy which he so much needed, was now dismissed. When
he returned to Khartoum it was to find the Viceroy already packing up to go north again. Thirty-two of his Albanian bodyguard
of sixty-five were down with what was, presumably, malaria;
and the courtiers were full of stories about the fatal consequences
of the climate upon those who were not native to it. There was
also a rumour that they who sojourn long in the Sudan ' can no
longer reproduce their species'. So Ferdinand had to rely on
the close companionship of the long journey back to Cairo, still
time enough to consolidate his position, particularly in that
Säid had been as good as his word and dictated what amounted
to a Constitution for the Sudan, together with various ordin-
ances designed to check the abuses which still went on. He had
even gone further and accepted as the new Governor-General
a man whom Lesseps supported, a very clear demonstration of
the influence to which Ferdinand had attained, particularly
since the candidate happened to be a Christian. Perhaps he
really had paid for bad luck in advance.

On the first stage of the journey the Viceroy's personal
physician fell ill, and with typical unselfishness it was Lesseps

who elected to stay behind to try to pull him through. Writing
to Madame Delamalle later he said wryly, that 'in spite of my
inexperience' he had bled the doctor – who recovered. It was
probably during this enforced break that he wrote his notes
on the subject of the journey into Equatoria along the White
Nile. Some of them seem rather naïve for such a man of the
world:

"'Adolescence begins at twelve or thirteen. Women do not bear
children after forty. Polygamy is universal and prostitution unknown. In Senaar during childbirth they are suspended by cords
against a wall. No travellers or natives have heard of the men
with tails (*coccyx saillant*).' He also records what must be one of
the earliest European references to Lake Victoria, 'M. Heuglein
showed me a manuscript map which had been sent to him by
M. Rehman, a Protestant missionary at Monbar on the Zanzibari
coast. This missionary seems to have gathered accurate information about an inland sea called Uniamesi, about which there has
been speculation for some time past. It occupies twelve to thirteen degrees from the north to the south, and would consequently
be bigger than the Black Sea.'"

By the time the doctor was fit to travel the Viceroy had such
a good start that Lesseps failed to catch up with him. They next
met in Cairo, where Ferdinand arrived on the 5th of March,
grateful that in all those miles he had met with no single
instance of hostility, or even lack of generosity among 'these
people called barbarians'. He found Säid with the new leaf still
turned:

"7th of March, 1857.   Residence of the Viceroy at Mit-Bire
                                    (Damietta Branch)
His Highness was waiting for me, and we were at once occupied
with orders for the continuation of the work. During our absence
all that had been asked has been excellently well done. . . .
Captain Philigret has completed his mission; in spite of very bad
weather his ship remained in the Bay of Pelusium on one anchor.
I shall publish his observations. The route of the Freshwater Canal
has been surveyed by M. Conrad and Linant Bey: the plans are
ready. The Viceroy is once again full of confidence, and no one
has yet tried to take it from him. Because the Princess his wife
has caused me to be thanked in a letter she dictated to Madame
Stephan Bey, it seems that he has been speaking in the family
circle of the proofs which I have given him of my genuine
affection."

Two days later Lesseps prepared to go to England for another campaign.

"9th March, 1857.   Note for His Highness the Viceroy.
Intending to leave for Europe within a few days, it may be as well to proceed with the collection of baskets, picks, etc., of which the numbers have been estimated, and we may now continue with the improvement of the working-sites, the making of bricks and the collection of timber."

It was on such a note of confidence, soon to be rudely shattered, that de Lesseps again left Egypt, to drum up recruits among the men of power and money.

Chapter 9. OFFENSIVE

Although the election of February 1857 had returned Lord Palmerston to power with a greatly increased majority, Ferdinand de Lesseps with fanatical zeal continued to mobilize British mercantile interests. Far from cooling off during his absence, he had found his welcome warmer than before. On the 24th of April he wrote from London to his old friend Barthélemy St. Hilaire, second-in-command of the canal's incipient hierarchy: "Yesterday evening I was invited to a big banquet at Goldsmiths Hall. One of the leading bankers of the City, Mr. Gladstone, was in the chair. The guests included the Bishop of London, General Williams, Sir Roderick Murchieson President of the Royal Geographical Society, Mr. Gladstone lately Chancellor of the Exchequer, and Mr. Ellice a Director of the East India Company."

Both the Gladstones spoke for de Lesseps, who said in his reply:

"'I am very much touched by your warm welcome; and since I owe it to my position as the promoter of the Suez Canal, may I say a few words on the subject of that enterprise, which is moving very close to realization? If some people still have doubts about the possibility of completing the work, I would ask them to read the report of the twelve engineers and shipping experts of the International Commission, whose competence is incontestable; and also the recent paper from the French Academy of Sciences, prepared by Baron Charles Dupin. To those who would object that the enterprise may be financially barren, I would say that they never achieve anything who do not believe in success. In that respect the firm offers of capital which I have received from all parts (of Europe) guarantee the success of the financial operation.

"'As to the motives of the political opposition, in my opinion there ought no longer to be any. It is difficult to see how any Power could sustain it. I certainly do not suspect England of jealousy against other countries, or of imaginary fears about foreign alliances which might affect her commercial and maritime prosperity. On the contrary, as the result of several visits to England during the past two years, I am happy to be able to record that public opinion completely refutes such arguments. The goodwill with which I have been received by this distinguished and numerous gathering is new proof that the canalization of the Isthmus of Suez, which will bring India closer to Europe and increase the importance of sea-power, will be especially profitable to the interests of Great Britain, which has more colonies, more commerce, more seamen, and more ships than all the other countries of Europe together.'"

He concluded the letter in high heart: "These words were warmly applauded by the audience. We may congratulate ourselves upon a good augury for the campaign which I am about to undertake. It seems to me to be a faithful echo of the true state of English public opinion." In which judgment he was substantially correct, since the public he had in mind were not the masses but men of influence, particularly the rich and thrusting middle classes. To them the canal meant only one thing: business. To the man in the factory it as yet meant nothing. As for the politicians, those of the free-trade, Liberal persuasion, such as Gladstone, were naturally inclined to favour it; but the diplomats cared nothing for business nor for free-trade neither. Their concern was with peace and war. Ignoring them, Lesseps began a tour of the Provinces where, at a series of meetings organized and attended by the chief trading interests in each district, he whipped up something approaching enthusiasm for the canal. Such a response, particularly to a foreigner, represented an extraordinary tribute to his powers of persuasion and the impression of straightforward, honest competence which he made everywhere. But there were also more hard-headed reasons for supporting the canal scheme. An expanding export market was now vital not only for individual trades or firms but for the country as a whole. What Director would not be ready to nod to a proposal which, at no cost to himself, promised to lower costs and raise profits?

In his speeches Lesseps kept strictly to practical considerations. He made no emotional appeal. He did not mention his friends at court, or the fact that the Pope had given the canal his goodwill, if not his blessing – an act quite remarkable enough to deserve mention. Lesseps did not imply a religious aspect to the enterprise, though it had always been in the forefront of his mind, not in terms of a narrow Christianity but also for the sake of Islam. If the canal opened a new missionary route to the East, it would also bring the Meccan pilgrimage within reach of many more of the Faithful. He chose his first platform where a favourable reception was most certain, in the Gladstone stronghold, Liverpool; and he was not disappointed. The canal would mean much, not only to the cotton industry but also to the shipping interests which brought the raw material and delivered the manufactured articles. With Mr. Laird, de Lesseps toured the docks and discussed the type of vessel which would best suit the new route. Mr. Laird's firm had just completed a small steamer, with a directional screw, designed for Dr. Livingstone's use in Africa. She was called *Day Spring*, and in her Lesseps, with Laird and Livingstone, puttered up and down the sprawling docks. Laird evidently wished to sell a sister to *Day Spring*, but Ferdinand concluded that she would be of no particular advantage to him, and he transferred his interest to the largest vessels afloat. The biggest he saw was the *Persia* of 3,500 tons, drawing 20 ft. Since in his view 'length and breadth increase but depth tends to decrease, a development which, among other advantages makes for higher speeds' and the canal had a working depth of 26 ft., he left the Mersey convinced that he would be able to pass the largest ships ever built.

Continuing his campaign, Lesseps in every city found a local bigwig to take the chair and enough of the right kind of people to fill even the largest hall available. His output of words, his mobility and momentum were prodigious. In just a month from the last day of April he attended eighty-four meetings or meals, without counting impromptu speeches and informal calls. To a second visit to Liverpool he added Manchester, Dublin, Cork, Belfast, Aberdeen, Edinburgh, Newcastle, Hull, Birmingham and Bristol, each of which passed substantially the same resolution: "That this meeting approves the project of a canal across the Isthmus of Suez, and is of the opinion that it will be of the greatest importance for the commerce of the world, and that it will bring about facilities to trade which no railway could achieve."

So great was the effect of this propaganda on the country as a whole that when he returned to London it seemed as though his cause must be already won, so far as English public opinion

was concerned. Had Ferdinand not been supremely confident
he would never have been so tactless as to allow Palmerston to
become his personal as well as his official enemy. Up to this
time, though necessarily opposed to each other's point of view,
the two men had treated one another with wary respect and
Lesseps had been socially accepted. He was not surprised therefore to receive an invitation from Lady Palmerston, as a result
of which the following interview took place:

"Lord Palmerston accosted me with, 'And so you have declared
war on us! You have worked up England, Ireland and Scotland
to agitate on behalf of the Suez Canal.'
"*F de L:* 'Certainly, my lord. I have profited from your freedom
of speech, which I admire because it has enabled me to discuss
everywhere in public subjects which are by no means pleasing
to the Government.'
"*Lord P:* 'You realize that I am quite definitely opposed to
your project?'
"*F de L:* 'I believe that the power of public opinion, which I
have just tested, will break down the resistance of individuals. I
would add that, more than ever, opposition is one of the greatest
factors in success. Only this morning I had a remarkable example
of it. I intend to print a large number of copies of the proceedings
of my meetings in all the big towns of the kingdom which have
approved the project of the canal. I asked the largest printer in
London for an estimate of the expense which might be incurred
in order to give the whole subject the widest publicity. When he
gave me his estimate I saw, I admit with some surprise, that the
largest item was for *attacking the work.*'
"*Lord P:* 'So you want my opposition? I am glad that our
relations are not to be disturbed on that account.'
"*F de L:* 'I want it so much that had I a hundred thousand
francs to give you for every speech you make against the canal
in the House of Commons; and if you were the man to accept
them, I would hasten to offer them. It is your opposition that will
stimulate the flow of capital to the enterprise.'
"However, in spite of his civility, I saw that Lord Palmerston
was not happy about the results of the meetings; and since I
realized that he still believed that the canal would damage
England, I waited for fresh news of attack by him. And next
morning he sent one of his agents to the Lord Mayor of the City
of London to ask him not to preside at a meeting which was to
have been held at the Egyptian Hall, the great room of the *Hôtel
de Ville*, and not to permit this to be used for the meeting.
The Lord Mayor, having told me of the embarrassing situation in
which he found himself, I said that it seemed to me that the Prime

Minister was striking at the liberties of the City. At the same time
I said I would gladly release him from his engagement and that
I would not make use of the Egyptian Hall. This incident, when
told to Members of Parliament for the City, caused them to
nominate one of their number to preside at the meeting, to be
held in some other place I was to select. It was much better
attended than it would have been at the *Hôtel de Ville*, and took
place at *la Grande Taverne de Londres*, usually employed for mass
meetings."

*   *   *

Lesseps now felt that he had such a following in England
that he could afford to ignore the attitude of the Government
and he accordingly went back to France with two main objects
in view, the next stage in the organization of the Company,
and to force the Emperor's hand by placing the work under
his personal protection. Napoleon had asked de Lesseps to
'conquer' England. It had been done – in terms of public
opinion. Now he could hardly have any justification for withholding official encouragement. Also a new factor had been
added to the complex equation of power. At Meirut on the 10th
of May the Indian Mutiny began, and now Delhi had fallen.
The British garrison were dead and a Moghul emperor again
sat upon the Peacock Throne. To Palmerston these events were
not only serious in themselves, they suggested that his worst
nightmare was about to become reality, that history would
recur, and the new Napoleon follow to the east the footsteps of
the old. More and more British troops would have to be sent
out to India, and, no matter by what route, they must inevitably
be difficult to withdraw. In comparison with France, England
would be temporarily weakened; so much so that if a crisis were
to occur, intervention in the Middle East would be out of the
question. Because of this sepoy revolt, not only would Napoleon
be able to make his canal, he could set about it with Egypt
already in his pocket. Nor would he have to wait for the triumph
of Lesseps before lending practical support to the new régime
in India. The first Napoleon had sent to Tippoo Sahib a
Phrygian cap – to that autocrat a singularly inappropriate
symbol of Liberty, and in his effort to follow it up he had
conquered Egypt. What would this Emperor send to Delhi?

For once Palmerston was quite wrong in his suspicions. The Emperor of the French had no such intentions. On the contrary, he looked to the new situation as a means of strengthening the Anglo-French alliance on which he had set his heart, and upon which depended his policy in Europe. He was aware of the British Government's misgivings and was determined to do nothing which could give them the illusion of a foundation. Much as he would have liked to take a stronger line over the canal, which threatened to become as embarrassing to him as it was to Säid, he could no more bring himself to do so than Palmerston could think differently. Between these two giants stood poor Lesseps, who, as usual looking straight ahead, could not appreciate the point of view of either of them. Plaintively he wrote to Napoleon to say that he did not even ask for a change of policy at Constantinople, only that the Ambassador there should be less openly Anglophile. And he had so much in hand that for the time being he could not even follow up this request; for, as the result of a question in the House of Commons on the 7th of July, his honour had been impugned.

"Mr. Berkeley, Member for Bristol, asked, 'Whether Her Majesty's Government would use its influence with His Highness the Sultan in support of an application which has been made by the Viceroy of Egypt for the sanction of the Sublime Porte for the construction of a ship canal across the Isthmus of Suez; for which a concession had been granted by the Viceroy to M. Ferdinand de Lesseps, and which had received the approbation of the principal cities, ports and commercial towns of the United Kingdom; and if any objection were entertained by Her Majesty's Government to the undertaking, to state the grounds for such objection.'

"The Noble Lord replied: 'Her Majesty's Government certainly cannot undertake to use their influence with the Sultan to induce him to give permission for the construction of this canal, because for the last fifteen years Her Majesty's Government have used all the influence they possess at Constantinople and in Egypt to prevent that scheme from being carried into execution. It is an undertaking which, I believe, as regards its commercial character, may be deemed to rank among the many bubble schemes that from time to time have been palmed off upon gullible capitalists. I believe that it is physically impracticable, except at an expense which would be far too great to warrant the expectation of any returns. I believe, therefore, that those who embarked their money in such an undertaking (if my hon. friend has any constituents who are likely to do so) would find themselves very grievously deceived by the result. However, this is not the ground upon which the Government have opposed the scheme. Private individuals are left to take care of their own interests, and if they embark upon impracticable undertakings, they must pay the penalty for so doing. But the scheme is one hostile to the interests of this country – opposed to the standing policy of England in regard to the connection of Egypt with Turkey – a policy which has been supported by the war and by the Treaty of Paris. The obvious political tendency of the undertaking is to render more easy the separation of Egypt from Turkey. It is founded also on remote speculations with regard to easier access to our Indian possessions, which I need not more distinctly show forth because they will be obvious to anybody who pays attention to the subject.

" 'I can only express my surprise that M. de Lesseps should have reckoned so much on the credulity of English capitalists as to think that by his progress through the different counties he would succeed in obtaining English money for the promotion of a scheme which is in every way so adverse to British interests. That scheme was launched, I believe, about fifteen years ago, as a rival to the railway from Alexandria by Cairo to Suez, which, being infinitely more practical and likely to be more useful, obtained the pre-eminence; but probably the object which M. de Lesseps and some of the promoters have in view will be accomplished, even if the whole of the undertaking should not be carried into execution. If my hon. friend the member for Bristol will take my advice, he will have nothing to do with the scheme in question.' "

In the debate which followed, Robert Stephenson, now an M.P., put the great weight of his own and his father's reputation behind the Premier's contention that the canal was impossible, and if by some miracle it should be finished, then it would be useless to the world at large and dangerous to England in particular. When the subject again came up in the House he went even further, and as a result of his remarks received a challenge from Lesseps dated the 27th of July:

"I send you a literal translation from *The Times* of the speech which you delivered on the 17th of this month in the House of Commons on the subject of the Suez Canal. I ask that you inform me whether the account is accurate. The engineers of the International Commission, who all their lives are concerned with problems of ports and canals, will themselves reply to the technical part of your remarks, but there is a passage to which I would call your immediate attention because it concerns me personally. According to *The Times* you said, '*I share the view of the first lord of the Treasury.*' And that Minister, whose office prevents me

from demanding satisfaction from him, had just uttered the following words, ' I think I am hardly likely to be wrong when I say that
the project is one of those chimeras so often formed to induce
English capitalists to part with their money, the end being that
these schemes leave them poorer, though they may make others
richer.' I ask you, Sir, for a written explanation of this matter,
either in person or by two of your friends whom you will put in
touch with me. I do not doubt but that you will make haste to give
the necessary explanation. I have come from France expressly to
demand it from you. I have the honour, Sir, to place myself at
your disposal."

At no time had Lesseps publicly suggested that he would be
prepared to receive money or to issue shares, and his speeches
had been confined to the construction and advantages of the
canal. Even had he wished to do so, there was as yet no organization which could have dealt with financial matters. If Lord
Palmerston, following Ferdinand's tactless remark about bribing
him, had exactly understood the jesting intent, he would still
not have found it funny; but owing to the insufficiency of
Ferdinand's English, it is highly probable that he took it with
some seriousness. In which case he could hardly be blamed for
concluding that Lesseps was no better than a crook. Of this
excuse, if such it be, Stephenson was ignorant, and so, of course,
was Lesseps himself. Possibly he forgot that he had even mentioned capital to Palmerston, certainly he thought that he had
been gratuitously insulted in the most public way imaginable
and under circumstances which prevented any recourse to the
law. It must have seemed to him that at last the years of exercise
with sabre and *epée* would bring their reward. If the choice
should be pistols he had ground for equal confidence. No doubt
Stephenson would be aware of his opponent's reputation in that
context.

Somewhere in London next day Robert Stephenson must have
sat down heavily with that letter in his hand. He was a sick
man. The law would be no protection nor public opinion a court
of appeal. He took up his pen and wrote:

"Dear Sir, nothing could be further from my intention in speaking of the Suez Canal the other night in the House of Commons,
than to make a single remark which might be construed as having
any illusion to yourself, and I am confident that no one who heard
me could regard what I said as having any such bearing when I

said that I concurred with Lord Palmerston's opinion. I referred
to his statement that money might overcome almost any physical
difficulties, however great, and that the undertaking, if ever finished,
would not be commercially advantageous. The first study which I
made of this subject, in 1847, led me to this opinion, and nothing
which has come to my knowledge since that period has tended
to alter my view.

Yours faithfully,

Rob. Stephenson."

The apology was duly confirmed and amplified by his seconds,
Mr. Charles Manby, Secretary of the Institute of Civil Engineers,
and Mr. MacClean, who was a member of the International
Commission. So Lesseps had to put his weapons away, but the
memory of the insult he could not erase, and it continued to
rankle, guiding his policy so that he decided not to attempt to
reap the harvest of his hard sowing all over the country. He
had of course intended, when the time came to open the lists,
that England should take up a large block of shares, proportionate to her maritime ascendancy. Now he resolved to con-
summate the union of the seas without her aid, financial or
otherwise. Alone if need be, he would drive his ditch against the
greatest power in the world; for not only had he personally been
insulted, through him the Legion of Honour, and *La Patrie*
were also impugned. Though nearly all the other trumps seemed
to be in English hands, he still held the ace, the Concession
itself. He would go ahead with the organization and with the
practical work. He would take the risk that the Viceroy might
turn against him, even at the price of offending France and
losing much 'face' because he had failed to keep his word. So
if Ferdinand had been cheated out of his duel, he could now look
forward to battle on a bigger scale. He stiffly acknowledged
Stephenson's apology, adding darkly that the International Commission would soon have something to say. Then, after a decent
interval, he went back to France and set about the mobilization
of all his resources, intending to launch them against the
Isthmus at the earliest opportunity. Not in London nor in Paris,
but out there in the desert was the place to heal the wound to
his chivalric pride.

*   *   *

Within four months, that is to say by the beginning of

November 1857, de Lesseps achieved on the Continent more than he had lost in England. All the chief towns and cities of France petitioned the Government on behalf of the canal. Prince Jérôme Bonaparte, the Emperor's cousin, became the Patron of the enterprise, and though Eugénie did not like him, between the two of them the Emperor found it increasingly difficult to remain neutral; particularly since Jérôme was 'nearest to the throne by blood, furthest from it by sentiment'. Born at Trieste, he was a tubby bachelor of twenty-six, with strong progressive ideas and a power of oratory. He had opposed the Emperor's *coup d'état* and although apparently tamed by royal generosity, remained a potential leader of the opposition, a man the more to be feared by the dictator because he was virtually beyond the law – at least until Eugénie should produce a direct heir. So Jérôme had to be humoured whenever possible, as for instance in the matter of the canal; for which he now solicited, at Ferdinand's request, those firmer instructions for the Ambassador at Constantinople which had not yet been drafted. Thouvenal, most anxious to help, was still there, and the position must have been most galling for him when Ferdinand, forced to look elsewhere for a lead, accepted it from a country with which France would soon be at war – Austria. But Ferdinand would now accept help from any quarter. He even tried to obtain American intervention:

"His Excellency Mr. James Buchanan,
    President of the United States of America   Paris.
       at Washington.   21st October, 1857.
                     Private

The honourable representative of the United States at Alexandria has shown himself most favourably disposed, in his own name as in that of his Government, towards the enterprise for cutting the Suez Canal. This consideration, and my family connections with the United States, where several of my close relatives have established themselves and become American citizens, authorize me personally to commend to you to-day the official letter which I have the honour to address to you on the present situation of the enterprise of the Suez Canal, which will shorten by more than 2,800 leagues the sea voyage from Bombay to New Orleans, Boston and New York.

"The liberal and generous policy of the American Union has always defended the freedom of the seas, and if another power, selfish and exclusive, should come to interfere with free transit

between the Mediterranean and the Indian Ocean, the principle
of the freedom of the seas would be seriously compromised. In
such a case the intervention of the representative of the United
States at Constantinople would be entirely justified in terms of the
national interest as regards the commerce and shipping of the
Union. Furthermore, the completion of the canal between the two
seas will one day be the most useful complement to the American
canal between the two oceans, which will later give the United
States the reason and the right to intervene in European diplomacy,
in order to ensure, with the help of France, this inevitable principle: Respect for private property on the high seas and the
abolition of blockade of commercial ports; extension to commerce
of an enemy the law which already regulates neutral shipping."

Among the skeins of power from which Lesseps was so
passionately winding, none is more significant of his determination to triumph if not with England, then against her, than this
evocation of a then recent grudge, this appeal for a global policy
which would require nearly a hundred years to develop. Much
though Mr. Buchanan would have liked to take England down
a peg, there were more pressing matters which required his
attention. The slavery issue was already becoming acute and
the country was in the grip of a great financial crisis. 'Almost
every bank in the United States was compelled to suspend payment in cash. In New York money was only procurable at an
interest of sixty per cent. Institutions in this country (England)
which had extensive dealings with the United States nearly all
felt the crisis. In the latter half of October and the first half
of November banks and other institutions in Liverpool and
Glasgow were compelled to suspend payment. The Bank of
England on November 12th was forced to raise its rate of dis-
count to 10 per cent; and, at the close of the day, its reserve –
the aggregate of coin and notes in the banking department –
was less than £600,000."[1] So this was no time for America to
embark upon an adventurous foreign policy which might commit her to both economic and military investment in Europe
and the Middle East. In spite of an industrial boom, it was
an almost equally unfavourable moment for British foreign
speculation.

So, in spite of having won over the business men of England,
in spite of the royal favour on both sides of the Channel and

[1] *Cambridge Modern History.*

of his widespread contacts in the highest diplomatic and social circles, Lesseps was still something of a Lilliputian figure on the world stage, and a mere petitioner at the feet of the Sultan. Neither the famous Lesseps charm, nor his unquestionable ability; neither his real power in Egypt nor the authority of his International Commission, could make any impression upon Stamboul, where the present was still but an echo of the past, sliding back towards Byzantium.

"The affair is in an impasse. Everyone is afraid. The Viceroy dare not authorize construction before receiving the Turkish sanction, and this the Porte dare not give, because of fear of England, and dare not refuse, because of fear of France. And England hesitates to force Turkey into a categorical refusal, while France dare not demand from the Sultan a definite approval. All the Governments are inhibited, and all their representatives complain. Each wants his colleague to take the initiative which he himself cannot take. Lord Cowley (Ambassador to France) states that in Paris the hindrances placed upon the Suez Canal are the cause of much bitter feeling. Lord Redcliffe, uneasy as to what French pressure might accomplish with the Grand Vizier, is asking London to make it easier for him to oppose it. However, this French pressure simply does not exist. . . ."

France was now in no position to exert pressure even had she wanted to do so. Following Napoleon's interference, however justified, in the elections of the newly created State of Rumania, diplomatic relations had been broken off. Nor was England much better placed, because it was now evident that the Mutiny and its aftermath would commit large British forces indefinitely to India. Under such circumstances not even Lesseps could hope to do more than mark time. Any other man might have given up altogether. Instead, he determined to attempt, single-handed, what influence and public opinion had failed to accomplish. At the sound of his trumpet the walls of Constantinople should fall like those of Jericho to Joshua, a bold, almost desperate act of faith to conceal from friends and enemies alike this echo of the Viceroy's sentence: "Your canal is a lost cause." Though to the world he kept up a show of confidence, he must now have come close to giving up the work which no one seemed to want because of base motives thought to be behind it. He was on the point of forming the Company. To draw in his horns now would hurt hardly anyone but himself. It would be much more painful to do so when the organization was functioning; and once the capital had been subscribed it would be impossible.

Before going to Constantinople he retired to La Chenaie for a brief interlude of domestic life, which must have added to the temptation to have done with the accursed waterway. He had hardly seen his children in years, and instead of the green countryside of France, rich with forests and rivers, he had been living in cities, which he had always disliked, or in the desert under even more trying circumstances. Moreover he had been always alone in the sense that there had been no one with whom he could safely share his secret thoughts. But his dream was still stronger than both his judgment and his desire. Instead of retiring again, as though after another Rome, he accelerated the growth of the Company's organization and himself began a third campaign of exhortation. Yet he by no means renounced the pleasures of being a parent:

"As I write, Victorinet is fishing, under the eye of keeper Pâris, from the bank of a pool. He is absorbed, and will doubtless bring us some huge fish. This afternoon we are going for a long walk in the gardens and through the woods. The keeper's ass will follow in case Victorinet gets overtired after the long run this morning. I hear on the stairs the voice of your young brother. He is shouting that he has caught a miraculous fish. He comes into the room where I am writing and shows me seven superb carp on a line. While jumping around he repeats that it was himself, his very own self, who achieved the exploit. After this explosion of joy and his account of the catch, he sits himself down at the poor piano, which is close beside me, and accompanies himself while singing the air of *Le Sire de Framboisy*. I embrace you, my son, and also your excellent grandmother, whom you cannot love too much. Shake hands with our good friend Saint-Hilaire. This morning I was remembering the walks we used to take with your dear mother. One need not think sadly about those one has lost. One should always be able to see them smile across one's cherished memories of them."

Early in November, Ferdinand left for Turkey *via* Vienna, and took young Charles with him. Almost at once his morale received a much-needed fillip and his mission a good omen, recorded in the Vienna Press: "M. de Lesseps arrived in our city at eight o'clock on his way to Constantinople. On the morning of the ninth a deputation waited upon him to invite him to a formal banquet. This deputation was composed of M. le Baron de Rothschild, M. le Baron Jean de Sina, M. le Baron Eskeles and M. Maurice de Wodianer." An account of the banquet follows. Lesseps sat at the centre of a horseshoe table with the most important men in Austria on either side of him. Having toasted, 'The Emperor of Austria and the Imperial Family', he spoke of making the canal a triumph of modern technique, a demonstration that what had hitherto been beyond the capacity of man was now, in this as in other fields, within his grasp. Other speakers emphasized Austria's particular interest in the canal, but omitted the obvious point that in the event of war with France it would prevent effective blockade. Finally, "Baron de Bruck, amid universal applause, offered a last toast – to the success of British arms in India. 'The celebration this evening,' he said, 'gives us occasion to celebrate that victory. And if at the beginning of the Mutiny the Isthmus of Suez had been cut and ships been able to follow the short route, then torrents of blood would not have flowed and most savage acts of barbarity would not have been committed. The events in India should be for us an additional motive to support with zeal and perseverance the most excellent work of civilization.'" The account ended with another testimony to Ferdinand's position in society: "Before leaving for Trieste, M. de Lesseps was to-day received in private audience by His Majesty."

There had been an unintentional irony in the reference to the Mutiny, which from the beginning Ferdinand had thought of as a decisive factor in breaking down England's opposition; particularly when it was reported that Nana Sahib had proclaimed that the Viceroy would close Egypt to the passage of British troops. The notion was serious enough to alarm the Viceroy of India, Lord Canning, though Säid would not in fact have dreamed of doing such a thing. Instead he had eagerly accepted the British troops and given every facility for further railway construction on their behalf, until the Alexandria-Suez line was complete save for a gap of some thirty miles, and the use of ferries instead of bridges. With this Lord Palmerston remained obstinately satisfied, and continued his personal and official opposition to the canal as though he had no notion of the enormous effort and expense of transferring large numbers of men and vast quantities of supplies from ship to rail and rail

to ship. Lesseps, he declared, was a knave and a crook, his project the greatest swindle of modern times.

Arrived in Constantinople, Lesseps for once moved with slow
caution, taking infinite care, through purely social activities, to
discover who were the men of real power in the land and what
were their sympathies. While this was leading up to direct
business talks with the Grand Vizier and the members of the
diplomatic corps, he sent Charles, who was seventeen, off to
Syria. On his return the youth was to begin his career at the
Embassy, much as his father had begun years before in the
consulate at Lisbon. Though Ferdinand usually made detailed
plans to which he rigidly adhered, on this occasion events in
Europe were moving so fast that he could not wait until Charles
returned before breaking off his reconnaissance and going back
to the other flank of the battlefield. Accordingly he wrote down
the paternal advice of which otherwise there would have been
no record:

" As soon as you arrive, go straight to Therapia with your baggage. The Ambassador has prepared for you at the *Palais de
France*, a very pleasant apartment of two rooms which will suit
you very well. The furnishing has been supervised by Madame
Thouvenal. I have no need to commend you to be with M. Thouvenal as you are with me, that is to say conscientious and ready
to do, with the greatest care and attention, any work or mission
with which you may be charged; but also, above and beyond work,
to serve with willing good humour, and never to show boredom or
bad temper. Being the most junior, you will always help the secre-
taries and attachés in their duties. They are well disposed towards
you and have accepted you as a friend. I have particularly suggested to M. de Vernouillet that he should be your friend. He is
a very capable young man, intelligent, and with his heart in the
right place. At any time when your inexperience puts you in need
of advice, he is well placed to give it to you.

" Take particular care in the translation of despatches. You know
how important it is to please M. Thouvenal in this. Our friends the
Aréons will give you the money you need for your personal
expenses. More than that I have nothing to say, having complete
confidence in your good sense and integrity. Your horse will be
kept in the Ambassador's stable. He has told his head groom to
look after it. You will yourself settle with the groom every fortnight or every month as to the expenses of fodder, etc., and you
will suitably reward his services. Keep your rooms tidy. See that
your belongings are properly set out and do not harm any of the
furniture. Be careful not to burn the rugs with dropped matches,

which should never be thrown down. Do not smoke indoors in the presence of M. or Mme. Thouvenal, even if they suggest it. If you do acquire this bad habit, which it is better to avoid, only indulge it in your own rooms, in those of your friends, or out of doors. Do not smoke in the houses of Europeans, or in the presence of ladies, even when other people are doing so.

"Forward to me all letters which may come to my address while I am away. Open them, and send to Paris only those which you think are worth it, that is to say those which contain interesting information, or which need a reply. I will write to you from Paris to say when I return to Constantinople. I suppose it should be a month if the debate in the English House of Commons on the 1st of June has a favourable result. Keep contact with all the families which welcomed us, but whenever possible stay in the French Embassy in the evenings. You know what the habits of most of these gentleman are like. It would be a good idea to make it clear that you are not among them in this context. I do add, however, that the rule makes for exceptions, but that the exceptions confirm the rule.

"At present Madame Thouvenal has her mother with her. You will show these ladies the care, attention and respect which your age, and their kindness to you, indicate. It would be difficult to find a finer or more distinguished woman than Madame Thouvenal. Her son Louis is friendly and pleasant. Treat him as a younger brother. You will write to me by every post from Marseilles and Trieste, even if it is only a few lines; but, before anything else — keenness, accuracy, and conscientiousness in your job at the Embassy."

*   *   *

In spite of his failure to make any impression on the Porte, Lesseps had every reason to feel some moderate return of confidence, for the political picture in Europe had changed considerably since he left France for the Middle East. When he told Lord Palmerston, at that unfortunate interview, that he admired the English freedom of speech, he had paid a sincere compliment. In France there was no such thing: "the liberty of citizens was placed at the disposal of the Government. If men talked politics they ran the risk of arrest, and there were spies everywhere, even in drawing-rooms."[1] The Press was rigidly controlled. Without Government sanction it would not have been possible for Lesseps to have carried out his campaign in his own

[1] *Cambridge Modern History.*

country. Much the same was true of Italy, which, since 1849, had fallen prostrate under the weight of reaction, and endured a discipline founded upon the bayonets of Austria, which Lesseps and the Triumvirate had so nearly turned aside. Police and soldiers held up the façade of law. In France they had done their work so well that virtually all potential resistance-men were in cells or in exile. Only the new pressure-groups, products of the Industrial Revolution, were still largely out of reach of coercion, and these provided an inevitable rallying point for the underground which, as always, became more desperate with each successive loss of liberty.

It was from such a ferment that the Orsini plot emerged, to shock all Europe on the 14th of January, 1858, when a bomb in the Avenue de l'Opera nearly killed not only the dictator but also his ingenuous, charitable, well-meaning wife, who was so beautiful. But Orsini was not mad, and his bomb, made in Birmingham, was highly efficient. The explosion, which took place just as the Imperial carriage pulled up at the steps of the Opera, killed eight people and wounded a hundred and fifty. The Empress stepped unhurt out of the smoke and the shambles. With her husband she went into the building as arranged, entered the Royal Box, and there received a great ovation. Her coolness probably prevented a panic among the audience who had heard the explosion but, until the Emperor and Empress appeared, had no idea what had happened to them.

Reaction was swift. The hitherto muzzled Anglophobes of France clamoured that the plot had been hatched in England. "On the morning following that tragic evening all France was shaking with emotion."[1] Such temper was very much resented in England, particularly since there had as yet been no judicial inquiry though it was known that warning of an assassination attempt had been communicated from London to the Paris police. When one of Orsini's accomplices, Bernard, came up for trial, his counsel made a winning point when he reminded the jury that no foreign power could intimidate a British court. Bernard was acquitted, and the furore in France reached the verge of war. A group of Colonels even wrote to Napoleon offering their services for the extermination of the ' nest of traitors ' in London. More restrained, the French Ambassador demanded

[1] Edgar-Bonnet, *Ferdinand de Lesseps*.

the extradition of Bernard, which was refused on the ground
that he had been acquitted. Then the French Press worked up
a campaign of wide accusations having little or nothing to do
with Orsini and his plot. The alleged root of the complaint was
Britannia's insufferable vanity and domineering manners. So
unfair stood the wind from France that Lord Palmerston, who
owed his power to his uncompromising insularity, was unseated
for his failure to take an even stronger line. He fell in February,
on the issue of the Conspiracy to Murder Bill, and the Queen
asked Lord Derby to form a Government, which he did; giving
to Disraeli both the Foreign Office and the leadership of the
House. It was his intention to include Gladstone in his Cabinet,
and had that occurred the policy over the canal would very
probably have changed; but Gladstone decided that he could
not compromise his Liberal principles to the extent which Derby
required, and so Lesseps was again left without a friend in the
seats of power. His prospects in the forthcoming debate were
no better than they had been before. Palmerston still took every
opportunity to remind the business world that in his view the
scheme was either an obvious swindle or the cloak for dark
intrigue; but he was now opposed by many people who felt that
he had gone altogether too far with his abuse, with the result
that Britannia had suffered a considerable loss of dignity.

*   *   *

When on the first of June, the Member for Sheffield, Mr. Roebuck, rose 'to draw the attention of the House to the matter of
the Suez Canal', he said that though at first sight the motion
might seem to be concerned with the actual execution of the
work, such was not his intention. The purpose of the motion
was to defend the honour of England, whose name was in the
mud because of her disreputable conduct in blocking the scheme
at Constantinople. We had, he said, conducted ourselves in a
base and selfish manner; and he went on to describe the situation much as Lesseps himself might have done, only to be confronted by an unrepentant Stephenson, who made a long speech
to much the same effect as on the previous occasion – thereby
changing the ground of the debate entirely. Claiming that he
had covered the whole country on foot, and that he spoke for all

British engineers, he reiterated that the cutting of the canal was beyond human resources, and that a single fact would suffice to demonstrate the impossibility of maintaining the labour force: "a desert eighty miles long, without supplies, without a drop of water." He added, "We shall see that this scheme can end only by ruining its supporters."

Though Mr. Roebuck did his eloquent best to bring the House back to his point, the national honour, the debate bogged down in semi-technical considerations and unanswerable conundrums such as one set by Disraeli – who must have known the answer. How did Mr. Roebuck know *at the present time* that the British Ambassador at Constantinople was preventing the Sultan from giving his sanction to the canal? The House evidently sensed that somewhere in the maze there was an unknown quantity, and also that in approving the motion it might seem to their constituents that they were yielding to French influence, a dangerous accusation against any Member. Of course the Government knew perfectly well that for the time being, after more than fifteen years (as Lord Palmerston had stated) the British Ambassador was in fact no longer actively hostile to the canal. If the Sultan remained inert, it was due less to outside pressure than to the fact that he was safe only if he stood quite still. Movement in any direction was bound to offend someone, and he was too weak to risk the consequences, particularly where England was concerned; for he at least realized, if the House of Commons did not, that the Ambassador's quiescence was not due to any change of heart but to the fact that while India remained in ferment Egypt must not be offended, lest Nana Sahib's fiction became fact and the gate to the East be shut in England's face.

In spite of a brilliant effort on the part of Lord John Russell, the result of the division was an overwhelming Government majority of 228: Ayes 62, Noes 290. Anyone but Lesseps would have concluded that he had lost everything, for the obvious corollary of the division was that new pressure would now be exerted on the Porte and the canal be finally vetoed. But either he had private information which pointed the other way, or else he just put on his blinkers, as he was apt to do when things went wrong, and galloped straight ahead. At any rate he wrote to his closest supporters on the 8th of June: "The debate in

Parliament, which has made a favourable impression on public opinion, will be followed by new motions. The Ministry will be harassed until the end of the session. The quality and persistence of the Members in favour of the canal ensure a moral success. The general opinion is that the progress of the Company cannot be prevented and that the opposition cannot be sustained. I shall soon be leaving for Vienna, Egypt and Constantinople." And to show that he had no intention of accepting the result either as a personal defeat or as the Government's last word, he wrote on the 16th, the day before he left London, to Lord Lyndhurst with the object of getting him to carry the battle into the House of Lords.

Not that Lesseps had the least intention of waiting longer for the obstinate men to change their minds. He proposed to press on with the formation of the Company and to develop the work in the isthmus as though there were no bar whatever to further progress. In view of the fact that Lombard Street was virtually the world's bank, not only British capital but capital from any other country was now likely to be most difficult to raise. Because of the very obstinacy of his opinion, Palmerston's slander seemed about to come true; for it had become crass folly to invest in an undertaking which the British Government intended should never make a start, still less be brought to a successful conclusion. No one could imagine that Lesseps might find the money elsewhere, or that, if he did, he would dare to start construction. But Ferdinand, though a zealot, was no fool. He must have had some secret hope to justify his brave decision. Possibly he thought to make the Viceroy underwrite the Company, while at the French court his influence at last might make Napoleon the protector of the scheme, and therefore of Säid, even at the risk of war. If so, he was very nearly right. Säid did take up the shares which should have been British, and Napoleon did find himself in a situation where he could do no other than protect the Company, even at the risk of war; but both these developments came about by means more devious than any simple *démarche* by Lesseps.

Chapter 10. THE RUBICON

If in spite of the adamantine attitude of the British Government, Ferdinand de Lesseps could still persuade himself that success was possible, for once he was unable to persuade others. Even his oldest friends and closest collaborators did not disguise from him their conviction that the debate in the House of Commons had been a death blow.

"Like everyone else, they were nearly all against his foolhardy plan. Among others, Barthélemy Saint-Hilaire said so frankly. That brilliant man of letters had given all his heart to the work which he so much admired; but now for weeks he tried, not indeed to convince his great chief to abandon the project, but to let it sleep. Lesseps would not budge. With death in his heart, Saint-Hilaire wished his friend the success in which he personally no longer believed, and dissociated himself from the enterprise which for more than three years he had served with skill and devotion." (Edgar-Bonnet.)

There was no quarrel between the two men, and after the break, they continued to correspond. It was typical of Ferdinand that where some men would have accused Saint-Hilaire of disloyalty, even of desertion in the face of the enemy, he quietly allowed his old friend to leave as he had joined, in freedom. But the sense of being let down must have cut the more deeply because at last Lesseps had to admit to himself that he was not facing facts. Saint-Hilaire was a highly intelligent man of the world. He would have carried on had he thought there was the slightest chance of success. But he believed, as did everyone who thought about the matter at all, that until England changed her tune, it was folly, almost criminal folly, to proceed with the attempt to float the Company. Saint-Hilaire could see no ray of light ahead, but Ferdinand still kept intact the vision from which all his effort sprang. In heroic folly he hunched forward into the storm.

To take the place of Saint-Hilaire he chose M. Merruau, a

journalist by profession, who seems to have believed in Ferdinand rather than in the canal. Even so he accepted his appointment under protest:

"After all, money is the sinew of war, and the greatest misfortune that could happen would be for capitalists, both big and small, to refuse their support. Or supposing that is avoided, the Company formed and the work taken in hand. Then what happens? England tells the Sultan that it amounts to contempt of sovereignty, that the matter is no longer a question of the canal but of international law. As a signatory to the treaty of 1841 (which established Mohammed-Ali) she will insist that the Sultan bring his vassal to heel. . . . And then you will see all the other powers acting in concert, even France. Has France strongly supported you at Constantinople? By whom have you been supported? The French Press will have nothing to say. You know better than anyone else how the most competent, keen and loyal conduct can be misrepresented when the means of publicity either criticize or simply fail to praise. Forgive this bluntness but the thing is serious. . . . Still, if you have really set your heart against such arguments, then there is nothing to do but to support and follow you."

Merruau was evidently a man to whom loyalty and affection were more important than all the cold argument in the world. Lesseps may have been a fool about money. He was so clever at propaganda that he came close, in that context, to being a knave; but whatever he undertook was in the service of his vision, and there can be no doubt that it shone out of him for those with eyes to see. Nothing else can explain his capacity for inspiring personal devotion, not only in good times but the more so in bad; not only among his own class and kind, but among polyglot workers on the isthmus and the gamut of Europeans of every persuasion. The same quality goes some way to explain the unreasoning hatred which he inspired in some people, who reacted to the same quality in the opposite way. There are very few men who have such an aura of vision, faith, spirituality, *mana*, genius – whatever the quality may be called which impresses those who can sense it as something beyond the reach of intellect. Moreover to such a stimulus it is virtually impossible to react rationally. As history often shows, the man or woman who has, or is credited with, this 'divine fire' can hardly be ignored. Instead, irrespective of their class, condition or colour, of success or failure, such extra-sensory individuals are both loved and hated. They are in the world but not of it, and the world, like a woman scorned, in fury tries to give them hell.

*   *   *

From Paris, Ferdinand began his preparation for the floatation of the Company, the subscription for which he resolved to open before the end of the year (1858). Already his agents were active all over France, and his many contacts in the rest of Europe required only to be alerted. Nevertheless he did not rely on them alone, but began another personal campaign on the principle which had served so well in the British Isles. In addition to all his other preoccupations he found time, between the beginning of July and the end of October, to hold meetings or attend banquets in Vienna, Corfu, Odessa, Trieste, Venice, Barcelona, Gerona, Cette and Marseilles. Everywhere he was well received, as much perhaps because of England's dog-in-the-manger atti-tude as because of the long-term benefits which the canal was expected to confer. The canal issue became a pretext for accusing Britannia of an insatiable greed for other people's property.

Lesseps also spent a good deal of time at Constantinople and Alexandria. In neither country did he find the situation encouraging, though some changes had taken place which might turn to his advantage. At the Porte two old enemies had quitted the scene, Lord Stratford de Redcliffe and Reschid Pasha the Grand Vizier. The former had merely finished his period of duty, but the latter was said to have been the victim of *mauvais café*, or had expired as the result of 'an abuse of that institution which by a prudish euphemism is called a Turkish Bath'.[1] At all events he was dead, probably poisoned. Ferdinand found his successor, Aali, a charming, cultivated, French-speaking gentle-man; but one who made no secret of his belief that under no circumstances should Turkey take action over the canal until France and England had agreed about it.

Stratford de Redcliffe's successor, Sir Henry Lytton Bulwer, though without the enormous personal influence of his pre-decessor, was necessarily tied to the policy of Westminster, so

[1] Edgar-Bonnet, *Ferdinand de Lesseps*.

that for all the change which the succession of these two great officers implied, there was from the point of view of Ferdinand de Lesseps no gain at all. So he soon left Constantinople for Paris, where from his old apartment on the fourth floor of No. 9 Rue Richepanse, he set out to fulfil – or so it must have seemed – Lord Palmerston's vaticinations about the ' bubble ' scheme. But first Lesseps had the excellent notion of putting the whole financial situation up to his old friend Baron de Rothschild, who was uniquely placed to decide whether in fact anything should be attempted. It might still be possible for great international bankers to carry the Company. They might even be strong enough to prevent British opposition from bringing to a stop the work on the isthmus. By creating a canal credit behind the new Bank of Egypt they might even bring Säid and his Government into a new power group, the influence of which might allay British suspicions by providing an international patronage of Egypt to replace the French. Whether fortunately or not for the canal, Ferdinand took it upon himself to turn down the Rothschild proposition, which in later years he reduced to something of a joke. At the time it can hardly have seemed funny:

" I began by telling M. de Rothschild of my intention to proceed with the subscription, which ought to amount to 200,000,000 francs. The Baron interrupted to give me warm congratulations, and spoke enthusiastically about the project itself and the magnificent benefits it would confer upon the world. He expressed his particular willingness to be of assistance to me and ended by saying, 'If you think that we can be useful to you, and you would like us to do so, we would accept applications over our counters both in Paris and elsewhere.' I was delighted. After thanking him effusively I was just going to withdraw when it occurred to me that to his way of thinking the services he proposed might not be entirely free. And so I asked, ' What would you want in exchange? '

" 'Mon Dieu! Evidently you are no man of business: the usual five per cent.'

" 'Five per cent! But for 200,000,000 that means 10,000,000! Ten million francs of my shareholders' money for your devious channels! Thank you very much. Stick to your counters. Our issue will be made without you. I shall find some place from which to make it where I'll pay 12,000 francs a month, and it will be all we need.'

" 'You will not succeed! '

" 'We shall see.' "

Bertrand et Ferrier conclude this version of the interview with: " And so, now that the issue had been decided upon, M. de Lesseps went back to his travels, conferring upon everyone, as a kind of sacred fire, his faith in the future and in the excellence of his enterprise." In fact his prospects were worse than ever. If the big financial houses were not to be with him, then certainly they would be against him. How could he personally hope to raise such a vast sum, about 3,000,000,000 francs to-day? Had he not believed utterly in his canal, he would not at this juncture have pressed on with what to any other eyes must have appeared a hopeless case. It was just because he believed, not only that the canal would be cut, but that it would bring fortune to all connected with it, that he could write:

" What can a dozen big bankers do, whose idea would be that I should part with the Concession? They propose that I share with them a certain number of millions, which they will then distribute, with fat bonuses attached to the 500-franc shares to put them right up; which is fair enough because one day they will bring in 15 to 30%. Why not appeal direct to the public? Do you think that subscribers, whose interests have been protected in advance by those who are resolved to conduct the business in all honesty, will be lacking? When they realize that the enterprise as now presented to them has no taint, nor likelihood of the slightest irregularity; that not a centime has been paid out in Egypt or at Constantinople to obtain or to ratify the Concession; that thanks to the generosity of the Viceroy the surveys and all the preparatory work have cost nothing at all, they will see in the principles which we serve the best guarantee for the future. . . . My object is to allow the greatest possible number of small subscribers to participate in all the benefits of the Company."

Brave words, but as though the forces against him were not already overwhelming, Fate was busy with a secret weapon to destroy anything which might survive when his declared enemies had finished with him. Lesseps was at Alexandria when he heard the details of the massacre at Jidda, the flare which first showed how tense were religious tensions in the Middle East, tensions which found their echo in the political and racial ferment of Europe, helplessly drifting towards war. On the 9th of July Lesseps wrote to Barthélemy Saint-Hilaire:

"I was with the Viceroy when the news of the terrible massacre at Djeddah came in. When I expressed my indignation the Prince said quietly, 'You who have known the Orient for so long should not be astonished. Your experience ought to have taught you that when fanatical and barbarous populations are not held in a tight grip, one day they will give themselves over to the most deplorable excesses. Even here, many of the people who greet you with respect would tear out your heart if they were not held in fear of the consequences. British policy took the administration of Syria out of my father's hands: perhaps we shall see plenty of other examples of unleashed fanaticism. But as for Djeddah and Arabia, our canal will bring them to order by forcing Arabia to become part of the European movement.' These observations are so apt that they ought to be preserved in our archives.

"It may be of interest to give you some account of the events at Djeddah. I have them from Mlle Elisa Eveillard and M. Emerat, who escaped the massacre but whose wounds are still unhealed. Five thousand rioters converged on the consulates of England and France. The English consul was literally torn to pieces. Two of his dragomans and a servant had their throats cut. The French consul, M. Eveillard, was killed with thrusts from knife and sabre. Having killed one *hadramant* and wounded another, his wife received a mortal wound in the breast. His daughter, in the middle of this frightful scene, had her father's head, already laid open by two sword-cuts, on her knees. Seeing M. Emerat, already wounded three times, struggling hand to hand with one of the murderers, she had the courage to throw herself at him, digging her nails into his face and so biting his arm that he was forced to drop his weapon; which then served M. Emerat until he fell under the redoubled assault. Mlle Eveillard had suffered a great gash in her cheek from a *yatagan* and she fainted. The murderers, thinking that they had accomplished all of their butchery, dispersed to loot the consulate. Mlle Eveillard drew over herself and the blood-soaked bodies of her parents the cushions and covers of a divan. There she waited.

"In this room where reigned the silence of death, a new horde of robbers entered a few minutes later. Seeing legs sticking out from the end of the divan covers, they thought to make sure by sword-thrusts that the bodies lying under them were really dead. Mlle Eveillard bore this ordeal with the courage which never left her. But her sufferings were by no means over. Wishing to discover whether a big cupboard contained anything of value, four or five of the bandits stood upon the pile of human flesh. One may imagine what it meant for this young woman in a lake of blood between the bodies of her father and mother. At last, drunk with pillage and with blood, the second band also went off. Then came a young negro, sent to the rescue by the women of a neighbouring harem. to whom, only a few days previously, Mme Eveillard and her daughter had taken some medicine. This young negro, the only

friend among so many savage enemies, had to wait until sunset
before he dared show Mlle Éveillard that he was a friend, and to
get her out of the near-tomb in which she had been covered up
alive. After surviving many dangers, he arrived at the harem, where
the rescued girl was taken in. As to M. Emerat, he was saved by
an Algerian Muslim who had served for twelve years in the French
army. Seeing the invaders cut down the Tricolor and defile it with
their feet, he hurled himself upon them with such fury that from
that moment the personnel succeeded in defending themselves.
They even recovered M. Emerat and took him to a place of safety."

*   *   *

Ferdinand de Lesseps had a rare trait indispensable to great
commanders. He could dismiss from his mind worries with
which he was unable to cope, and so concentrate his forces for
effective action at decisive points, in this case the various
agencies which he had set up, and which he now briefed as to
the constitution of the proposed Company. The subscription was
to be opened in November, war or no war. On the 28th of July
he wrote to Ruyssenaers, his agent in Alexandria:

"We have reason to congratulate ourselves because I am about to
raise the curtain upon our last act. By the two copies attached you
will see that there was no time wasted in fruitless negotiations with
the Turks, but that, profiting from their protestations, I bear witness
to their tacit consent. And I have placed my interests and those
of the Company under the infallible protection of the Emperor of
the French. Baron Prokesch the Austrian Ambassador, M. Bou-
tenieff the Russian Ambassador, General Wildenbruck the Prussian
Minister, M. de Souza the Spanish Minister, and the representatives
of the other Governments at Constantinople approve my attention,
will communicate it to their respective Courts, and will be joined
at need by the Ambassador of France. I ask you to communicate
this information to the Viceroy. It is clear-cut and definitely leaves
him the best rôle."

If he understood the realities of the situation, Mohammed-
Säid could hardly be expected to rejoice; for the rôle in prospect
was now very far from that of the gracious patron for which he
had originally cast himself. It seemed as though he would be an
unheeded figure – for no one listened to him – in the still centre
of a tornado about to break. Whether, after it had passed, there
would be a canal across the isthmus, must have been for him a

consideration quite secondary in comparison with the prospect
of being able to keep his seat upon the throne. His anxieties
would have been further increased, and even Ferdinand would
have had to postpone his Company's formation, had it leaked
out that war was now imminent. Napoleon had recently met
Cavour, catalyst for United Italy, at Plombières. There in deepest secrecy the Emperor had agreed to attack Austria at the first
available opportunity.

If Lesseps had any misgivings about Russian intentions, they
seem to have been set at rest in the course of a series of banquets
and discussions, chiefly at Odessa in August, where the focal
point, as described in the local paper of the 9th, seems to have
been set in a singularly modern light:

"In the great European family all noble enterprises are sisters.
They link arms, and, without rivalry, each contributes to the well-
being of all the other members of the family. . . . As in the old
days, the Doges, from the height of their superb *Bucentaure*, were
married to the Adriatic as a symbol of their command of the seas, it
was on board the most superb ship, the *Wladimir*, dressed with the
flags of all the nations, that a splendid banquet was given for M.
de Lesseps. We shall not go into the details of the magnificent
entertainment. We shall say only that at this dinner, at which were
present His Excellency the Governor-General of New Russia and
Bessarabia, Count Strogonoff, General Besak, Baron Mestmacher
acting Governor of the town of the Odessa, M. Yourieff Director
of the Imperial Bank at St. Petersburg. . . ."

In spite of having lost their war against France after much
bitter fighting in the nearby Crimea, the Russians, who had
only evacuated Sebastapol in September 1855, now went out of
their way to refer to French arms in terms of admiration. This
forgiving attitude may well have been accounted for on the
ground that the ex-enemies had recently opposed England at
Bolgrad, only ninety miles from Odessa, the headquarters of a
Commission established to re-define the frontier between Bessarabia and Moldavia. That England was against him, would
have made de Lesseps even more popular; yet in all probability
he would have had just as warm a welcome had England supported him. He must have been especially grateful for the
implication of official Russian support. Though Odessa hardly
represented Russia more than Bristol represented England, in

spite of the entente no Director of the Bank of England had sat down to dinner at Bristol, nor did the Lord Lieutenant of Gloucestershire represent his Sovereign as did the Russian Governor-General. Quite apart from politics, the commercial interests of the port had every reason to favour the construction of the canal, and it could hardly have been coincidence that the dinner simultaneously celebrated the formation of a Steam Navigation Company, based on Odessa, whose captains would make excellent clients for M. de Lesseps. If the thought had not previously occurred to him, he must now at last have seen a real chance to win through in spite of British opposition, for the *rapprochement* between France and Russia over the frontier dispute continued through later negotiations of the same sort, which were still going on in Armenia. When the time came to open the subscription, might not Russia take up the shares which otherwise would have gone to England? Such an act would be a severe blow to British prestige in the Middle East and would confer both commercial and strategic advantage upon the Russians, who, together with the French, could then afford to disregard the Sultan's wishes – and those of the British Ambassador behind him; for the canal from start to finish would then be under their control.

Lesseps had every reason to think along such lines, though it is unlikely that he carried the argument to its logical conclusion, a Russo-French alliance on the lines of that which the first Napoleon, thanks to Barthélemy de Lesseps, so nearly succeeded in making the bedrock of an impregnable hegemony. Ferdinand admired the British, particularly their sang-froid in face of crisis, a characteristic which he also possessed. He believed in the entente for the sake of peace, but if Russia elected to play the part which England disdained, he could hardly be expected to mourn on that account. Confident again, he went back to Rue Richepanse and began the actual business of launching the Company. He filled his long day to overflowing. When he came home, even late in the evening, he would put in half an hour with the *epée* instead of taking a rest. And if someone wished to see him without an appointment, about the only chance would be before six in the morning. Even then the visitor, having climbed the three flights of stairs to Ferdinand's modest apartment, would be more likely to have the door opened by an athletic figure, eyes flashing, moustache bristling, sword in hand, than by a servant. Indeed it seems doubtful whether he kept any staff, perhaps because he was so little at home; if home is not too gentle a word for his spartan setting. He luxuriated only when there was no work to be done. Though horses had been his hobby since childhood, and he still had his stud down at La Chenaie, he did not even keep a cob in Paris. This ungentlemanly lack of circumstance, no servants, no horses, may have been tactless in a society which took both so much for granted. But Ferdinand, though punctilious, conventional even, and certainly no ascetic when off duty, disliked ostentation and used social occasions chiefly as a means to an end.

* * *

The floatation of the Company was eagerly awaited by the public, and it is hardly an exaggeration to claim that between its partisans and their opponents the civilized world was divided. In every town, every board-room, every club, there were *canalistes* and *anti-canalistes* whose arguments were topical in workmen's cottages as in the courts of Europe. Ferdinand announced the decisive act in a circular to the French and foreign Press dated 15th of October, 1858. On the same day he issued his prospectus, with a covering letter to all the agents and correspondents of the Company, asking them to arrange for the leading banker of their nearest town to receive applications for shares. The prospectus was in the form following:

"M. Ferdinand de Lesseps, Concessionaire for the Suez Canal, pursuant of the mandate which he has received from His Highness the Viceroy of Egypt, is offering a public issue, having been assured of the approval of European financial interests. The Suez Canal is destined to re-establish the short passage between the two worlds, which the discovery of the Cape of Good Hope caused to fall into desuetude. To confer upon the undertaking the grandeur and universality which it deserves, M. de Lesseps appeals to investors in all countries.

The object, commercial and financial advantages of the enterprise are as follows:—

1. The right to open across the Isthmus of Suez a canal for the shipping of the high seas, to unite the Mediterranean with the Red Sea and the seas of India, China, etc., etc.

2. The joining of the Nile to the Maritime Canal by a navigable fresh-water canal.

3. The reclamation of 133,000 hectares of land ceded to the Company, of which 63,000 hectares constitute a strip two kilometres wide on each bank of the canals and around each port.

4. The canal across the Isthmus of Suez will shorten by 3,000 leagues the voyage between Europe and the Indian Ocean, and will effect enormous economies for long-distance shipping. The due of 10 francs per ton, which was fixed by the decree of Concession for the right of navigation along the canal, is moderate. It will be applicable to a traffic of the order of 4 million tons, and will produce a very considerable revenue, independently of the profits from the canal derived from the Nile, and of the evaluation and sale of 133,000 hectares of the ceded land.

The capital of the Company is limited to 200 million francs apportioned as between 400,000 shares of 500 francs each.

The registered offices of the Company are in Paris.

Conditions of Investment

On application, 50 francs per share are payable. A second payment of 150 francs per share is payable on publication of the allocation.

On payment of the 200 francs per share investors will receive temporary certificates, convertible to bearer bonds at a date to be determined later.

While the work is under construction, and as from the dates of the temporary certificates, the paid-up portion of the shares will bear interest at 5% per annum.

No other issue will be made within two years. Surveys already made suggest that before a new issue is required a navigable passage will already have been made between the two seas.

The investment will be controlled from Paris. A Committee will decide the allotment of shares without distinction of nationality.

The subscription will open on the 5th of November and will close on the 30th of the same month, in order to give all the countries of Europe time to reply.

All payments or requests for shares shall be considered null and void if, after the 30th of November, the instalment of 50 francs per share shall not have been paid.

Applications will be received at:—Paris, the Offices of the Company, Place Vendôme 16. In the Départments and abroad, at the offices of MM. *les Banquiers et Correspondents de la Compagnie.*"

And on the same day, Ferdinand de Lesseps wrote to his faithful lieutenant Ruyssenaers, quoting the words attributed to Caesar at the crossing of the Rubicon: *Alea jacta est,* the die is cast. No understatement. Not only was the dream of Lesseps on offer to the world for purchase; an heroic association with generations gone was, as it were, attached as a bonus to the shares. Those who pushed across the counter a modest speculation in the money of the Second Empire would share a romantic history and become participants in the founder's dream. To the old order this dream was now an open challenge: forward or back? Lesseps himself had decided long ago; nor had he ever wavered in his arduous approach to this decisive river-bank. But would his men follow him past the point of no return? Would they abide by the consequences of the decisive act?

*   *   *

Of the 400,000 shares on offer, 222,000 were taken up before the books were closed, and thanks to a verbal understanding with the Viceroy, a further large block was booked to his account. So the operation had been a success. Yet, for various reasons, the only troops who can really be said to have crossed the Rubicon with Lesseps were 25,000 relatively small French investors, many of whom were motivated as much by the thought that their action might annoy the English as by hope of reward. Edgar-Bonnet crisply sums up the situation:

"Undoubtedly the capital had been subscribed. Unfortunately the fact did not prevent financial embarrassment. In law everything was clear. In action everything was uncertain. To subscribe was one thing, to pay up was another; and at the first appeal for funds collective defaulting began. Neither the English, in deference to the stand taken by their Government; nor the Americans, out of indifference; nor the Russians, out of timidity; nor the Austrians, because of their politics, were able or willing to honour their signatures. As things turned out, the universal character of the operation, so much desired by Lesseps, was much diminished. The President was not responsible, and he regretted the fact more than anyone. In order to avoid it he made every possible effort. It was in vain."

The French share preponderance, which would call forth much shaking of wiseacre heads saying, "I told you so" in support of the theory of the secret purpose imagined by Palmerston, is represented by the allocation as given by Lesseps in his first official communication to his Egyptian agent. It is dated the 1st of January, 1859:

France	207,111
Belgium	324
Denmark	7
Naples	97
The Ottoman Empire, including the personal subscription of the Viceroy of Egypt .	96,517
Spain (Barcelona)	4,046
Rome	54
Low Countries	2,615
Portugal	5
Prussia	15
Tunis	1,714
Piedmont	1,353
Switzerland	460
Tuscany	176
Shares held in reserve for the subscriptions of: Austria, Great Britain, Russia, and the United States of America . .	85,506
for which I am responsible according to the Viceroy's undertaking to take them for his account should they not be placed	
Total of Shares forming the capital of the Company	400,000

Ferdinand read the figures with typical optimism:

" So it is made clear that I have not sought to monopolize for France and Egypt the merit of subscribing to the great universal enterprise, which, in spite of everything, does not, by its results, fall short of being universal. My last letters from England warn me that in the matter of funds Great Britain will completely default on us. The words of Lord Palmerston and of the engineer Stephenson in Parliament have produced their effect. But since we shall march on in spite of the policy of our dear allies, I shall not be put out when I succeed without their financial help and in spite of their hostility. It will serve to put down a little their insular presumption."

So there was an overwhelming French control of the equity, with the Viceroy's personal holding easily ranking next. In spite of the founder's efforts towards internationalism, once again that ageing English statesman had shown an almost uncanny capacity for prediction. The canal was French, so French that its construction would necessarily make Egypt more the appanage of Napoleon than of the Sultan. Lord Palmerston may have permitted himself a wry smile; but then he had often complained that few men could 'anticipate the consequences of events which have *not* happened'. As one of the few, even he could hardly have guessed that this apparent triumph would do as much to bring the enterprise to ruin as his own parliamentary opposition; for the matter of the Viceroy's holding was to cause a serious breach between Säid and Lesseps. The facts are recorded in various letters, some quoted by Edgar-Bonnet. The Viceroy's intention was evidently to take up only a modest number of shares. No doubt both he and Lesseps were convinced that at the close of the issue very few would remain, and on Säid's part the verbal offer to take up the surplus was therefore primarily a generous gesture to his old friend; particularly since Säid was no longer rich, in fact he was scarcely solvent. Circumstances beyond their control had caused a relatively enormous deficit, chiefly through the complications of international politics, and accordingly it became extremely important for Lesseps to know to what extent the Viceroy was prepared to implement his engagement. Though certainly it would never have occurred to Ferdinand that the shares in his canal were not excellent things to have, and the more the better, he must also have been aware that Säid might not feel the same way; particularly in view of the heavy commitments which he had already made to the Company under the Act of Concession. Perhaps Lesseps ought to have secured Säid's written consent before adding the huge surplus to his account; but that would have taken a long time, time which he could not afford. For if the surplus were not taken up, French law would not be complied with as to registration and the international reaction might be disastrous. So Lesseps did what must have seemed to him the only possible thing. He relied upon Säid's willingness to take up all the surplus and entered the shares to his account – which explains the curious wording beside the allotment just quoted, which in the original reads: "*pour lesquelles je suis porté fort, d'après la déclaration du vice-roi, de les prendre pour son compte dans le cas où elles ne seraient pas réalisés.*" This is not quite the same thing as saying that Lesseps *guaranteed* those shares, as Crabités has it, but rather that he booked them pending confirmation. What might happen should Säid refuse to accept them was a possibility to be considered later. All that mattered for the moment was to show on paper and in principle that the Company was properly constituted, having the required capital fully subscribed.

In fact, as far as real money was concerned, the capital was at least forty-two million francs short. Moreover the Viceroy's existing personal holding, which must have been the vast majority, if not all, of the 96,517 shares allocated to 'The Ottoman Empire', was not real money either, part being in exchange for ceded lands and so forth, part payable in kind, as by the *corvée* and part in Egyptian bonds, which were not likely to prove readily convertible. So, with minor international defaulters added, the Company in fact began operations with something less than half its capital, and that half was almost entirely from small investors. The Rubicon had been a symbol chosen well. Shadowed by approaching war, undermined by the implicit veto of the Porte, the gallant 25,000 followed de Lesseps into hostile territory. They were unlikely to be able to obtain any further supplies, and would be lucky to escape defeat, if not at the hands of the enemy, then by starvation.

Lesseps, the brave captain, put on his boldest face and proceeded, in the most confident manner imaginable, to register the Company and to hold the first General Meeting, which was convened, in compliment to the Empress, on what he thought was the feast of St. Eugénie, the 22nd of November. Oddly enough the usual date is given as Christmas Day, which he would surely have taken as an excellent omen.[1] As President he was in the chair for the first of many, many times. In his speech he avoided matters financial, implying as he no doubt sincerely believed, that all was for the best in the best of all possible worlds. He dwelt rather on technical progress and the speed of the work, which was to provide small-ship navigation, *via* the Freshwater Canal, within two years. He made use of the most propitious day, Christmas, to date the papers which he had to submit to the *Ministre du Commerce et des Travaux Publics*, and followed them with a formal application for the Company's registration. If the share position was not likely to give the Minister great confidence, the names at the head of the organization must have done much to reduce his misgivings, and the request was granted. For his part, Ferdinand would not rely too much upon the great names which were associated with his enterprise. He knew how precarious was their support. The original muster was as follows:

[1] There is another date in September.

CONSEIL D'ADMINISTRATION

Patron: S. A. I. Monseigneur le prince Jérôme Napoléon.
Présidents Honoraires: MM. Jomard Bey, Président de la Societé imperiale de géographie, membre de l'Institut
le baron Charles Dupin, Senateur, membre de l'Institut
le marechal Navaez, Duc de Valence
Elie de Beaumont, Senateur, secrétaire per-petuel de l'Academie des Sciences.
Président: M. Ferd. de Lesseps, Ministre Plenipotentiare.
Vice-présidents: MM. le Duc d'Albuféra, Deputé du Corps legis-latif
Forbes (Paul), de la maison R. B. Forbes, banquiers a Boston, Etats-Unis
le chevalier Revoltella, Banquier, delegué en Autriche.

There followed a list of thirty-one members of the Committee, eight members of the sub-committee of works, and eight of the judicial sub-committee. Such were the officers of the gallant little army which now marched, figuratively, upon the isthmus defended by the world's paramount power. They were neverthe-less no *corps d'élite*. As the London *Globe* put it: "The principal shareholders are hotel waiters who have been deceived by the papers they have read, and petty grocery employees who have been beguiled by puffs. The priesthood has been victimized, and 3,000 day-labourers have been induced to pool their savings to buy these shares. The whole thing is a flagrant robbery gotten up to despoil the simple people who have allowed themselves to become dupes." Palmerston could not forbear to gloat; "little people have been induced to take up little shares". Lesseps retorted: "If the Company is composed of little men it will not be the less honourable on that account, or the less honoured." For there had been truth in the taunt. By far the greater pro-portion of shares were held in blocks of 100 *i.e.* of 50,000 francs. There were twenty-four investors with 200 shares each and only two with 400. To Palmerston it must indeed have seemed a contemptible little army; but such judgments are sometimes inept.

Ferdinand was proud of his command. Its morale was high. Supplies and ammunition were at least sufficient for the immedi-

ate objective, to start work on the isthmus. Had it not been for
the death of Madame Delamalle, at fifty-nine, this would have
been a time for joy. At the end of December it became instead
a time for sorrow, not only because of his affectionate gratitude
to his mother-in-law, but because the boys would miss her so
much. While at eighteen Charles was quite capable of looking
after himself, Victor had only just gone to school – the Lycée
Napoleon. "I left you yesterday," Ferdinand wrote to Charles,
" with great sorrow. I have never had to leave you so much alone
with your little brother. You two are my most prized possessions,
and the most effective consolation in my loss."

Except when in retirement at La Chenaie before the death of
his beloved Agathe, domestic interludes had always been brief.
Time had never been more pressing than it was now: so much
to do, so many places where he was needed. Victor would have
to settle down as best he could while his father's dream at last
began to crystallize in terms of earth.

"To M. S. W. Ruyssenaers at Alexandria.

Paris, 16th February, 1859.

I pass on to you a copy of the agreement with M. Hardon, the
contractor. It has just been completed so that preparatory work
can be begun on the Suez Canal. I am leaving for Egypt *via* Vienna,
Trieste, and Corfu. I shall be met at Alexandria by the Commission nominated by the Committee of Administration to take
possession of our Concession."

Chapter 11. ATTRITION

The Emperor must have realized that the new Company was unlikely to survive the war which he was about to launch, but he received de Lesseps before the latter left for France and as usual confined himself to vague expressions of goodwill. So Ferdinand, unwarned, departed with a sense of achievement which was, to say the least, premature. At Berlin, Vienna, and Trieste there was no presage of the coming storm. From Corfu he wrote to Constantinople in a personal style which was not appreciated by the recipient:

"My dear Grand Vizier,—So the Company has been regularly constituted and has the necessary funds to carry out the works, a situation which might prove embarrassing to the Porte had I not taken care to instruct the Committee of Administration to confine operations to the continuation of surveys and preparatory work; for which the costs have been paid, these four years past, by the Viceroy himself. We are therefore going to be concerned only with the first phase of the programme as drawn up by the Committee of Works, which consists in opening a service channel from Pelusium to Suez, a channel which will at the same time serve as a pilot destined to prepare the isthmus for ocean shipping."

The greater part of this long letter is taken up by a counterblast to the renewed hostility of Lord Palmerston; but the novelty and importance of it consists in a few words defining the meaning of 'preparatory studies', the phrase which, in the original firman of Concession, limited the work which could be done without the express sanction of the Sultan. Clearly Lesseps proposed to go full steam ahead, just as though there were nothing to prevent him; for the idea of a small channel (*rigole*) running the whole way could so easily lead to a full-scale excavation. And who would be able to say when the work of preparation became the forbidden act of construction?

Meanwhile Säid had taken an unexpectedly firm stand on

behalf of his old friend. When the new British Consul, Mr. Green, asked the Viceroy to dissociate himself from the Company, Säid replied that Mr. Green was quite wrong if he supposed that M. de Lesseps was responsible for the idea of the canal or the formation of the Company. On the contrary, both were due to Säid's initiative, for the prosperity of Egypt and the glory of his name. The wind taken out of his sails, Mr. Green could only ask whether he might officially report the conversation, and was told to do so. But Säid was in fact far from sure of himself, and his attitude towards the Company was qualified by reservations over Ferdinand's handling of the surplus shares. When Lesseps arrived at Alexandria and presented his Committee, Säid was affable; but both sides wisely confined themselves to the exchange of compliments. These were tactfully followed up by an official letter which, after praise and thanksgiving, went on to promise repayment of the considerable sums which Säid had generously expended upon the work to date. Whether intentional or not, the implication was that the preparatory phase was now at an end, for practical purposes, and that Lesseps proposed to get on with the major works. For Säid had offered to pay for the 'preparatory' effort only. Perhaps he had done so in order to minimize the grounds for objection at Constantinople. If the Company now proposed to reimburse him, it must be because the second stage of development had already been reached; a conclusion borne out by the rapidity with which material began to accumulate at Alexandria.

The Viceroy had every reason for anxiety. The Franco-British impasse was such that whichever side he chose, his throne would be in danger. In such a situation a strong man would at all costs have come to some decision; but if he had been strong at the beginning of his reign, Säid was so no longer. His health was beginning to fail. Adiposity, personal indulgence and extravagance had prematurely aged him. He could not decide, and therefore, whether consciously or no, became a man divided. Yet he had complete insight into his condition, and there appears to be no justification for the rumour, which found its way into the English Press, that he was out of his head. Lesseps turned his back upon all such side-issues and put his whole momentum behind the job. Owing to the financial situation he was above all aware that the work must be pressed forward with the utmost speed. No doubt even now he would have much preferred to wait for a fair wind, but he could not afford to do so. So while the contractors built up their base at Alexandria, with an advanced base at Damietta for the attack upon a sand-spit destined to become Port Said, Lesseps himself organized a survey for the Freshwater Canal. He has left a note of his establishment:

"The surveys will be made by 3 units on the following basis:

One tent for 3 Europeans	
„ „ „ 6 Arab levellers	
„ „ „ 6 „ measurers	
„ „ „ cookhouse	

3 camels for Tentage	
4 „ „ Water	
2 „ „ Rations	
2 „ „ riding	

10 kegs of water

(In all, 12 camels, which the Company will have to buy.)[1]

Apparatus

3 spirit levels	3 measuring chains
6 survey instruments	50 landmarks
2 measuring squares	1 theodolite
1 post with white calico	
1 „ „ red „	1000 small headed nails
1 „ „ blue „	

*   *   *

In one such primitive party Ferdinand followed the line of a section of the proposed canal drawing water from the River of Moses. He was almost half-way to what would be the junction of the fresh with the salt canals when the consequences of Säid's schizoid attitude began to make themselves dramatically apparent and he had occasion to write the first of many protests against hostile acts which, because they had no discernible origin, were the more effective on that account.

[1] Presumably one camel was a spare.

"To His Excellency Zulficar Pasha,
         Governor of Cairo.   25th March, 1859.

It was entirely agreed with His Highness that during our
journey we should continue the studies begun several years ago.
The day before yesterday we were in the desert close to the cultivated land at Tell-el-Ouady, where we still are. . . . When all my
companions were away at the village, imagine my astonishment
when the dragoman told me that a Turkish officer named Abderrahman Effendi had followed us all the way from Cairo. He had
collected about fifty bashi-bazouks and armed Bedouin, who fell
upon our drivers, bound them and led them away. I immediately
had a mount made ready and went to the village. There I lodged
a strong protest to Abderrahman Effendi. I told him he had be-
haved like a bandit. I said that if he needed any information he
had only to ask me, and I insisted that he should release the
prisoners to me, which he did. . . . I am certain that His Highness
is quite ignorant of the mission of Abderrahman Effendi. You
must understand that should such incidents recur I cannot possibly
be responsible for what might happen; because if armed men come
into my area without warning and conduct themselves like robbers,
I have the right to reply with rifle fire.
    "PS.   Permit me to put before you the terms of the decree of
His Highness dated the 5th January, 1856 (Art. 22): 'As witness
to the interest we have in the success of the enterprise of the Suez
Canal, we guarantee to the Company the loyal co-operation of the
Egyptian Government, and we expressly require by these presents
that the officials and agents of all the services of our administration
shall give under all circumstances their aid and protection.'"

Though Lesseps of course received a most courteous reply,
it was not long before another incident occurred, the excuse
probably being the same as that offered on the first occasion.
Though Lesseps did not mention it to Zulficar, there had been
no trouble so long as the party confined their activities to survey work as such. But within a few hours of the time when
the drivers had been set to digging – clearly a mere experiment,
such as a test of subsoil, Abderrahman had evidently acted
on orders. It may be inferred that the Viceroy, like his Sultan,
reasonably regarded survey and survey alone, as being within
the authorization of the original Concession. The dragoman
next reported Abderrahman as stirring up trouble with local
sheiks, whom Lesseps promptly invited to take coffee at his
camp:

"After we had washed, I showed them a six-barrelled revolver.

They had never seen anything like it. I had half a dozen bottles
set out at a considerable distance, and when the sheiks saw me
break them in succession I told them, 'My good friends, I am
given to understand that a Turkish officer, who says he has been
sent by the Government, told you this morning to refuse me
supplies. I would ask you patiently to explain to this individual,
who is nothing but an impostor, that we are now going into the
desert, that we are twenty in number, among whom I am by no
means the best shot. Tell him that any black spot we may see
upon the desert is likely to be mistaken for a gazelle.'"

The survey of the Freshwater Canal was accomplished without further trouble and Lesseps with his party returned to
Cairo, where he left them for Alexandria, and thence Damietta,
en route for the site of Port Said:

"We arrived this morning (April 19th) with our little flotilla,
sailing under the French flag, to which was added the boat of the
French vice-consul. After receiving calls from the Governor and
all the foreign consuls, including the Englishman, I proceeded as
far as Lake Menzaleh, whence four fishing-boats will take us to
Port Said to-morrow. There we shall encamp. The vice-consul of
France, whom I appointed twenty-five years ago, invited me to be
his guest. I am installed in a charming room which forms a belve-
dere at the top of the house. All my travelling-companions, to the
number of fourteen, are coming to dine, and I can see that a great
celebration is being prepared. At Port Said we shall openly inaugurate the works. The local authorities are everywhere most
anxious to please. The Governor of Damietta, whom I have known
for a number of years, told me he has orders to give me every
assistance."

On the following day Port Said was founded. On the 25th,
Ferdinand de Lesseps shifted some earth between two lines of
pegs and so inaugurated, with one cubic foot out of a hundred
million, the excavation of the Suez Canal. At peak as much
dirt would be moved in a month as might fill the Champs-
Élysées to the tree-tops, all the way from the Obelisk to the
Arc de Triomphe; a rate which was as yet unimaginable, even
to de Lesseps, who was still thinking in terms of men rather
than machines. In token of which he passed the pick to the
next senior European, and so through all the staff. The inaugural
pick then went to the senior of the hundred and fifty native
workmen, and so to each of them until the youngest had made
his ceremonial knock upon the desert's door step. It would

have been pleasant for Lesseps to have given the ritual a wide publicity, but not only would it have been singularly tactless, the Press suddenly had something far more important to put on the front page.

Leaving behind him four merchant ships riding at anchor in the virgin roadstead, unloading timber for jetties and the iron components of a light-house, in high heart Ferdinand sailed back to Alexandria – to be struck down on his arrival by the news that Europe was on fire. Almost while the inauguration of Port Said was in progress, France and Piedmont had declared war on Austria for the liberation of Italy. England and Russia stood aside, alert and opportunist. None could guess how far the conflict would spread or how long it would last; but at least one thing was tolerably certain: no more money, no more material for the canal. And what had already arrived or was on order might well have to lie idle for lack of skilled labour to put it together, to make the basic establishments without which further progress must be indefinitely held up.

That his Emperor, the heir to whose throne was the Patron of the Company, should have unleashed this turmoil without the least hint even presumably to Jérôme Bonaparte himself must have seemed singularly callous to Ferdinand; if only because it must entail the ruin of those faithful thousands of their countrymen who, to fulfil a patriotic dream, had defied the maledictions of Britannia and the anathema of the Sultan. Yet on the 7th of May, when as yet no offensive action had been taken by either side, Ferdinand could write to the Duke of Albuféra in the most matter-of-fact manner, without even mentioning the war:

" In my last letter, dated the 3rd, I had no time to tell you about the gains we made at the end of our excursion. The surroundings of Port Said offer us considerable areas covered with salt-wort (*plantes de soude*), which makes excellent firing, and the ashes are a by-product. There are fish in Lake Menzaleh and they will provide our workmen with a basic diet which is healthy, plentiful and cheap. Finally we shall not have to cut, at our own expense, a canal between the Nile and Lake Menzaleh because the Viceroy has surprised us. While we were at Port Said he started, with ten thousand workers, a canal 15 metres wide, 1·25 metres deep and 2 kilometres long, for the sake of communication between Lake Menzaleh and Damietta."

As to the financial situation, Lesseps said he had gone further into the matter and that "the result cannot be anything but the complete capital". On the 11th of the same month he claimed "our work on the isthmus goes forward without the least obstacle". But that was the last occasion on which even he had any grounds for cheerfulness. On the 29th April Austria invaded Piedmont, and British diplomacy, profiting by France's concentration on the war, intensified diplomatic pressure against Säid and against the canal. By the middle of May, work was virtually at a standstill, not for lack of men or material but because local authorities, including the Governor of Damietta, refused to provide transport or to furnish supplies. Even water for Port Said was sometimes held up, threatening death by thirst for those who laboured there. When at last he gave up the attempt to get satisfaction from the Egyptian authorities, Lesseps complained officially to his Consul-General, that same Sabatier who had represented the Emperor on the occasion of the award of the Legion of Honour. Unknown to Lesseps, Sabatier had long been won over to the British view, and if not actively engaged in furthering Säid's machinations, was at least a passive enemy. So Lesseps, like Canute, struggled against a rising tide. Had there been people he could reach with tongue or sword there might have been some hope for him, but, so far as he could discover, there was no individual enemy at all. Mysteriously, almost by accident, the simplest movements broke down, the easiest work became impossibly difficult. This was the Egyptian version of the boycott, far more effective than the Irish original because the power behind the scenes was not outraged tenantry but an absolute monarch. Officially Säid still supported the canal, but he used his personal authority secretly against it; and sometimes publicly denounced Ferdinand, who recorded the following story. After a stormy audience a man stayed behind when the others thankfully trooped out. The Viceroy demanded to know why. "Sire," said the frightened man. "You spoke with such violence that I thought you could not be expressing your real views." Säid paused, then said, "You may be right. But if you let anyone suspect that you are aiding Lesseps, you will have to reckon with me."

The boycott soon achieved what no amount of open hostility

could have done, and even Ferdinand, though still fighting, was beginning to lose the faith which had for so long sustained him. Then the Prime Minister, Cherif Pasha, formally wrote to him as President of the Company and ordered him to cease work. Lesseps protested, quoted the Concession, and struggled on. But by now even the foreign labour force was almost extinct and of course there had been no call-up. He felt that he was not entitled to keep from the war any men willing to fight against Austria, or rather for the United Italy in which he had always believed. He even paid the fare for every volunteer from his labour force. The remainder carried on. Finding their attack parried, albeit by a man nearing the point of exhaustion, his enemies decided finally to break him. Pressure upon Säid was increased until, desperate, Lesseps was driven to threaten him that, if he allowed the canal to come to nothing, then he personally would have to refund to the investors every centime they might lose. Glad of the excuse, Säid promptly broke off all contact with Lesseps. It seemed as though he must have come down firmly upon the enemy's side of the fence on which he had for long enough been trying to sit. When this news reached France it caused even more gloom among the *canalistes* than had *The Times* when it declared that the canal scheme was "already approaching dissolution", and again that "England has little reason to be concerned with the acts of this turbulent person". The person responded by becoming even more turbulent. He published a letter which 'deeply wounded' the Viceroy; who took the drastic step of demanding, through Sabatier, that Lesseps be reprimanded from Paris – presumably by the Emperor since he was no longer responsible to the Quai d'Orsay. The effect of this was that the English Consul soon remarked 'in his bearing an unaccustomed nervousness which broke through his bragging air'.

Edgar-Bonnet states that quite apart from the boycott and the diplomatic offensive, there is in the archives of the Abdin Palace evidence of other secret measures taken by the Viceroy against his sometime protégé, who seems to have been fortunate therefore not to have suffered a similar fate to that of the 'turbulent priest'. Murder in the Cathedral is, after all, a more serious matter than the 'accidental' demise of a stranger who has outstayed his welcome in a strange land. Ferdinand must

have dined in fear of '*mauvais café*', but still he fought the
Egyptian Government and its secret agents, while in the isthmus
his lieutenants strove with the obstinate earth, their determination matched by the grim conditions under which they had
to work. Säid felt that he had failed to bring the work to a
standstill and therefore must have offended England. On the
other hand, so long as a token effort was going on, at least
he would not risk that indemnity with which he had been
threatened. Though of doubtful validity, the theatrical threat
that Säid might have to reimburse the shareholders, had been
effective. Like most of his countrymen at that time, the Viceroy had but little understanding of European law and
commercial practice. But he had learned to be critical of simple-
sounding propositions, and to dread the penalties which might
be concealed among the subordinate clauses of an apparently
straightforward contract. It did not seem to occur to him, nor
to his advisers, that since the cutting of the canal was illegal,
there could hardly be a legal claim when the work ceased.

So Säid got back on the fence, hoping that the canal would
fail without any further action on his part; but this did not
satisfy England, whose Government arranged with the Sultan
for Säid's deposition. The excuse was to be the Sultan's proposed visit to Bayreuth. He would stop at Alexandria on the
way, summon the Viceroy and, with the backing of a British
squadron, quietly remove him from power. The squadron duly
appeared, and Säid, unwilling to obey the Sultan's command
yet reluctant to refuse it, shivered in Cairo. Meanwhile the
friends of the Company in France were almost equally alarmed,
among them Victor Delamalle, a lawyer by profession, who
was almost as devoted to Ferdinand as his mother had been.
Victor wrote to Ferdinand, "You tell us to keep going. That's
fine. But with what? While we wait, the capital evaporates. To
say, 'maintain the rights of the shareholders' is all very well
in conversation, but one cannot implement impossible statements. If within a few days our Emperor does not come strongly
to our support the upshot will be calamitous." The young man
concluded by signing, "Yours to the end."   And indeed it
seemed like the end, not an heroic one, but with ignominy.
"Even those whom the founder had recruited at the very beginning of the enterprise had lost all faith and all courage." It

seemed that not only the canal but the pro-French régime in Egypt would be defeated, that the dream which was to have paved the way for peace and plenty would bring instead another war. On the 6th of July the new Prime Minister of Egypt, Nubar Pasha, wrote to Bulwer at Constantinople, to put down that last card with a light hand: "France wants the Suez Canal. England does not. If they cannot agree, one day the affair will be settled with guns."

*   *   *

Amid this seemingly hopeless state of affairs, the Fates decided to introduce a new thread, a scarlet thread, into the sombre pattern of de Lesseps. At the battle of Solferino on the 24th of June, France won an unqualified victory. But there was still no sign of the war coming to an end. Indeed it seemed likely to spread, for Prussia became uneasy. Then, against all probability, an armistice was signed at Villafranca. There the two Emperors, in brotherly concert ignored Cavour, for whose aspirations France had begun the conflict, and made an amicable settlement of their differences. This unlooked-for development immediately altered the situation in Egypt. The British squadron sailed away, and Säid was able briefly to relax, aware that with her large army fully mobilized and free to turn away from Austria, France could now confront England with a power which she would be slow to challenge, a very different power to that envisaged when Lord Palmerston's policy for Egypt had been formulated. On the isthmus the boycott ceased as mysteriously as it had begun. Lesseps sighed with relief and restarted major works. Then he went to France, claiming, " I leave Egypt with the honours of war ".

The boast was premature. Even as he rallied his shaken following and by sheer force of leadership closed their ranks to meet the still threatening future, there arrived in Egypt a special envoy from the Sultan. This official, Muktar Bey, with the approval of the Viceroy called together all the Consuls and read out to them a formal edict from the Porte. Forthwith each was required to recall from the isthmus any of his countrymen who were there working for de Lesseps. The move was completely unexpected. It created a precedent. There was silence in the room. No one was willing to bow to such an arbitrary demand, humbling his country before the Sick Man of Europe in the presence of his own colleagues. Then someone spoke in French. It was the voice of Sabatier accepting the order.

So, at the moment of what must have seemed almost miraculous deliverance, Ferdinand was again stabbed by the representative of his own country. All the rest of the *corps diplomatique* held back, even the British, rather than accept the authority of the Sultan over their own nationals; and also perhaps because of the fact that the Company's senior officer, in the absence of the President, was also Consul-General of the Low Countries – Ruyssenaers. Alone Sabatier carried out the order, and through his Vice-Consul at Damietta, who so recently had been a generous host to de Lesseps and his party, gave instructions that all French citizens were to cease work forthwith and await evacuation. To this the senior officer on the spot, engineer-in-charge Laroche, replied with a firm refusal, and, at the risk of prosecution on his return to France, went on with his hopeless task. In Paris the news reached Lesseps by telegraph. At first it must have seemed that this decisive intervention by the Porte was no more arguable than an earthquake, and that the result would be equally destructive. Only in one place was there concentrated sufficient power to weigh in such a scale: Napoleon. So Lesseps was forced to risk everything upon a single throw, upon the turn of a phrase. Urgently he sought an audience of the Emperor, and when the request was granted, took with him a group of his closest associates.

"To M. S. W. Ruyssenaers
    at Alexandria   Paris, 24th October, 1859.

I have the satisfaction of being able to tell you that yesterday we were received in audience by the Emperor at Saint Cloud. MM. Elie de Beaumont, Baron Ch. Dupin, our honorary vice-presidents, were accompanied by members of the Council. We formed a semicircle round the Emperor, who seemed well disposed. His Majesty, who already knew the object of our visit, spoke directly to me, saying: 'How is it, Monsieur de Lesseps, that so many people are against your enterprise?'

"'Sire,' I said immediately, 'because everyone thinks that Your Majesty has no intention of supporting us.'

"Twisting the ends of his long moustaches, as he has a habit of doing when he is pondering, after a few moments of silence the Emperor said: 'Very well; don't worry. You may count upon my support and my protection.'

"In the matter of English hostility and a recent communication from London which he termed 'stiff', the Emperor said: 'It is a squall. We shall have to take in a reef.'

"We then asked whether he would authorize us to announce to the shareholders that negotiations had been begun and that the General Meeting would be postponed; failing which we should be obliged to go into liquidation and refund the monies. He accepted our suggestion, and permitted us to adjourn the General Meeting as from the beginning of negotiations. He gave us to understand that he had already given orders to his Minister for Foreign Affairs that our rights and our operations in Egypt should be supported. We then thanked him.

"We complained about the conduct of the consul-general of France in Egypt, who had completely failed to protect our interests, and we handed over a note in support of our complaint. Then, judging that the moment had come to withdraw, I signed to my colleagues, and said to the Emperor that I thought it best that I should go to Constantinople and to Alexandria. He replied, 'That is very important.'

"Each of us then filed past His Majesty. With the Duke of Albuféra I waited until the end, having noticed that the Emperor evidently wished to speak privately with us. With an air of great *bonhomie*, he said, 'What do you think we ought to do now?'

"'Sire,' I answered, 'transfer the consul-general of France, who, being an agent of great capacity, should be posted somewhere else.'

"'*Eh bien!* If that is all, it is easily done. Tell Walewski so.'

"On leaving the audience I made haste to send to Count Walewski a note in which I gave the full account of which I have given you a summary. I ended it thus, 'The practical result of this audience seems to me to be as follows, apart from the political questions which will be worked out through diplomatic channels:

1. That M. Thouvenal receives instructions to ask the new Grand Vizier (whom I believe to be sympathetic to our project) for a letter to the Viceroy authorizing the continuation of preparatory work as defined in the letter which I sent to Aali Pasha, the ex-Grand Vizier, on the 3rd of March from Corfu in 1859; which definition was accepted by the Viceroy and acted upon over several months.

2. That the services of M. Sabatier are utilized elsewhere than in Egypt.

"'It was very fortunate that I happened to be in France rather than remaining in Egypt, since the action of Muktar Bey, which

caused you so much worry, has resulted in you giving to me new
proof of your tact, your spirit, and your devotion to the Company's
interests.'"

*   *   *

As usual the Fates gave Ferdinand only enough encouragement to carry him on to the next crisis, which was not long
delayed. Though Sabatier, who, in the nature of the instructions which he had received, had some reason for his apparently
unpatriotic behaviour, was duly removed; and though at Constantinople Thouvenal was instructed to lend his official support to the canal project; once again the situation crystallized
without anything having been done to alter the *status quo*.
This was hardly surprising in view of the fact that Walewski
told the British Ambassador that while France hoped England
would abandon her opposition, yet the Emperor preferred to
see the Company wound up rather than prejudice good relations between the two countries. The French Foreign Minister
added that His Majesty, faced with a formal demand for protection by his subjects engaged upon the venture, could do nothing
but respond; but he had 'on several occasions' told de Lesseps
that if England continued her opposition the Company ought
to go into liquidation.

Constantinople settled down again on the old basis, with
British influence predominant and the bias of the Porte inclined
towards the veto, which, after such a long delay and so much
bitterness, would be much easier to pronounce than the firman
of positive approval. An added complication was due to the
increased French understanding with Russia, which Turkey
naturally distrusted, and so tended to choose England. On the
other hand the Austrian war had made France more formidable, and so the canal became a mere focus for far wider issues.
For instance, French influence might detach Egypt from the
Ottoman Empire. To counter such a drift, British diplomacy
opened up the whole question of the settlement of 1841, which
was to be annulled so that once again Egypt should become
a mere province of the Turks. In that case the canal would
come directly under the authority of the Porte, and the present
issue would be by-passed. Had this proposal been made before
Solferino, or even before Napoleon – perhaps in consequence

of his victory – ventured upon the stronger line at Constantinople, it might well have been accepted. As it was the Sultan
found himself too much in awe of the French armies to take so
definite a step.

And so, with pipes and cups of coffee, conferences, committees,
and a flood of words from Lesseps himself, the old wrangle
persisted at a higher voltage. The Vizier was dismissed, probably for being too sympathetic to de Lesseps. Diplomats
engaged in an increasingly futile correspondence. In Egypt
Säid still 'hid behind a tree', while on the isthmus the work
went slowly forward; the fall of Sabatier having proved a deter-
rent to any further attempts at boycott. The Porte proposed
an inquiry should be held to re-interpret all the various agreements which at one time or another Lesseps had entered into
with the Viceroy. Lesseps refused to co-operate. Then it was
suggested – brilliant procrastination – that the issues should be
referred to the Powers for a prior agreement between them.
Clutching at this straw, Count Walewski proposed to take the
initiative in appealing to the other interested countries through
their Foreign Ministers, so leading up to an international
conference at which it was just conceivable that a majority vote
might decide for or against the canal. Such a conference might
prove to be the only way in which to prevent the further
deterioration of Anglo-French relations, and under these circumstances the Low Countries became of particular importance as
the potential casting vote. They were vitally interested in the
eastern trade, and not being a Mediterranean power, considered
the canal from very much the same standpoint as did England.
Accordingly Lytton Bulwer sought out Ruyssenaers when the
latter was visiting Constantinople, and the result was reported
to the Dutch Minister on the 30th of November:

"Further to my last communication I offer to Your Excellency
an account of a personal interview with the British Ambassador
about the Suez affair. Sir Henry asked me whether I had heard
anything from the Hague about Count Walewski's request to several
Governments for their support. I replied in the negative, and when
he desired further information I told him that in my opinion the
affair with us was never a political issue. At the outset it was in
high favour, but serious investigation of its advantages and dis-
advantages to the Netherlands ended unfavourably, and so on
balance I would tend to be against it. I added that my Govern-

ment had refrained from all interference. We had adopted a neutral attitude, and in all probability that would remain our policy in the future. Should the French Ambassador ask me the same question I would give him exactly the same answer."

At first sight such a declaration seems extraordinary on the part of one who for years had been a passionate *canaliste*, and now occupied a most responsible position as Ferdinand's adjutant and confidant. No doubt Sir Henry had been aware of this, and at the back of his mind may have hoped to play to his own advantage the contrast between official Dutch neutrality and this Dutchman's personal rôle. If so he must have been disappointed. Ruyssenaers was perfectly content to be diplomatically neutral, and had recently informed his Government that he would most strictly adhere to their renewed instructions to that effect. He was aware that a recent committee of experts had reported unfavourably on the canal in terms of the benefits it might confer on Holland. Owing to the dangers and difficulties of navigation with sail in the narrow seas, and in the canal itself, they concluded that there would not even be a significant saving of time by the new route. Lord Palmerston soon heard of this, and was equally unable to foresee the developments in steam which would completely remove the objection.

So Ruyssenaers, who did believe in such developments, and also in the usefulness of the canal, if not to Holland, then to many other countries, was able to pursue in honesty two apparently irreconcilable lines of conduct without in the least damaging his considerable reputation or embarrassing either his Government or the Company. He had considerable influence with the Sultan, and it must have been galling for Sir Henry to realize that in spite of the genuine Dutch neutrality Ruyssenaers was working as hard as ever for the canal, in a position which was diplomatically impregnable. But even he could not alter convictions which by now had set like concrete. Walewski's appeal was a foregone failure unless someone important changed sides. Only a completely new development could bring that to pass. Every argument had been used over and over again. Every legitimate pressure had been applied where ever it had the slightest chance of success: deadlock. In a chastened but still determined mood, Lesseps left for Egypt.

He had at least a crumb of good news, though by now even he was too cautious to make much of it:

"To His Excellency Zulficar Pasha
          at Cairo.   Alexandria, 3rd January, 1860.

I arrived from Constantinople to see His Highness before my return to Paris, where I am expected, and where I shall follow up the negotiations begun by the Government of the Emperor. This evening I take the Cairo train and to-morrow morning I shall call upon you to find out if His Highness will receive me. I have good news to give him about the enterprise, in the accomplishment of which I do not cease to demonstrate to him my devotion to his interests and to his person.

"The Ambassador of France at Constantinople has asked the Porte, in the name of the Emperor, to express officially and fully its opinion upon the execution of the project which has been submitted to it by the Viceroy, to cut through the Isthmus of Suez a canal for the shipping of the high seas. After sixteen sittings of the Council of Ministers it was unanimously agreed by the Members of the Divan that the Viceroy's project would be helpful to the interests of the Ottoman Empire, and, so far as the Porte was concerned, there was no obstacle to the realization of the project."

Here was a real victory – at its face value. But behind the belated and surprising decision there was of course the unchanged international situation. In fact the decision of the Porte was arrived at less for the sake of Lesseps, or even for the Viceroy, than in the hope of profiting from the threatening political atmosphere. Moreover, the approval of the canal scheme was conditional, and the conditions must have been regarded in Constantinople as virtually impossible. So the Porte had in effect made its grave pronouncement without saying anything significant at all. *If* the Powers agreed among themselves to guarantee the neutrality of the canal, and, incidentally, to support the existing régime in the Ottoman Empire, then obviously there would be no further objection to the canal from the Porte or from any other source. On the other hand, should the Powers continue at loggerheads, the Porte would lose no 'face', the canal would be postponed indefinitely, and everyone except Lesseps would be happy. The Sultan felt secure whatever happened. Lytton Bulwer did not. The very fact that the Porte had shifted the plane of negotiation high into the international sphere went far towards taking the matter out of his hands. It was one thing to bring pressure to bear at Constantinople, another to have to defend England's attitude at European conferences, where, as in the case of Palmerston's interviews with Lesseps, the real reasons behind the negative attitude – all in terms of mistrust of France – could not be openly aired owing to the entente. The result would be to suspect British diplomacy either of folly or of fear.

So Bulwer conceived a plan by which, whether or not the Powers reached any agreement, whether or not the firman authorizing the canal were finally granted, England would retain her dominant position; and, if necessary, have the veto promulgated. His suggestion amounted to a proposal to buy out the French interests and form a new Company based on a new concession, not from the Viceroy but from the Sultan. The Company would then be under British control and would owe nothing either to Lesseps or to his canal. This plan failed, probably because of the obstinate patriotism of the ordinary French investor. The Powers did not even trouble to start conferences about the canal, so obvious was it that there would be no chance of agreement. Again the irresistible force was up against an immovable object. Edgar-Bonnet says: " So ended the year 1859, which saw the first practical progress in the isthmus, but has been almost fatal. The worst has been avoided. The Emperor's initiative, at last deployed, cleared the air. The work is in theory at a standstill, but in fact, and with the tacit approval of the Viceroy, Lesseps and his heroic phalanx plod on that the flame may not completely die. Nothing is lost: nothing is secure."

The last sentence is applicable to the next three years, during which, as though within a cloud of invisibility, the quantities of men and material on the isthmus gradually increased, and the line of the *rigole* crawled southward from the terminal shanty-town, Port Said; while at the other end of the line the Freshwater Canal also advanced. Yet so complete was the deadlock abroad that neither Säid nor the Sultan, nor France nor England, seem to have been officially aware that anything was being done. This suited both Lesseps, who was quite happy to go on working in the dark, and Säid, who took courage in the silence. Also he was very much relieved to be left alone to do what he thought fit. Even the arrows of Lord Palmerston gradually lost their power to wound, though on occasion Lesseps still found it necessary to try to shield his people from them – as in the matter of those surplus shares:

"To the Company's Correspondents.　　　Paris, 31st August, 1860.

I have been charged by the Committee of Administration to inform you of a decision taken by it with the object of meeting the allegations made by Lord Palmerston in the House of Commons of England at the session of the 23rd of August, 1860, in reply to a question concerning the Suez Canal. These allegations bear upon three subjects quite distinct from one another, to which His Lordship, in a spirit of malevolence towards the canal, implied a relationship which does not exist.

1. Lord Palmerston declared that a certain number of shares booked to the Viceroy's account were transferred without his knowledge or consent. This accusation is completely false. It is only necessary to cite the report which I made to the shareholders at the General Meeting on the 15th of May this year. After explaining all the facts relative to this transaction and having traced its history, which has received the widest publicity, I said, 'We consulted with the Viceroy to the end that he should definitely take for his account the shares which had been set aside for foreign bankers who, through force of circumstances, could not fulfil their engagements.' Not only did this statement draw forth no protest from His Highness' Government; on my recent visit to Egypt the agreement on this matter as between His Highness and myself was confirmed by the Egyptian Government.

2. Lord Palmerston claimed that the work already done shows that it will be impossible to complete the canal without such an expenditure of both time and money that no Company would be able to bear it. The contrary is true. The experience already gained permits no doubt but that the Maritime Suez Canal will be open for navigation much sooner than was expected, and at rates less than those forecast by the International Commission of engineers.

3. Lord Palmerston tried to suggest that the loan recently arranged between His Highness and a well-known financier was rendered necessary by his investment in the canal. That is not the case. The Suez Canal is quite distinct from the transaction which has just been completed. The ordinary income of the Viceroy permits him to fulfil his engagements with the Company, engagements which, incidentally, he, with good reason, regards as a new source of credit and of revenue."

Less than a year later the commitment of money and material on the isthmus was such that labour became an acute problem, in the absence of the call-up which, under pressure from the Porte, Säid had not dared to make. But the Sultan had reckoned without Ferdinand's extraordinary personal influence in those parts, added to the attractive terms and conditions which, according to the original arrangement with the Viceroy, were applicable equally to free labour and the *corvée*. Lesseps wrote to the Duke of Albufera in Paris:

"I have just completed my tour of the whole of the Isthmus. The six working sites are complete and their machines are being erected with great keenness. Each of them has between 200 and 250 free native workers, which is all we need for the moment. At Kantara the working site employs between 500 and 600·Arabs from the Syrian frontier, who are installed in a village we have built for them, to which they have brought their wives and children. A hundred girls and boys from 10 to 13 years old go at their tasks with remarkable zeal and energy. At Port Said I only paused to see the result of the decision which I took last December, when I made all the necessary arrangements. There are at the moment in the Arab village of Port Said 600 fellahs with their families. They expressed to me their satisfaction with the good treatment they are getting, and they assure me that they will not leave us during Ramadan. In all the camps the Arabs have their music of tambourines and flutes. Even a few dancing-girls have turned up at the working site of Seuil.

"The Viceroy is quite calm and his attitude towards us is excellent. I have arranged with him that the Inspector-General of Works in the villages of Egypt will assist recruiting. M. Joseph Vernoni will be going to Zagazig as soon as our recruiting system is properly organized. I was afraid that the sudden death of the Coptic Patriarch at Cairo would produce difficulties about the recruitment of Coptic workers; but there is going to be no hanging back. I am sending into the villages of Middle and High Egypt a prominent Copt who is loyal to me and highly intelligent. He will leave with the necessary orders and introductions."

When Lesseps himself went recruiting in Palestine, his journey became almost a royal progress because of his personal prestige dating from the time when he delivered the men of Bethlehem from the galleys. It was essential that there should be no call-up in Egypt until the Porte approved construction, for such a move could not be kept quiet in a country thick with Turkish informers. Even if Säid had agreed, which was unlikely, to use the *corvée* before the 'preparatory' period came to an end, it must have involved losing another trick to the enemy. Meanwhile Ferdinand's desire to carry his affair into the House of Lords was gratified. On the 6th of May Lord Caernarvon opened a debate which proceeded on lines singularly discouraging to the *canalistes* and included some remarks, delivered by Lord Ellenborough, to much the same effect as those which Lord Palmerston had been reiterating for years – that the Company was a swindle and that Lesseps was a crook.

As with the unfortunate Stephenson, so with the noble lord, as soon as Lesseps heard about it he issued a challenge, but, being much occupied by business in Egypt, caused two friends of his, an admiral and a general, to handle the 'affair of honour' on his behalf. They proved less touchy than their principal, to whom they wrote pointing out that if he were to reach for his sword every time someone made a rude remark he would be issuing challenges every day. They might also have pointed out that in England, though an occasional duel had been fought up to a few years before, the custom was now definitely out of fashion, and, apart from the risk of being hanged by the neck, it would not do Lesseps any good to be concerned with such a *coup de théâtre*. But, though they may have wished to write in such terms, the two seconds were constrained to be very formal. Indeed, Ferdinand himself was unusually ponderous in his style, and carefully refrained from mentioning the name of the man whom he judged to have insulted him; presumably because the challenge itself would become an insult, the name being given, if in the opinion of the seconds there was no valid ground for it.

Later in the year the Porte's idea for a prior agreement among the Powers was carried a stage further by the proposal to set up an international commission to consider the subject; which caused Lord Palmerston to write the following letter to his Foreign Secretary, Lord John Russell, whom Lesseps described as 'a small man, thin and melancholy'. The letter so clearly summarizes the situation as viewed from London that it is quoted in full in the *Lettres, Journal et Documents* (iv, 123) both in French and in English:

"74 Piccadilly. 8th December, 1861.
MY DEAR RUSSELL,
            The proposal of a French, English and Austrian commission to inquire into the practicability of the Suez Canal sounds fair and plausible, but it would be a dangerous measure.

There are three aspects under which this scheme may be looked at. First, as to the commercial advantage of it; secondly, as to the engineering and the financial practicability of executing it; thirdly, as to the political effect of the canal, if completed. Now we cannot deny that if no objection could be urged against the scheme on the second and third hands, no valid objection could be made to it on the first. Looking at the matter purely with reference to the commerce of Europe, any great work which would shorten considerably the voyage to India would be advantageous to all nations trading by sea to Asia. Even on this ground, however, there is something to be said against the scheme, because it was demonstrated by a Dutch engineer that owing to the difficulties of navigating the Red Sea, in consequence of coral reefs, prevailing winds, and the intense heat, the navigation round the Cape would, except with regard to very powerful steamers, be cheaper and shorter than through the canal.

"But the second point hardly admits of a doubt. The Lesseps Company have now been ostensibly at work for nearly ten years at a canal that is to be a hundred feet wide and thirty feet deep from sea to sea, with ports for sea-going vessels on the Mediterranean and Red Sea ends, and yet up to this moment, though a very large part of their nominal capital has been spent, not a single spadeful has been turned up for the construction of the canal. Lesseps has begun what he calls his *rigole*, a boat canal twelve feet wide and four feet deep, of which one-third, beginning from the north end, has been finished; a second third may be completed next spring or early summer, and the remaining third would be more easily finished by letting the water of the Red Sea into a salt marsh some way to the north of Suez. Lesseps is eager about this, because he thinks that his shares would rise in the market at Paris if he could show that he had actually floated a boat from sea to sea. But he will not tell his shareholders what is nevertheless the fact, that this boat canal or *rigole* is not to form any part whatever of the ship canal; the ship canal is to be dug in a line parallel with this boat canal, and the boat canal is only to be used like a railway, for the easier conveyance of workmen, provisions and material as the great work goes on. I understand there is scarcely one among the French engineers employed who would not, if he told the truth, acknowledge that the ship canal could not be made without an amount of money and a period of time far exceeding all the calculations hitherto made, and that if completed, it never could be made to pay the interest on the cost incurred. It may be safely said, therefore, that, as a commercial undertaking, it is a bubble scheme which has been taken up on political grounds and in antagonism to English interests and English policy.

"Well then, we come to the last point, namely the political objects of the enterprise, and these are hostility to England in every possible modification of the scheme. It requires only a glance at the map of the world to see how great would be the naval and military advantage to France in a war with England to have such a short cut to the Indian seas while we should be obliged to send ships and troops round the Cape. Thouvenal proposes, indeed, that the passage of men of war should be forbidden as at the Dardanelles, but I presume he does not expect us to receive such a proposal without a decently repressed smile. Of course the first week of a war between France and England would see 15 or 20,000 Frenchmen in possession of the canal, to keep it open for them and shut for us. But then, moreover, so strong a military barrier between Syria and Egypt would greatly add to the means of the Pasha for the time being to declare himself independent of Turkey, which would mean his being dependent on France; and lastly, if the canal should ever be made, the French Company is to have a large grant of land in the middle of Egypt and would establish a colony whose complaints against the Egyptian Government, well or ill-founded, would give the French Government pretences for interfering in all the internal affairs of the country.

"I should say therefore, on the whole, that it would be best for the French and English Governments to have this scheme as a commercial and engineering question to be settled by the result of experience and the money markets of Europe; and that, as regards the political question, all we ask of the French Government is not to interfere in the matter, but to let all questions between the Sublime Porte and the Pasha be settled according to the mutual rights and reciprocal obligations of those two parties.

Yours sincerely,

PALMERSTON."

Chapter 12. ADVANCE

Turning his back upon the international wrangle, Ferdinand de Lesseps concentrated upon making the quickest possible demonstration that the great canal was feasible. Accordingly, he spent most of his time on the isthmus, ceaselessly planning, organizing, rallying. At night he continued the flow of his river of letters. If he had no training in engineering, his informed general ability had given him particular understanding of the problems to be faced between Port Said and Suez; and if he delegated to contractors the specific tasks of excavation, he retained an overall command which was singularly efficient, both as regards the flow of work and the growth of the organization which came into being behind the lines. The contractors became the executive officers of one commander, who also represented the various committees and the shareholders. By any standard, the build-up of the Suez Canal excavationary force was a task which only an exceptional individual could have achieved, particularly since it was without precedent and had to operate under such adverse conditions of climate and communication. Owing to the opposition from Constantinople he still could not make use of the call-up, and as a result the number of men he could set to work was below the minimum necessary for the rate of progress required by the financial situation. Even so the scale of operations was soon of the order of that of an army in the field, and not the smallest indication of Ferdinand's capacity for organization is the lack of red-tape. Not only because of lack of typewriters but also because of the language difficulty, paper work was avoided as much as possible and initiative allowed on the widest scale consistent with the progress of the work. For instance in the matter of supplies other than rations forming part of the worker's pay; instead of setting up a Company monopoly, traders were encouraged to go out into the desert, competition between them being relied upon to keep down prices. In this way Stephenson's primary objection was met to the satisfaction of both employers and employed.

As for the Viceroy, seeing that no further action was being taken against him, the enemy being content to reiterate the old charges, he again began to receive de Lesseps. He finally agreed to take the shares which had been put to his account when the subscription fell short. So until now, even if there were no question about the legality of their allocation, it is clear that Säid had been prepared at need to repudiate it. They were to be paid for over several years, and by no means all of them in cash; so in spite of the fact that he had regularized the position in the eyes of his shareholders, if not of all the world, Lesseps remained in urgent need of progress sufficient to justify a further appeal for money. Though no admission seems to have been made in writing, he must already have realized that he would be most unlikely to succeed without additional capital. On the other hand it is certainly untrue that he went on with dishonourable intent. He still had faith not only in the nobility of the project and its practicability, but also in the means. If truth lies between his apologists and his enemies, it must be much nearer the former. For if Lesseps obtained money and money's worth from Säid to an extent which embarrassed the Prince, he did so not for himself, nor even for the shareholders, but for the sake of a work which he believed – among other things – would be the saving of Egypt. Whatever they may have been at the time of the floatation, the finances of the Company were now upon a firm basis; for though Egypt, with a national debt of 160,000,000 francs, was happily in possession of an excess of income over expenditure amounting to some 40,000,000, the outlook was even better. As for Säid's personal expenditure, if he spent a matter of ten million francs on a drawing-room at the Abdin Palace, his personal contribution to public works was vastly greater, and to a large extent justifiable. Apart from the civil list, he had a huge income derived from inherited estates. And if the enemy is allowed to make the point that Säid was grossly extravagant, it must still be admitted that the rates of interest on his borrowing were extortionate. If Säid and his successors are blameworthy for borrowing, the lenders, who should have been

in loco parentis to the infant State, must enter the dock on
the more serious charge of financial vampirism.

*   *   *

At the beginning of 1862 the immediate objectives were the
extension of the ancient River of Moses from the neighbourhood of Zagazig to make fresh water available at Timsah in
the centre of the isthmus, and the extension of the *rigole* from
Port Said to the lake. This involved the deployment of two
labour divisions, widely separated; but Lesseps never seems to
have lost his personal control over them, even at the cost of
much personal hardship and lack of sleep. As early as January,
before any call-up had taken place, he had a total of 20,000
volunteers; but he needed 50,000, the number which had originally been agreed between the engineers, the Viceroy and himself. The rate required of them was one cubic metre per man/
day, which in view of the fact that as much as 2·5 cubic
metres was quite usual, suggests that he did not seek to drive
the men harder than was fair. Even so there were frequent
desertions, including that of a military contingent which
Lesseps was glad to be rid of because the men were such trouble-
makers. Nor was the incidence of the labour demand unduly
harsh on the country. Lesseps calculated that, allowing for the
foreign volunteers, if every village in Egypt furnished between
three and five men he would have all the labour he needed.
As for pay and conditions, in spite of the enemy's accusations
there seems no doubt but that in general both were good, not
only in relation to geographical conditions but also in comparison with what the fellah was accustomed to at home. And
it must be borne in mind that it was Säid who put an end to
the serf-system, a reform which, by freeing the fellah from
the residence and land ties which had held him down in one
place all his life, produced a great shift of population. To
facilitate this movement, internal customs dues were done
away with, and this in turn made a significant reduction,
temporarily, in the national income. Egypt was in effect passing very rapidly from a medieval to a modern state. Disorganization and abnormal expenditure were inevitable, and would
have occurred even if Säid's character had been quite other-

wise. As for de Lesseps, he had no part in the country's
economics except in so far as he became the greatest single
employer and headed the greatest single investment. If the
business had turned out as well as they had reason to expect,
it would have gone far to realize the dream of both of them,
a prosperous contemporary Egypt, no longer the whipping-boy
of Europe nor the chattel of the Sublime Porte.

Even to-day the enemy still suggests that the canal was ruinous
to Egypt, largely because she had no adequate control over it.
But the intention as between Ferdinand and Säid was certainly that Egypt should have control, if not of the equity,
which was to be spread as widely as possible in the interests
of internationalism, then of the direction. It was the fault of
neither of them that force of circumstances—that is to say
force of creditors, robbed Egypt of the reward which the
founders of the canal had jointly planned for her. As for the
political aspect, which has caused so much trouble, the original
intention was to give the Viceroy such personal influence, in
part by his shares but chiefly through his position as the person
appointing the President of the Company, as would assure
Egypt's political rights and contribute to the balance of interests upon which the perpetual neutrality of the waterway must
ultimately depend. Had human nature been even a little less
murky than it proved to be in this context, then Ferdinand's
reasonable forecast would have been justified, and instead of
the Canal Zone being a perpetual bone of contention, its
integrity would have been a focus of peacemaking. For, just as
the Powers with astonishing unanimity had agreed to support
Turkey, so, according to de Lesseps they ought to support the
new Egypt. Finally the human fact remains that between the
ports of Said and Suez, where before his time the desert
remained inviolate save to an occasional tribe of nomads, there
now live and work nearly two hundred thousand people.

During February 1862 the Freshwater Canal reached Timsah
and was formally inaugurated by Lesseps, who travelled along
it from Cairo in a matter of forty hours, at a cost, he said, of
200 francs; in comparison with the vast expense to which he,
or rather the Viceroy, had been put not so many years ago,
on his first survey. Then the only water was in kegs between
the tents, where it had to be guarded day and night by armed

men. Now the 'blessed water' was not only enough to meet the needs of fifty thousand men in the middle of the desert; along it would float the boats which would save them a dreary march, and bring all they needed to the site. Before the end of the month Lesseps wrote of seventy boats, 'passing and re-passing under my window'. Such were the first-fruits of his dream, and they did not pass unnoticed in the enemy camp. 'If so much can be done by volunteers,' the enemy must have thought, 'what will happen when the call-up takes place? We must at all costs put a stop to that.' But for once the enemy had left it too late, the initiative was at last with Lesseps. In March the call-up began in an orderly manner, and the flow of men to the working-sites (*chantiers*) proceeded with commendable smoothness. Pay, conditions and accommodation came up to the requirements which Lesseps himself had laid down in agreement with Säid – for the purpose, among others, of not giving the enemy cause for complaint. The work promptly leapt ahead. It seemed that the enemy were for the first time on the defensive, and that they had used up the last of their ammunition. Blithely Ferdinand went back to Paris to preside at the third General Meeting, held on May Day, at which he was able to give to his shareholders a most encouraging picture. In his speech he described how, with the arrival of the *corvée*, even simple machines, wheelbarrows and the like, had to be withdrawn because of the fellah's preference for his traditional implements, the pick and the basket, unchanged since Pharaoh reigned.

There were at this time six separate *chantiers* at El Guisr alone, which because it represented a great step of hard rock, thirty feet in height, was soon known simply as le Seuil, the threshold. The overcoming of this obstacle would do more for the prestige of the Company than many miles of canal along the flat, and in itself would tend to prove that the canal was a practical proposition after all:

"When the cutting of Seuil has been achieved the rest of the work will be comparatively short and easy. Once the water of the Mediterranean has reached Lake Timsah we shall begin the extension of the *rigole* from the Lake to Suez, parallel with the continuation of the Freshwater Canal as far as the Red Sea. These works are not difficult and should not take long; they should easily be completed within nine months. And so, within a year in all, if the supply of workers does not fail us, the two seas shall mingle, the problem of their meeting solved."

He did not have to explain to his shareholders that Lord Palmerston had made a mistake in thinking of the *rigole* as parallel to the ship canal, thus involving the Company in a double task. Rather, the *rigole* was an essential technical achievement without which the ship canal could neither be sited with certainty nor dug with speed. Once the *rigole* showed the actual water-line, then also it would serve, not only to bring the men and material which otherwise must go, at impossible costs and labour, by camel-back; but also would permit the use of dredgers which, even of the most primitive type, would greatly facilitate the work. Not only would dredgers cut the channel wider and deeper, they, or barges alongside, would be able to get rid of the spoil. They could not, however, dig ahead, so that whether for the *rigole*, which was in fact 8 metres wide – more than twice Palmerston's figure, and 1·2 metres deep, or for the ship canal into which it grew, the forward movement had generally to be done 'dry'. At this time powered machines hardly existed. At Port Said there were in all four dredgers with cranes, but the canal itself was a pick and basket job. The work was necessarily arduous, the climate an added strain. The enemy made great play with both factors, foretelling a terrible toll of suffering which the construction must necessarily entail. Here again Lesseps was able to confound them. Among Europeans the mortality was less than half that in France. Among natives the rate was only one in five thousand. The hospitals, which had been established as part of his medical welfare service, were largely empty, a result due no doubt to the strict attention to field hygiene; upon which experience had taught him to insist because of the overriding need to prevent a cholera epidemic. Still no one seems to have thought of that disease as water-borne, and the medical profession generally remained in ignorance of John Snow's conclusive researches, done at the peril of his life in the Soho outbreak of 1854 which killed 10,738 people, almost all of them the victims of contaminated Thames water. The hygiene principle, though in practice generally effective in the absence of cholera, was still understood only in archaic terms: "The pathologist knows no difference of operation between one decaying substance and another; so soon as he recognizes organic matter undergoing decomposition, so soon he recognizes the most fertile soil for the inception of epidemic diseases." Reliance upon this inadequate hypothesis would be worse than useless in the event of a water-borne epidemic.

As for the financial situation, though the need for speed was still imperative, Lesseps was able to show that on paper the Company was much better off than the enemy had predicted; to demonstrate which he announced a most advantageous purchase of land, the famous Ouady Estate athwart the Freshwater Canal. It was certainly impressive that the Company could afford to lock up in the ground a matter of almost a million francs, representing 200 francs per hectare (2,471 acres) for 9,000 hectares belonging to the Prince El Hamy Pasha. The Prince must have been well disposed towards Lesseps, for the price was evidently a very fair one, in spite of the expectation that the estate would become much more fertile in the near future. Also the owner could legally control the flow of water, and might have forced Lesseps to bid to a ruinous figure.

*   *   *

Lesseps could not forbear to quote earlier great works in comparison with his own humane and efficient organization. He pointed out that, according to Herodotus, in Necho's time the Seuil cost 80,000 lives; and as for modern times, the haste with which the British pushed ahead the railway during the Indian Mutiny resulted in much suffering and a high mortality through the inefficiency of Indian man-management. Even so he was attacked on the ground that because conditions had been bad in the past, therefore they must always be so, particularly when the corvée was employed. It was implied that Lesseps was no better than a slaver, and the passionate feelings which many people uncritically vented on this subject tended to focus on him. On the 23rd of May he wrote a spirited protest to Mr. Layard, Under-Secretary of State for Foreign Affairs:

"It is in a country enjoying the most advanced civilization that the following things happen. 'Young children are apprenticed by their parents, who receive the wages stipulated in the contract; and the apprenticeship, at no matter what age it begins, goes on until twenty-one. If they resist, magistrates compel the children to keep the contract by which they are bound, although their consent to it need never have been asked. As long as he is under twenty-one the apprentice forms part of his master's property, and in the case of the master's death the heirs inherit him. Thus the apprentice has been bought by one man from another, for the sum of twelve francs. It is not unusual in the case of an impecunious employer for the apprentice to be let to someone else for more money than would be due to his parents. An apprentice can be beaten and starved. . . .' This picture has been painted by one of the most popular writers in England, and the country where such things happen is England. . . . They are trying to make out that both the Company and the Egyptians are guilty. I am ready to defend them. Look under what conditions this so-called forced labour operates. I invoke a speech by Lord Henry Scott, whom you yourself have praised. He said, 'It is true that without the intervention of the Government no public works can be undertaken in an oriental country, but while remembering that the workers on the isthmus are regularly paid and well fed, one cannot say that they are exactly forced labour. On the isthmus they live much better than they do when they are engaged in their usual occupations.'"

At this time of rapid expansion, when the scale of operations was becoming gigantic – though still officially 'preparatory', there were certainly places where, temporarily, conditions were not so good. Nor did all men take to the work with eagerness, as the desertion-rate shows. But they were healthy, and they did receive their wages '*de la main à la main*' and not, as was alleged, have them withheld, or even paid to the overseer. Most surprising of all, and as great a tribute to Lesseps as anything could be in this context, they willingly worked through the month of Ramadan, during which the Koran says that only soldiers and the sick may abstain from the rule of fasting from sunrise to sunset, abjuring smoking and scent.

So, taking the broad picture of the work in progress and its financial backing, together with the complex management problems, it is evident that Lesseps and his shareholders had reason to be satisfied. It did seem, too, as though at last they might be left alone to get on with the work and confront the world with a *fait accompli* which would make the Sultan's firman a mere redundancy. As usual they were too optimistic. Far from being content to see the enterprise as a going concern about which there was hardly any point in further argument, England again secretly increased pressure at the Porte; this time with the object of having the *corvée* completely suppressed on the ground that it was a form of slavery. But this slow-moving sap was less of an immediate threat than a new under-cover thrust against the Company's shares, which were standing around 470 against 500 par. It would soon come to light that another attempt was on foot to break de Lesseps and form a new Company, not on this occasion through British initiative but by the action of financiers in France, at least one of whom had access to the Emperor. When the time was ripe, Napoleon was to be asked to disown Lesseps and lend his support to the new venture which London would not oppose.

As yet both these movements went unobserved by Ferdinand, who for the first time began to feel himself relatively secure. England was officially silent. Napoleon remained friendly, as did Säid. Every week brought more material, more workmen. Wonderfully the great ditch grew and the heart of the dreamer was lifted up. At eleven o'clock on the morning of the 18th of November:

"'By the grace of God,' he declared in the presence of a multitude, 'and in the name of His Highness Mohammed-Säid, I ordain that the waters of the Mediterranean enter Lake Timsah.'

"There was a moment of solemn silence. Everyone's attention was concentrated on the embankment. Suddenly water came boiling out of the cut which had just been made. Growling and carrying away the earth, the flood moved on. A great shout went up. Emotion kindled every heart. I saw tears on cheeks the sun had turned to bronze. Mingling openly with all the rest I heard the reiterated hurrahs of the representatives of England. The band played the Egyptian national anthem. Standing, the Ulemas invoked Allah at the tops of their voices. The chiefs read the *fetva*, a kind of religious witness to the great event, which will also be read in all the mosques of Egypt. In the chapel at Seuil a *Te Deum* was sung by the Bishop of Egypt."

Lesseps preserved a copy of the *fetva*, which reads in part:

"Surely the great feats of antiquity and the search for means to increase the material well-being of peoples have been good actions. Surely also the putting into practice of an idea which serves the industry and progress of the world, as with great discoveries which facilitate communication between peoples; they are admirable things which everyone ought to admire. But all that has been sur-

passed. Among the great Powers, Allah has deigned to choose the
land of France, whose rank and dignity are so high. And He has
looked upon a man of high birth, and has revealed to this man
His will for the creation of a great and useful enterprise, which on
completion will bear such good fruit. The chosen of Allah has
worthily discharged the mission with which he has been entrusted,
and he has brought to the accomplishment of the will of Allah his
high intelligence. He has straightly followed his road, with neither
slowing down nor halt; and thus it is that this great work has come
to the state of completion which to-day we see. This result is due
to Mohammed-Säid, to him whose power gives to his people happiness, prosperity and all security, by night and by day. May God
protect his reign and his days. In the name of almighty God, master
and author of all creation, so be it."

But the days of Säid were already numbered short, and with
their term the canal which his Act of Concession had made
possible, would again be at the mercy of the enemy. It would
soon seem that neither Allah nor Jehovah were any more
attentive to the needs of their servant than was the muse of
the poet Bornier, who, earlier in the year, had won a prize
offered by the *Académie Française* for an epic on the canal.
It may be that the artistic merit of the piece is not to-day rated
very high, and its nationalism – typical of the epoch, is quaint;
but the poet had something in common with the attitude of
the bishop at his *Te Deum*, with the Ulemas and their *fetva*,
and with the personal mystique of Lesseps himself. All of them
believed, as did numbers of private individuals, that above and
beyond questions of commerce, or even of politics, the canal
was an act of faith, a pilgrimage in sand:

> Au travail! Ouvriers que notre France envoie,
> Tracez, pour l'univers, cette nouvelle voie!
> Vos pères, les héros, sont venus jusqu'ici;
> Soyez ferme comme eux intrepides,
> Comme eux vous combattez aux pieds des Pyramides,
> Et leurs quatre mille ans vous contemplent aussi!

> Oui, c'est pour l'univers! Pour l'Asie et l'Europe,
> Pour ces climats lointains que la nuit enveloppe,
> Pour le Chinois perfide et l'Indien demi-nu;
> Pour les peuples heureux, libres, humains et braves,
> Pour les peuples méchants, pour les peuples escalves,
> Pour ceux 'a qui le Christ est encore inconnu.

Occasionally Säid seemed to catch a glimpse of his friend's vision, but his was not the kind of character to follow his heart against his head, and when the going became rough he took refuge in expediency; which must have irritated Ferdinand, who was never very good at appreciating another person's point of view if it happened to be expressed on a different emotional wavelength. Yet basically Säid had remained loyal to Ferdinand in spite of their quarrels, and now that success had been demonstrated to the world the two men were closer than ever. In Ferdinand's phrase, 'the situation could not be better'. There is no more satisfying occupation than mutual congratulation, and they two had reason for it. In the past few months enormous progress had been made, and not only in terms of labour. A potential enemy, Sir John Hawkshaw, President of the Institute of Civil Engineers, had recently visited the works and afterwards issued a written report in which he concluded that virtually all of the Lesseps claims would be made good. As Sir Arnold Wilson says:

"The skill and resource of Voisin Bey, the first engineer-in-chief, and his assistant, Laroche, had worked wonders. A French contractor, M. Lavalley, had devised and constructed a fleet of powerful trough-dredgers, the prototype of modern steam excavators, which deposited silt by long shoots at some distance from either bank of the canal, without the intervention of barges. These and other mechanical appliances totalling 10,000 h.p., capable of removing two million cubic metres a month, had the effect of reducing by three-fourths the number of workmen needed."

The quotation, though of the period, nevertheless runs ahead of what Säid and Lesseps knew in early January. Then the dredgers were still building, but on the other hand the *corvée* seemed assured.

Even Sir Henry Bulwer's visit only served to increase the confidence of these two, the prime movers of the whole vast enterprise. In duty bound, Bulwer took occasion in a speech to reiterate the hostility of England, but he himself seems to have felt that it was too late for such words. England was faced with a very solid fact, and he knew better than anyone else that Britannia had no need nor desire to *force* Marianne to give up her pet, any more than had Napoleon the need or desire to break up the entente. Words, words, words, there had been so many of them! And now there were none left which could be expected to call halt to the ant-like, irresistible progress of the dig.

Sir Henry met the Viceroy at the Nile Barrage on the 3rd of January. Four days later, still at the Barrage, Säid entertained Sheik Abd-el-Kader, for whom he gave a formal dinner party:

"But scarcely were we at table than he asked me to take his place. He felt very weak and went to his room. As soon as Abd-el-Kader had gone I went to the Prince. I passed the night with his doctor, who has been devoted to him all his life, having known him since childhood. The sick man is stricken by pains which rack him from time to time, starting at the neck and running down to the heels. He thinks it is the forerunner of the end. I tell him it is only sciatica and that he will be better in the morning. What seems to have given him most confidence is that when he begged me to get him to sign, as soon as possible, the deed for the settlement of his financial obligation to the Company, I told him there would be plenty of time to deal with the matter. I said we would consider the question when I returned from an expedition I was about to make into the isthmus. I would see him at Alexandria, where his doctor recommended that he should go.

"However, the next morning, Doctor Haage-Bey took me aside and advised me to take advantage of the offer which had been made, because, he said, death would soon follow if two abscesses failed to drain exteriorly. I would have committed a heinous action had I undeceived him after inspiring so much confidence in the invalid. Since he seemed much better than on the previous evening, we went out of doors to smoke a pipe in the garden. He leaned upon me as we went, but, once installed in a large armchair, regained all his old cheerfulness. But at the same time he told me what he thought of his approaching end, without betraying the least regret or anxiety about it. He said he had just completed a settlement for the Princess his wife, for whom he had the greatest respect; also for his son Toussoum and his mother. He related how Bulwer, after his visit to the isthmus, had made out that it was in the Viceroy's own interest that the British Cabinet opposed the completion of the canal — because it would so much emancipate Egypt that he would no longer be master in his own house. 'You can guess,' said the Prince, 'that I did not fall into the trap. I also learned that the Ambassador had recently called upon my nephew and heir. I do not know whether he received any assurances but I am sure that they were asked for. If I go: you have been warned. You will have to defend yourself, not against him personally, because he has always been well disposed towards you, but against the political pressure which will be brought to bear upon his Government.'

"There passed in front of us the servant who looks after the pipes. In a low tone the Viceroy said to me, 'See that fellow? He is watching me very carefully because, according to custom, it will be he who announces my death to my successor, and that will mean a good *bakchich* (present).' The illness hung fire for two days more, and then, all my preparations having been made, I set out for Suez, putting some hope in the strong constitution of the Prince and upon his resignation."

Extract from the Journal of de Lesseps, 17, 18, 19, 20 January, 1863
"I left Ismailia this evening, on horseback, so as to reach Kantara quicker than I could by boat, and though it was a very dark night, in which only the Pole Star served to give direction, I crossed the desert, followed by my faithful Hassan. After two hours' sleep I was awakened by a messenger. I opened his despatch. It informed me that Mohammed-Säid had arrived very ill at Alexandria and was at the last extremity. If I wished to see him alive I had not a moment to lose. I went to saddle my horse. Instead of taking the desert route I followed the banks of the canal, which are still unfinished and have several breaks in continuity. In spite of the darkness, my excellent mount saved me from any false step and I arrived at Ismailia with the dawn. Ordered by telegraph, a boat was waiting for me, drawn by two dromedaries. In an hour I was passing Ramese. As I reached Tel-el-Kebir a boat met me. Jules Voisin, sent by Guichard, our estate manager at Ouady, who did not care to break the news to me personally, told me that the Viceroy had died during the night of the 18th.

"I am in despair: not on account of our enterprise, in which I still have the most serene faith – in spite of all the difficulties which are likely to arise, but because of this cruel separation from a faithful friend who, over twenty-five years, has given me so many proofs of his affection and his confidence. Until my arrival at Alexandria I passed in review all the circumstances of our relationship since his childhood, his carefree life as a young man and his beneficent reign. Before trying to get any rest, I hastened to ask the noble and worthy Princess, his widow, to allow me to go into the family mosque where they had just laid the body of the Prince. There, without witnesses, I remained for an hour, with my head touching the turban of the dead."

*   *   *

The contrast between the foregoing account and that representative of enemy opinion of Säid is significant as illustrating the great gulf between the two points of view. To Lesseps, who had every reason for resenting the Viceroy's double-faced attitude, his arbitrary moods, and his easy swaying to the draughts of politics, the Viceroy was above all a human, humane character in a position where both qualities had in the past been most rare. Lesseps took his orientalism for the inevitable thing that it was, especially with Säid's easygoing character. That huge man, as Ferdinand knew, possibly better than anyone, was a child in the affairs of ' progressive' industrial civilization and its financial structure. But he believed in it, and did his best to bring what he thought would be its blessings to his country. Tormented by too many advisers, most of whom were as much concerned to discredit others as to follow their own policies, Säid still managed to keep faith in the three most important matters, with his family, with his friends and with his people. It is true that he was unpopular in England for very reasonable reasons, based on those European standards which he did not understand. He had been extravagant as a Prince is expected to be in such a country as Egypt then was; and his attitude in that respect was not far from Napoleon's. For the building of palaces, and their decoration, at least keeps people in employment; a principle of such antiquity that it has been held the Pyramids were built to prevent unemployment during the inundation rather than as colossal follies or mystic tombs. Whatever the final assessment of Säid, it can hardly be closer to the following ' enemy' version than to that of de Lesseps: "He had mounted the throne a gay, hopeful, ardent man, with vigorous health, boundless power, and almost inexhaustible wealth. He left it but nine years later for a premature grave; his health wasted by disease and trouble; hope, fortune, friends, all lost; and, with a soul as sick as his body, welcomed death as a release from suffering."[1]

[1] Cameron, *Egypt in the Nineteenth Century.*

Chapter 13. ARBITRATION

Ismail Pasha came to power in Egypt:

"The country had entered a period of extraordinary prosperity. The war of secession in America discovered new markets for Egyptian cotton, and the spinners of Europe were clamouring for the supply of the raw material. Ismail reaped a harvest from the boom. No whim was so fanciful that he did not indulge it. He built noble residences for the members of his family, and he assigned to dependents sufficient incomes to maintain a royal household. He flung himself into the most imprudent enterprises, emerging from few either with profit to himself or with benefit to his subjects. Following Säid's example, he began almost at once to borrow money at heavy discounts and ruinous rates of interest. The interest charged was fantastic: never less than seven per cent, it gradually advanced to double that rate."[1]

Of the foregoing, which fairly sums up an historical view of the new Viceroy, only the first three lines are strictly relevant to Lesseps at the beginning of 1863. But the character of the new Prince was already set – he was thirty-three, and Ferdinand might well have suspected from the beginning that in this queer figure was a streak of unreliability which augured ill for the canal. Though he had passed through St. Cyr, there was nothing military about Ismail's bearing. He was short, seemed flabby, and had a trick of sitting with eyes half closed. When he opened them they were not in agreement about the subject focused, a trait which disconcerted his visitors. Behind this unprepossessing façade there was a fine if cynical mind. Already he had seen through the myth of European 'protection' for his country, but could contrive no better alternative. It seemed to him that, because the previous heir had been accidentally drowned, he had succeeded to a very comfortable trap. Had he not seen Uncle Säid, on paper such a monarch, running like a mouse between feline Ambassadors? They might

[1] Cameron, *Egypt in the Nineteenth Century.*

225

have been gentle had he not so firmly believed that the great canal would make his country strong. Whether poor or rich, in the view of Ismail Egypt must remain under the hand of the Sultan or else in the claws of the cats. He had not the least objection to the canal, but he did not intend to carry it through in face of British or Turkish opposition, and he insisted that, if ever it should come to completion, then 'the canal must belong to Egypt, not Egypt to the canal'.

In his own right, de Lesseps was now a man of power. If in Europe he was something of a legend, among the general population of Egypt he was regarded with awe. Under such circumstances Ismail went out of his way to be civil. When they first met after Säid's death, Lesseps did not mention the canal, and his only request was on behalf of the family of the late Viceroy. Ismail at once replied that they would all be treated as though they were of his own household. He then assured Lesseps that he was a convinced *canaliste*, and that there was no question but that the great work would be carried on. In letters which urgently followed this interview, Ferdinand professed that he was completely satisfied with the position. Perhaps he had already fallen under the extraordinary charm for which this rather uncouth Prince was to become notorious. At all events his confidence in the future exorcized the ghosts which, at the news of Säid's death, had emerged in the Company's offices: fear that work would be stopped, fear of liquidation, fear that the Act of Concession would be revoked.

Ismail went off to Constantinople for his investiture, and Lesseps back to the isthmus; where he drove himself harder than ever because he needed constant activity to dull the sense of loneliness and insecurity. He travelled incessantly, often in extreme discomfort, slept little and lived in solitude. His 'home' was a modest hut at Ismailia which was also his office. From there he ran the organization which now employed 20,000 men, spread out from Port Said to Suez. At the same time he contrived to keep in touch with Paris, London, and a number of private individuals. Even his enemies in France, who were patiently maturing the plot to buy up his Company, had to admit that it would be next to impossible to find an adequate successor for him.

At Constantinople Ismail learned, without surprise or emotion, that he was not to be master in his own house. Egypt was increasingly regarded as a Turkish province, and the new Viceroy would hardly have protested, in view of what he believed to be the sole alternative. As for the canal, instead of allowing it to plague him as it had plagued his uncle, the thing might well be turned to his advantage. As he saw it, everyone else wanted to control the waterway, which was now certain to be completed if Lesseps were allowed his head. Very well, instead of obstinately defending the Frenchman, why not sell the canal to the highest bidder? Then, whoever won the tug-of-war at Constantinople, he could hardly fail to gain by the result; and Egypt could hardly lose. First, however, he must consolidate his personal position. The Concession might conceivably lapse or be set aside unless confirmed in his own name, and so, immediately on his return to Cairo, the new Viceroy filled to the brim the Lesseps cup of confidence by signing two deeds of far-reaching importance. One of them, possibly to Ferdinand's surprise, accepted on behalf of the Egyptian Government all the shares which Säid had to his name, including those which he had intended formally to accept only a few days before his death. There was, however, a consideration for the acceptance, and one dictated less by reasons of state than by Ismail's experience as a practical farmer. The Company were to release the lands on either side of the Freshwater Canal. In return the Government agreed to complete that canal, at its own expense, as far as Suez. This gesture at once made Ismail master of the situation with regard to the Canal Company in Egypt and at the same time made him popular in the country, where the blessings of fresh water had recently come to be so much appreciated that de Lesseps had been receiving more praise than the Viceroy. Arabs who had known only the brackish water of the wells, or the even nastier beverage resulting from water carried for weeks in kegs or skins, treated the clean stream with superstitious reverence. It was inevitable that the maker of such a miracle should gain great stature, a new Moses to Ismail's Pharaoh.

*   *   *

London's reaction to the report of Sir Henry Bulwer ushered in a last attempt to crush this turbulent Lesseps; not because the

report was unfavourable, but because Bulwer frankly confessed
that while in the early stages the enterprise had been

" more prepared than pursued. Now I am bound to say, after my
recent inspection, that in Europe we have not in general sufficiently
understood the circumstances under which the work is carried out,
circumstances which are without parallel in modern times. . . . At
the head of the enterprise is an extremely active and intelligent
man, always good-humoured and indefatigable. Little by little he
is being surrounded by capable men, keen and competent in their
special fields, and imbued in the highest degree by the greatest
national stimulus, *amour-propre*. All of which I have seen, and I
admit that, until I had seen it, I did not believe it. All that is
possible to art, science, and perseverance can be done here."

It was a handsome tribute, but it could not change what
England believed to be the strategic realities, and Lord John
Russell determined to take drastic action. Pending a general
increase of British power in the Middle East and the fortifica-
tion of Malta, Lesseps must be stopped.

The first definite result of the new enemy drive struck the
isthmus in the form of an order from the Porte to the Viceroy,
telling him that the *corvée* was illegal. Deprived of labour, what
could even Lesseps do? Simultaneously the plot to force the
Company into liquidation was carried a stage further. Though
the initiative appeared to be French, the international interests
behind the Duc de Morny were not without British inspiration;
for if a new Company could be based upon an English control
of the equity, then the Government would be able to encourage
the project, under certain conditions, and so please the influential
men of business concerned with eastern trade. But because
French patriotic feeling was running high, the manœuvre had
to be most discreet; so in Paris there was no more than a
suggestion, made personally by the Duc de Morny to the
Emperor, that Lesseps was mismanaging the whole concern.
To save the prestige of France his Company should be com-
pulsorily wound up and the assets handed over to a new one.
An attempt had already been made to buy an interest through
the acquisition of individual holdings, but this had met with
negligible success because shares were not on offer in any
quantity. Now it was to be another story. Lesseps would be
forced into liquidation and then the new Company could take

over in the guise of a rescuer, not only of the canal but also of French prestige.

As it developed through successive stages, each more drastic than the previous one, Lesseps faced the issue boldly. By September he was ready to hit back, and in a long memorandum to the Viceroy quoted *The Standard*, *The Spectator*, and *The Saturday Review*, all of which said bluntly, if in different words: "Lesseps is ruined. The canal is vetoed." And it is evident that the Press fairly represented the situation as it appeared to the public. Lesseps, however, had two last cards to play, both still unknown quantities to the world at large. The first was the rapid development of mechanical excavators – just in time to take the place of the picks and baskets of the defaulting fellaheen. The second was his influence on the Emperor through the faithful Eugénie. Had the situation been as simple as it appeared, he might have thought with reason that even yet he could win through; but unknown to Lesseps, and to the Viceroy, a new factor had been added to the equation in the person of Nubar Bey, now the effective Prime Minister of Egypt. Nubar was a Christian Armenian of great ability and an uncompromising ambition to create for himself a dominant rôle in Egypt. To this end he worked secretly to gain British support in exchange for his help in arranging the canal issue to the satisfaction of Westminster.

In the following month, October, Nubar and Lesseps were both in Paris, each intent upon a personal bid for power, the one operating under cover of an official mission from the Viceroy, the other as the President of the Company. So the fight now reached a climax upon two distinct levels, the first that official plane where the weapons are diplomatic notes and official interviews, the second a secret diplomacy based upon private contacts close to the decisive power, that of Napoleon III. He was now almost as hog-tied as the Sultan between opposing herdsmen. Even Queen Victoria, on her recent visit to France, had begged him to have the Suez business wound up because, she said, all her Ministers were so insistent upon it. Alone among the tradition-bound courts of Europe, that of Victoria and Albert had accepted Napoleon socially. In return he had been loyal to the entente, which he still relied upon for the success of his adventurous foreign policy in Europe. But, much

as he would have liked to throw Lesseps to the wolves, the
canal had now become a symbol of national aspiration. Its
failure would have the most undesirable political consequences
at home. Napoleon's dictatorial régime needed all the popular
acclaim it could get, and to abandon the canal at this stage
would be a positive encouragement to the underground opposition, headed by the patron of Lesseps, Prince 'Plon-Plon'
Jérôme.

By midsummer it became evident to both sides that no solution was possible on the political level, and the only result of
Nubar's plots was to infuriate Ismail, who could not understand
why the accounts he received from his special envoy in Paris
differed greatly from those reporting the same negotiations
through official channels. He therefore decided to withdraw still
further from the scrummage, and even went so far as to break
off relations with Lesseps; much as Säid had done under somewhat similar circumstances. The situation was now as follows.
France still hesitated to cross England. England dared go no
further for fear of offending Napoleon to such an extent that
he would adopt the policy which England so much feared.
Having decided that from a domestic point of view the canal
would be an asset, the Sublime Porte continued to refuse ratification of the Concession in the hope of profiting from whatever
international agreement – or disagreement – might eventually be
reached. The Viceroy of Egypt still looked to the canal as an
eventual source of revenue and influence in world affairs; but
he was now as much opposed to being a mere appendage of
the Ottoman Empire as to being the protégé of England or
France. Desire for independence had grown with experience
of power. Through this impasse he trusted Nubar to find a
way, and even to make a profit out of the deadlock. It had
not yet occurred to him that Nubar might be playing a secret
game of his own, with no paramount regard for his master's
interests. Ferdinand de Lesseps, sure now that the cessation of
the *corvée* would not after all bring the work to a standstill,
was content to press on with mechanization, recruiting of free
labour, and firm leadership of the shareholders. Sooner or later
some sort of arrangement would be arrived at, and in the meanwhile it seemed that time was again on his side. Each month
that the wrangles continued the canal came nearer fulfilment,

particularly since the *corvée* did not suddenly cease but was gradually withdrawn.

Then the enemy launched a surprise frontal attack upon the one position in which Lesseps thought himself completely safe – the legal title of his Company. Prompted by Nubar, the Viceroy sent to Paris specific instructions that the legality of the whole proceeding, from the first Concession to the matter of the ceded lands, be challenged in the French courts. It was a bold stroke, made in expectation that on the ruin of Lesseps the Duc de Morny would succeed him, albeit in a manner pleasing to Lord Palmerston. In view of the Duke's position as the Emperor's half-brother and President of the Corps Legislatif, there seemed a good chance that, whatever the rights of the case, the plaintiff might well succeed. It was by the merest chance that the case opened in favour of the defendant, for Lesseps was able to show that certain documents put in by the plaintiff had been altered from the originals. At once public feeling, already smouldering, flared up unmistakably in favour of the Company; and, after some more or less dignified wrangling, it was established, at least in French law, that what the Company had it might hold.

Lesseps hardly had time to celebrate this victory when a fresh *démarche* came from the Porte through the Viceroy. This time it was less a direct attack upon the Company's position than a trap for the Emperor himself. It was a request that Napoleon should arbitrate as between the claims of Egypt and those of the Suez Canal Company. Had it not been for the Morny plan, Lesseps might have welcomed this proposal, for he was quite willing to make concessions if only he were allowed to finish his work in peace. Indeed he may well have begun to think that, at least as regards the lands ceded to the Company, there was much to be said for the Egyptian point of view. Whatever the legal status of the occupier, they ought not to constitute French enclaves within Egyptian territory. For Lesseps was almost as pro-Egypt as he was pro-France. He would never intentionally detract from the inheritance which, in part thanks to Mathieu, Mohammed-Ali had left behind him. Morny utterly changed this picture. It would be easy now for the Emperor to save his face, and at the same time solve the problem, by making his judgment conditional upon the

Morny faction's take-over; which might indeed save the canal for posterity, but not for Lesseps. Accordingly he drew up a formal protest:

Petition to His Majesty the Emperor
6th January, 1864

" SIRE,

The Suez Canal Company peacefully pursues its operations. It has opened up the Maritime Canal for 75 kilometres from the Mediterranean to Lake Timsah. It is in process of completing the Freshwater Canal, which is also navigable, and will soon permit the completion of the Maritime Canal as far as the Red Sea, as well as irrigating the desert. In fact one may already take small ships direct from Port Said to Suez. The eminent engineers of the Imperial Department of Roads and Bridges have just brought to completion work which is essential for the excavation of the Maritime Canal for ocean-going ships between the two seas. The Company is in possession of important contracts such as would assure achievement of the whole project within four years. The results to date are due to the protection of Your Majesty, who in 1860, when the Company was beginning operations, saw to it that they were not brought to a standstill by an irregular order from the *Porte Ottomane*.

"The Company has no cause whatever for anxiety, because, being bound by agreement with the Egyptian Government, the Egyptian Government is equally bound towards the Company; and by public deeds which the new Viceroy of Egypt formally confirmed in two special contracts dated the 18th and 20th of March, 1863. We have no need to concern ourselves with international and political questions, nor with treaties of neutrality, which are the business of governments. Such is the situation when, under the pretext of the persistent refusal by the Porte to ratify the Concession, a recent letter from the Grand Vizier seeks to place the Viceroy in a position to demand from the Company the surrender of some of its rights, without compensation of any kind. . . . In the same way that in 1860 Your Majesty countermanded orders which had been officially given with the object of bringing these works to nothing, the undersigned dare to hope that again on this occasion, and with more reason, the Emperor's will shall not permit the accomplishment of intentions hostile to the Company; and that he deign to protect the French shareholders in the Suez Canal as much as the interests of the Egyptian Government itself, whose administrative independence is the result of French political initiative formally recognized by the conventions of 1841."

So now the Emperor had been asked to arbitrate by both sides! Lesseps lost no time in exerting personal influence, and sent his petition privately through Eugénie, accompanied by the following request:

"Monsieur Ferdinand de Lesseps begs the Empress to be so good as to deliver and support his petition to the Emperor, and to let him know, by M. Damas Hinard, whether she would receive him on Sunday; in which case he will hasten to ask the *Chamberlain de Service* for an audience. It would be highly desirable that the Emperor should be present with the Empress if she would deign to receive M. de Lesseps. The principal object of the petition of the Council of Administration is to oust M. le Duc de Morny from his intervention in the Suez business and to place the negotiations in the hands of the Minister for Foreign Affairs."

Wheels within wheels! And none could freely turn. Ferdinand promptly sought out the Duke and had a frank conversation with him – which, though extremely polite, accomplished nothing at all. It began to seem as though Napoleon had been manœuvred into a position where he could do no other than become the unwilling executioner, if not of the canal project as an engineering feat, then certainly as the concern of Ferdinand de Lesseps, and perhaps of France. In such circumstances even Lesseps had to compromise. On the 22nd of January, having heard nothing from Napoleon, he wrote to the Foreign Minister, Drouyn de Lhuys saying that he was prepared to give ground. Nubar, he said, was alarming the shareholders. No doubt the Emperor would be giving his orders in the sense required by the petition. . . .

In appealing to the Foreign Minister whose scapegoat he had been over the Rome affair, Lesseps betrayed his desperation. Even Eugénie had failed him, and now he was constrained to appeal direct to this cold official who, holding no personal brief for Lesseps, would do no more than his duty. And unless the Emperor took decisive action, nor would the Foreign Office. It seemed once again that Lesseps was lost. Then, as had so often happened, help came from an unexpected quarter. On the 11th of February (1864) the shareholders gave a banquet to Ferdinand to demonstrate their solidarity in the face of all opposition, even of disaster; though it is doubtful if any of them understood the real position. To the general public the issue was still in terms of the *corvée*, and, being ignorant of the capacity of the new machines, it was on this ground alone that Jacques Bonhomme was shaking his head about the Company's prospects.

In the vast hall of the *Palais d'Industrie* sixteen hundred people sat down to dine, and shivered through an elaborate meal because the heating system had gone wrong and the weather outside was bitter. Looking round from his place of honour, it must have seemed to the President that his people were remarkably cheerful under the circumstances. He must have wondered how long his popularity would endure when the full story was known. If he told them now, would anyone think there was a chance left to save the day? How useful it would be now to have the House of Rothschild on his side – or was it too late even to hope for money with which to carry on? Then rose His Imperial Highness the Prince Napoleon Bonaparte, Patron of the Company, an unprepossessing figure. Ferdinand would have applauded without enthusiasm. Plon-Plon was apt to be long-winded. There was nothing practical he could say. It was very cold. He was a figure-head and nothing more.

In fact Plon-Plon said many things, which if they were not directly practical, had the effect of warming up the audience, and then kindling their enthusiasm until, in the flare of their united loyalties, all physical discomfort was forgotten. Always an exceptional orator, Plon-Plon was now making the speech of his life – for the shareholders, for the Emperor, for France. It lasted an hour and a half, during which he never lost his grip on the audience; and as it came to an end, Ferdinand de Lesseps knew that a power had been released which could force the Emperor to act in obedience to public opinion. Plon-Plon claimed as much:

"Permit me, as I bring this too-long speech to an end, to insist that you attach no official inspiration whatever to what I have just been saying. If I have a fault, and I have, it is one of extreme frankness. All that I have told you is my personal opinion. It constrains no one but myself. However, I am so much convinced of the worthiness of the cause which I have been defending, of the justice of the ideas which I have just voiced, that, should public opinion adopt them, I dare to hope that the Government also may approve of them. I have confidence in the Government of the Emperor, the natural protector of the rights of French citizens abroad." (Prolonged applause.)

With a sense of deliverance, often experienced before, de Lesseps went out into the cold night. He knew, none better, the force of public opinion, not as it had been roused in England, in a democratic spirit which, except in the last resort, can hardly influence the planners of secret strategy, but in Imperial France. There the Emperor was the only strategist, and he needed the approval of the masses; if only for the excellent reason that should he falter in what they thought was his patriotic duty, they might yet choose Plon-Plon in his stead. The thought was an Imperial nightmare, and so was an echo of recent history, muttering out of the shadows in the Tuileries, 'Remember the Four June Days'.

*   *   *

During the months which had followed the Porte's declaration of the previous April that the call-up in Egypt was illegal, Lesseps had quietly been making arrangements to minimize the effect of the total loss of the *corvée*; and by the time the Extraordinary General Meeting took place, on the 1st of March, 1864, these had already proved effective. Sir Henry Bulwer had not been alone in confessing amazement that the great work seemed capable of fulfilment, even with the *corvée*. It seems to have occurred to no one, not even in the circle round Lesseps, that it could be carried on with free labour only. Yet such was now the case. Not only had mechanization made numbers of unskilled labourers unnecessary, it also created a demand for specialists, who, earning better wages, were eager to take the work. Just as the usefulness of the canal depended to a large extent upon the development of marine propulsion, so did the steam engine save the Company from failure during the period of construction – a factor which had been left out of account until recently, not only by the enemy, but by Lesseps and all the experts on his side. And a further benefit accrued from the new system: instead of contractors taking relatively small tasks of excavation as their responsibility, leaving the Company with the overall organization of labour, now virtually the whole of the technical work was passed to contractors. The Administration was therefore free to concentrate on the co-ordination of the entire enterprise, with its manifold ramifications abroad. The extent of the progress on the isthmus may be illustrated by the following notes taken from Sir Arnold Wilson's book. They apply to the year 1864.

Port Said: 530,000 cu. ft. of stone taken from quarries at Mex (Alexandria) for the Port Said quays and embankments. Dussaud Frères establish their plant for the manufacture and submersion of artificial stones for moles. Tonnage of port (January-July), vessels 124, tons 35,220.

Maritime Canal: General Works. Telegraph system finished; 13,000 natives at work first three months only; Borel and Lavalley, who afterwards carried out such vast operations, employed in planning their work.

North of Lake Timsah. Port Said to Timsah; excavation by natives, 23,000,000 cubic feet; Aiton's excavations (with Company's plant), Port Said 1,050,000 cu. ft.; in the Canal, 8,100,000 cu. ft.; Couvreux's excavations 2,200,000, using 2 excavators, 4 miles of railway, 4 engines and 30 trucks.

South of Lake Timsah. South of Chalouf; excavation by natives, 48,000,000 cubic feet; transverse cut to Serapeum, 3,200,000 cu. ft.; transverse canal to Chalouf, 425,000 cubic feet.

Freshwater Canal and Water Supply. Junction at Ismailia, 1,300,000 cubic feet; water supplied Port Said from 10 April, reservoir Plateau of El Guisr 110,000 gallons, reservoir Port Said 154,000 gallons.

When at the Annual General Meeting he rose to give his Presidential address, Ferdinand de Lesseps must have known that, far from the suppression of the *corvée* doing harm, he would now have preferred to do without it, had he enough machinery and enough money, for the new methods were quicker and more efficient. Dramatically, the Suez Canal presented the whole meaning of mechanization, political, social, and technical. But of this the world at large was still ignorant, and in England particularly the enemy was jubilant. Having quietly and accurately described the actual state of affairs on the isthmus, and so brought the meeting under his hand, de Lesseps quoted a selection of comments by the British Press, of which the following excerpt from *The Standard* is typical:

"In future the work cannot be carried on except at enormous expense. What will the shareholders say then, these poor speculators in France, Egypt and Turkey? *They will be ruined.* (Laughter.) When the 200,000,000 has been spent the enterprise will fall of itself for lack of funds. M. de Lesseps, and the adventurers who have supported him with their money, would do well to withdraw promptly from a bad business, and to make the best bargain they can with the Pasha; because the enterprise on which they based so many hopes is found to be as empty of commercial results as the tunnel under the Thames." (More laughter.)

Lesseps then reviewed the whole progress of the work from the beginning, and without making accusations against individuals, such as Nubar and the Duc de Morny, traced the financial history and its political exploitation. He then played the ace of trumps:

"We are authorized to inform you that in reply to various communications which have been made to him, the Viceroy has declared that he is in complete agreement with the Emperor as to the amicable and definite settlement of all the questions in dispute at law" (interruption, *explosion de bravos*), "and that His Majesty has deigned personally to undertake the supreme decision on all these questions." (Indescribable movement, enthusiasm at climax, arms waving, hats in the air, the hall shaken by long and enthusiastic acclamation. Vive l'Empereur! Vive l'Empereur! Vive l'Empereur!)

"*Monsieur le Président:* 'Yes, Gentlemen, Vive l'Empereur! We all have confidence in the Emperor.' (Redoubled cheering.) 'And we need not desire a happier result than that in accord with the views expressed by His Imperial Highness the Prince Napoleon at a recent banquet, whose noble and eloquent words so ably defended our cause.' (Bravo! Bravo! Bravo! Vive le Prince Napoleon! Renewed cheering.) 'It is as a friend of Prince Ismail and of the Company also that His Imperial Highness made his appeal for conciliation. And we replied, "Conciliation? We are willing, but we look for it in the terms which our noble protector has himself defined – with the recognition of our acquired rights, with the honouring of contracts, with respect for public confidence, with the satisfaction of those interests which have been confided to our honour."' (Bravo! Bravo! Prolonged cheers.) 'Such will be the principles which guide us in the negotiations which are now proceeding. Success will be due to your constancy, your firmness, to your unshakable unity, of which so many striking examples have given power to your Directors.' (Yes, yes. Go on. Applause.) 'As for ourselves, Gentlemen, we are all conscious of having done our duty towards you, and we now ask you for a vote of approval for the past and of confidence in the future.'" (All, all. We will give you all. You shall have it. Bravo! Bravo!)

*   *   *

Napoleon III appointed an arbitration committee under the chairmanship of Thouvenal, now a Senator, which met for the

first time on the 18th of March. A few hours later the Turkish
Ambassador produced a telegram from the Porte. The message
was to the effect that the procedure was unacceptable, and had
it arrived in time, the session would have been postponed pending investigation of the Sultan's objections, which, of course,
were really those of England. As a London paper put it: "The
Sultan controls the Pasha and Lord Palmerston controls the
Sultan. M. de Lesseps cannot do anything without the Sultan,
and the Sultan cannot do anything without Lord Palmerston."
That events had moved too fast for all three potentates is
emphasized by the tact of the Turkish Ambassador, who had
prudently kept the telegram for two days lest its delivery hold
up the arbitration which was now clearly in Turkey's interests.
For if the Emperor could go so far, he could go farther, and
an independent Egypt under his aegis was the last thing which
the Porte desired.

Understandably, the Committee was in no hurry, and so
the enemy was again able to snatch the initiative, during a period
when Lesseps hardly opened his mouth for fear of seeming to
anticipate or prejudice the Imperial judgment. In June the
Viceroy finally shut down the *corvée*, leaving not a single called-
up man at work. This gesture, rather belated from the Porte's
point of view, because almost a year had elapsed since the standstill order had been given, was for Lesseps well timed. The work
could now go on without interruption. On the 19th the Committee made its detailed recommendations to the Emperor, and
judgment was given on the 6th of July. It upheld the legality
of the Act of Concession and of the contract concerning the
corvée. On the other hand it recognized the validity of Egypt's
desire – but not necessarily the legal claim – to repossess certain
territories which had been ceded to the Company. The Committee added a rider that their recommendations were only in
general terms, since they had been unable to establish exact
boundaries.

The suppression of the *corvée* naturally became a matter for
compensation, and so, in view of their legal possession by the
Company, did the restoration of the various pieces of property.
Napoleon, accepting the Committee's recommendations in their
entirety, fixed Egypt's liability to the Company at 84,000,000
francs, say £3,360,000. It was a brilliant stroke. It infringed

none of the rights of the High Contracting Parties, and if it seems odd that Egypt had to pay for what was, after all, her own sovereign territory, the fact remains that without the inducement provided by the vision of fertile tracts where before there had been only desert, the Company might never have been able to attract the needed capital. Now the compensation guaranteed sufficient funds for the completion of the great work, and so the question of these territories, principally along the course of the Freshwater Canal, was by no means so important as it had been, say at the time of the purchase of the Ouady Estate. And from Egypt's point of view, being still sure of adequate participation and control in the finished canal, the liability could be set off against future dividends. At all events, both Nubar and Ismail accepted the Emperor's ruling, an accord which alarmed the enemy in London although Ismail had prudently stated that he could not answer for the Sultan.

Sir Henry Lytton Bulwer, writing to Lord John Russell, exclaimed that the act of arbitration was an abuse of sovereignty –the Viceroy's and, by implication, the Sultan's. If the Emperor of the French dared to interfere like that, what might he not do? "If the Emperor can pronounce upon the validity of a concession made against the laws of the Turkish Empire . . . the authority of Constantinople over Egypt is transferred to Paris." The obvious counter to this was to impose British ascendancy upon the Sultan to such an extent that he would have to set aside the Napoleonic judgment, and accordingly an alternative plan was prepared at Constantinople. Its object was to deprive de Lesseps not only of his workers, but also of his territory; and with no such compensation as he now would deem himself entitled to receive. Upon the initiative of the Grand Vizier it was proposed to appoint a Turkish Committee of Arbitration, which would proceed as the French had done, but from the standpoint of Ottoman, not European, law. If at the end of their deliberations there should appear to be a shred of legality in the Company's position, the fact would be due entirely to the Sultan's clemency.

So once again, just as it seemed that he was safe, Ferdinand found himself under a falling sword. Even if the Ottoman inquiry in the end made just and reasonable recommendations, they were likely to be too late; for in the meantime the Com-

pany would founder through lack of confidence, and the Duke's
faction would have joined forces with the Grand Vizier. But
Lesseps had reckoned without the deep and devious mental
processes of the new Viceroy, who had by this time realized
that Nubar had been pursuing an independent line in Paris as
the result of which he, Ismail, had been deprived of his rightful
place as a prime-mover in the matter. He now decided to move
without reference to Nubar or anyone else, and did so in a
singularly simple and effective way. It emerged that Aali
Pasha, the Grand Vizier, was personally in debt to the House of
Oppenheimer, and one morning it so happened that he received
his quittance from the creditors to the tune of £20,000. As
a result of this mysterious windfall, his views on the subject
of the canal underwent an immediate transformation. No more
was heard of the proposal to withold the Sultan's approval of
Napoleon's award, nor did the Ottoman Committee come into
existence. So the sword missed Lesseps, who now thought that
his course was at last clear. It is true that the firman of ratification was still withheld, but as he had come so far without it,
he did not doubt but that if need be he could go on to the end.
As 1864 drew to its close, it must have seemed to him that the
enemy had now reached a point of exhaustion which would
prevent them from offering any further effective resistance to
the advance of his own forces, whose morale and equipment
had never been better, even if their numbers were smaller. At
Aali's request, Lesseps, on the basis of the arbitration award,
drew up detailed proposals for the disposal of the various matters
affected only in principle by the ruling about the territory in
the Company's occupation. He had no more to do. The business
was settled. Happily he returned to Egypt, and was there confronted by a series of counter-proposals which the offended
Nubar had drawn up, and which, as might have been expected,
were entirely unacceptable. Nor was this the fruit of a private
understanding only between Nubar and Bulwer. Somehow the
Sultan's approval had been obtained. To all intents, the
Emperor's ruling had been set aside: "it counted for nothing;
it was an *auguste simulacre*."[1]

Accustomed by now to be winning at one moment and losing
the next, Lesseps refused even to discuss the counter-proposals

[1] Edgar-Bonnet.

and formally appealed to the French Foreign Office. It seemed inevitable that the issue would be taken to the final extremity, a direct struggle for Egypt between England and France, in which, from the moment of diplomatic failure – which might almost be said to have already occurred, lay the seed of war. As it had done over the Orsini affair, temper in France was running high. Drouyn de Lhuys, 'insisted upon a prompt execution of the ruling, which was binding upon all parties and had been accepted as such by the Viceroy of Egypt'. Ismail sent for Lesseps and offered him a document for signature. It was Nubar's. Lesseps refused to sign. Ismail took offence. Lesseps let it be known that, 'he regarded the issue as closed and confidently placed himself at the disposal of the Emperor'. Sir Henry Bulwer transferred his headquarters from Constantinople to Cairo. The French demanded immediate implementation of the award as originally given: deadlock.

For some months neither side would move, while between them Ismail sat anxiously upon the throne which might so easily collapse under him. For fear of offending one he dared not make the least gesture of conciliation to the other, and Lesseps had to be treated like a leper. Then, quietly as the bribe had slipped into the hands of Aali, Egypt made the first payment due under the arbitration award; and so sealed the bargain with France. Lesseps, who all this time had been getting on with the work in the isthmus, hardly looked up. By now of a certainty he knew, after so many crises, that neither England nor France would go to war over the canal, no matter how much irresponsible people talked of it. He knew that the deadlock was such that neither side could gain any worthwhile advantage by further effort, and meanwhile at least he was left alone. It was all he asked.

As an engineering feat the eventual success of the canal was now generally considered to be no longer in doubt, so the enemy concentrated upon attempts to slow the work and embarrass the Company's finances. The political impasse extended into a wrangle between England and France, not over the canal as such, but for the domination of the Middle East. France desired an African empire based upon a 'French' Egypt, but she was not prepared to go to war for it. England still believed that, under certain circumstances, war might become inevitable, and one of those was French control of the canal when completed. As for public opinion as opposed to Ministerial policy, on both sides of the Channel the canal became an emotional issue, not the less potent in England because the motive was negative, a patriotic jealousy tinged with fear; which was fairly rooted in the past. On the French side the motive was also largely jealousy. Eminent men, such as Alexandre Dumas, preached that it was time to put a stop to England's rôle as the prim governess of Europe.

Upon such an exalted stage as that, even Ferdinand de Lesseps was not qualified to act. With the Sultan and the Viceroy he could only stand in the wings, for the most part remaining in almost complete ignorance of the trend of the play. In any case he was fully occupied with practical matters. The excavation must be pressed on with the utmost speed if funds were not to run out, as the enemy continued to claim they would do. He summed up his attitude in two short sentences: "Let us mind our own business. The Emperor's Government will do the same." So well did he follow his own advice that by the first week in April 1865 he was able to conduct a party of eighty-five Chamber of Commerce delegates by boat from sea to sea. They came from almost every country in Europe. The New World was represented by Cyrus W. Field from the United States – as they would be in the following week, when General Lee surrendered at Appomatox. Field was the maker of the transatlantic telegraph. And from South America came M. Gilly (Brazil). There were two Englishmen. Though the boats were drawn by camels and a great part of the route was along the Freshwater Canal, the event was still a powerful symbol of the shape of things to come, and the prestige of de Lesseps benefited accordingly. His spirits rose, his youthfulness returned. He galloped happily from *chantier* to *chantier* and took particular care in the entertainment of '*une jolie Californienne*', an excellent horsewoman beside whom he led the admiring delegates through the maze of works. Occasionally the pair of them left the delegates behind, and the canal also.

And now another 'chance', as had so often happened before in this racked destiny, did what all manner of pressure had failed to do. It made Napoleon take direct action against the

Porte. The circumstances were trivial, but, to the oriental mind, involved a serious loss of face:

"It appears that when Napoleon III arrived at Marseilles, April 30, 1865, to embark on his yacht *Aigle*, on his way to Algeria, the Grand Vizier, who had come to the south of France to recruit his health, was among the crowd of notables who were grouped around the Emperor, who took no notice of him, and did not reply to his bow. Going up to the Emperor, he inquired if His Majesty had any cause for complaint against him or his Government. The only answer he received was an expressive gesture accompanying the single word, 'firman'."[1]

Though the Sultan still required certain assurances from France and England, it is quite possible that the incident was eventually decisive as the speck of dust which immediately crystallizes a supersaturated solution. Lesseps at this time was still in Egypt, but in June he returned to Paris, less in the hope of being able to do anything to break the deadlock than to discover what was the inwardness of the situation and to encourage his supporters. One evening, at a Foreign Office party, a friend showed him a confidential note which had just arrived, giving the first news that cholera had again broken out in Egypt. And Ferdinand, who had every excuse for staying in France, took the next boat back to Alexandria, where he arrived to find panic at the port, which was besieged by people trying at any cost to get out of the country. Within eight days a tenth of the population succeeded, and Ferdinand dryly commented that 'fear did more harm than the disease'. Ismail had been one of the first to flee the country, and his example was followed by a large number of Europeans – but the officers of the Company were not among them. As for Ferdinand, the unusually staccato style of the following letter indicates the strain under which it must have been written.

"To M. le Duc d'Albuféra
      Paris   Port Said, 6th July, 1865.

Arrived at Alexandria on the 25th of June, I found the senior administration had matters well in hand and that I had only to approve the action taken by M. Sala. We have had only one case of desertion, that of M. —— whom I ask you to have removed by

[1] G. B. Smith, *Life and Enterprises of Ferdinand de Lesseps*, London 1893.

the Personnel Department from our establishment. At Alexandria
the cholera seems to be in the ascendant. I have given all our people
the praise which they deserve. They have, with the staff of the
consulate of France, set good examples of courage and devotion
to duty. I was in Cairo on the 28th, where the cholera was beginning to make serious ravages. Our excellent agent, M. Vernoni,
as also his staff, displayed the best possible attitude; and I must say
the same of M. Cazenaux, who has established the headquarters of
his section of the Freshwater Canal in the neighbourhood of the
Agency, and who is continually on a tour of inspection of the line
of works from Cairo to Bulbeis.

"On the 29th I was at Zagazig, a town ravaged by the cholera.
In the middle of the general flight the government doctor had left
his post and his hospital. Our two junior employees – for posts,
telegraph and transport – had remained firm, and by their example
held in check the Arabs, labourers and sailors, whom I compli-
mented and thanked. Their names deserve citation. They are MM.
Pages and Guerin. They were much exhausted. A young employee
from the transport section at Ismailia came to help them and to
keep an eye on the convoys of boats and the flow of supplies. I
left him at Tel-el-Kebir with a severe attack. I learn that he has
come through, thanks to his constitution. He is called Autran.

"I reached Tel-el-Kebir on the 29th after noon, and, reassured
about the situation on the Isthmus by telegrams from M. Voisin,
arranged to leave for Ismailia the next day; but at eight o'clock in
the evening another telegram from M. Voisin informed me that
the plague was beginning to find victims at his post, and he asked
me, in view of the insufficiency of hospital accommodation, if we
might make use of Sciama House, still not occupied by the Government. So I set out immediately with Doctor Aubert-Roche. From
the morning of the 29th sixty cholera cases were received in the
reception rooms and bedrooms of Sciama House, and a few hours
later they were all full. We had a lot of trouble to get the place
ready, find medical orderlies and bury the dead. The first day there
were thirty deaths, forty-three the second, and thirty the third. At
the end of that day few new cases were brought in and these were
less severe than the others. The epidemic is decreasing, but nearly
all the working population had fled towards Port Said, our base
of operations. It is there that the danger still threatens. The people
are restless, and there may be complete disorganization at the
chantiers. For two days they have been begging me to go there
but I have not been able to leave Ismailia.

"On the night of the 2nd I took a boat and arrived in time to
calm down the working men of all nations whose fears the admirable bearing of Larousse and Lavalley had not been able to control.
Deserters from the interior had spread the panic. For several days
past I have had more trouble with the scared who are well than
I had with the dying at Ismailia. At last things have quietened

down. I believe that the squall has passed. Here as everywhere the Company's servants have set a good example. As for M. Voisin, the two notes which he wrote me yesterday and to-day – and which I am sending you together with various telegrams – will sufficiently show you how efficient he is. We chose our man well when we put him at the head of the works. And now let us talk about the works. . . ."

Again the competent courage of Ferdinand de Lesseps had made the vital difference in a major crisis. Again cholera had apparently been conquered, but this time there were no rewards. Ismail came back to Cairo. Lesseps returned to the canal. Puzzled because cases continued to recur, he noted that an Arab encampment of 3,000 people near Port Said had not had a single case. The Arabs had a well of their own, but the port was connected to one of the Nile's minor mouths by a line of iron pipes across Lake Menzaleh. He still failed to suspect that the disease was water-borne and no boiling or filtration was practised. The idea was not an easy one to grasp, partly because the epidemics had died down, partly because clean, wholesome-looking water was completely above suspicion. Snow's work still went unrecognized. And so the continued incidence of cases was regarded as a mere aftermath of the epidemic, which must peter out in time and about which nothing further could be done.

Charles de Lesseps was now the Company's manager at Ismailia where he lived with his wife and son, the second 'little' Ferdinand, to whom 'old' Ferdinand had evidently given all the accumulated affection which had grown round the memory of Agathe. It was after the hot weather, in December, that the boy contracted the disease. At the news 'old' Ferdinand rode like a demon through the night, sixty miles from Zagazig, but he arrived too late. 'He found only the dead body of his grandson. And at the sight, for the first time in his life, his vitality failed. He fell senseless beside the body.' Six years later Robert Koch, working in Egypt, isolated *vibrio cholerae*, the 'comma bacillus', so called from its shape, confirming Snow's empirical work to deliver mankind from another 'scourge of God'.

Chapter 14. ACCLAIM

It was gradually borne in upon the diplomats that war over the canal would be a crowning folly, and that the great work might yet become what Lesseps had always claimed for it, a guarantee of peace through the necessity for international co-operation. On February 22nd, 1866, with the approval of both France and England, a final convention was signed between the Viceroy and the Company, by which all outstanding questions, particularly with regard to compensation and territorial rights, were settled. In the following month the Sultan issued his firman, a document the preamble to which is of singular simplicity:

"To my illustrious Vizier, Ismail Pasha, Viceroy of Egypt, having the rank of Vizier and being decorated with the Orders of Osmanie and of Medjidieh, First Class with Brilliants. The accomplishment of the great work, destined to confer new facilities on commerce and navigation by the cutting of a canal between the Mediterranean and the Red Sea, being one of the most desirable events in this century of science and of progress, for some time past conferences have been held with the Company desirous of permission to carry out the work. These have just terminated in conformity with the sacred rights of the Porte and of the Egyptian Government, in the past and for the future. . . . This present firman, given from our Imperial Divan, is drawn to give effect to our sovereign approval for the execution of the canal by the said Company and according to the conditions set out in this contract, with all associated acts and agreements here designated and set out, and which form an integral part of it. Given the 2 zilqudje 1282 (2nd March 1866)."

If Lesseps was delighted, Ismail chose to be affronted. Did not the preamble refer to him as a mere Vizier? While Ferdinand, at last free from the need to defend himself against the Porte, concentrated all his forces in the hope of avoiding voluntary liquidation, Ismail set about the long and extremely expensive business of getting himself a better title. In due course he became the Khedive, an archaic term originally used to

designate a Persian prince, and something far less than the
Aziz to which he aspired – tactlessly in view of the Sultan's
title *Abd el Aziz*, the Slave of the Gracious. Ismail's lavish
presents and increased annual contribution to the Porte had
in effect brought him only an old word for his Viceroyalty,
while his conceit to be called The Gracious, making his
Sovereign *his* slave by implication, caused a further deterioration in the already strained relations between Cairo and Constantinople. Lesseps, however, was free to rejoice, not only on
account of the long-awaited firman, but because his two greatest
enemies were dead: Lord Palmerston, whom Lord John Russell
succeeded, and the Duc de Morny. Had it not been for the
fact that, as usual, the money was running out – just as Palmerston said it would, the great canal might have seemed as good
as finished; for there could no longer be any doubt but that
the means for excavation were now sufficient and would complete the job if free to do so. But machinery, in particular the
'gigantic inventions' of Borel and Lavalley, required highly
paid operators. The climate was almost impossible for European
labour, and an army of Syrians, Arabians and the like was
still maintained, for the most part in circumstances which, for
the times, were expensive; certainly far more so than had been
envisaged when the *corvée* had been relied upon as a basis for
costing. Some of the work was terribly hard, particularly at
a place near Tineh (Pelusium) where: "The vigorous race of
fishermen on its borders, accustomed to sun and mud, scooped
up the clay in their hands, rolled it into balls on their chests,
and then carried it on their backs with the arms crossed behind.
In this way they raised some 400,000 cubic metres, until the
first dredger, let down into the mud by sections, carried forward the work, followed by twenty others. The sulphurous
exhalations of the mud were almost unbearable, but they caused
little sickness. The men who had toiled all day in the mud
with their hands, slept on rafts. They were paid the current
rates (three piastres a day) with free rations of rice, millet, dates
and onions. Even so, labourers flocked in from all sides."[1] Since
the suppression of the *corvée* the overall cost of work had
doubled; but the Sultan's writ ran only in relation to employment by the Company. Ismail still called up all the men he

[1] Sir Arnold Wilson, *The Suez Canal*, London 1933.

required, and even used some thousands of them to complete that part of the Freshwater Canal which he had agreed to dig at the country's expense. For the years 1864-66 the general situation is concisely represented by Rabbino:

Port Said: Plan of harbour modified; instead of two parallel moles 1,300 feet apart, eastern mole started from shore at a distance of 4,500 feet from western mole, gradually approaching to 1,300 feet, and thus forming a fine port; pass of Port Said 200 to 300 feet wide, 16 feet deep; entry of basin 600 feet wide, 16 to 20 feet deep. Tonnage of port, 15th July, 1865, to 15th June, 1866, vessels 595, tons 108,539. (Work during June much hampered by an outbreak of cholera and the subsequent flight of 4,000 labourers.)

Maritime Canal: General works: Borel and Lavalley; 32 long trough dredgers at work along 35 miles of canal; native contingents abolished May 1864, replaced with almost no delay; in 1866 7,954 European labourers; 10,806 Africans and Asiatics, viz: Arabs, Syrians, etc.

North of Lake Timsah: Canal from Port Said to Timsah widened by 325 feet, thus allowing formation of strands for the protection of banks from passing vessels, and economizing stone embankments; El Guisr ridge trench widened and deepened by Couvreux, 6 miles by Gioja on account of the Company.

South of Lake Timsah: Timsah to Suez, first excavations by hand, afterwards by dredgers from Timsah to south of Toussoum; from Toussoum to the Bitter Lakes trench opened 5 miles; rock of Chalouf removed 1,100 feet long, earth 3,200,000 cubic feet, stone 1,000,000 cubic feet. (The seuil of Chalouf is a hard bank of rock some 2 feet thick at a depth of 6 to 16 feet below sea-level and four miles across. The clay here was full of fossil remains of the elephant and the dog-fish, mixed with layers of bicarbonate of magnesia. Nearly all this section was worked by hand, and fifteen hundred men from Piedmont were specially employed on the work.)

Freshwater Canal and Water Supply: Viceroy set 80,000 men to work at canal from Cairo to Wady (Ouady), 5t'i October, 1865, 70,000,000 cubic feet; subsequently 105,000,000, leaving 70,000,000 allowing of the passage of Nile Water at all seasons; the Company finished 30,750,000 cubic feet, placed to its charge by the imperial award.

With so much accomplished in spite of such tremendous obstacles, it might have been thought that the Company would have no difficulty in making a fresh share issue; but Lesseps' high-handed waving aside of the Rothschild offer, aggravated by his frequent criticisms of the whole system of international finance, especially as applied to Egypt, resulted in the Company creating round itself a financial vacuum. Had the position on the isthmus been even better, it is doubtful whether a straightforward offer would have been sufficiently taken up, if only because the existing 500 franc shares stood at only half that amount on the Bourse. With characteristic audacity, Ferdinand charged straight at the opposition, and, largely thanks to Eugénie, was able to get a bill through the Chamber, enabling the Company – with the implication of the Emperor's blessing, to issue preference shares. The parliamentary debates had the effect of giving the canal immediate and excellent publicity, which, owing to the decisive voting in its favour, amounted to a vote of confidence by France in Lesseps. When the issue opened, success was already assured, and within three days the books were closed. Now, at long last, Lesseps had both the means and the money to fulfil his dream; a fact which was soon recognized in England, where the P. & O. Company prepared to re-route their Indiamen and the chorus changed its tune. Instead of maledictions, paeans of praise were heard on every side, particularly among merchants concerned with the eastern trade and their associated interests. Only the ship-owners lost enthusiasm as they came to realize that re-routing would not be enough. The new course required a new type of vessel, and so favoured new firms which had not capital invested in ships which might soon become prematurely obsolete.

Lesseps turned his back upon London and Paris. Better than anyone else he knew that, in spite of the future seeming so assured, many things could still prevent, if not the justification of the work, then its completion on time. Financial success for the Company could not be assured until dues began to roll in, and the sooner that happened the better. So the work pressed on, even in the dark, when the dredgers operated by lantern-light. Distinguished visitors began to arrive: the Duke of St. Albans, Prince Tewfik (Ismail's heir), the Prince of Wales, and finally Ismail himself. All of them regarded the work as a wonder of the world, an achievement already past doubt. The future Edward VII even went so far as to comment that Lord Palmerston, 'had been guilty of a lamentable lack of foresight'. Almost as convincing as the canal itself was Port Said, now a town of ten thousand people with 'depots, workshops, market, post-office, hospitals, baths, schools, churches, mosques, hotel, club, theatre'. Ten years before there had been nothing but a barren, waterless sand-spit, close to the treacherous mud of Pelusium. Ismailia was also a flourishing township, backed by fertile land newly reclaimed from the desert. It was as though the momentum which Ferdinand had brought to the original plans had endured until it was now shared by everyone connected with the enterprise. In such circumstances the work rapidly accelerated. The great moment when the two seas should meet could not be long delayed, and on the 15th of August, 1869, it took place with impressive ceremony.

The Khedive had invited a number of distinguished visitors, and a large native crowd, augmented by workers from other parts of the line, spontaneously assembled where the waters of the Red Sea were held back by a dyke at the northern end of the Bitter Lakes. A kilometre or so farther north was a similar dyke, penning the Mediterranean. The plan was to release the Red Sea and allow it to find its own level before the second dyke was breached. Ferdinand said: "Thirty-five centuries ago the waters of the Red Sea drew back at the word of Moses. To-day, at the order of the Sovereign of Egypt, they return to their bed." Ismail gave a signal. A prepared place in the dyke gave way. Boisterously the Red Sea poured through it, and, widening the breach, appalled the watchers by the force and pace of the rushing water; which swept like a bore towards the other dyke, inundating the banks of the dry canal, over-turning machinery, threatening to undo in a few minutes the work of months. And if the second dyke were to break under the strain, the boiling waters, laden with mud and sand, might silt up miles of the canal. Every available man hurried to the northern dyke to reinforce it. The water was lapping towards them as they began to work. Night came and they still laboured. Next morning there was a still lake on either side of the barrier. Without sound or ceremony the two seas, already level, were allowed to mingle.

Little more than a month later, on the 25th of September, de Lesseps voyaged from sea to sea in fifteen hours, and a few days afterwards he was followed by an ocean-going ship, *Louise et Marie*. Soon the Khedive, all bitterness forgotten, was professing himself 'full of admiration' for de Lesseps and the work. Almost at once he began to make plans for a European tour, in the course of which he would be able personally to invite the most important people to attend the canal's inauguration.

In spite of some doubt whether the remaining technical difficulties could be overcome in time, this had been provisionally
fixed for the following November. Lesseps was anxious to rush
the last stages of construction, because in spite of the high rate
of extraction in recent months the work was already a year
behind schedule. And it would not be possible for the Company to raise any more capital until the usefulness of the
waterway could be commercially demonstrated. Meanwhile
victory was generally considered to be so certain that the Sultan
took opportunity to restrict his vassal's authority, lest Ismail
should get above himself because of it. So, in spite of his new
title, Ismail found himself virtually demoted to the status of
a provincial governor. Understandably in view of what *Khedive*
had cost him, he took this as an insult and appealed to Lesseps,
who, by publicly supporting him, only increased the suspicion
that Ismail still meant to become another Mohammed-Ali. For
the sake of the old delusion that Lesseps was a secret agent
of French imperialism, it seemed as though the jealousy between
France and England might yet break out again. Only when
rumour was already circulating the possibility of another war
did Ismail finally accept his subordinate position, on paper. In
practice he still remained very much master in his own house;
and to demonstrate the fact made the forthcoming inauguration the excuse for a series of entertainments of such magnificence that the Sultan himself would hardly be able to command,
or to afford, them.

*   *   *

As patroness of the enterprise, it was natural that Eugénie
should take the first place at the canal's opening, the date of
which, 17th November, was chosen to be as close as possible to
her Saint's Day – and perhaps also to Ferdinand's birthday.
Perhaps in deference to England, the Emperor avoided making
political capital out of the event and did not accompany her
when in mid-autumn she set sail for Venice, Athens and Constantinople, *en route* for Egypt. She had tremendous personal
success everywhere she went, of the kind which in modern
times is associated primarily with actresses; for Eugénie was
literally a beauty Queen, and her wit was the equal of her looks.

In fact she gained such a reputation for light-heartedness that the more solemn members of her entourage, and their opposite numbers in other royal circles, began to think there was no serious purpose within her. Such was certainly not the case. She won a diplomatic victory out of her visit to Constantinople, as the result of which tension with Egypt sharply decreased, though the Sultan would still not be represented at the inauguration. Perhaps with the idea of outshining Ismail, he gave her the most magnificent reception. When she sailed for Alexandria she must have been tired and surfeited with formality *de luxe*. She did not stay long in Cairo, though in her honour the capital had been turned into a fantasy of luxury. Verdi wrote *Rigoletto* for the occasion, and it is said that the jewels worn upon the stage were all genuine, to the tune of several million pounds. In six weeks a road had been built out to the Pyramids so that she could go there in a carriage. Perhaps she would have been less comfortable had she realized that all the labour had been *corvée*, and that the remarkable speed had been due in part to the lash. In any case she had no particular interest in antiquities, though an egyptologist had been attached to her suite for the sole purpose of instructing her. He must have been a disappointed man, for in the week's journey she made into Upper Egypt he had small opportunity to impress upon her the glories of the past. Even her closest companion, the Comtesse de Nadhaillac, seems to have been unable to appreciate that Eugénie had already had too much pomp and circumstance to be concerned with the evocation of ancient splendours.

The Countess thought Eugénie took too much trouble over her toilette and described her as, 'nervous, excitable, demanding, accustomed to upset protocol for a whim'. She would slip away to talk with unworthy persons, such as a group of students designated by the damning phrase *mal élevés*. In fact Eugénie had every need and intention to relax, and she did so in the common-sense way, by throwing formality to the winds and revelling in what must have been as near to private life as she had known since her marriage to the Emperor, to whom she wrote wistfully: "Far from people and affairs one can breathe the peace that heals. I do not wish to recall the shadows in my life which have dulled the lovely colours of illusion."

Illusion? The word is hardly one likely to be used by a shallow person, and there are other reasons for supposing that she was by no means so light-headed as Cécile de Nadhaillac imagined. It is more likely that the Empress already had a presentiment of the coming storm in Europe, and regarded her Egyptian progress as something of a charade. At least she thoroughly enjoyed the 'illusion', and returned to Alexandria more beautiful, more gay, more charming than ever.

Ferdinand saw to it that his cousin's confidence was not shaken by news of what had been happening in the isthmus during her absence. Perhaps it would have been better had he told her, for she would be sure to hear the rumours, which were far more damaging than the truth. They said there was a huge rock in the channel and nothing could move it; that Ismailia had been completely destroyed by fire; that the claim to have made tracts of desert fertile was all nonsense; that Lavalley had committed suicide out of despair and that his chief engineers had fled rather than face disgrace; that de Lesseps was out of his head; that the Empress had gone back to France rather than face public humiliation through the failure of the enterprise, and that everyone else would do well to go home, in order to avoid great discomfort and bitter disappointment.

In fact the situation was well in hand, despite administrative worries due to a greater influx of people than even the Khedive desired, or Lesseps could cope with through the organization set up for that purpose. Ismail had personally invited six thousand persons, paying for their journey to and from Egypt as well as for all their expenses while in the country. There were thousands more Europeans who had not been invited, but were irresistibly drawn by the promise of so great a wonder. Every town in the Delta was overflowing. Public transport was inadequate. The waterways were congested and the harbours crammed. And still the guests poured in, some of them saddened by four days of storm in the Mediterranean which had kept their ships almost continuously hove-to. Even so they were outnumbered by the influx from the countries of the Middle East:

"People from Asia Minor, Ukrainians, men of Bokhara, Turks, Tartars, men in caftans, sheiks with green turbans, women, children, old men, the sick, the paralysed. Bashi-bazouks with their high

hats and cummerbunds swathed from chin to crutch, their weapons
within the folds, their leggings partly covering down-at-heel shoes.
. . . A few veiled, white-robed women, whose long, less bold eyes
do not suggest the Egyptian: they must be Turkish."[1]

In the area of Lake Timsah alone there were thirty thousand
Arabs, with their families, flocks, camels and horses. If the
orientals appeared quaint, the occidentals were not less so:

"Helmets of double thickness, with a flap coming down over the
back of the neck in the manner of the ancient Saracens, and with
a doubled visor in green; caps of unbleached cloth with flaps to
protect the cheeks and neck; Syrian *couffiehs*, Panamas with enormous brims. . . . Théophile Gautier describes all the products of
human ingenuity designed against the imaginary enemy whom one
must at all costs keep at bay, even though the temperature of
Lower Egypt does not, in the month November, exceed that of
Marseilles or Algiers. The hotels were carefully patrolled so as to
guard their visitors from the divine murderer. Shepheards was a
great monument, bare and austere, more like an English barrack
than an oriental caravanserai; a vast monastery in which the staircases were hardly lit and the rooms resembled cells."[2]

The isthmus was equally crowded. The canal was lined for
almost the whole of its length by encampments; while at Port
Said, Ismailia, and Suez there was much the same turmoil as
at Cairo. The five hundred cooks with a thousand waiters, whom
Ismail had specially imported, were as inadequate as existing
accommodation, which had to be supplemented by army tents.
Everywhere there was a sense of tremendous importance, an
emotional tension as though before an earthquake. How wise
Eugénie had been to go into Upper Egypt! The pace of social
life was killing. Not that Ferdinand saw much of it. There
had been some foundation for the rumour about a rock in the
channel. By sheer bad luck a pair of soundings only a hundred
or so feet apart had fallen each side of a ridge of hard stone
which broke the buckets of the dredgers and still projected
five feet above the permissible maximum. When Ferdinand
went to inspect he was told the position was hopeless in so
far as the opening day was concerned. Such an obstacle could
never be moved in time. "Get powder," Ferdinand said, "masses
of it. If we don't manage to blow it up, then we'll go up."

[1] *Fromentin. See* Edgar-Bonnet.   [2] *op. cit.*

Somehow they managed to get the charges in, and, perhaps as much by luck as by calculation, the blasting was successful. Ferdinand had hardly satisfied himself that all was well when a fire was reported in Ismailia and he hurried there to mobilize the military, whom he kept at watering the wall surrounding the outbreak. It had begun in a timber-yard used for storing a quantity of fireworks to be used during the celebrations, and the fire-fighters were not over-eager on that account. They might well have left their duty had they known, as Ferdinand did, that buried under the sand of the yard was a dump of gunpowder, enough of it to make a shambles of the town. The water quenched the fire, preventing it from spreading, and soaked down into the sand, rendering the powder harmless. Only in rumour was the town destroyed, but it had been a near thing. Ferdinand was only just in time to collect his two sons and meet the Empress when the imperial yacht *Aigle* steamed into the Port Said roadstead on the morning of the 16th.

Over eighty vessels, many of them warships, had assembled to welcome her. They were dressed overall, with rails and yards manned, and as *Aigle* entered harbour, each fired a salute, through which the cheering of the multitude broke in waves which brought people near to tears. As *Aigle* dropped anchor Eugénie exclaimed, "Never in my life have I seen anything so beautiful! " The weather was superb, the shores gay with thousands of pennants fluttering above the heads of the dense crowd of many nations, many shades. In the foreground was the paint-shop perfection of the royal yachts, the definitive accuracy of naval craft in an unofficial contest for the smartest ship. Beyond them were the newest of passenger ships, each chosen by some delegation or group for this particular honour. Standing out to sea, as though to emphasize the real focus of power behind the regatta, were 'two enormous English frigates'; and there were twelve other British naval vessels in the anchorage, among them five ironclads: twice as many ships as the French.

Following the Khedive, the Emperor of Austria, the Prince of Holland, and a roll of near-royalty which must have been unique even for those regal days, Ferdinand went aboard *Aigle* to greet his cousin, his Empress, his loyal agent. The arrangements were now working well. The channel was clear. Eugénie was radiant and the Khedive at his very best, both treating a retired consular official on terms of equality. This surely was his climacteric hour. Nothing which could follow would match its importance to the man who had for so long fought, not so much for the completion of an engineering feat as such, but for the friendly intercourse of peoples. That afternoon, perhaps for the first time in history, Allah and Jehovah were worshipped side by side, in a setting rendered the more dramatic by an unusually high tide, which isolated the tribunes of the priests and set a rippling barrier between them and the congregation. Islam was represented by the Grand Ulema of Egypt, Christianity by the Archbishop of Jerusalem; but the principal sermon was delivered by Monseigneur Bauer, Apostolic Delegate and confessor to the Empress. He evidently held his audience, perhaps less by eloquence than because they too caught a glimpse of what the world may be when men forgot their fears, and so have no more need of jealousy or cruelty.

"He began, 'Monseigneur, Madame, Sire' (the Khedive, the Empress of France, the Emperor of Austria), 'it is perhaps permissible to claim that the hour which has just struck is not only one of the most solemn in this century, but one of the greatest and most decisive which humanity has witnessed since there has been history here below. In this locality, where hitherto Asia and Africa met without touching, takes place an august and cosmopolitan celebration, attended by all the races of the globe. All the flags, all the banners, float gaily under this bright enormous sky. And there stands the Cross beside the Crescent! What marvels, what striking contrasts, are produced when dreams, reputed to be illusions, become palpable realities! In this gathering together of so many prodigies, what subjects there are for the thinker, what joys in this present hour, and for the future, what glorious hope!

"'There at last in view, there at our very feet, is this work of giants which, because people would not believe the things of which man is capable when he wills in truth, was said to be impossible. There it is, made by created beings, the river which shall be for the perpetual astonishment of generations. There it is, achieved by science, by courage, by treasure, and through all manner of conflict; by perseverance, the genius of man and the manifest protection of God. There ride the vessels of all the nations, ready to cross for the first time this threshold which makes of the Orient and Occident a single world. The barrier is down. One of the most formidable enemies of mankind and of civilization, which is distance, loses in a moment two thousand leagues of his empire. The two sides of the world approach to greet one another, and in greeting recognize that all men, being children of one God, tremble with the wonder of their mutual fraternity. . . . Henceforth the Indian Ocean and the Mediterranean Sea are a single flood. The history of the world has reached one of its most glorious stages. As in the past chronology was divided between the centuries before and after the discovery of America, so the chronology of the future will say: " This was before or after the Orient and Occident met across the half-open flank of Egypt; this was before or after the 16th of November, 1869; this was before or after the opening of the Suez Canal. . . ."

" ' Madame, those who have closely followed this great work know the part which Your Majesty has played. That part is immense. It is proper to your devoted soul to accomplish great things in silence; but we are under no obligation to be accomplices of this silence, which might falsify history and put posterity upon the wrong track. It is important for history to know that this great work is to a large extent yours. In bearing such witness history will be telling strictly the truth. And history may add, Madame, that in lending your powerful support to the Canal of the Two Worlds, you have been completely in tune with the thoughts and sympathies of all France. . . . Now that the unbelievable has become a fact, now that the pretended chimera is there, a splendid accomplishment before our enchanted eyes, what must be passing in the mind of him who was the soul of that which now we see? God knows. But it seems to me that in his eyes I see a glitter of tears, and I would that I could preserve them, because they belong, first to France, and then to all humanity. Let us declare the name of this man who belongs to History – which, by a rare Providence, he enters while yet alive. Let us declare to all the world that France, which is far off but by no means absent, is proud and content in her son. Let us add that, just as the New World, discovered in the fifteenth century, will always pass from mouth to mouth the name of its discoverer, so in this nineteenth century will this name pass, which I am about to utter to the four winds of heaven, the name of Ferdinand de Lesseps. . . . Almighty and eternal God, creator of the world and the Father of all creatures, bless this new highway which you have permitted man to open in the midst of your creation. Make of this river not only a passage to universal prosperity, but make it also a royal road of peace and of justice; of the light, and of the eternal truth. O God, may this highway bring men together, but above all may it bring them to Thyself; and may it be to everyone propitious, for time and for eternity.' "

*   *   *

When the religious ceremonies had ended, two pilot vessels, *Latif* and *Salamandre*, left for Suez. They had covered only thirty kilometres when an error of pilotage put *Latif* aground,

and though *Salamandre* was able to work past her, it was evident
that *Aigle* would not be able to do so. And, at the request of
the Empress, in the morning she was to lead the van; followed
by fifty-one ships a cable's length apart. If *Aigle* were held up,
none of them would be able to turn, and without steerage way
must inevitably run aground. *Latif* had been proceeding at the
speed ordered for the procession, which, at ten kilometres an
hour, was quite fast enough under the circumstances; and
though there was no damage nor injury, she bit deep into the
soft side of the canal. Even so, her Captain thought that he
would be able to get her clear, and no doubt realizing that the
Khedive would hardly be likely to overlook such an incident,
decided against reporting it. He did so only when all his
resources had been exhausted, and by that time the fireworks
were going up from Port Said after a State dinner and a ball.
The Khedive had already boarded his No. 1 yacht, *Mahroussa*,
and was about to start for Ismailia when Ferdinand got him
out of bed to hear the news. Far from flying into a princely
rage, for which he might easily have been forgiven, Ismail at
once agreed to go with Lesseps to the scene of the mishap, and
said that if there were no alternative, he would have *Latif* blown
up rather than delay the procession. They arrived in the small
hours and found a thousand men at work under a clear sky.
Latif was refloated in time for Lesseps to get back to Port Said
just before *Aigle* weighed anchor, a little after eight o'clock.
As she entered the canal, followed by the Emperor of Austria's
yacht, Ferdinand ' calm and smiling' was on the review platform
with the Empress. He made no reference to the night's emer-
gency, even though he knew, better than anyone, how likely it
was that the grounding of the frigate had so narrowed the
effective channel, by shifting sand from the banks to the bed,
that even now *Aigle* might not be able to pass: "It was only
five minutes before we arrived at the scene of the grounding
that an Egyptian admiral, sailing in a small steamboat, signalled
that the way was clear. And when we arrived at Kantara, which
is forty kilometres from Port Said, the *Latif*, dressed overall,
saluted us with her guns. Everyone was enchanted with the
gesture of so placing this big frigate."

The Captain of *Aigle*, Surville, took extraordinary care. He
left the bridge and conned his ship from the starboard paddle-

box; from which he could follow the line of the banks, and even of the bottom, at close quarters. His helm-orders were passed from mouth to mouth, and in the same way the Company's pilots on the bridge, often Lesseps himself, communicated with the Captain, whose responsibility did not end with keeping the ship afloat. It must have been extraordinarily difficult to maintain constant speed, failing which the ships astern were bound to get into trouble. With her 99 metres of length, 18 of beam, *Aigle* must have been awkward, particularly owing to the extra beam represented by her paddles. The tension soon communicated itself to the Empress, who went below, saying that she felt as though there were a circle of fire around her head. The shouting of the crowds, the booming of the guns, the blare of military bands, were left behind. The Captain insisted upon strict silence. There was no sound but the slow splash of the paddles and terse orders: this was no pleasure trip.

As *Aigle* approached Ismailia, Eugénie again appeared on deck to acknowledge the cheering which began again long before they reached the lake. But she was still so upset that she failed to make any gesture of recognition to Ferdinand, who was standing beside her, to show her gracious pleasure. He would not have cared, but the fact that the incident is recorded suggests that Cécile de Nadhaillac was even then concerned for the manners of her Empress. But even Cécile was not proof against the high voltage of the hour: "We bore upon our shoulders a part of the heavy burden which bowed down our brave and excellent Captain. Suppose *Aigle* went aground? What disasters! Without speaking of the national honour, tarnished. The future of the canal would be destroyed, and France be made a laughing-stock for having lent her support to the idea. The hours passed full of imagined misfortune for the ship and for ourselves."

That afternoon all the vessels anchored in Lake Timsah, not one among them having had the least difficulty. Relieved of anxieties, at least in so far as this first section of the journey was concerned, the passengers went ashore, further to enjoy the fantastic hospitality of the Khedive; at whose orders the entire town had been garlanded with fresh green-stuff, to symbolize the fertile land won back from the desert. A palace had been built for the occasion, in the halls of which Ismail that evening received between four and five thousand of the *élite,* while the lower orders also enjoyed themselves at his expense. The desert Arabs increased the commotion by bringing in with them their own shrill orchestras. Though up all night – after a long night at Port Said, and what must have seemed one of the longest days in her life – the Empress was out at eight o'clock next morning. She rode to the famous Seuil of El Guisr on horseback, but for the return journey insisted upon mounting a camel – which must have been something of an achievement sartorially as well as in terms of equitation. It is hardly likely that Eugénie had ever been on a camel before. The authorities who watched over her evidently considered it a somewhat undignified procedure, and so she was followed all the way home by a carriage drawn by eight white dromedaries.

Her next engagement was a visit to the gabled chalet where Ferdinand, austere as any anchorite, had worked and slept during the hard years. Then, after holding court at which many distinguished ladies were presented, she rejoined *Aigle* for the remainder of the voyage to Suez. Much of the anxiety was now past, though Ferdinand still had reason to worry, particularly at the rock of Serapeum, where he knew there was barely enough water. When *Aigle* reached that place a crowd of workmen were waiting with much the same thought in their minds, that the ship might touch bottom. When she did not, they gave her a tremendous ovation, which caused Ferdinand to declare that 'there was not a camel-driver among us who did not consider himself to be an agent of civilization. That is why we succeeded.' A little later Captain Surville noticed that de Lesseps was no longer present and a search was instituted when he could not at once be found. He was eventually discovered fast asleep in one of the cabins, a circumstance ascribed to his magnificent confidence in his work. Still no one, except perhaps the Captain, knew about *Latif*.

After spending the night at anchor off Suez, the long procession steamed back to Port Said, making the passage in fifteen hours. Then:

"The Sovereigns and the Princes expressed to Ferdinand de Lesseps their great admiration. On the waters of Lake Timsah the Empress had already invested him with the Grand Cross of the Legion of Honour. The Khedive now gave him the Grand Cordon of the Order of Osmanie. The Emperor of Austria gave him the

Grand Cordon of the Order of Leopold. A few days later, the King
of Italy sent the Grand Cross of the Order of St. Maurice and
Lazare. Besides all this the Empress gave him a silver cup, *chef
d'œuvre de l'art*, executed by Fannières, upon which was inscribed,
' l'Impératrice Eugénie à Ferdinand de Lesseps 18 Novembre
1869.' Congratulations poured in: from continents, countries, cities,
towns, companies and individuals the world over. As the Viceroy
of India, Lord Mayo, said in his message, this was ' universal
acclaim'. He added that Ferdinand had ' just title to the gratitude
of all peoples, and high esteem among the most distinguished men
of modern times'."

*   *   *

Aigle steamed back to France, taking the beautiful Eugénie
to an ugly destiny; for war was already in the air. Within nine
months she would in council give her assent to the attack on
Prussia, too much believing in those who urged that national
honour demanded a blood-sacrifice. Even then the peace might
have been saved had not France stood alone in Europe. And
perhaps she would not have been alone if, in order to preserve
an effective British alliance, Napoleon had abandoned, or at
least postponed, the cutting of the great canal. For Eugénie the
' illusion' was ending. For Ferdinand it would soon begin. Meanwhile he did nothing to exploit his triumph, neither in publicity,
in money, nor yet in power; all of which were open to his hands.
He declined the Emperor's proffered title ' Duke of Suez', sought
no favours at the Egyptian court. and did not go to Paris to
listen to the echo of the cheers which had resounded from Port
Said to Suez and Suez to Port Said. Instead, he went to meet a
woman to whom he had been writing love-letters even while
the suspense was mounting to climax. Her name was
Mademoiselle Louise-Hélène Autard de Bragard, and she was
twenty years of age. He was sixty-four but looked ten years
younger, square, strong, debonaire. His keen eyes and generous
vitality seemed to lift from his big grey head the weight of the
lonely years.

Hélène's father was an old friend who had an estate in
Mauritius, where Hélène was born. Her father now found himself a British subject – since the island was in English occupation,
but she had been educated in Paris, and had first encountered
Ferdinand at one of the Empress' ' Mondays'. In the family

tradition he fell in love with her at first sight; but, realizing that it would be unfair to bring her out to the isthmus, had waited upon the realization of his dream before proposing. Only a few weeks before the inauguration, he had assured her that she would never leave Egypt except as Mme de Lesseps. And he was accepted, evidently, on his own merits rather than for his fame. Otherwise how could the marriage, from which came twelve children, the last born in his eightieth year, have been so happy?

The marriage ceremony took place in the chapel at Ismailia on the 25th of November, and the civil formality afterwards at the French consulate. The Press was not represented. There were no distinguished guests. It was a very quiet wedding.

Chapter 15. IDOL

In June 1870 Ferdinand de Lesseps emerged from the obscurity of his second honeymoon into a spotlight reserved for the Lion of the London Season; but he did not take Hélène with him, an understandable decision. She knew none of the crowd of big-wigs who were now so anxious to make him forget the old hostility. She knew nothing about the business of the canal. It may even have occurred to her that the obvious discrepancy between her husband's age and her own might well raise English eyebrows, and perhaps start uncharitable rumours; though their first child, Mathieu-Marie, was not born until the 12th of October. On the day after Ferdinand's arrival, the 24th of June, he wrote to Charles:

"My evening at M. Pender's yesterday was a real ovation for the canal. The most important people were continually being introduced. The Prince and Princess of Wales have asked me to dinner on my return from Liverpool, where I go this evening to attend a Mayoral banquet. During the Pender evening, where all the *élite* of London was gathered, I had opportunity, quite apart from the formal presentations, to meet many acquaintances and to take note of the great success of the canal. I congratulate myself on having come here. A telegraph to the Governor-General of India had been installed in the ballroom. The first message was sent out at eleven o'clock, and before midnight we received Lord Mayo's reply, dated at five in the morning of the 24th, from his residence in Simla. Lady Mayo, who was at the ball, then sent a message to her husband. I also sent one to Lord Mayo, presenting my compliments. Invitations are pouring in from London and other places."

If Ferdinand was a lion of the season, certainly his canal was one of the two topics of the hour, both in the popular Press and among serious councillors. The other was the probability of war between France and Prussia over the Spanish succession; which still seemed so far-fetched that it hardly gained serious consideration; particularly since Queen Victoria had been instrumental in getting William of Prussia to withdraw in face of French umbrage at the idea of a Hohenzollern candidate for the throne. Besides, England had never known such an acceleration of prosperity at home and of power abroad. She was too busy to be concerned with quarrels among foreigners, and the season was too brilliant to be shadowed by macabre speculations. The only serious interlude which Ferdinand seems to have had between soirées was an interview with the Board of Admiralty, where he was consulted about various technical matters arising out of their Lordships' recent decision to make the canal the normal trooping route to India. To all appearances, what a change of opinion was there! But Lesseps himself must by now have realized that nothing had in effect changed. England would still have preferred there to be no canal rather than one under French control.

In the first week of July the Directors of the Crystal Palace promoted a colossal demonstration in favour of de Lesseps and his creation. The huge greenhouse, surrounded by exuberant gardens, all brilliantly lit, became the swarming-place for between thirty and forty thousand people. In almost royal state he led a procession of carriages on a circuit of the grounds, before being set down at the main entrance; from which he was conducted, *via* the Queen's Corridor, to meet the select company with whom he was to dine. Afterwards the famous fireworks gave added grandeur to stupendous jets from the fountains, rising to almost three hundred feet before feathering into a fine spray of rainbow colours. The Prince of Wales presented Lesseps with a gold medal, and he was then called upon to accept an 'Egyptian Salute', which proved to be a pyrotechnic novelty in the hands of two hundred boys from the Lambeth Industrial Schools, who in unison waved four hundred coloured flares while themselves remaining invisible. The display ended with a set-piece consisting of a pyramid flanked by huge palm-trees which changed colour, a flight of two thousand large rockets, and 'a cataract of golden fire covering half an acre'. England had taken Lesseps to her heart.

France meanwhile, besotted with the false idea of glory which had long permeated the Empire, and full of blatant over-confidence in her military power, allowed Prince Bismarck to provoke her into declaring war. The irrevocable decision was made at a secret meeting between Napoleon, Eugénie, and their

Foreign Minister, the Duc de Gramont, at Saint-Cloud on the 13th. Years afterwards Eugénie admitted that she had been carried away by the hysterical temper of the people, which, after so much repression at home, demanded satisfaction abroad : "You cannot imagine what an outburst of patriotism carried all France away at that moment. Even Paris, hitherto so hostile to the Empire, showed wonderful enthusiasm, confidence and resolution. Frantic crowds in the boulevards cried incessantly, 'A Berlin! A Berlin!' No, I assure you, it was beyond human power to prevent war any longer." Though the Government was aware that the army was ill-equipped and unprepared, the formal declaration was made a week later, on the 19th; but the London season did not pause in its stride, and on the thirtieth, while both sides were still mobilizing and setting out their order of battle on the frontier, the Lord Mayor handed to de Lesseps the Freedom of the City, contained in a box of fine gold. "The ceremony of presentation prevented me from writing to you yesterday," wrote Ferdinand to Charles. "Everything went off very well. My reception was enthusiastic, and after the presentation I had to parade down the banqueting-hall amid my fellow-citizens (*et surtout mes concitoyennes*), who kept putting out their hands from the crowd to shake mine." With the letter was enclosed a copy of his speech, which ended as follows :

"In according to me this honourable title, this rare and valued distinction, you have consecrated and enlarged the enterprise of the Suez Canal, and you bear witness to its success and its advantages. If Egypt and France have brought this universal work into being, it is for England to give life to it by lending that support which previously had been lacking; so that the commerce of all nations may follow the decisive lead of British ocean shipping. . . . Sincere friend of England and her worthy emulator, France is one of the standard-bearers of civilization and of liberty, in time of peace as of war. And we may expect of her in the struggle now unfortunately inevitable, that the worthy blood which will be shed by both sides shall not be useless to the cause of the well-being of humanity."

Almost as he was speaking, what little glory there was left began to depart from this last of the 'romantic' wars in which armies were led by kings.

"The reservists who should have filled the depleted ranks were posting up and down France looking for uniforms and arms: the railways were blocked by supplies still lacking at the front: officers could not find the units they were to command: generals at the front telegraphed to say they had plenty of maps of the German side of the frontier but none of the French; that they had no canteens, ambulances, nor baggage-carts: 'there is an utter lack of everything'. Louis Napoleon himself was almost too ill to travel: nominally in supreme command, he was no soldier and his generals knew it. . . . With the easy capture of Saarbrucken, two miles inside Germany (August 2nd) the French offensive, upon which all plans and hopes had been based, came to an end. On the German side everything was ready; and it was they who, unexpectedly the aggressors owing to French dilatoriness, now advanced across the frontier. They had never counted on taking the offensive, and entered upon the campaign with more anxiety than confidence." (Thompson.)

A few days later, Ferdinand was back in Paris, to find that already the tide of war had turned; for on the day he arrived the Germans gained a decisive victory at Wissembourg. So high ran emotional tension in the capital that at first the news was treated as unbelievable, then, as the inefficiency of the French organization became manifest, opinion soured overnight, turning against the dynasty which had, in more ways than one, driven it into this miserable adventure. Charles de Lesseps was in Egypt. Victor's unit was still in Paris, which, following a telegram from the Emperor, was already preparing for a siege. In his usual calm way, Ferdinand set about organizing an ambulance unit, while trying to keep an eye on Eugénie, who was acting head of State, and bursting with schoolgirl notions of military glory. The end of the campaign in the field came on the 1st of September at the village of Sedan. In an almost illegible hand Napoleon wrote to the King of Prussia: "My brother, not having been able to die among my soldiers, there is nothing left for me to do but to place my sword in the hands of Your Majesty." To Eugénie he telegraphed, "The army is defeated and made prisoner, not having been able to get myself killed among my troops I have had to become a prisoner in order to save the army." And that night he wrote:

"My dear Eugénie, I cannot tell you what I have suffered and am suffering. We made a march contrary to all the rules and to common sense: it was bound to lead to a catastrophe and that is complete. I would rather have died than witness such a disastrous capitulation; and yet, things being as they are, it was the only way of avoiding the slaughter of 60,000 men. Then again, if only my torments were concentrated here! I think of you, of our son, of our unfortunate country. May God protect you! What is going to happen at Paris? I have just seen the King. There were tears in his eyes when he spoke of the sorrow I must be feeling. He has put at my disposal one of his *châteaux* near Hesse-Cassel. But what does it matter where I go? Adieu: I embrace you tenderly."

Socialist reaction in the capital was immediate and potentially as dangerous as such movements had been in the past. Ferdinand, alert for any rumour that might point to danger for Eugénie, heard of a plan to raise the suburbs and march on the Tuileries. On the 4th he insisted upon seeing the Empress alone, and urged her to abandon her constitutional powers. She refused, partly out of pride, partly because she could not see deep enough into the emotional state of her people, who would inevitably shift the force of their hatred from the triumphant enemy to the leaders whom they regarded as responsible for the disaster. Apparently unmoved, Ferdinand stayed to luncheon, though Eugénie did not come down. "*Eh bien*, M. de Lesseps," said a fellow-guest as they sat down to table, "and what do you think of the situation?"

"I think, my dear General, this is the last lunch you'll ever get at the Tuileries."

The meal is inadequately described as 'short and silent'. While the guests were leaving, Eugénie was impatiently waiting for a key to be found to a private door which led from the State Apartments into the Louvre Museum. For years no one had had occasion to use it. Meanwhile the mob, of which Ferdinand had warned her, bore down upon the palace and made it impossible to leave the building by any of the usual doors. At last the key was found. With only Madame Lebreton in attendance, the Empress slipped through into the public galleries, and anonymity. On reaching the street, they were fortunate in being able to stop a passing cab, which took them to the house of M. Besson, a Member of the Council. He was not at home. They could not even gain entry, and the cab had gone. So they had to walk until they found another one – and still the beauty that was the paragon of Europe went unrecognized. They arrived at M. Peinne's apartment. He too was out. For safety in her own capital city, which should have been full of friends, the Empress could now think of only one place, the American Embassy. But she could not recall the address, nor could Madame Lebreton, nor could the cabby. Was there no one at all to whom she could turn? Her American dentist lived in the Avenue Malakoff. There they found refuge for one night.

Early next morning Dr. Evans took his 'invalid sister' out of Paris in his carriage. She was accompanied by a nurse – Madame Lebreton, and her 'doctor', a reliable friend called Crane. Evans and he drove their horses to exhaustion. They hired another pair, and another. They changed carriages. Avoiding the obvious escape routes, they were making for Deauville. It must have seemed that the shade of 'The Austrian', Marie Antoinette, travelled with them. Having had hardly any rest, they arrived at three o'clock the following morning. So the first stage of the journey was completely successful; but there was still no way of getting Eugénie out of the country, even though she had a forged passport, supplied by Pietri, the Prefect of Police.

Next day two men, Evans and Crane, displayed great interest in Sir John Burgoyne's yacht, which was riding in the harbour. Sir John, thinking no doubt that their interest was only nautical, asked them aboard. No sooner were they on deck than Evans begged urgently for a few words in private, and then said that the Empress was concealed on shore. Would Sir John give her passage to England? Sir John was not to be jostled into any show of surprise:

"After consulting with Lady Burgoyne, and considering the scanty accommodation available, I at once agreed to the request. Later it was arranged that the Empress should come aboard just after midnight, and so she did. She was very much agitated and sobbed bitterly. On my saying to her, 'N'ayez pas peur, Madame,' she replied in English, 'I am safe with an English gentleman.' I then introduced her to my wife, who told her the last three days' news and read the papers to her."

After a rough crossing, she landed at Ryde, Isle of Wight, before seven in the morning of the 8th.

*   *   *

Of all this Ferdinand de Lesseps was inevitably ignorant. He did not even know that Eugénie had left the palace, and, believing her to be still there, did his best to shield her from the rabble. When they saw him before the main doors, with soldiers on either side, the leading elements became reluctant; but they were helplessly pushed on by the press of those behind. Even so, Ferdinand had time to recognize two loyal faces, though the uniforms were those of the insurgent National Guard. Two more friends of the Empress had taken a great risk to help her. Ferdinand could only exchange glances with them, but it was clear that the plan was to pretend to lead the crowd while in reality trying to gain time. The pseudo-National Guards parleyed with the picquet, whose Commander was induced to withdraw in order to avoid provocation, which would inevitably have involved the sacking of the palace. Only enough men remained to line the two sides of the forecourt. They could have been overwhelmed in a few moments – or they could have saved their skins by siding with the mob. Ferdinand recognized among them the badges of Victor's unit, to whom he made himself known. Thanks to the two bogus insurgents, the silent steadiness of the picquet, and their own lack of a specific purpose, the crowds, instead of whipping up to riot-pitch, as must have happened had there been the least incident to encourage them, contented themselves with merely occupying the forecourt, which had been closed to the public since the time of Louis-Philippe. At last they dispersed, without even touching the great doors. Not until then could Lesseps have gone in search of the Empress. And when he did so, no one knew what had happened to her.

That same day, amid vociferous tumult, the Third Republic was proclaimed; and though there was between the Left and the Moderates so little respect that in any other circumstances a civil war might have followed; facing the alien enemy Paris became, almost overnight, one vast entrenched camp. On the nineteenth the Prussians invested the city, and soon demoralizing famine tightened winter's hold. Red flags appeared, and down the silent streets a new cry echoed, ' Vive la Commune! ' In Louis XIV's famous *Salle des Glaces* at Versailles, the King of Prussia was proclaimed the first Emperor of Germany. From the unhappy city a balloon ascended, wafting Gambetta over the lines to carry on resistance should the city fall. On the 18th of January Ferdinand was at his field hospital when he heard that Victor had been wounded. He immediately went with an ambulance to the park at Buzenval, where he found his son, and, with sudden intuition, took him back not to the casualty clearing station but all the way to Rue Richepanse: this in spite of continuing loss of blood. A musket-ball had shattered the kneecap and penetrated the thigh. Warned by a galloper, the family doctor arrived almost at the same time. Between them and the driver they must have carried Victor up those long three flights of stairs to the familiar apartment. After a careful examination, the Doctor told Ferdinand that had his son been taken to the field hospital he would certainly have had an amputation; but since the recovery rate from such operations was only twenty per cent, the risk of sepsis was preferable to that of the saw. The Doctor was proved right. In due course Victor recovered, to be made a Chevalier of the Legion of Honour for his distinguished conduct in the field. Meanwhile the last sortie from the city had failed, and so did a communist *coup* attempted by the National Guards, fifty of whom were killed outside the *Hôtel de Ville*. A week later France sued for peace, and in the shadow of national abasement, for which he was as unprepared as anyone, Ferdinand left for Egypt, where at least with work he could cover up his wounded pride.

The canal was slowly gaining traffic, but there was as yet no sign of it reaching an economic level, and capital was again running out. Though the actual cost of construction, in spite of all delays and difficulties, had amounted to a relatively modest 291,330,000 francs against the original estimate of 200,000,000, other factors had added as much again, making a total of 453,000,000 francs. Consequently the Company had to skip its dividend for 1870 and the shares fell to 250 thence to 208, a calamitous decline due as much to scurrilous propaganda as to the war. Even during the siege pamphlets were widely circulated under such titles as *The Agony of the Suez Canal: its Approaching Ruin*. Deprived of his social influence in France by the fall of the Empire, Ferdinand must have been ready to read into English sympathy, for him and for his country, more than was intended. This was particularly true when, on the 3rd of July, 1871, he was invested with the insignia of a Knight Commander

of the Order of the Star of India: " I arrived at Windsor, where
the ceremony went off perfectly. The Queen had on her right
the Prince of Wales and on her left Prince Arthur. The Prince
of Wales put the cordon over my shoulder and the Queen pinned
the jewel to my chest. Afterwards the Prince of Wales took me
back to London in his carriage." It was not unnatural for Ferdin-
and to infer from the gesture a change in the attitude of Her
Majesty's Government, and he even considered changing the
Company's address to London in expectation of official support.
It was with pardonable exasperation that he learned there was
no more behind his Freedom and his Order than a polite expression of admiration. At the Foreign Office Lord Granville
remained firmly Palmerstonian in his attitude to the canal, and
it was therefore useless to expect financial help from the City.

An attempt to raise fresh capital in France had completely
failed, only five out of twenty million being subscribed. The
Directors considered liquidation inevitable. Charles de Lesseps
was at his wit's end, and therefore in no mood to receive strangers
at the office; so when a certain M. Lebaudy tried to see him
the door remained shut. This happened again. Even on the third
occasion Charles probably received the fellow only for fear that
otherwise he might make an enemy. The visitor had not stated
his business on either of the previous occasions. He was probably just one more shareholder with a grievance. As M. Lebaudy
came through the door he announced, " I have come to bring
you the money." He then explained that he was indeed a shareholder, but, having complete confidence, he said, in the Company, far from pulling out he wished to save the situation,
personally. It was a big claim but Lebaudy seemed to be in
earnest. " What," he demanded, " is the minimum needed to
prevent failure? "

" Seven million," Charles answered, and must have thought
he was dreaming.

" You shall have it," said the astonishing M. Lebaudy – and
was as good as his word. At the Annual General Meeting (1872),
which took place a few months later, Ferdinand frankly
admitted: " It is pure chance that the Company is not in liquidation." Lebaudy's gesture had been well-timed. From that day
the commercial success of the canal became gradually assured
as traffic receipts continued to rise, until, in the following year,

they no longer admitted of doubt as to the profit-making capacity of the concern. Even then the actual traffic was less than half the original estimate of three million tons. Politics were another matter. Britannia, faced with a *fait accompli*, now demanded her lion's share. Ferdinand was only too willing to allow her to take part in the enterprise, to sit on the Board. He had always insisted that British interests in the Company should be proportionate to British preponderance in shipping; but he had never been prepared to surrender his personal authority, which now became the crux of the issue. England did not want a share, she wanted control.

After prolonged negotiations, Lesseps proposed that the canal be purchased jointly by all the maritime Powers; but this scheme, if ever it had a chance of success, was quashed by the Porte, which claimed that, as Egyptian territory, the canal and its zone could not be sold. Though traffic was satisfactory, the Company needed still more money for the development of the amenities and essential services. So Ferdinand, undismayed as ever, next proposed a private deal by which he would sell a substantial interest to a syndicate headed by the Duke of Sutherland and Mr. Pender. This in turn was prevented by the British Government, which still feared military commitments in the Middle East even more than it desired control of the road to India. In a mood of cynical disappointment, Ferdinand gave up the attempt to get English backing. Perhaps his sense of frustration affected the working of the canal. Led by the British, customers complained that the dues were too high, the service too slow, and the lavatories insufficient. This attitude was, to say the least, unreasonable in relation to the financial muddle. As Sir Arnold Wilson says: " We forced the Company to meet capital expenditure out of revenue; our opposition had, more-over, already had the effect of almost doubling the cost of construction. The French regarded our financiers as hypocritical, and our shippers as unreasonable." The British Government did not now care a rap what the French thought, but did want to lower canal dues so that the voyage to India could be made to pay better dividends in Lancashire. In the end it was through the Egyptian Government, prodded by the British, that the required changes were brought about – but only through the use of force. In 1874 ten thousand Egyptian soldiers occupied the isthmus and took over the administration of the canal. Lesseps had no alternative but to do what he was told, even at the risk of having more trouble with his shareholders.

Then, as so often happened, a new factor came into the situation in time to bring some relief. France was already recovering from her defeat, and naturally looked to Russia for support, in particular as an ally in the Middle East. So England, after all, did not have the field to herself. Then, in 1875, the Sultan went bankrupt, and Ismail promptly followed his example; finding in exile shelter from his people, who began to realize the implications of the rise in the National Debt from three to nearly a hundred million sterling, during his reign of thirteen years. Sixteen million had gone to the canal, and were represented by shares, but there must have been other ways in which the enterprise had cost him money. It was in the hope of staving off ultimate failure that he had sought a purchaser for the big block of shares which, owing to the somewhat eager action of Lesseps years ago, still stood to Ismail's private account. They ought to have been worth the sixteen million, but officially France refused to make any offer which was at all acceptable, while private speculators, foreseeing the *débâcle*, waited like vultures for the financial death which would allow them to gorge for nothing. They were confounded by Disraeli, aided by the personal initiative of Charles de Lesseps; but the fact remains that what England was now so delighted to purchase had been on offer from the very inception of the canal scheme, to be repeatedly and discourteously refused. Never more feminine, Britannia had a sudden craving for an article which had been in the world's shop window for years – since 1854; but had never seemed likely to suit her, and now she wanted no one else to have it.

On the 24th of November Disraeli wrote to Queen Victoria:

"It is just settled. You have it, Madam: the French Government has been outgeneralled. They tried too much, offering loans at a usurious rate which would have virtually given them the government of Egypt. The Khedive in despair and disgust offered Your Majesty's Government to purchase his shares outright: he would never listen to such a proposition before."

On the following day he wrote to Lady Blandford:

"As you complain sometimes, though I think unjustly, that I tell you nothing, I will now tell you a great State secret, though it may not be one in 4 and 20 hours (still you will like to know it 4 and 20 hours earlier than the newspapers can tell you) – a State secret, certainly the most important of this year, and not one of the least events of our generation. After a fortnight of the most exacting labour and anxiety, I (for, between ourselves, and ourselves only, I may be egotistical in this matter) – I have purchased for England the Khedive of Egypt's interest in the Suez Canal. We have had all the gamblers, capitalists, financiers of the world, organized and platooned in bands of plunder, arrayed against us, and secret emissaries in every corner, and have baffled them all, and have never been suspected.

"The day before yesterday Lesseps, whose Company has the remaining shares, backed by the French Government, whose agent he was, made a great offer. Had it succeeded, the whole of the Suez Canal would have belonged to France, and they might have shut it up! We have given the Khedive four millions sterling for his interest, and run the chance of Parliament supporting us. We could not call them together for the matter, for that would have blown everything to the skies, or to Hades. The Faery (the Queen) is in ecstasies about 'this great and important event', wants 'to know all about it when Mr. D. comes to town to-day'. I have rarely been through a week like the last – and am to-day in a state of prostration – coma – sorry to have to go down to Windsor – still more sorry not to have had a line to-day, which would have soothed.

Your affectionate,

D."

"PS. Though secret here, the telegraph will send the news from Egypt, I doubt not, to-day."

So long as Ismail had been in Ferdinand's pocket, those shares might as well have been in his own name in so far as influence over the Company was concerned; and so when the Khedive sailed into exile in June 1879, he left his old friend naked to the wind. The new Khedive, Tewfik, amenable and conscientious, could never take Ismail's place. The old order had perished, and with it Ferdinand's personal power, not only in Egypt but in France also. He had prestige and fame of no common order, but there is no substitute for power.

*   *   *

The eagerness of England, France and Austria to help Egypt out of the morass into which Ismail and his creditors had led her, was partly due to the fact that it was Bismarck who had taken the initiative, ostensibly on behalf of German financial interests. About the only thing which could have welded Franco-British policy into something positive was a mutual resolve not to give the German Emperor an excuse to meddle with the Middle East. And a prostrate Egypt was just such an excuse. The country had to be jerked to its feet and held upright by main force. This, with commendable efficiency, the Dual Control set out to do. But it could not create confidence, and the inevitable social reaction caught the well-meaning Powers before they could cure the fundamental ill, poverty. The focus of the inevitable revolt was Arabi, a Pasha of fellaheen origin, who for that reason had been sent back to regimental duty when a lieutenant-colonel of Ismail's palace guard. Having been a soldier all his life, since being conscripted at the age of fourteen, he would have been in a fair way to become not only the ruler of Egypt, but perhaps of an African empire, had he not been, 'in camp a poor disciplinarian, in the field an unenterprising commander'.[1] Even so he came close to winning Egypt for the Egyptians because of the widespread and in large measure justifiable belief that it was not Ismail but Turks and alien money-lenders who had brought the country to ruin. Get rid of the foreigners, and prosperity must be just around the corner. In that prevailing frame of mind, particularly among army officers who had long been without pay, and whose troops consisted of men ground down, they and their families, by the most ruthless taxation, it would hardly have been possible to get nearer to the truth. Even now it is not easy. Europeans had indeed taken out of the country a great deal more than they had put into it, yet, after Ismail, they did in general honour the broad principle of common welfare – finance from abroad for prosperity at home. From the beginning of Dual Control, England and France meant well; but Egypt could hardly be expected to believe that as an act of faith, or even to understand it as natural solicitude for the great investments still in the country. Anti-Christian, anti-foreign riots inevitably occurred, and, according to the methods of the times, war therefore became inevitable.

It began with the bombardment of Alexandria by the British fleet, an action due to the fact that, despite orders to the con-

[1] Cameron, *Egypt in the Nineteenth Century*.

trary following riots in the town with loss of foreign life and
property, Arabi's garrison had continued to strengthen the sea-
ward defences of the port. Ferdinand de Lesseps, then on the
isthmus, immediately saw the consequences to his beloved ditch
and implored the French Government to defend it. His plea
made no impression. When the issue was debated in the
Chamber not a franc was voted for the cause. Having so recently
emerged from her humiliation, France could not spare a single
rifle from the Rhine. England had tried to get her to co-operate
in the action at Alexandria, but the commitment was adjudged
too great, and she had withdrawn from the Dual Control. To
act unilaterally now in defence of the canal, perhaps even against
England, would have been politically impossible and strategically insane. So, without an ally of any kind, Lesseps with his
lame son prepared to defend the canal against all comers. The
isthmus was unquestionably Egyptian territory and England was
technically acting in loyal support of the Khedive whom she
had in effect appointed. Nevertheless Lesseps telegraphed to
Arabi: "The English shall never enter the canal: never. Make
no attempt to block my canal. I am here. Not a single British
soldier shall disembark without being accompanied by a French
soldier. I answer for everything."

Arabi replied in accordance with tactical requirements:
"Sincere thanks. Assurances consolatory but not sufficient under
existing circumstances. Defence of Egypt requires temporary
destruction of the canal." Ferdinand's state of mind may have
been as hysterical as it had been at Rome. The physical calamity
would be bad enough, but far worse would be the blow to his
visionary's pride in the canal as a way of peace, a symbol of
goodwill towards men. Typically he had ignored, when he sent
that telegram, the realities of the situation for the sake of an
ideal; often but not invariably a trait as admirable as it is rare.
For the plain fact was that while Arabi required the destruction
of the waterway to prevent a flank attack by England, it was
more than ever in England's interest to make use of the canal.
With admirable dash a British squadron, ignoring Horatius and
Son, sailed from Port Said to Lake Timsah before Arabi could
cut the line – which would have been a simple matter once he
had his guns within range and a blockship across the channel.
Troops were disembarked at Ismailia. Arabi cut their life-line

by damming the Freshwater Canal. Sir Charles Wolseley's first objective was to capture and destroy that dam, failing which he would have had to re-embark. But he brilliantly succeeded, and then, after hard fighting, destroyed the enemy's main forces behind their earthworks at Tel-el Kebir. After that the occupation of Egypt became inevitable, as Lord Palmerston had foreseen . . . but not by France. And the primary reason for it, strategy apart, was not further exploitation but to create out of the remnant of the country's corrupt administration a sound and just system, the foundation for permanent prosperity. At long last British policy was the same as that which France had followed since the Battle of the Pyramids, towards a strong and independent Egypt.

*   *   *

Hardly had the canal traffic settled down again after all the excitement, than Lesseps had to turn from it to meet another threat from London, where public opinion, inflated by imperial enthusiasm, was in no mood to leave what was virtually a French enclave in Britannia's new dominion. Faced by the Company's legal title, which England herself was now bound to protect, it was proposed to construct a second canal. The irony of this plan must have struck Ferdinand with considerable force; but for all its absurdity at a time when the existing canal could still not pay its way, the threat was real. For what consideration would the English drop this uneconomic scheme? The answer soon became all too clear: for the control of the equity of the existing canal. Leaving Charles to administer the Company, Ferdinand with Victor went to London to seek a compromise. In all probability they did better than Ferdinand had dared to hope. Then came a summons from his old ally, Mr. Gladstone, who since 1880 had been Prime Minister, that is for three years. He told Ferdinand that the temper of the country was such that if the terms of the settlement became known the Government would almost certainly fall. Without hesitation the Frenchman withdrew his claims, and a new series of negotiations began; the result of which still left de Lesseps at the head of the Company with the equity in French hands, but British representation was a good deal stronger than the possession of the

Khedive's shares warranted. It may even have been as strong as Lesseps himself would have wished had his original plan succeeded and England shared in the construction to the extent by which her commerce was likely to benefit. As in his earliest proposals, the number of Directors was to be thirty-two instead of the existing twenty-four, and of the new seats seven were to be British. The total would be: Belgium 1, Dutch 1, England 10, France 20.

So the idea of the second canal was dropped, and the newly constituted Board promptly put in hand a number of improvements to the old one, thus initiating a policy which has been maintained ever since, of keeping pace with technical developments in world commerce and ship-building. In 1870 the Company's revenue from all sources was 9,270,000 francs. In 1880 it was 41,820,000, and continued to rise until, in the last year before France went off the gold standard, 1927, the annual earnings were more than three times the original estimate of capital required, and nearly twice as much as the canal actually did cost; in spite of every liability that Fate and enmity could contrive. The revenue for 1927, in post-war francs, was 785,510,000. And so the enterprise which for years had been regarded as, at best, the biggest wild-goose chase ever put before the investing public, resulted in the capture of an immortal bird which continues to lay a plethora of golden eggs. But the mighty hunter who first dreamed that such a bird might in fact exist, omitted to put any eggs into his own pocket, and, instead of being content to look after his fairy-tale prize, he eagerly began, at the age of seventy-three, to look for a new adventure.

Chapter 16. FIGUREHEAD

As early as 1873 Ferdinand had sent Victor, now a foreign service officer in the family tradition, to explore the possibility of a railway joining Paris with Moscow, Pekin and Bombay. At first the Russians gave encouragement to the idea and provided Victor with all the visas he required. He did reach Kashmir, no mean journey in those days, but before he could report the irrefrangible Himalayas the scheme was dropped for political reasons. England and Russia were coming into conflict over Afghanistan, and also in northern China as a result of British ascendancy following the Taiping rebellion. Next, Commander Roudaire came forward with a plan to create an inland sea in north Africa. There is a narrow ridge of land separating the Gulf of Gabes from a depression almost as big as Spain. Flooded, it would certainly provide an excellent eastern frontier for Algeria, but there was little prospect of commercial success, and again the scheme fell through before any definite steps had been taken. The King of the Belgians, a passionate anti-slavery campaigner, was in process of creating an international organization to combat the beastly traffic at its sources in Africa. With a donation of five thousand francs, Lesseps started a French effort in that direction. It was the money received from the Academy as a prize for his *Lettres, Journal et Documents pour servir à l'Histoire du Canal de Suez*, as being, ' the work which did most honour to France, an inspiration to creative thinking, behaviour and character'. With some Government as well as private assistance, he set up a series of check-posts in central and western Africa; but the scheme, though admirable in principle, had no revenue and was gradually forced to close down.

Ferdinand was by now one of the most famous men in the world, and in France he was an idol representing all that was peaceful in the dominant national concept of *la Gloire*, which had been badly shaken by the events of 1870. "It seemed that henceforth nothing in the universe would be impossible to

279

Ferdinand de Lesseps. No public meeting was complete without him. Societies of every sort competed to have him as a member or as President. The highest honours hardly seemed sufficient to match his renown. Hardly a project of any kind was considered practicable unless Ferdinand de Lesseps had at least cast his eye over it; or its sponsor had been received and encouraged by him. He was a kind of arbiter for all new schemes." Inevitably many attempts were made to harness this prestige to politics. In 1868 his name had been officially put forward as a candidate in the Marseilles election, but he had refused to stand. The Minister of the Interior insisted. He again refused. Then the Emperor intervened, and, unable to disobey, Lesseps allowed his candidature to go forward. He was by no means disappointed when his opponent, Gambetta, was returned by a large majority. He was fond of quoting ' the scalded cat fears cold water ', and he had seen much of the seamy side of politics. He even refused candidature of the Senate, and when in spite of this his name went forward, he wrote:

" To the President of the Senate.   Ismailia, 24th March, 1876.
    Having read in the papers an account of the session of the 15th, I would ask you to thank the members of the Senate, who, in spite of my declining the candidature, have honoured me with their votes; and also those who have increased the power of the Marshal (President Mac-Mahon) in voting for M. Ricard."

To other importunate demands he truthfully replied that he could not leave the canal to look after itself, and that he ought not to take up responsibilities in France while it remained necessary for him to spend much of his time in Egypt. But to his son Charles he telegraphed a more revealing answer: "Desiring in freedom to integrate all the questions by which the parties are divided, I am not in a position to serve any one of them." Coming from a lesser eminence such sentiments would have invited attack, but for the time being he was unassailable; though all over France there remained potential enemies of this man, "with an incorrigible, perilous passion for human welfare ".

*   *   *

It was under such circumstances that Ferdinand was drawn

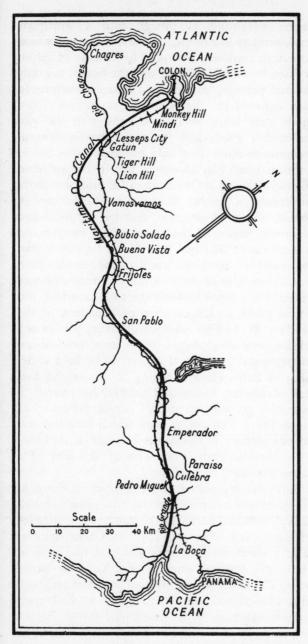

THE
ISTHMUS OF
PANAMA,
showing
proposed
canal route
and part of
Panama, a
state of the
Federated
Republic of
Columbia.
A sketch map
based on
Bertrand et
Ferrier, 1887.
Many
watercourses
not shown.

into the Panama adventure as though into a whirlpool.
Humbled before Germany in Europe, France had lost every foot-
hold on the American continent. It would be a stroke of genius
to make a new Suez between the North and the South, not only
in terms of national prestige, but also as a business venture. In
this decade men believed in 'the poetry of capitalism'. New
financial methods were being evolved to cope with the vast
increase of commodity goods and the rapid development of
transport and communication. Not only geographically, but at
every level of the national life, adventure was in the air. And
de Lesseps, *le Grand Français* as Gambetta called him, was above
all things an adventurer, a pioneer. Moreover he still believed in
the Saint-Simonian notion of progress, that by technical and
industrial achievement universal peace and plenty must ensue.
His canal was a means to that end, his rôle as he saw it was,
Aperire terram gentibus: open the world to the people – than
which there was no worthier cause. Inevitably therefore he supported the clamour for a canal between the two Americas; but
he did so at first solely in his capacity as President of the
Geographical Society. He had no intention of taking part in any
commercial development which might follow from the deliberations of the international congress of experts to be held under
his chairmanship in Paris. He was getting on for seventy-five.
After a lifetime of posting hither and thither, he wanted to
watch his new family growing up at La Chenaie. Also he had
to keep an eye on the golden goose, upon which England was
still casting envious glances. It was in the summer of 1878 that
the savants assembled in Paris, when already the idea of a
second Suez canal was being mooted.

The Geographical Society placed at the disposal of the delegates all the information available on the American isthmus,
still largely unexplored; and in particular presented a detailed
report on a recent survey recommending the Colon route as
against nearly fifty alternative schemes which at one time or
another had been put forward since Spanish galleons loaded
silver at Panama. The experts were divided into five technical
committees with various sub-committees, which studied every
aspect of the undertaking in all its practicable forms. At the
end of their deliberations Ferdinand de Lesseps called them all
together and put the following resolution: "That this Congress

is of the opinion that a canal on the level between the two oceans is feasible and most desirable in the interests of commerce and shipping; and that, in conformity with the indispensable require- ments of access and operation, it ought to be cut between the Gulf of Limon – on which is situated the town of Colon, and the Bay of Panama." Out of ninety-eight votes there were seventy-eight Ayes, and most of the Noes fell short of affirmation only because they believed locks to be essential. Had an amend- ment been passed to delete the phrase 'on the level', the voting would almost certainly have been unanimous.

The results of the Congress were front-page news, and the pro- posed Panama Canal became, almost overnight, practically the only subject upon which every shade of opinion in the country was agreed; the more so because it was known that the United States had begun preliminary surveys for a cut through Nicaragua. For national prestige, for adventure, for profit, the idea of the Panama Canal stirred the imagination of the French and rekindled the smouldering fire of their collective aspiration. Immediately there emerged proposals for the floatation of a Company, which would have the incalculable advantage of being assured, from the beginning, of the protection of the Govern- ment, no matter what the political colour of the hour. Inevitably the whirlpool began to draw Ferdinand nearer and nearer to its vortex. At first he struggled against the current, even when he was offered the Concession which had been brought back from Columbia by the two men, Wyse and Réclus, whose survey had 'been the deciding evidence before the Congress. Charles de Lesseps led the family opposition.

"At the time when we were going to decide about making the second canal, I was in the office of Henri Bionne – who was to die of yellow fever between Colon and New York. Henri Bionne was one of a group which had done a great deal to persuade my father that his intervention was necessary to the incontestably great and attractive idea of Panama. I begged my father to have nothing to do with the project and spoke to him as follows: 'What are you going to look for in Panama – money? You will not be any more concerned with that at Panama than you were at Suez. Glory? You have already enough of it to be able to leave some for others. You believe that everyone ought to strive to the end of his strength for the good of his fellow-men. Well, you have paid that debt. You have the right to rest. The Panama project is grandiose. When achieved it will certainly benefit the human race. I believe that it is feasible and that when finished it will reward those who lent to it their capital. But what a risk they will run who head the enterprise and devote themselves to it! Remember the Suez Canal, how through all the ten years of construction it was almost every day next door to calamity. Even when Suez was opened up the earnings did not come in quickly enough, and the shareholders were soon saying that you had been bribed by English shipping interests to reduce the transit-dues. Your enterprises are unique in that you rely only upon your own credit to bring them to a successful conclusion; while the smallest railway, of only local importance, is begun only after subsidies and guarantees have been obtained. The Panama Canal may be a very fine idea, but what becomes of it when one day the Company is unable to find the funds of which it will stand successively in need? One cannot imagine raising the whole lot on the very first day.

"'After the opening of the Suez Canal, on the eve of the prosperity you had promised, and which was only a few months away, you had to ask for twenty million to stop the Company going into liquidation. The public brought you five. The share and bond holders nearly found themselves ruined through their lack of confidence. By a miracle you succeeded at Suez. In the course of one life is it not enough to have one miracle without counting on a second? If you decide to go on. If nothing will stop you. You know that if you have no need of me I shall ask you for nothing. But if you want me to follow you, then gladly I will take whatever comes, without complaint. All that I am I owe to you, and what you have given you have the right to take away.'

"My father replied that he had already decided. With such a valiant heart it could not have been otherwise."

A level-headed and experienced man of over forty, Charles knew the inside story of Suez better than anyone except his father; but it was evidently not upon business arguments that he relied. He knew that, appearances to the contrary, Ferdinand was growing old, that soon the eagle's vision might become the mere projection of blind faith. Ferdinand himself may have had a degree of insight, but he hesitated and was lost. Having vacated the Chair at the final session of the Congress he said, "I must admit to you that I have been through a most perplexing time. Two weeks ago I little dreamed that I should be asked to put myself at the head of a new enterprise. My best friends tried to dissuade me. They told me that after Suez I should take a rest. Well, if one asks a General who has won his first victory whether he wants to win a second, will he refuse?" The temporary chairman then ended the proceedings with the following words:

"Gentlemen, May 29th, 1879, will mark the beginning of one of the greatest undertakings of modern times. Permit me, as we depart, to close this meeting with a wish that is already in our hearts. That illustrious man who has been the heart and soul of our deliberations, who has captivated us with his charm and who is the personification of these great enterprises, may he live long enough to see the end of this work which will bear his name for ever. He has not been able to refuse the direction of it. In doing so he continues to carry out the mission which has made him a citizen of the whole world." (Prolonged ovation for several minutes.)

*   *   *

As though he had just received an injection of the elixir of life, Ferdinand de Lesseps set about the task so inescapably wished upon him. One of his first acts was to interview the two men who had brought back the Concession. At risk and with pain they had surveyed the route. At seventy-four Bonaparte Wyse had for eleven days ridden over the mountains to reach Bagota and obtain the all-important document for which, presumably, he paid out of his own pocket. Clearly he and his partner were entitled to speak to de Lesseps, who had never seen Central America, as an equal; but the old man would have none of it.

"'Messieurs,' he said, 'I am desolated that I am unable to undertake such an enterprise with others who might limit my responsibility. You are highly honourable persons. I do you full justice. But when I take up such a duty as this I cannot share the responsibility with anyone. I have my own ideas, and they are not always shared by others; therefore I need complete liberty of action. I started my diplomatic career as an attaché close to Mohammed-Ali, the regenerator of Egypt. One day he said to me, "My dear Lesseps, you are very young. At any time in your life when you have something important to accomplish, remember that if there are two of you there is one too many." We have made a binding contract, and that is the condition under which I undertake this enterprise. I alone am responsible. No one but myself has any responsibility.'"

His next action was equally characteristic. Entirely on his own initiative he borrowed two million francs for preliminary expenses, which included paying 700,000 to the Columbian Government; evidently because Wyse had only put down the money for an option. Reiterating his old principle that he would ignore the professional financiers, and the Government, he next made an appeal to the small investor to the amount of 400,000,000, on which to register the Company. The issue was a complete failure, only 30,000,000 being subscribed, and these monies were returned to the would-be shareholders. To them who knew the old man well, the sign must have been extremely significant. He had lost touch with his times and his judgment was no longer sound. They must have been even more anxious for the future when they read in the *Bulletin* which he had begun to publish: " Two million francs have been given to me, and I may say *given*, in an entirely disinterested manner, in the service of this work which is so attractive to great spirits." For the fact was that the ' great spirits' were to receive as a consideration fifteen per cent of the eventual net profit of the enterprise. The contrast, which is cited from reliable sources, *Bertrand et Ferrier* and *Coureau* respectively, does not imply that Ferdinand de Lesseps had turned crook. There was no compromise with his principles, but his light had failed. He could no longer see the disagreeable detail of reality in the picture he held in his mind. And that picture was essentially an idealization of Suez. He probably did not realize that the consideration required by the 'great spirits', persons 'devoted to the creation of grand enterprises', was more than a token. They had doubtless made it look like a gift, and he probably felt himself impelled to offer a little something in exchange. Lesseps had no longer the desire, nor the patience, to read the small print at the bottom of the page.

It was much the same with the Concession. Not only did he have to pay out that huge sum to Columbia for what, after all, could be of no value until the canal was in being, or at least in sight of completion; his brusque treatment of Wyse and Réclus rebounded to the tune of 10,000,000 francs, their price for handing over the Concession instead of collaborating with Lesseps. Had it not been for public eagerness at levels higher than those of the savings of the 'little men', the Panama Canal Company might well have failed before the work began. But as soon as Ferdinand's personal appeal showed no response, financiers in all shapes and sizes, from the Crédit Lyonnais to the sinister

Baron Reinarch, offered their services. They thought they could
not lose. The canal was a matter for the national honour. If the
Company got into difficulties the Government of the day would
have to come to the rescue. So in August an unparalleled appeal
went out, with the whole force of the Press and every bank in
France behind it. Six hundred million was asked for. In three
days twice that amount rolled in. Taking this as a sign that his
star was still ascendant, Lesseps forthwith made arrangements
to carry out a personal reconnaissance of the route which Wyse
and Réclus had pioneered. And just to show that there was
nothing behind the rumour of a climate murderous to white
people, he took with him, in addition to a technical committee,
Hélène and her three children, Mathieu, Ferdinand, and Ferdinande, aged nine, eight and seven. Considering that neither of
the previous 'little' Ferdinands had lived to reach his teens,
this was another gesture of brave folly.

*   *   *

At the very end of 1879 Ferdinand wrote to Charles:

"The reception they gave us at Colon, and all along the railway
line, has been a series of indescribable ovations. Here in Panama
we have now been celebrating for three days with illuminations,
decorated windows, fireworks, troop-reviews, and excursions in the
beautiful Bay of Panama. This bay is at the mouth of the Rio
Grande where the exit of the maritime canal will be."

And the following announcement appeared in the local Press:

"Under the authority of the United States of Columbia, with
the benediction of Monseigneur the Bishop of Panama, in the
presence of the delegate of the Central Government of the United
States of Columbia, and in the presence of the technical commission of the Universal Interoceanic Maritime Canal, there will
be given this day, the 1st of January, 1880, by M. Ferdinand de
Lesseps, the first blow of the pick-axe on the place which will become the entrance of the maritime canal from the Pacific Ocean.
All those present will in succession give a blow with the pick as a
symbol of the alliance of all the peoples who will contribute to
the union of the two oceans for the benefit of humanity."

With a Gallic *coup de théâtre*, it was in fact little Ferdinande
who inaugurated the canal – it is to be hoped with a pick scaled
down to size.

Since Lesseps and his experts had hardly time to look over the route let alone prepare detailed plans, the formal ceremony of commencement may seem somewhat premature. No doubt it was dictated by the recognition that nothing would be more likely to prevent the Americans taking a similar step with their Vanderbilt project farther north. The English were still agitating for a second canal at Suez, and it would not have been at all desirable to have the United States bent upon the same sort of competition in the New World. The publicity proved excellent. The committee got down to work, and in six weeks, thanks largely to the railway which, because of the nature of the terrain, necessarily followed closely the proposed route for the canal, they were able to confirm the judgment of Wyse and Réclus. Lesseps himself was greatly impressed with the contrast between these wooded hills and the bare deserts of that other isthmus. In his lifetime he had seen enough of sand, thanks to which water supply had been his biggest single administrative worry – until the completion of the Freshwater Canal. Here was certainly no lack of water, nor of wood, which had been almost equally difficult to come by in Suez. Then there was the railway, almost as though it had been constructed with the canal in mind. True, the ridge of Culebra was three hundred feet above sea-level,[1] but then the whole canal would be barely fifty miles long; and there was already at either end an anchorage and a port, while for most of the distance considerable saving might be effected by making use of the numerous existing waterways. As for the climate, the large population, which had been so hospitable, at least proved that it could not be so bad as all that. During the whole time that the Lesseps family was on the isthmus, not one of them was touched by the least malaise. As for epidemics, had Ferdinand not fought two cholera outbreaks and beaten them? It would not have crossed his mind that there might be a different means of infection in the case of malaria and yellow fever, for the deadly rôle of the mosquito *Aedes aegypti* would remain undiscovered until the turn of the century. At this time all 'putrid fevers' were still regarded as the result of decay and its effluvia. Adequate attention to hygiene should therefore protect the workers even in the wet season, those seven months from May to November, in which three

[1] See page 304: profile of the canal route.

times the rainfall of England's year soaks the forests and turns each runnel into a river, each footprint into a puddle, from which a million insects may hatch out to seek for victims on the cool night wind.[1]

Aware that though honoured in North America, he was by no means welcome to the Government, which was almost committed to the support of the Vanderbilt scheme, Lesseps toured the principal cities of the United States much as he had done with the towns of the British Isles at the beginning of the Suez adventure. Everywhere he was acclaimed with the heart-warming admiration of those who tend to believe that the best is always the biggest, save by an evil chance. But behind the popular welcome were business as well as political reservations. While appreciating the French effort to the full, Americans could not help feeling that if there were to be a canal at all it ought to be their own. Though they were delighted to cheer the great pioneer, they were by no means prepared to lend him money for the purpose of doing what they felt they ought to be doing themselves. After all, they had thought of it first. As early as 1876 they could have started work in Nicaragua. President Hayes, in a special message to Congress, reflected the national sentiment when he declared: "The policy of this country is to advocate a canal under American control.'

The rebuff was obvious, but, the cheers still ringing in his ears, Lesseps in the *Bulletin* referred to the 'enthusiastic and unanimous adherence to our cause . . . The Message of the President had assured the security of the canal.' Blithely he left New York, where the cable ended which would, from Paris, be his quickest link with Panama, and continued his propaganda campaign in England, Belgium and Holland; from none of which was capital forthcoming. Particularly in view of the fact that he still held, in theory, autocratic control not only of the nascent organization at Panama but also of the complex Suez affair – where the question of neutrality was still nagging and British interests remained unsatisfied – this was an extraordinary feat; perhaps an unnecessary one. Panama was to be 'twice as big as Suez, three times as profitable'. It needed Ferdinand's complete attention from the very beginning. But in spite of his own claim to share responsibility with no one, he began almost

[1] Annual rainfall: Egypt 9", Panama 128".

at once to shed it on to the devoted shoulders of the Vice-President, his son Charles. As for the engineering works, they were, very properly, passed entire to the best and biggest contractors of the day, Couvreux & Hersent, who had proved their competence, and their honesty, on that other isthmus. They sent out their own surveying team, which came back with the depressing view that instead of finding the work easier than Wyse had believed it to be, they expected the amount of excavation to be double what Ferdinand's committee had allowed for. However, they confirmed all the essential findings of their forerunners and accepted the contract on a cost-plus basis. So the beginning of the practical effort was theirs, and Lesseps was content that it should be so. A distinguished figure, both in his dealings with Panama, where he became Director of Works, and as regards his qualifications, Bunau-Varilla described Ferdinand's attitude as follows: "He was not an engineer, and he did not like engineers. He preferred what are called practical men. He never understood that such people have no sure understanding beyond the extent of their personal experience. Their limited intellectual endowment prevents them from conceiving and assessing hitherto unknown factors which bring with them new problems." Certainly the old man tended to resent discussion and was apt to interrupt with some *ex cathedra* pronouncement, usually based upon a Suez precedent which might or might not be applicable. Such a manner, added to his irascibility, did not make it easier for those closest to him to tell him unpleasant facts. He became more and more a mere figurehead, driving on a course he knew not, but thought he knew, by power pressing from behind. This was a complete reversal of the situation in Egypt, where his really was the prime-moving force, his the initiative and the far sight.

If a figurehead is hardly human, it is also incapable of doing harm. It cannot even alter course or speed. So long as the contractors were in full control of the work, and Charles was behind his desk in Paris, the influence of Ferdinand was negligible except in the field of publicity, where it was absolutely dominant. Unfortunately Charles could not go back to the page which his father had turned when making the original bargain with Wyse over the Concession. Among the 'small print' there was a clause which made the Railway Company virtually a concessionaire in its own right; so that, having paid the Columbian Govern-

FIGUREHEAD 291

ment, the Canal Company was now faced with an ultimatum from the Railway. What made the situation even more irritating was that the Railway, which had been opened in 1875, had in its turn bought out the stock of a French Company which had failed. Now, far from getting the line at the upset price which would reflect its value after the completion of the canal, de Lesseps paid over a hundred million francs for it. Par would have been forty millions.

The contractors duly performed the enormous task of assembling on the sites, men, machines and their supplies, while the Company took a great deal of trouble to ensure the health and welfare of the staff and labour force. Since there could be no question of a *corvée*, it was necessary, even from a purely business point of view, to provide the best working conditions which the climate and terrain allowed. At whatever level a man was employed, he would not be likely to stay long unless relatively well paid. The labourers were mostly Jamaicans, men of the Antilles, South American Indians, or Chinese; officered by Frenchmen, with some technical people from other European countries. As for the medical side, the following eye-witness report is evidently representative. It refers to Panama : " The hospital has been sited in the healthiest place of the locality, on the slope of a great *butte*. . . . It consists of five separate buildings, lightly constructed in wood, between which air and sunlight play without restriction. Excellent water is laid on in abundance. The hospital has its own farm, abattoir, and icehouse. Every night the soil is removed and taken down to the sea. The wards are so large and well-ventilated, even those occupied by negro patients suffering from fever, that the most sensitive olfactory nerves cannot perceive the slightest odour. There are private rooms for the Company's employees, and in the most expensive nursing-home you would not find more comfortable accommodation. There are five experienced and devoted medical officers. The administration and nursing, day and night, is in the hands of thirty sisters of Saint-Vincent-de-Paul."[1]

Yellow fever first appeared in epidemic form during the wet season of 1882, and though perhaps as much as ten per cent of the relatively few Europeans were affected, with a fairly high death-rate, it seemed that the medical services were generally

[1] R. Coureau: *Ferdinand de Lesseps*. Paris 1932.

adequate; for with the dry weather the incidence of cases fell. The reason, of course, was the drying out of the *Aedes* breeding-places; but to those in charge of hygiene, and to Ferdinand de Lesseps, it must have seemed that, as with cholera in Egypt, they were masters of the situation. This opinion probably did as much as any other single factor to make a worse epidemic inevitable. But before that could happen there must be more stagnant water, the works must be further advanced. Under normal conditions the sun kept the mosquitoes down in the dry season, while in the wet so much water was in movement down the steep slopes that *Aedes* was severely handicapped. Mosquitoes as a rule will not breed in moving water.

If the Company came through the year full of confidence, the same was no longer true for the contractors. There had been a revolution. Their best man had died of yellow fever. There had been an earthquake, followed by a tidal wave which did immense damage to their installations. The soil and subsoil had proved far more difficult to handle than had been expected, turning under the torrential rains into a soapy mass which clogged machinery, bogged rail-track, and made every cutting crumble unless the slopes were either revetted or cut to a much wider angle than had been allowed in the estimates. This last was technically the most serious, for it meant that in the deeper cuttings the amount of excavation would not only be doubled or trebled, but would go up in a geometrical progression which can be illustrated by imagining a cone standing on its point. Each successive slice through the cone contains a much greater volume, which in this case was rock and earth, time, money and life. So disheartened were Couvreux & Hersent that they decided to pull out before being committed any further, a blow which to any ordinary Company might well have been mortal. But the enterprises of Ferdinand de Lesseps, as Charles had told him, were not like others. In the last analysis they were sustained not by the cool assessment of technicians, nor by the common sense of shareholders, but by the emotional response to Lesseps himself. He had in the past demonstrated that his vision was often a better guide than the calculation of experts. Now his mind's eye was dim. Instead of instituting a fresh inquiry to determine why the contractors, who had every reason for going on, had decided otherwise, the Company bought from them all

their equipment and installations, paying a million francs.
Lesseps then looked round for a successor to Couvreux, but
could not find any big firm willing to stand upon such a slippery
slope. True to his old principle, Ferdinand forthwith decided
to take the whole business under his own control, from Paris,
working through a Director in Panama. In financial terms this
decision would prove as disastrous as, in the medical field, did
the conviction that hygiene and nursing would by themselves
beat yellow fever.

With inadequate means of communication and in the absence
of any clear discipline, to prevent waste and inefficiency, if not
downright robbery, would have been almost impossible, however loyal the majority of the personnel might be. For by this
time, in addition to the Company's staff and employees on the
isthmus, there were swarms of every sort and kind of opportunist, from the seller of clean water to the purveyor of prostitutes
– whose arrival was wired in code from one working site to
another: " *langoustes arrivées*." Even the good wages and conditions, which Ferdinand had so properly insisted upon, began to
twist into a vicious curve. Gambling and drinking became hectic
relaxations among men who for weeks had battered their way
through mud. Commodity prices, in any case high because of
the locality, moved upward as organized shopkeepers made their
killing, and so tended to force wages still higher. Again Suez
provided a false parallel. There free enterprise had resulted in
competition which kept prices down. Here it produced a ring
which kept prices up.

By this time Arabi Pasha had put Suez back into the melting
pot and Anglo-French relations were rapidly deteriorating. For
fear that somehow the British might steal his golden goose,
Ferdinand could not concentrate on Panama, while Charles had
all his work cut out to keep track of the intricate organization
that was growing up around him. He was Adjutant and not at
all the Commanding Officer. In any case his father would not
have allowed him to display any initiative, and so another fatal
trend began. Instead of leadership coming from the Board, it
came from outsiders: contractors with something to sell, capitalists with something to lend; from journalists and politicians with
real or imagined influence – for sale. Meanwhile on the isthmus
an equally pernicious system was developing. Small firms would

contract for short sections of the canal, and because they had
not the necessary resources, the Company had to buy their equipment and consequently supervise the works so that the most
use could be made of it. This swelled the administrative staff to
something over six hundred, the majority of whom, in spite of
all handicaps, resolutely pursued the goal with competence and
integrity. This fact is of the greatest importance, for it represents the redeeming feature of the whole story: how Ferdinand
de Lesseps still inspired devotion, and how men, touched by
the embers of his fire, were still willing to give their lives in the
hope that, because of the canal, the world might be a happier
place.

This attitude was in sharp contrast to the cynicism prevailing
in France, particularly after the failure of the Union General
Bank in 1882, which involved the loss of some 500,000,000 francs.
Siegfried wrote:

"'What people most feared was to be considered simpletons. I
still shudder to think of the damning formula, "You are not much
of a Parisian!"' Evidently a 'Parisian' was a wide-boy, an unscrupulous exploiter of other people's positions. Siegfried continued, 'A low, dishonest Press kept hounding the Company, and
a little rag called The Panama hounded it like a wolf. Charles de
Lesseps soon gave way. He got into the habit of paying for favourable publicity, and his monthly cheques were sometimes even the
price of silence.' 'The whole world battened upon Panama,' wrote
Drumont in La Dernière Bataille. 'The top hats arrived first with
enormous demands. Then came smaller hats, and then little ones—
mere children's caps. Finally some vague reporter would appear,
and he would get a little cheque for having inserted a single line
in a review, mentioning The Great Frenchman, or Tototte, or
Ismail, or other members of the de Lesseps family. Some did not
contribute anything, but they got their cheques just the same. This
was hush-money from the Company which was thankful to be left
alone.' Soon the Company was to busy itself with members of
parliament as well."

So much was learned only afterwards. At the time, the surface
of the great concern appeared almost unruffled, and Ferdin-
and's personal prestige had never been so high. It was therefore
with some confidence that he approached the Government with
a view to getting a bill through the Assembly to permit him to
offer Lottery Bonds. There was really no alternative, for recent

issues, even with additional attractions, had not been successful, and the cost of works continued to mount. Originally the excavation was to be at the rate of five francs per cubic metre, but it was already costing eight francs; and the total number of cubic metres was still increasing as the 'abyss' of Culebra gradually revealed its true character; which, in fairness to the many competent men who surveyed it, could hardly have been anticipated. Since the Government, through Crédit Lyonnais, was directly interested to the extent of approximately ten per cent of the capital, and indirectly concerned because, in the eyes of the world, the effort was, first and last, a French national undertaking, it was decided that before preparing the required Bill, a fresh survey should be made, this time by a Government mission. Though Ferdinand fretted at the delay, he could do nothing but agree; and so it was arranged to send a first-rate man, M. Rousseau of the *Ponts et Chaussées*, a Councillor of State and former Under-Secretary for Public Works. Prudently he decided not to reach Panama until the dry season at the end of the year, so increasing the delay and driving the Company to more desperate measures to keep up face until the Lottery issue could be made.

If the anxiety of his vast responsibilities affected Ferdinand, he did not in the least betray the fact. Everywhere he played the part of the demi-god, above the limitations of the petty world at his feet. To any complaints or arguments he had but one answer: 'the canal will be made'; but he continued to forget that it was not he who was making it. When, in April 1883, he was elected a Member of the Academy, his cup of fame brimmed over. This was his public noonday, though in fact the night was close upon him. Ernest Renan, then as much the conscience of the country as he was her foremost man of letters, delivered a eulogy which, among the compliments, contained some pertinent observations:

"The word religion is not too strong to express the enthusiasm which you engendered. For some years your work was a kind of gospel of redemption, of grace and pardon. The idea of rehabilitation, of a moral amnesty, always takes an important place in religious origins. The outlaw is ever grateful to him who preaches forgiveness, who puts things back in their places. . . . One day a whole gang of convicts, escaped from some Austrian gaol on the shores of the Adriatic, descended upon the isthmus of Suez as though upon Eden. The Austrian consul demanded their surrender. You kept the affair hanging fire. After a few weeks the consul had nothing else to do but to forward the cash these fellows wished to send to their poor parents, perhaps even to their victims. . . . I read in the account of one of your meetings, 'M. de Lesseps stated that when men have enough to live on they are loyal and not at all base. Man does not become debased save through hunger or fear.' One should add, 'or when he is jealous'. To a sceptical generation you have demonstrated the efficacy of faith and given practical meaning to these high words, 'I say unto you that if ye have faith no greater than a grain of mustard seed, ye shall say unto this mountain, go, cast thyself into the sea, and it will do so.'

"The King of Abyssinia has said, 'Lesseps is of the tribe of light.' Surely the King was speaking gold. It is an army order to march towards the guns, from whatever direction they may be heard. We others have for our law to go towards the light, often without knowing where it leads us. . . . I suppose that, after Lamartine, you are in our century the man most beloved, around whose head have formed the greatest number of legends and of dreams. We thank you. . . . The nation which knows how to love and to admire is not near death. To those who contend that within the breast of this people nothing beats any more, that they no longer know how to worship, that the experience of so many failures, so many deceptions, has extinguished in them all confidence in what is good and great, to them we shall cite you. . . . That is what consoles us, that is what upholds us and gives us strength to say, 'Poor, cherished France, you shall not fall; for you still love, and are beloved.'"

*   *   *

M. Rousseau duly returned to France, but no report was made public although it was known that, having made all due allowance for miscalculation and misconception, he was ready to advise the Government that the canal could and should be completed. This independent view by a Government expert did a great deal to stabilize the situation for the time being, and to give extra weight to a confident pronouncement which Ferdinand had made at the General Meeting of the previous July. He then said, "At Panama we have means which we did not have at Suez. According to the returns, we possess 57,000 steam horses, which, at ten men per horse-power, represents the work of 570,000 men. So there is an army of 570,000 added to the 20,000

labourers who we have on the site. *Eh bien!* With that we are
going to make, between now and 1889, a waterway for all the
vessels afloat to-day."

Arrived on the isthmus in 1886, Lesseps again made an almost
royal progress, but did not on that account skimp his tour of
inspection, which, for the benefit of provincial delegates and
a *commissaire vérificateur* representing the shareholders, was
particularly thorough. By water, on foot, by rail, on horseback,
the party went over every inch of the route; and though the
season was dry, the delegates could not have failed to take into
account the effect of torrential rains. There must have been
plenty of people only too anxious to tell hair-raising stories of
what happened when the clouds opened and all the land steamed
like a swamp at evening. The delegates would also have considered the incidence of fever and inspected the medical services. Had there been an epidemic they would not have been
able to ignore it. But there was no epidemic, and the work was
going forward with efficiency, even with enthusiasm. Already
the senior staff began to see the end in sight, and their loyalty to
Lesseps approached idolatry. Riding like a general along a
battlefront, he was everywhere cheered, less perhaps for what he
was than for what he represented. The far-off godling in Paris
had become present, human, and inspiring.

The whole line of the canal was now simultaneously under
construction. The delegates were awed by the magnitude of the
effort and its means: "We came to Culebra, the most striking
of all the *chantiers* which we visited. It is only 1,800 metres
long, but 20 million cubic metres have to be cut out of the hills
to a width of 140 metres beyond the axis of the canal, and to
an average height of 88 metres. There is an ant-like activity
of men and machines working at different levels: hand work,
mines, Decauville wagons, excavators, ballast trains coming and
going; two thousand workers spread over the site. It is an
extremely busy scene. The Culebra col forms the watershed
between the Atlantic and the Pacific. Our third stage, from
Paraiso to the Pacific, begins at kilometre 55·800 where the
current effort has already excavated 500,000 metres out of a total
of 1,400,000 metres. From Paraiso to Pedro Miguel (kil. 61) work
is continuous. It is an easy stretch, where between 1,000 and 1,500
labourers are employed. The diversion of the Rio Grande is

almost finished. From kilometre 61 to la Boca (kil. 69), the mouth of the Rio Grande, there is nothing more to do than to raze an outcrop, clear woodland and set up marks. This ground is all low-lying, boggy and easy to dredge . . ." In much the same terms the report covers the entire distance, and the general impression of the party is summed up by the member for Rouen, M. Ferry, whose final paragraph reads: "And so it is with confidence that we who have seen what has been done up to this time, await in the near future the crowning glory of him who has been called *le Grand Français*."

The delegates sailed away, Ferdinand attended the inauguration of the Statue of Liberty, and in that cordial atmosphere might reasonably have believed that, as with Suez, his faith had won the day against all odds. Even the health question was a matter which, if still a source of anxiety, was no longer something likely to embarrass the total effort. On his return to France, Lesseps wrote for the *Bulletin*:

"The data furnished by the Railway Company show that during the construction of the line there were only 253 deaths among European workers, and that the number of Chinese employed never exceeded 4,000. What becomes of the tale that under each of the 80,000 sleepers there lies the body of a Chinaman? If the work was more killing in the old days it was because the Bay of Colon, now so populous, was then deserted; and the work had to be done, not with the aid of powerful engines, but by excavation made painfully with pick and wheelbarrow, by men ill-housed, often without shelter, and also without adequate services. From the 1st of April, 1885, to the 31st of May, 1886, when there were fourteen thousand people employed at various points along the route of the canal, there were only 735 deaths, that is to say a mortality of 5¼%. Such a figure is not greater than the mortality usual in public works, and definitely lower than that of the navy over the whole of our colonies, which is 7%."

Even as the shareholders read this, with satisfaction made warmer by the rest of the report, dealing with technical and financial matters, the rains began on the isthmus of the Americas. On the stagnant waters created by the work, *Aedes* began to breed in billions and soon there was no lack of infected blood on which to feed. Those neat, odourless hospitals became the focus of a plague the origin of which remained utterly obscure.

"The clinical features of yellow fever show great variety. In a population immune, or partially immune, the symptoms may be slight, not unlike influenza. The usual clinical picture is a sudden onset with fever reaching 104° F. on the second day and dropping to between 98° and 99° F. on the third to the fifth days. . . . The second stage of the disease, called by some the period of calm, is characterized by cold, clammy skin, bradycardia, hemolytic icterus of the sclerae and skin which may persist into the period of convalescence, and a peculiar odour of the skin which has been likened to 'gun-washings'. . . . Other findings are melena, hematuria, albuminaria, anuria, oliguria, delirium, nausea, vomiting, torpor, coma, black hemorragic vomit which is painless and sometimes projectile. To quote Manson-Bahr: 'Everything is congested at the beginning: everything bleeds at the end.' Death usually occurs between the fifth and the sixth day. . . . The prognosis is favourable if the initial temperature does not exceed 105° F. There have been no deaths reported with a fever under 103° F. and no recoveries with a fever going above 106° F. In epidemics the mortality has reached 50%. It is below 10% in natives of the endemic zones of yellow fever. . . . The incubation period is from five to six days, rarely longer. The period of communicability is two days before and two or three days after the onset of the fever. There is a high degree of communicability when infected mosquitoes abound and there are many susceptible persons. Recovery from an attack is regularly followed by immunity, apparently for life."[1]

On the isthmus in that fearful year, the first of several, there was certainly no lack of mosquitoes nor susceptible persons. "Of thirty engineers disembarked in October 1886 from the packet-boat *Washington*, 13 died of yellow fever in the following month. In spite of the fact that his predecessor had died at his post, the second Director of Works had brought out his family to demonstrate that the unhealthiness of the climate was greatly exaggerated. He had a new bungalow built. There his wife fell ill and both the children died. Broken-hearted, he sailed for France, but his wife died. He was then publicly assailed for having wasted the Company's money on his home and his travelling office, a railway coach. M. Boyer took up the Directorship. He died in this year, 1886, and his last words were: "Never abandon Panama." His was just such an evocation of courage as *Ils ne passeront pas* at Verdun: but this enemy was a mosquito, unsuspected. Reinforcements continued to come out,

[1] E. K. Albrecht, *Modern Management in Clinical Medicine*, London 1946.

nor were they all engineers: "The Mother Superior of the Sisters of Ancon arrived with twenty-four helpers. Twenty-one disappeared. Sir Claude Coventry Mallet, the British Consul at Panama, tells of going with an engineer into the upper valley of the Chagres. They were accompanied by a group of 22 men. Of these 20 fell ill and 10 eventually died. The Consul and the engineer returned alone. Next morning Sir Claude waited in vain for his friend whom he had invited to lunch. He eventually went over to his hotel to inquire, only to find that he was already dead."[1] Had it not been for the fact that the coloured races were largely immune, though prone to the less fatal but incapacitating malaria, the enterprise must have ceased. Perhaps it is a pity that it did not do so. Perhaps if Ferdinand had gone out there again, in the wet season, he might have concluded that all the money in the world would not be worth having if bought with so much misery. He did not go. In all probability he did not comprehend what was really happening. People did not tell him disagreeable news, and it was all he could do to keep the Company afloat. While the following advertisement was appearing in Panama, he was probably drawing up the Prospectus for the Lottery Bonds.

Attention!

I have the honour to inform the inhabitants
of this town that I am always able to supply
Coffins of any Size. Prices from 6 to 100 piastres.

*   *   *

When the Government committee met to authorize the presentation of the Lottery Bonds measure, it was negatived by six votes to five, pending the production of further documents. Ferdinand promptly declared:

"They have adjourned me. I do not accept the adjournment. Faithful to my past, when they try to stop me, I go on. Not alone, but with 350,000 Frenchmen who share my patriotic confidence. . . . So six Deputies have by their attitude prevented me from going forward, from marching with you to the conquest by France of the Isthmus of Panama! We shall pass over the obstacle. Together we shall go to this second victory. We shall issue the necessary 600 million. . . . The dogs bark: the caravan passes."

[1] Coureau: *op. cit.*

But everywhere the enemy was coming into the open. Throughout the country the topic of the day was no longer the success of the great adventure but its imminent failure – in spite of the fact that officially, i.e. according to Rousseau, the canal was now certain to be completed by 1891. This early date was justified by the abandonment, in face of Ferdinand's obstinacy, of the plan for a canal without locks. Already at Culebra massive concrete frames were being prepared for the huge gates that Eiffel had designed and was now building in France. The resulting economy of excavation would be enormous. Technically speaking, from a purely engineering point of view, victory was again in sight. But the issue failed. Again applicants had to have their subscriptions returned to them. Forced now to wait upon the Government, the Company became even more entangled with those who, for a consideration, claimed they could bring influence to bear in high places. Even in the Assembly the enemy spoke up. One Deputy claimed, of what was after all a national humiliation: "The failure is going fine. There is only fifty per cent more to lose."

The Committee duly met again, and this time, somewhat mysteriously, the vote went the other way; and so, after due debate, the Lottery Bonds became legal. *Crédit Lyonnais* then stipulated that the entire sum authorized, 720,000,000 francs, must be solicited all at once. That figure represented Rousseau's estimate of the total required to complete the work, but all the Company needed was enough to keep them going for the time being, a fresh issue being made when there was more progress to report. That much could be raised with certainty, but it would be utterly impossible to raise the whole sum; for in all France there was not so much available money. *Crédit Lyonnais* remained adamant: all or none. Hoping for sufficient response to justify the appeal, the Company gave way. The issue was publicized.

Now the enemy abandoned all discretion, even decency. No abuse was too violent, no scurrilous rumour too far-fetched. On the morning that the subscription opened, every town in France received a telegram announcing the death of Ferdinand de Lesseps; and the lie was sufficiently believed to ensure the death of his Company. The issue failed utterly. "In the de Lesseps circle all hope was lost. But the old President, who was eighty-

three, refused to bow to the inevitable."[1] He went on the war-
path for the last time, believing still in his star, and at least
knowing, on independent authority, that, given the money, he
must again succeed. No mention was made of fever. Had he
known he must have given in; for no Lesseps ever believed that
money maketh man. His still resonant voice challenged all
Frenchmen: "You know by what abominable means success
was prevented. To-day 500,000 of our compatriots are directly
interested in the coming achievement of the enterprise. If each
one of them took up only two shares, the canal would be made."
And so great was his power to inspire against great odds, that
even now, when nearly a thousand million francs had already
been soaked up by Panama, the 'little men' rallied to him.
They set up committees. They organized meetings. In war there
could have been no better response. Ferdinand himself travelled
all over the country, and if he occasionally used a theatrical
gesture, such as pulling a telegram out of his pocket and
announcing to the audience its message of new success, unquestionably he was entirely sincere. In November 1888 he played
his last card:

"To-day I offer the remainder of the shares. If the subscription
is completed you are henceforth freed from all anxiety as to the
realization of your project. But the response must be sufficient to
assure the proper continuation of the work, that is to say it must
attain a minimum of 400,000 shares. I have given my life to two
things which people said were impossible: Suez and Panama. Suez
is made and has enriched France. You wish to finish Panama?
In your hands is the choice. Decide."

The minimum was not achieved. Hoping that at least the
politicians would remember the words of Renan and put *la
Patrie* above party, the Company begged for three months
grace. But the men of substance had had enough of the 'poetry
of capitalism' and the have-nots were agitating for a new order.
Gambetta was old in power – he had been President of the
Chamber in 1879, and against him two great waves were rolling.
One wave was crested red, the other was intended to carry
General Boulanger to power. A clash, even another revolution,
seemed probable. For any sort of investment, particularly

[1] André Siegfried, *Suez and Panama*, London 1940.

abroad, the time could hardly have been less favourable. Over the Rome affair Lesseps had been sacrificed to the secrets of a dictator, and now he would be the scapegoat for a democracy. The Left would not support him because he was rated something of a reactionary, and the Right still distrusted him because, though he had been forgiven by the Pope, it was difficult for some churchmen to forget Rome. Facing dissolution, the Company tried to create a successor to take over the wreck and keep it afloat until salvage could be begun; but the big bankers recalled how Lesseps had criticized their methods and their ethics. Why should they now run grave risks to save the man who boasted that he could succeed without them?

Even in this extremity Ferdinand could rise above the storm and ignore his own worries. Franco-German tension was running dangerously high, and he personally intervened to save the peace. He went to Berlin and spoke to the Emperor as perhaps no other individual in the world would have dared to do. "Sire," he said, "if Germany declares war on us I will carry a rifle and arm all my children. We will all go to the frontier to die for *la Patrie*. And there won't be a family in France of which the mother will not say to the son: go and fight. There won't be a woman who fails to devote herself to the care of our wounded, or an old peasant who does not battle to the end. It will be a war terrible and without quarter. God save you from provoking it!"

The affairs of the Company were now passing out of the control of the Board, and, through a series of humiliations, the day drew inexorably nearer when the Directors must resign. On the 5th of February, 1889, the *Tribunal de la Seine* ordered liquidation, and for the first time in his long life Ferdinand de Lesseps had to admit defeat. He telegraphed to the isthmus that work must cease. As a healthy man in his right mind it was almost his last action, for soon afterwards he had a stroke. Thereafter, to the end of life he lived in twilight, while the Company crashed down upon those for whom it had been erected, the 'little men' his shareholders, the workmen whose conditions he sought to improve, the friends whose loyalty was a large part of his strength.

Chapter 17. SCAPEGOAT

Far from quieting the outcry, public reaction to the news that the Panama Canal Company was in liquidation raised it to an hysterical pitch. Common sense and common decency were equally lacking. This was a national *crise de nerfs* in which reason had no place. Culebra, mud and fever were forgotten with the men still out there. Only money mattered. No voice dared

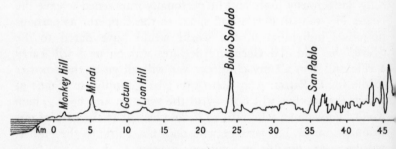

PROFILE OF THE PANAMA CANAL ROUTE
(Heights × 100, based on Bertrand et Ferrier, 1887.)

to suggest that perhaps the Company had been defeated, not so much by its own weakness or wickedness, nor even by Nature, as by the avarice of Frenchmen in high places. There was suspicion of corruption spreading out from the Company as though from a septic focus in the body politic; but the Company, and particularly Ferdinand de Lesseps, was regarded as the cause of all the trouble. Though in the aggregate losses were enormous, they were so widely spread that among half a million shareholders, the average was only about 3,000 francs. But big figures suggest dramatic tales of ruin, and these the Press duly supplied. One man was said to have killed himself after pinning a note to his chest: "I put my future in Panama. The Company went bust. So do I." It was inevitable under such circumstances that scapegoats would be found, guilty if possible, innocent if need be. Even so the Government hesitated to take action until after the Boulangist bid for power had failed and there could no longer be any excuse for procrastination. In fact they had to act or abdicate. But how to act? If they took over the completion of the canal and failed, the Government would surely fall. If they succeeded, the United States would be most unlikely to allow France peaceful enjoyment of such strategically important property. If they washed their hands of the whole business and handed Lesseps over to the mob, then in the course of the judicial proceedings, political scandals were almost bound to come to light. The position was further complicated by a belated letter from Sir William Russell, a special correspondent for *The Times*, which made it impossible to take refuge in the convenient notion that the state of the work on the isthmus was irredeemable.

"To M. Ferdinand de Lesseps.

New York, 9th July, 1899.

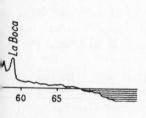

I have wanted to write to you ever since I sighed over the works of the Panama canal while on my way here from the Pacific Coast of South America. I was spellbound by what I saw. I was angry at the thought of so many false reports which have been circulated all over the world. Of course I am not an engineer, but the progress of your great enterprise was clear before my eyes, and free from the difficulties which I saw you overcome in the past, as at the entrance to the Bitter Lakes. I was surprised to see construction so far advanced, but my astonishment was mixed with sorrow when I thought of the vast enterprise being in suspense. So many unproductive millions! Silence and solitude where there ought to have been such activity, the utilization of so much capital, industry and thought! I cannot believe that such atropy will be permitted to continue. It would mean dishonour for the whole world if the canal were not completed. For my part I am certain that it ought to be. I have heard repeated *ad nauseam* that old story of lack of traffic, catastrophe, and physical obstacles. I told those who gave me such information that I had already heard the same arguments, made with far greater force and on the highest authority, before you succeeded in cutting the isthmus of Suez. They have exaggerated all the objections, the river Chagres, the mountains, fever; and I regret to say that their voices have been echoed by some of my friends in England. . . . I cannot help but write to give you my sympathy and my hopes. I pray that you may live to see completed the *opus maximum* of your lifetime, which has been so fertile in great achievement."

By now a 'salvage' Company had successfully been formed, and the wreck was being kept afloat, a very necessary step in view of the considerable assets represented by the Concession, the railway, buildings and equipment of all kinds, together with the work already done. No doubt the United States might have been induced to make a take-over bid, but no one seems to have been in a position to display so much initiative. The new concern was effectively tied down by the liquidators of the old one, who in turn were bound by political considerations. Charles was still fighting, but the old man, his father, was largely out of touch with this world. He had aged ten years since he had ordered work to cease. He was deaf and senile. But that did not prevent him from playing the chief part in the drama which the Government were getting ready to produce if sufficient legal grounds could be found. On the 5th of January, 1892, the Assembly unanimously voted for 'the energetic and rapid prosecution of all those who have incurred responsibility for the Panama affair'. Soon afterwards Ferdinand was required to appear before an examining magistrate, M. Prinet, whose duty it was to submit a full report to the Attorney General upon which a legal decision would be taken as to whether there was in fact enough evidence to justify proceedings. The interview with Prinet was to be the last occasion on which Ferdinand appeared in public. Charles left an account of it.

"When the inquiries were directed at my father, his health began to deteriorate. He often kept to his room, even to his bed. The day he had to go to see Councillor Prinet I went to look for him and found him with Doctor Moissenet, who had been authorized to accompany my father and to remain with him during the interrogation. My father, very feeble, had only just got up and was not yet dressed. He was taking a token breakfast. Doctor Moissenet was of the opinion that it would be most unwise for my father to go out, and asked me to warn M. Prinet. However, sooner or later this visit would have to take place. I had some hope that it would prove to be the only one, and that thereafter I would alone face the magistrate in my father's place. So I thought it best that my father should bear this ordeal which otherwise would only be postponed.

"I went up to my father and explained that he had been summoned by M. Prinet who was going to examine our administration of the Panama Company. I said that we might congratulate ourselves on that account, and that if he felt well enough I thought he ought to go. My father got up, and, looking me in the eye, said, 'I'll go.' Then he got dressed and arrived at M. Prinet's as though he had recovered all his powers. He stayed three hours in M. Prinet's study – for M. Prinet was the victim of an attack of gout and so received us at his own house, 68 Rue Bonaparte. My father came out with his face full of geniality and vitality, just as it used to be in his fighting days. But the reaction was not long delayed, and it was terrible. From the next day, for three weeks my father never spoke and never left his bed. One could see that he was obsessed by a train of thought which could not be broken and which further lowered his health, making him weaker, and giving Doctor Moissenet cause for concern. I tried every day, unsuccessfully, to discover what this train of thought was. At last I had the idea of trying a particular phrase which I had often heard him use: 'The one thing which is certain is that good prevails over evil.' My father answered, 'If that were not so, it would mean self-destruction.'

"I embraced my father, took his hand and said, 'What I have just said is the truth, and I hold you to it. You impressed it upon me with such force that I shall always believe it. It is not at your age, I imagine, that one alters one's principles.' My father's expression changed, and from that moment his condition rapidly improved. He gladly gave himself up to that faith which he had always shown to me. But those few words, 'If that were not so, it would mean self-destruction', show the mental suffering which my father was going through. He who was so good, who was concerned only for others, could not understand how the least suspicion could fall upon a life of service and of honour; unless, contrary to what he had always believed until that moment, evil prevailed over good. When I had to ask him to request the Tribunal to nominate liquidators, he said, 'So long as honour is safe.' Life without faith in humanity did not seem possible to him. After passing through so many dangers in his long life, and having always expressed a horror of suicide; what a wound there must have been in his soul for him to pronounce, at the age of eighty-five years, the phrase 'self-destruction'."

*   *   *

On the isthmus thousands of men began to be in want. Had it not been for local efforts, particularly by the British Consul, who fed and gradually evacuated the Jamaicans, starvation on a large scale must have ensued. As it was, the entire social and economic organization of Panama was disorganized, for, directly

or indirectly, the majority of the population now depended for
their livelihoods upon the canal. But in France the isthmus was
now completely forgotten. The talk was only of venality, bribery
and corruption; now not so much in relation to the Board of the
Company as to those who had battened upon it, abusing positions of trust to extort large sums of money. The Minister of
Public Works was involved, and around him gyrated a whole
coven of more or less clearly defined figures, some in politics,
some on its fringes, but all in contact with what is loosely termed
'the financial world'. Of such was Baron Reinarch, sometime
secret adviser to the Exchequer, and his parasite, Cornelius
Hertz. Renan had been mistaken; France was no longer beloved.
She had become a mere chattel for exploitation by cynical
opportunists, hell-bent for power at the price of their own souls.
In such a context the Panama scandal was a symptom not a
cause, a symptom of the chronic sickness of French politics, prevented by the trauma of the past from rising above party
jealousies in the service of a national ideal. Under such circumstances scapegoats were all the more necessary. Openly in the
Chamber, Deputy Delahaye had stated that a hundred and fifty
of his colleagues were involved in unsavoury deals with the Company. After shouts of, "Names!   Names!" the Chamber,
thoroughly alarmed, appointed a committee of thirty-two to
investigate Delahaye's charges and to act.

Though the Attorney General was still doubtful whether he
had enough evidence upon which to prosecute de Lesseps,
warrants for the arrest of both father and son were issued,
together with the Company's Secretary, Fontane, a Director
named Cottu, and Eiffel 'of the Tower' as a contractor for
Panama. The warrants were executed on the 17th of December.
With the exception of Ferdinand, who was now too ill to be
moved from La Chenaie, the accused were placed in solitary
confinement at the Mazas, where they were not permitted any
communication with one another. One meal a day could be
brought in from outside, but it must not cost, in all, more than
2 francs 50. It subsequently emerged that the arrests had been
made on the sole inspiration of the Minister of Justice, who had
not thought fit even to inform his colleagues. At a later stage
this Minister[1] would appear in court, accused by Madame Cottu

[1] Bihaut.

of conspiring with the Director of the *Sûreté Général* to promise her husband and his friends ' many benefits in their dealings with the magistrates; and doubtless they might avoid having to appear before the Court of Assize'. The consideration, oddly enough, was not in money. Protection was to be conferred in exchange for a copy of the list of those politicians who had been milking the Company, to which were to be falsely added the names of ' several parliamentarians of the Right'. Whatever the basis for this accusation, from a source which could hardly be unbiassed, the Minister promptly resigned. It began to seem that the whole country was run by opportunists. The Company no longer filled the foreground of the picture. People began to feel that they had been betrayed, and their bitterness coloured the national thought. It seemed that there was no good in anything or anybody. The Press began a witch-hunt, irrational and irresponsible. It was inevitable that, because Ferdinand had been at the apex of the pyramid – which now began to appear as though it had been held together only by the proverbial thickness of thieves – he should attract the lightning. Not only was he treated as guilty before the case was heard, all manner of irrelevant baseness was attributed to him. It was at this juncture that his wife, who had hitherto kept quietly in the background, bravely defended him in print. Replying to a particularly venomous attack in *le Gaulois*, Hélène wrote:

"In your paper I saw a few words on M. de Lesseps, declaring that he has lived some weeks too long. I shall not stress that hardly Christian phrase, because he who wrote it can hardly have given thought to a wife and children who love, and profoundly venerate, this old man whose precarious life is dearer to them than all things. It is no crime to be brought down by age. . . . One fails to see, amid the hurricane of hatred unleashed against this ancient of eighty-seven, any solicitude for the Panama shareholders who have been misled, or any noble desire to salve a magnificent adventure destined to enrich the country. Instead, there is the gratification of I know not what jealousy by mediocrities in face of this disinterested character, unique in history. They will never find another human being who, having accomplished Suez, would have come thence with empty hands, without even providing for the future of his numerous family; a fact of which I am proud, and my children with me."

If openly Hélène was defiantly protective, in private she could no longer keep up even a pretence of confidence. She began to spend much of her day alone in her room, and when she came downstairs, it was sometimes evident that she had been weeping. Meanwhile in Paris all manner of dirt was being collected to provide ammunition for an unparalleled orgy of mudslinging. The sudden disappearance of Reinarch, then his mysterious death, provided a trigger for an explosion big enough to rock the Government and profoundly disturb the electorate. Reinarch's body, after being the subject of macabre speculation, was exhumed; but only years later was it established that his end had been suicide by poison. This German Jew, who acquired an Italian title and was naturalized French, had been a professional contact-man, a grafter on the grand scale and at the highest level. His creature Hertz, a Bavarian and sometime chemist's bottle-washer, had contrived to become a Grand Officer of the Legion of Honour; which did not prevent him from abstracting a million francs from Reinarch as his 'cut' of the Panama take.

With a new sordid story on the breakfast tray every morning, almost the calmest place in Paris was the Court of Appeal, by which alone a Grand Officer could be judged, on the analogy of a British Peer being tried by the House of Lords. If the proceedings, which began on the 9th of March, 1893, were relatively quiet, the revelations were none the less spectacular; though not particularly damaging to de Lesseps, either father or son, whose motives were never directly impugned even by the prosecution. The Attorney General began his case with a speech from which the following paragraph is taken:

"Among the men who are arraigned there is one whose personality dominates the others to a remarkable degree. I would for myself have spared him whom age and illness have kept from this hearing, who will not have to suffer its sorrows. He is a man who had too much confidence in his luck, in his superiority, in his star. He initiated, and conceitedly persisted in, the tragic adventure which swallowed up his fortune and his honour. That *Grand Français* who walked almost as an equal among kings, has not thought fit to acknowledge his error. His obstinacy led him on and brought him to the guiltiest devices. Aided by his lieutenants, he cast millions into the abyss and heaped up ruins along his way; while scandalous fortunes were made beside him as a kind of taunt thrown out to his victims. Without other preamble, Messieurs, I begin my heavy and dolorous task."

Though Charles admitted that he knew about the 'scandalous fortunes', in all probability his father did not, for the good reason that Charles would have tried to spare him further worry. Neither Lesseps could be shown to have made a centime for themselves, and Charles" evidence was clear on the vital point that the Company had not sought out the 'chequards'–men who took cheques for real or imaginary services. On the contrary 'chequards' had for years been persecuting the Company. Among the largest individual extortions were Hugo Obendoerfer's 3,850,000, Reinarch's 6,800,000, and 8,000,000 paid as 'commission' to the *Crédit Lyonnais*. The Minister of Works, Bihaut, had extracted a million for his goodwill, by methods which Charles described as highway robbery. The President of the Court protested, "But you could have called the police!" And Charles, with the forthright air which he bore throughout the trial, retorted, "Not when it is the gendarme himself who is the robber!" (Laughter in court.)

As the long process dragged along, it seemed more and more likely that both father and son must be acquitted. The most that could be sustained against them was weakness, folly perhaps, and certainly over-confidence. There was no evidence in support of the essential motive which the Prosecution had to prove: criminal intent. For lack of it, much was made of such matters as Ferdinand's estimated traffic for the completed canal–which was to prove, eventually, far below the fact. Perhaps the Defence made a serious mistake in not bringing forward expert opinion as to what had actually been accomplished on the isthmus, but that may have been in deference to the prevailing mood that in itself Panama was hardly relevant. It was with Paris that the court was primarily concerned. Perhaps counsel was also over-confident: certainly he was over long. During his final speech several people went to sleep–it lasted for four hours, and much of the time was taken up trudging columns of seemingly endless figures. Only at the end did he raise the level of his appeal, and by then it was too late to warm the chilled emotions of the Bench. Since this was a civil action, there was no jury.

"Beautiful illusions!" exclaimed Maître Barboux. "That is what the Attorney General would call all great adventures which do not succeed. But humanity has need of such illusions. And when a great people is no longer kindled by them, then it must resign itself to be but a stolid ox, head bowed to earth." He then went on to invoke Ferdinand as though he were already a ghost,

"I could have had him brought here in a chair, but I know what would have happened had I done so. This whole gathering would have respectfully risen to its feet to make way for such chivalry in such misfortune. And then perhaps a brief awakening would have come to that noble mind. He would have seen, as though by a lightning-flash, the horror of this spectacle. He might indeed have uttered a cry of protest against these men who would impugn his honour, and his son's. But then he would have fallen, never again to rise. Therefore I may speak freely, as though he were already in the tomb. No one could be easier to understand, or to depict. Mix together the spirit of adventure with incredible courage and invincible tenacity. Add passionate love for the glory of his country, and there you have the man, complete."

After announcing the verdict, the President of the Court was heard to mutter something to the effect that he was helpless to make his view prevail, that he had been outvoted by those who, for the sake of the mob, would not be cheated of their sacrifice. And yet the Prosecution had done its duty. The verdict of Guilty must be accepted as technically correct. Lesseps broke the rules, but had he broken faith? The sentence was the maximum penalty. Father and son would go to prison for five years and each pay 3,000 francs. Cottu and Fontane were given two years and 2,000 francs, Eiffel two years and 20,000 francs; the larger fine being due to the fact that he alone had misappropriated funds. At first silent with surprise, the public soon voiced its disapproval, if not of the verdict than certainly of the severity of the penalty for the Lesseps. In fury Maître Barboux exclaimed, "Never again will I plead before such people!" Then he gave notice of appeal and left the court. At La Chenaie the old man soon realized what had happened. He made no comment, and continued to sit motionless in his usual chair by the fire, a smoking-cap on his head and a sailor's double-breasted jacket buttoned high against the cold; but it was observed that there were tears at the corners of his closed eyes. Age was kinder than his judges. He soon forgot. His mind went wandering off down the long corridors of memory, and his pet monkey jabbered unsuccessfully for attention.

*   *   *

Shocked into the recognition that in decency if not in law the State was more culpable than its prisoners, Press comment was remarkably restrained. *Le Matin* went so far as to say, "The sentence of the court will mark in history a date of base ingratitude." *Figaro* and *le Petit Journal* accused the judges of ' lack of deference towards the name de Lesseps'. *Le Gaulois* said, "The Republic, which with both hands has been ransacking the Lesseps coffers, now, as though he were an old lag, inflicts upon him the maximum penalty." In London the *Daily Graphic* summed the issue in few words: "a judgment given under the pressure of popular emotion". The prevailing view, veering in favour of the condemned, seemed to be that if they had assisted at the ruin of so many hopes, they had not intended ruin. They had meant well – which was more than could be said for many people who were not before the court. Ferdinand no longer read the papers. He was too far gone to do more than keep up a semblance of normal routine. To Hélène he often complained that Charles was neglecting him; and she was able to use this as a plea to the authorities that Charles might be allowed to visit his father before beginning his sentence. Perhaps because they were secretly ashamed, the authorities agreed, and through the bitterly cold night of the 25th/26th of February, 1893, Charles, between two policemen in plain clothes, was brought down to La Chenaie. The nearest railway was thirty kilometres away, at Issoudun. From there the silent trio drove in a closed carriage, arriving a little before dawn. After two hours rest Charles faced his father. The old man was in bed.

"'Ah, Charles, it is you. Is there nothing new in Paris?' Then he embraced his son, still saying, 'Charles. Ah, Charles!' This was all, for he immediately fell back into his customary state of semiconsciousness. The Countess (Ferdinand had succeeded to the title) was present at the interview, and the two inspectors were just outside the door. At about nine, when the children had breakfasted, M. Charles de Lesseps took a walk with them. During this walk he told a reporter that he had given up hope of being able to revisit La Chenaie. 'I have rarely let a week go by,' he said, 'without coming to see my father, whom I all but worship. He could scarcely help being surprised at my long absence, and the Paris doctor, who examined him the other day, asserted that if I stayed away another week it was to be feared that his wish to embrace me might become such a fixed idea that it could bring on a fever, which might prove fatal. Now that he has seen me, he will be at ease about me for another two or three weeks. I complain of nothing, really of nothing, for I have a clear conscience.'

"During the morning, another son of M. Ferdinand de Lesseps arrived by train, and at the same time came the postman, with one hundred and two letters and nine telegrams. These were from all parts of Europe, and Madame de Lesseps expressed the consolation which she felt in the continued testimonies of affection and loyalty which are now pouring in. M. Ferdinand de Lesseps took his accustomed place at the luncheon table. One of the inspectors also sat at this table, the other in another room with the children. M. Ferdinand de Lesseps ate a good luncheon, frequently falling asleep, however, and resting his chin on the cane which now he always carries. Without saying a word, from time to time he looked at his two sons, Charles and Victor. Once he smiled at the former and opened his lips as if about to speak, but finally said nothing. Towards the end of the meal he fell asleep. After luncheon the old man was conducted to the adjoining room. He sat down with an old copy of the *Revue des Deux Mondes*, always the same, and tried to read but dropped continually to sleep. And so it is every day."

The above account is quoted by Schonfield, presumably from one of the journalists who haunted the place at this time, to one of whom Hélène gave her last defiance: "I am a fatalist as my husband has always been. He believes in the inevitability of events, coming in a predestined order. I am sure of only one thing, and that is the inflexible and absolute honesty of my husband and his sons. Mistakes and misconceptions? I know nothing about that. A dishonest action of any kind? Never! "

The law had not yet finished either with its scapegoats or with its proper prey. With Bihaut, Fontane, and a contact-man called Blondin, Charles was soon standing in the dock on a criminal charge, to go through the same humiliating examination all over again because the distinction between bribery and malpractice was such that the two could not be dealt with at the same time. As at the previous trial, his father's name was conspicuous, but the bribery charge could not be brought against him. There were seventy-eight witnesses, and so many interested parties that there were no seats for the public and standing-room for only two hundred. Minister Bihaut was deprived of civil rights and given five years of prison with 750,000 francs fine plus a 'civil indemnity' of 375,000 francs, payable jointly with

Charles de Lesseps and Blondin, both of whom were found "guilty with extenuating circumstances". Charles was given one year's prison, to run concurrently with his previous sentence, and Blondin two years. Fontane was found Not Guilty. In the little room reserved for the accused, Charles was standing, calm but very pale. His first action was to congratulate Fontane on his acquittal. Weeping, Madame de Lesseps threw herself into her husband's arms. They had to come and take her away in a *crise de nerfs*. Fontane was weeping. Bihaut, cold and contemptuous, rejected the condolences of his wife and two daughters, and kept feverishly pacing the room.[1] At La Chenaie the verdict was known that same evening. Hélène, who had long been able to appreciate the generosity and integrity of her step-son, had been counting on his acquittal before a jury free from political entanglements. At the beginning of March she had written to a friend: "I receive thousands of letters from all countries. There is a clamour of sympathy and I find that our name is more glorious than ever." She was cruelly surprised and very indignant at the verdict, but she bowed to the inevitable. "God's will be done," she said, "the future will judge us."

Meanwhile the Court of Appeal had heard, through hours of great solemnity, that there had been a technical error in the prosecution of the civil action. In such circumstances as these it appeared that a person could not be brought to trial more than three years after the alleged offence. The Lesseps had been arrested within that period, but no proper notification of the fact had been made at the time. Therefore the date of the conviction, in June 1892, had to be taken instead of the date of arrest – which involved more than the three years. And so, by a legal quibble, both Ferdinand and Charles were saved from the pit of degradation. The civil-suit prison sentences were quashed. There followed another appeal, against the sentence of the criminal court; but in that case the one year sentence on Charles was confirmed. Even so he was forthwith set at liberty because he had long been in 'preventive detention'; but he remained liable for his share of the civil indemnity payable by Bihaut, and because there was no possibility of raising the money he had to flee the country. Charles had made no more out of Panama than had his father, for whom Maître Barboux claimed

[1] Schonfield, *Life of Ferdinand de Lesseps.*

that when he died there would not be realizable from his estate three thousand francs for each of his children.

So Charles was in exile when, on the 17th of November in the following year, 1894, Hélène tried for the last time to break through into her husband's world. She arranged a little celebration *en famille* for the occasion of the twenty-fifth anniversary of the opening of the Suez Canal. The revenue of that concern for that year amounted to 76,950,000 francs. In the following week her silver wedding passed unheeded. The end was at last near, a welcome end. Peacefully, on the 7th of December, Ferdinand de Lesseps achieved death.

*　　*　　*

Charles was given a forty-eight-hour permit to attend his father's funeral in Paris, but he could not go down to La Chenaie, and so saw Hélène only while she was in Paris for the grim day when Ferdinand at last followed Agathe into Père Lachaise. As the silent procession shivered behind the coffin, some of his oldest friends would have remembered that other funeral, forty years before; but only Charles could have recalled the dream which he had while at school, and how, when he told his father, Ferdinand wrote: "Death does not give up his victims, but one day he will reunite us with those who now seem lost. For that one needs resignation, courage, confidence in God."

For once the Press, which had for so long been vociferous, could find few words; though *Figaro* published his will with the introduction, "It was short and straightforward as the man who signed it. It is dated 1st of May, 1889, and was the same day deposited with M. Champetier de Ribes." It had to be short because there was so little to bequeath by this man who, on behalf of others, had handled something like twelve thousand million pre-war francs, and whose dream at Suez was already earning more than even he could ever have imagined. He mentioned particularly the silver cup which Eugénie had given him ' on the waters of Lake Timsah ', making it an heirloom. He charged Charles and Victor to look after Hélène and her children. For the sake of family tradition he desired only: " that my descendants, in the person of the eldest among them, shall continue to use the title of Count, which was conferred upon my father by Napoleon I in 1815, by way of recognition for his patriotism when he refused to surrender Corfu to an English squadron ".

More or less belated, more or less shamefaced, the learned societies rendered appropriate eulogies, in the spirit, as one speaker put it, " of the Kings of Persia, who, when they came to a particularly venerable palm-tree, used to decorate it with a collar of gold, without concerning themselves with whether it had been struck by lightning ". But the learned societies made no practical gesture; that was left to the shareholders of Suez, without whose assistance Hélène and the children would have been in want. As it was, she was enabled to pay off the heavy costs of the legal battle, and for the future she was provided with an income which would set her free from anxiety. But it may be safely presumed that she would not have taken more than was sufficient to bring up her family with decency. Meanwhile Charles had at last been able to convince the authorities that there was no hope of him ever being able to repay his liability, and eventually they settled with him for 3,000 francs, which through friends he was able to raise, and so came back to France. He was in time to attend a solemn act of deference to his father's memory on the occasion of the unveiling of a more than life-size statue at Suez in 1897. Ferdinand is there represented in doctorial robes, gesturing from a massive stone plinth towards the entrance to his canal.

By this time a new Panama Company had been formed, and Ferdinand's old critic, Bunau-Varilla, who at twenty-seven had directed operations on the isthmus, campaigned throughout France for the work to be restarted. At his own expense he took whole pages of the principal newspapers to rouse the country to what he believed was her duty. Gaining no support, he left France for the United States, and toured much as Ferdinand would have done, urging the claims of Panama against the Nicaraguan scheme, which was now almost ready for practical development. In all probability it would have been begun had not two catastrophic volcanic eruptions in the area made the Government change its mind. And so, in 1902, having decided upon the Panama route, America bought out the French Company for 40,000,000 dollars, leaving Bunau-Varilla as the only living link between the old work and the new. Even so, he was not employed in an executive capacity, and so went back to the isthmus, where he played a conspicuous part in the bloodless revolution which created the State of Panama. Appointed Ambassador to Washington, he negotiated a treaty which defined the position as at 18th of November, 1903, so that work could at last begin again.

After an epidemic of yellow fever, it was proved upon the bodies of volunteers that the disease could not be transmitted by the excretions of the afflicted, but was carried from a sick person to a healthy one in blood taken up by that particular *Aedes* mosquito. The breeding-places of mosquitoes were sprayed, and all dwellings were screened. The isthmus became reasonably healthy. Even so, and with far better equipment than ever the French had, the canal was not ready for commerce until 1915. Ten years later the annual traffic amounted to some thirty million tons – a sufficient comment on the Attorney General's claim that because Ferdinand had forecast seven million tons he must have intended to deceive: the figure was self-evidently absurd.

Before Ferdinand de Lesseps, many men had thought along similar lines; it was his genius to condense their ideas into reality. Behind that was a more unusual quality, the capacity to inspire idealism and devotion. Behind that again was an innate authority which made people believe what he said, a kind of *mana* which he himself never understood. More than any other man of his generation, he is still thought of in terms of quantities – manpower, money, and earth. But individuals are valued by qualities and live not only under the law. To Ferdinand de Lesseps a re-trial is by grace allowed; and not for fear of the mob, nor by bank balance, but by the weighing of his heart 'against the feather of truth'. In those Ancient Egyptian scales his enthusiasm, his capacity for inspiring loyalty and affection, may more than counteract the deadweight of his Paris condemnation; even though it be admitted that from the inception of the Panama scheme his character was largely out of control and that even his merits overreached themselves. He was an old man. His rocket had reached ceiling at Suez, and the stick took an unconscionable time to come down. How much does that matter now, in comparison with such rare achievement by one

man among, and often against, the princes and the powers?
He expected to meet friends rather than enemies, yet was always
sword in hand, ready to defend a personal faith: that men are
fundamentally good, that good prevails over evil, that therefore
war at last will yield to peace. Among contemporary prophets
wailing over the fissionable future of the human race it may be
difficult to hear the cheerful shout of Lesseps: "Open the world
to the people!" Yet, even with the black record of the nations
since his day, he may still be right. For what shall it profit a
State to gain the whole world and lose its own soul?

"A new worship now I sing,
  You captains, voyagers, explorers, yours,
  Not for trade and transportation only,
  But in God's name and for thy sake, O my soul."
                                              WALT WHITMAN

BIBLIOGRAPHY

Albrecht (E. K.): *Modern Management in Clinical Medicine* (London, 1946).
Allemagne (d'): *Les Saint Simonians* (Paris, 1930).
     Prosper Enfantin (Paris, 1935).
Annual Register, particularly 1858.
Aubry (O.): *l'Impératrice Eugénie* (Paris, 1931).
Bell (H. C. F.): *Lord Palmerston* (London, 1936), 2 vols.
Bertrand (A.) et Ferrier (E.):*Ferdinand de Lesseps sa Vie et son Oeuvre* (Paris, 1887).
Booth (A. J.): *Saint Simon and Saint Simonism* (London, 1871).
Bourgeois (E.) et Clermont (E.): *Rome et Napoleon III* (Paris, 1907).
Breasted (J. H.): *History of Egypt* (London, 1906).
Bridier (L.): *Une Famille Française, les de Lesseps* (Paris, 1900).
Brunet (G.): *Le Mysticisme Social de Saint Simon* (Paris, 1925).
Bulwer (Lytton): *Life of Henry John Temple, Viscount Palmerston* (London, 1870-4), 3 vols.
Butler (E. M.): *The Saint Simonian Religion in Germany* (Cambridge, 1926).
Cambridge Modern History (1902-1912), 13 vols.
Cameron (D. A.): *Egypt in the Nineteenth Century* (London, 1898).
Charles-Roux (F.): *Autour d'une route, l'Angleterre, l'Isthme de Suez et l'Egypte au XVIIIme. siècle* (Paris, 1922).
Charles-Roux (J.): *l'Isthme et le Canal de Suez* (Paris, 1901), 2 vols.
Congressional Record (U.S.): vol. 93, parts 8, 10, 11.
Coureau (R.): *Ferdinand de Lesseps, de l'apothéose de Suez au scandale de Panama* (Paris, 1932).
Crabités (P.): *The Spoliation of Suez* (London, 1940).
Dubos (R. J.): *Louis Pasteur* (London, 1951).
Edgar-Bonnet (G.): *Ferdinand de Lesseps, le Diplomate le Createur de Suez* (Paris, 1951).
Elbée (J. d'): *Ferdinand de Lesseps, un Conquistador et Génie* (Paris, 1943).
Elgood (P. G.): *The Transit of Egypt* (London, 1928).
Encyc. Brit.: *The March of Man* (London, 1935).
Ghorbal (S.): *The Beginning of the Egyptian Question* (London, 1928).
Guedalla (P.), ed.: *The Palmerston Papers* (London, 1928).
Hallberg (C. W.): *The Suez Canal* (New York, 1931).
Hare (R.): *Pomp and Pestilence* (London, 1954).

Hermant (A.): *Eugénie, impératrice des Français 1826-1920* (Paris, 1942).

Illus. Lond. News, particularly 1869.

Jeaffreson (J. C.): *Life of Robert Stephenson* (London, 1864), 2 vols.

Lamartine (A. de): *Histoire de la Turquie* (Paris, 1854-5), 8 vols.

Leon (E. de): *The Khedive's Egypt* (London, 1877).

Lesseps (F. de): *Etude sur Don Jaime Balmés* (Paris, 1849).
   Considerations sur Egypte (Paris, 1856).
   The Isthmus of Suez Question (London, 1855).
   Recollections of Forty Years. Trans. (London, 1887), 2 vols.
   History of the Suez Canal. Trans. of a speech (London, 1876).
   Lettres, Journal et Documents pour servir a l'Histoire du Canal de Suez (Paris, 1875-81), 5 vols.
   Inquiry into the Opinions of the Commercial Classes of Great Britain on the Suez Ship Canal (London, 1857).

Life: *Picture History of Western Man* (New York, 1951).

Ludwig (E.): *Napoleon* (London, 1926).

Magnus (Sir P.): *Gladstone* (London, 1954).

Maurois (A.): *Histoire d'Angleterre* (Paris, 1937).

Morley (J.): *Life of Gladstone* (London, 1903), 3 vols.

Nelson (W.): *Five Years at Panama* (London, 1891).

Oman (C.): *Nelson* (London, 1947).

Pemberton (N. W. B.): *Lord Palmerston* (London, 1954).

Punch, particularly 1869.

Quentine-Bauchart (P.): *Lamartine et la Politique Etrangère de la Révolution de février* (24 février-24 juin) 1848 (Paris, 1907).

Rabino (J.): *Statistical Story of the Suez Canal* (Roy. Stat. Soc. Journal, vol. 50, 1887).

Rhoné (A.): *l'Egypte à petites journées* (Paris, 1950).

Saint-Hilaire (J. B.): *Egypt and the Great Suez Canal*. Trans. (London, 1857).

Saunders (E.): *The Age of Worth* (London, 1954).

Sencourt (R.): *Life of the Empress Eugénie* (London, 1931).

Siegfried (A.): *Suez and Panama*. Trans. (London, 1940).

Smith (G. B.): *Life and Enterprises of Ferdinand de Lesseps* (London, 1893).

Spencer (P.): *Politics and Belief in Nineteenth Century France* (London, 1954).

Thompson (J. M.): *Louis Napoleon and the Second Empire* (London, 1954).

Tocqueville (A. de): *Souvenirs* (Paris, 1893).

Voisin Bey: *le Canal de Suez* (Paris, 1902-6), 7 vols.

Wilson (Sir A. T.): *The Suez Canal* (London, 1933).

Worsfold (W. B.): *The Story of Egypt* (London, 1900).

Young (G.): *Egypt* (London, 1927).

FERDINAND DE LESSEPS, 1805-1894

1805	Nov. 19	born in the town of Versailles. The family soon moved to Pisa.
		Trafalgar, Austerlitz.
1807		massacre of the Mamelukes by Mohammed-Ali.
1814		fall of Napoleon: Lesseps family returned to Paris.
		Waterloo, Louis XVIII.
1818		entered Collège Henri IV.
1821		Napoleon died.
1822		left school, studied law, job in Army commissariat.
1824		Charles X.
1825		attached to French consulate, Lisbon.
1829		transferred to Tunis under his father the Consul-General.
1830		July Revolution, Louis-Philippe,
		French conquest of Algeria.
1832		Posted to Alexandria, then to Cairo. Father and uncle Barthélemy both died.
1834		Egypt at war with Syria.
1835		made Chevalier of the Legion of Honour for services during cholera epidemic in Egypt.
1836		on leave, fell in love with Mlle Agathe Delamalle.
	Dec. 21	married her in Paris.
1838		appointed Consul in Rotterdam.
1840		transferred to Malaga.
		Louis-Napoleon (future Napoleon III) given life sentence.
1842	June	transferred to Barcelona.
	Nov. 17	fighting began in Barcelona.
1843	Dec.	end of Spanish Civil War.
1844		on leave in France, much fêted for distinguished conduct.
1845		returned to Barcelona as Consul-General.
1846	May 26	Louis-Napoleon escaped from prison.
1846		Anglo-French entente broken by Spanish succession issue.
1848		Revolution of the Four June Days, Second Republic, Louis-Napoleon elected President.
		F de L recalled to Paris and appointed Minister at Madrid.

1849	Feb.		Roman Republic proclaimed by Mazzini.
	May		sent to Rome as special envoy.
	June		recalled to Paris, examined by Council of State, resigned from the foreign service.
1850			became land agent to his mother-in-law Mme Delamalle.
			Mohammed-Ali died, succeeded by his grandson, Abbas Pasha.
1852			Louis-Napoleon became Emperor Napoleon III.
1853	Jan.	30	the Emperor married, in Notre Dame, Eugénie de Montijo, cousin of F de L.
	June		his wife, Agathe, died of scarlet fever.
			Crimean war began.
1854	Sept.		Abbas Pasha died and was succeeded by Säid Pasha, whom F de L had in youth befriended.
	Nov.	7	arrived in Egypt as guest of the new Viceroy.
		15	Viceroy approved F de L's proposal to cut the Suez Canal.
		30	F de L authorized by Act of Concession to start preparatory work.
1855	Feb.		at Constantinople F de L failed to get Sultan's ratification to Act of Concession, without which canal must not be dug.
			Lord Palmerston Prime Minister.
	Oct.		International Commission appointed to report on feasibility of the proposed canal.
1856	Jan.		Commission reported in favour of F de L's plan. In a private interview with Lord Palmerston F de L sought to have British Government opposition withdrawn: failed.
	Mar.		treaty of Paris ended Crimean war.
1857	Mar.		F de L, encouraged by Napoleon III, toured British Isles to recruit commercial interests on behalf of the canal.
			Indian Mutiny.
			France broke off diplomatic relations with Turkey over Rumania, the new State created by the Treaty of Paris.
	Nov.		F de L again went to Constantinople to try to get ratification of Suez Canal Concession: failed.
1858	Jan.	14	Attempted assassination of Napoleon III by Orsini et. al.
		24	fall of Palmerston, succeeded by Lord Derby.
	June	1	Canal debated in House of Commons, big majority against.

1858	June 9	F de L came to London to challenge Robert Stephenson to a duel.
		F de L again went to Constantinople and again failed.
	Nov. 5	in spite of hostility of both Turkey and England, the Universal Company of the Maritime Suez Canal was founded on £3,200,000.
		Lord Palmerston again Prime Minister.
1859	Apr. 19	F de L founded Port Said.
	Apr. 25	In spite of Egyptian boycott, F de L with 150 workmen began excavation of the Suez Canal near Pelusium.
		France at war with Austria.
	July 8	armistice of Villafranca.
1862	Apr.	the town of Timsah founded.
1863	Jan. 18	Säid Pasha died, succeeded by Ismail Pasha.
	Dec. 29	Freshwater Canal completed to Suez.
1864	Mar.	Extraordinary General Meeting of Company because of crisis caused by diplomatic opposition to the work on the isthmus. The *corvée* had been suppressed to deprive the Company of labour.
	Mar. 18	arbitration between the Company and Egypt, under Thouvenal responsible to Napoleon.
	Apr. 30	Napoleon publicly snubbed the Grand Vizier because Turkey had still not ratified the Act of Concession.
	July 6	Napoleon awarded the Company 84,000,000 francs in lieu of the *corvée* and certain territory.
	Nov.	F de L stopped riots on the isthmus.
1865	Spring	Chambers of Commerce sent 120 delegates to be F de L's guests and inspect the work on the isthmus.
	June	cholera in Egypt again. Heroic work by F de L and Company's officers.
		Palmerston died, succeeded by Lord John Russell.
	Dec.	F de L's only grandson, 'little' Ferdinand, died of cholera.
1866	Jan. 30	the Viceroy formally accepted the arbitration award.
	Mar. 19	the Sultan at last ratified the Act of Concession.
1867		the Company raised another £4,000,000 but the 500-franc share was worth only 250.
	June 18	Ismail given the hereditary title of *Khedive* by the Sultan.
1869	Aug. 15	at Ismail's order, the Red Sea entered the Bitter Lakes

1869	Apr. 18	the Red Sea joined the Mediterranean.
	Sept. 25	F de L steamed from Port Said to Suez in 15 hours.
	Nov. 17	leading 51 ships, the Empress Eugénie inaugurated the canal.
	21	Eugénie left for France.
	25	F de L married Mlle Louise-Hélène Autard de Bragard at Ismailia
1870	Summer	fêted in London, F de L received Freedom of the City and was invested by Queen Victoria with G.C.S.I.
		Franco-German war began.
	Sept.	Sedan.
		Flight of the Empress from the Tuileries after refusing F de L's advice. F de L, not knowing she had gone, tried to protect the palace.
1875		Ismail bankrupt, exiled by the Powers (through the Sultan), succeeded by Tewfik.
1879	May	International Congress at Paris voted for Panama Canal. F de L reluctantly accepted Presidency of new Company.
	Aug.	ignoring Government and other financial assistance, F de L's share-issue failed: money refunded.
	Oct. 20	F de L registered Universal Interoceanic Canal Company.
	Dec. 8	with wife, 3 young children and technical committee, F de L embarked for Panama.
1880	Jan. 1	F de L's daughter Ferdinande inaugurated Panama Canal construction.
	Mar.	F de L toured United States.
		Gladstone Prime Minister.
	Dec.	new share-issue over-subscribed in three days: 12,000,000 francs.
1882		war in Egypt. F de L tried to hold the canal against all comers. British intervention. Tel-el-Kebir made British occupation of Egypt inevitable.
1886		F de L again visited Panama with representatives of French Chambers of Commerce. Almost half the work already done: canal to be opened in 1891.
1887		financial crisis in France over Canal Company.
1888	Autumn	F de L's last personal appeal failed.
	Dec.	Company in liquidation. F de L's health broken, he retired to La Chenaie.
1889	Sept.	political crisis in France, Gambetta failed at elections.
1891	Aug.	Panama shares 27½ for 500 par.

1891	Oct.		judicial inquiry opened, F de L's last public appearance.
	Nov.		prosecution of Directors and others set on foot.
1892	Jan.		Charles de L arrested, his father too ill to be moved, semi-coma.
	Nov.		civil trial, father and son each five years.
1893	Mar.		criminal trial, Charles one year, F de L not accused on this count (bribery).
	June		appeal, prison sentences were quashed on a technicality, but
	Sept.		Charles had to flee the country because he could not pay civil indemnity.
1894	Dec.	7	F de L died at La Chenaie, was buried in Paris.
1897			F de L's statue unveiled at the Suez entrance to the Canal.
1904			United States began work on the Panama Canal.
1914			Panama Canal inaugurated.
1915			Panama Canal opened to commerce.

THE DE LESSEPS FAMILY

In 1451 the family of Essep or Lessep was represented by one of the principal citizens of Bayonne. The first *de* Lesseps seems to have been

1. *Bertrand,* who in 1523 was a grown man. He had a son

2. *Esteban,* who married in 1620 and had a son

3. *Jehan,* born in 1621, married in 1675, died in 1708.
   (These three generations were all master-armourers and Captains of the Watch in Bayonne.) Jehan had a son

4. *Pièrre,* who became senior lawyer and Town Clerk of Bayonne. He was the confidant of the exiled widow of Charles II of Spain and through her met exalted persons. He was born in 1690 and died in 1759, having had fourteen children, among whom were

5. *Dominique* (1715-1794), Ambassador at Brussels in 1752. He was ennobled by Louis XVI and after the Revolution attended the States General. His brother

   Martin (1730-1809) married Mlle Cayzergues because she had seen him in a dream before they met – and because he fell in love. He was Consul-General at St. Petersburg in the time of Catherine the Great. He died in his eightieth year, of a chill caught while out shooting. He left two sons

6. *Barthélemy* (1766-1823), explorer and diplomat. He was Civil Governor of Moscow in 1812 and survived the retreat with the *Grande Armée.* His brother

   Mathieu (1774-1823) at seventeen was an Arabic interpreter, at twenty a Consul, and at thirty Napoleon's Quartermaster for the Egyptian Expedition sailing from Cadiz. In 1801 he married Mlle Catherine de Grivegnée, whose niece, Maria Manuella, was the daughter of a Jacobite Scot exile, Kirkpatrick. Maria became Comtesse de Montijo de Guzman, and her daughter, Eugénie, became Empress of the

French. Mathieu was made a Count of the Empire during the Hundred Days. His children were

7. *Theodore* (1802-1874), Comte de Lesseps, who became Director of Consulates, ranked Minister Plenipotentiary, was a Commander of the Legion of Honour, and held twenty-two foreign orders. He died without issue; so, late in life, the title passed to his brother, Ferdinand.

Adèle (1803-1879) who in 1821 married her cousin Eduard Tallien de Cabarrus. They had three children, one a girl. Both sons became diplomats.

FERDINAND (1805-1894), diplomat and canal-builder, married first Mlle Agathe Delamalle, who died fifteen years later, of scarlet fever. They had five children of whom only

   Charles, who was born in 1838 and followed his father into the canal ventures, and
   Victor, a distinguished officer in the Foreign Service, survived to manhood.

He married second, just after the inauguration of the Suez Canal in 1869, Mlle Louise-Hélène Autard de Bragard, of Mauritius. He was then sixty-four and she was twenty. They had twelve children, the youngest born in 1885, Ferdinand's eightieth year.

Jules (1809-1887) was for twenty-five years the Paris representative of the Bey of Tunis. He married a widow, Madame de Bertrand. They had no children.

INDEX